SECOND EDITION

Cassandra: The Definitive Guide

Jeff Carpenter and Eben Hewitt

Beijing · Boston · Farnham · Sebastopol · Tokyo

Cassandra: The Definitive Guide

by Jeff Carpenter and Eben Hewitt

Printed in the United States of America.

Published by O'Reilly Media, Inc., 1005 Gravenstein Highway North, Sebastopol, CA 95472.

O'Reilly books may be purchased for educational, business, or sales promotional use. Online editions are also available for most titles (*http://safaribooksonline.com*). For more information, contact our corporate/institutional sales department: 800-998-9938 or *corporate@oreilly.com*.

Editors: Mike Loukides and Marie Beaugureau	**Indexer:** Ellen Troutman-Zaig
Production Editor: Colleen Cole	**Interior Designer:** David Futato
Copyeditor: Jasmine Kwityn	**Cover Designer:** Karen Montgomery
Proofreader: James Fraleigh	**Illustrator:** Rebecca Demarest

June 2016:   Second Edition

Revision History for the Second Edition
2010-11-12:   First Release
2016-06-27:   Second Release

See *http://oreilly.com/catalog/errata.csp?isbn=9781491933664* for release details.

978-1-491-93366-4

[LSI]

This book is dedicated to my sweetheart, Alison Brown.
I can hear the sound of violins, long before it begins.

—E.H.

For Stephanie, my inspiration, unfailing support,
and the love of my life.

—J.C.

Table of Contents

Foreword

Cassandra was open-sourced by Facebook in July 2008. This original version of Cassandra was written primarily by an ex-employee from Amazon and one from Microsoft. It was strongly influenced by Dynamo, Amazon's pioneering distributed key/value database. Cassandra implements a Dynamo-style replication model with no single point of failure, but adds a more powerful "column family" data model.

I became involved in December of that year, when Rackspace asked me to build them a scalable database. This was good timing, because all of today's important open source scalable databases were available for evaluation. Despite initially having only a single major use case, Cassandra's underlying architecture was the strongest, and I directed my efforts toward improving the code and building a community.

Cassandra was accepted into the Apache Incubator, and by the time it graduated in March 2010, it had become a true open source success story, with committers from Rackspace, Digg, Twitter, and other companies that wouldn't have written their own database from scratch, but together built something important.

Today's Cassandra is much more than the early system that powered (and still powers) Facebook's inbox search; it has become "the hands-down winner for transaction processing performance," to quote Tony Bain, with a deserved reputation for reliability and performance at scale.

As Cassandra matured and began attracting more mainstream users, it became clear that there was a need for commercial support; thus, Matt Pfeil and I cofounded Riptano in April 2010. Helping drive Cassandra adoption has been very rewarding, especially seeing the uses that don't get discussed in public.

Another need has been a book like this one. Like many open source projects, Cassandra's documentation has historically been weak. And even when the documentation ultimately improves, a book-length treatment like this will remain useful.

Thanks to Eben for tackling the difficult task of distilling the art and science of developing against and deploying Cassandra. You, the reader, have the opportunity to learn these new concepts in an organized fashion.

— Jonathan Ellis
Project Chair, Apache Cassandra, and
Cofounder and CTO, DataStax

Foreword

I am so excited to be writing the foreword for the new edition of *Cassandra: The Definitive Guide*. Why? Because there is a new edition! When the original version of this book was written, Apache Cassandra was a brand new project. Over the years, so much has changed that users from that time would barely recognize the database today. It's notoriously hard to keep track of fast moving projects like Apache Cassandra, and I'm very thankful to Jeff for taking on this task and communicating the latest to the world.

One of the most important updates to the new edition is the content on modeling your data. I have said this many times in public: a data model can be the difference between a successful Apache Cassandra project and a failed one. A good portion of this book is now devoted to understanding how to do it right. Operations folks, you haven't been left out either. Modern Apache Cassandra includes things such as virtual nodes and many new options to maintain data consistency, which are all explained in the second edition. There's so much ground to cover—it's a good thing you got the definitive guide!

Whatever your focus, you have made a great choice in learning more about Apache Cassandra. There is no better time to add this skill to your toolbox. Or, for experienced users, maintaining your knowledge by keeping current with changes will give you an edge. As recent surveys have shown, Apache Cassandra skills are some of the highest paying and most sought after in the world of application development and infrastructure. This also shows a very clear trend in our industry. When organizations need a highly scaling, always-on, multi-datacenter database, you can't find a better choice than Apache Cassandra. A quick search will yield hundreds of companies that have staked their success on our favorite database. This trust is well founded, as you will see as you read on. As applications are moving to the cloud by default, Cassandra keeps up with dynamic and global data needs. This book will teach you why and how to apply it in your application. Build something amazing and be yet another success story.

And finally, I invite you to join our thriving Apache Cassandra community. Worldwide, the community has been one of the strongest non-technical assets for new users. We are lucky to have a thriving Cassandra community, and collaboration among our members has made Apache Cassandra a stronger database. There are many ways you can participate. You can start with simple things like attending meetups or conferences, where you can network with your peers. Eventually you may want to make more involved contributions like writing blog posts or giving presentations, which can add to the group intelligence and help new users following behind you. And, the most critical part of an open source project, make technical contributions. Write some code to fix a bug or add a feature. Submit a bug report or feature request in a JIRA. These contributions are a great measurement of the health and vibrancy of a project. You don't need any special status, just create an account and go! And when you need help, refer back to this book, or reach out to our community. We are here to help you be successful.

Excited yet? Good!

Enough of me talking, it's time for you to turn the page and start learning.

— Patrick McFadin
Chief Evangelist for
Apache Cassandra, DataStax

Preface

Why Apache Cassandra?

Apache Cassandra is a free, open source, distributed data storage system that differs sharply from relational database management systems (RDBMSs).

Cassandra first started as an Incubator project at Apache in January of 2009. Shortly thereafter, the committers, led by Apache Cassandra Project Chair Jonathan Ellis, released version 0.3 of Cassandra, and have steadily made releases ever since. Cassandra is being used in production by some of the biggest companies on the Web, including Facebook, Twitter, and Netflix.

Its popularity is due in large part to the outstanding technical features it provides. It is durable, seamlessly scalable, and tuneably consistent. It performs blazingly fast writes, can store hundreds of terabytes of data, and is decentralized and symmetrical so there's no single point of failure. It is highly available and offers a data model based on the Cassandra Query Language (CQL).

Is This Book for You?

This book is intended for a variety of audiences. It should be useful to you if you are:

- A developer working with large-scale, high-volume applications, such as Web 2.0 social applications or ecommerce sites
- An application architect or data architect who needs to understand the available options for high-performance, decentralized, elastic data stores
- A database administrator or database developer currently working with standard relational database systems who needs to understand how to implement a fault-tolerant, eventually consistent data store

- A manager who wants to understand the advantages (and disadvantages) of Cassandra and related columnar databases to help make decisions about technology strategy
- A student, analyst, or researcher who is designing a project related to Cassandra or other non-relational data store options

This book is a technical guide. In many ways, Cassandra represents a new way of thinking about data. Many developers who gained their professional chops in the last 15–20 years have become well versed in thinking about data in purely relational or object-oriented terms. Cassandra's data model is very different and can be difficult to wrap your mind around at first, especially for those of us with entrenched ideas about what a database is (and should be).

Using Cassandra does not mean that you have to be a Java developer. However, Cassandra is written in Java, so if you're going to dive into the source code, a solid understanding of Java is crucial. Although it's not strictly necessary to know Java, it can help you to better understand exceptions, how to build the source code, and how to use some of the popular clients. Many of the examples in this book are in Java. But because of the interface used to access Cassandra, you can use Cassandra from a wide variety of languages, including C#, Python, node.js, PHP, and Ruby.

Finally, it is assumed that you have a good understanding of how the Web works, can use an integrated development environment (IDE), and are somewhat familiar with the typical concerns of data-driven applications. You might be a well-seasoned developer or administrator but still, on occasion, encounter tools used in the Cassandra world that you're not familiar with. For example, Apache Ant is used to build Cassandra, and the Cassandra source code is available via Git. In cases where we speculate that you'll need to do a little setup of your own in order to work with the examples, we try to support that.

What's in This Book?

This book is designed with the chapters acting, to a reasonable extent, as standalone guides. This is important for a book on Cassandra, which has a variety of audiences and is changing rapidly. To borrow from the software world, the book is designed to be "modular." If you're new to Cassandra, it makes sense to read the book in order; if you've passed the introductory stages, you will still find value in later chapters, which you can read as standalone guides.

Here is how the book is organized:

Chapter 1, Beyond Relational Databases
    This chapter reviews the history of the enormously successful relational database and the recent rise of non-relational database technologies like Cassandra.

Chapter 2, Introducing Cassandra

This chapter introduces Cassandra and discusses what's exciting and different about it, where it came from, and what its advantages are.

Chapter 3, Installing Cassandra

This chapter walks you through installing Cassandra, getting it running, and trying out some of its basic features.

Chapter 4, The Cassandra Query Language

Here we look at Cassandra's data model, highlighting how it differs from the traditional relational model. We also explore how this data model is expressed in the Cassandra Query Language (CQL).

Chapter 5, Data Modeling

This chapter introduces principles and processes for data modeling in Cassandra. We analyze a well-understood domain to produce a working schema.

Chapter 6, The Cassandra Architecture

This chapter helps you understand what happens during read and write operations and how the database accomplishes some of its notable aspects, such as durability and high availability. We go under the hood to understand some of the more complex inner workings, such as the gossip protocol, hinted handoffs, read repairs, Merkle trees, and more.

Chapter 7, Configuring Cassandra

This chapter shows you how to specify partitioners, replica placement strategies, and snitches. We set up a cluster and see the implications of different configuration choices.

Chapter 8, Clients

There are a variety of clients available for different languages, including Java, Python, node.js, Ruby, C#, and PHP, in order to abstract Cassandra's lower-level API. We help you understand common driver features.

Chapter 9, Reading and Writing Data

We build on the previous chapters to learn how Cassandra works "under the covers" to read and write data. We'll also discuss concepts such as batches, lightweight transactions, and paging.

Chapter 10, Monitoring

Once your cluster is up and running, you'll want to monitor its usage, memory patterns, and thread patterns, and understand its general activity. Cassandra has a rich Java Management Extensions (JMX) interface baked in, which we put to use to monitor all of these and more.

Chapter 11, Maintenance

The ongoing maintenance of a Cassandra cluster is made somewhat easier by some tools that ship with the server. We see how to decommission a node, load balance the cluster, get statistics, and perform other routine operational tasks.

Chapter 12, Performance Tuning

One of Cassandra's most notable features is its speed—it's very fast. But there are a number of things, including memory settings, data storage, hardware choices, caching, and buffer sizes, that you can tune to squeeze out even more performance.

Chapter 13, Security

NoSQL technologies are often slighted as being weak on security. Thankfully, Cassandra provides authentication, authorization, and encryption features, which we'll learn how to configure in this chapter.

Chapter 14, Deploying and Integrating

We close the book with a discussion of considerations for planning cluster deployments, including cloud deployments using providers such as Amazon, Microsoft, and Google. We also introduce several technologies that are frequently paired with Cassandra to extend its capabilities.

Cassandra Versions Used in This Book

This book was developed using the Cassandra 3.X series of releases, along with the DataStax Java Driver version 3.0.

When discussing features added in releases 2.0 and later, we cite the release in which the feature was added for readers who may be using earlier versions and are considering whether to upgrade.

New for the Second Edition

The first edition of *Cassandra: The Definitive Guide* was the first book published on Cassandra, and has remained highly regarded over the years. However, the Cassandra landscape has changed significantly since 2010, both in terms of the technology itself and the community that develops and supports that technology. Here's a summary of the key updates we've made to bring the book up to date:

A sense of history

The first edition was written against the 0.7 release in 2010. As of 2016, we're up to the 3.X series. The most significant change has been the introduction of CQL and deprecation of the old Thrift API. Other new architectural features include secondary indexes, materialized views, and lightweight transactions. We provide a summary release history in Chapter 2 to help guide you through the changes.

As we introduce new features throughout the text, we frequently cite the releases in which these features were added.

Giving developers a leg up

Development and testing with Cassandra has changed a lot over the years, with the introduction of the CQL shell (cqlsh) and the gradual replacement of community-developed clients with the drivers provided by DataStax. We give in-depth treatment to cqlsh in Chapters 3 and 4, and the drivers in Chapters 8 and 9. We also provide an expanded description of Cassandra's read path and write path in Chapter 9 to enhance your understanding of the internals and help you understand the impact of decisions.

Maturing Cassandra operations

As more and more individuals and organizations have deployed Cassandra in production environments, the knowledge base of production challenges and best practices to meet those challenges has increased. We've added entirely new chapters on security (Chapter 13) and deployment and integration (Chapter 14), and greatly expanded the monitoring, maintenance, and performance tuning chapters (Chapters 10 through 12) in order to relate this collected wisdom.

Conventions Used in This Book

The following typographical conventions are used in this book:

Italic

Indicates new terms, URLs, email addresses, filenames, and file extensions.

`Constant width`

Used for program listings, as well as within paragraphs to refer to program elements such as variable or function names, databases, data types, environment variables, statements, and keywords.

`Constant width bold`

Shows commands or other text that should be typed literally by the user.

`Constant width italic`

Shows text that should be replaced with user-supplied values or by values determined by context.

 This element signifies a tip or suggestion.

 This element signifies a general note.

 This element indicates a warning or caution.

Using Code Examples

The code examples found in this book are available for download at *https://github.com/jeffreyscarpenter/cassandra-guide*.

This book is here to help you get your job done. In general, you may use the code in this book in your programs and documentation. You do not need to contact us for permission unless you're reproducing a significant portion of the code. For example, writing a program that uses several chunks of code from this book does not require permission. Selling or distributing a CD-ROM of examples from O'Reilly books does require permission. Answering a question by citing this book and quoting example code does not require permission. Incorporating a significant amount of example code from this book into your product's documentation does require permission.

We appreciate, but do not require, attribution. An attribution usually includes the title, author, publisher, and ISBN. For example: "*Cassandra: The Definitive Guide, Second Edition*, by Jeff Carpenter. Copyright 2016 Jeff Carpenter, 978-1-491-93366-4."

If you feel your use of code examples falls outside fair use or the permission given here, feel free to contact us at *permissions@oreilly.com*.

Safari® Books Online

 *Safari Books Online* is an on-demand digital library that delivers expert content in both book and video form from the world's leading authors in technology and business.

Technology professionals, software developers, web designers, and business and creative professionals use Safari Books Online as their primary resource for research, problem solving, learning, and certification training.

Safari Books Online offers a range of plans and pricing for enterprise, government, education, and individuals.

Members have access to thousands of books, training videos, and prepublication manuscripts in one fully searchable database from publishers like O'Reilly Media, Prentice Hall Professional, Addison-Wesley Professional, Microsoft Press, Sams, Que, Peachpit Press, Focal Press, Cisco Press, John Wiley & Sons, Syngress, Morgan Kaufmann, IBM Redbooks, Packt, Adobe Press, FT Press, Apress, Manning, New Riders, McGraw-Hill, Jones & Bartlett, Course Technology, and hundreds more. For more information about Safari Books Online, please visit us online.

How to Contact Us

Please address comments and questions concerning this book to the publisher:

O'Reilly Media, Inc.
1005 Gravenstein Highway North
Sebastopol, CA 95472
800-998-9938 (in the United States or Canada)
707-829-0515 (international or local)
707-829-0104 (fax)

We have a web page for this book, where we list errata, examples, and any additional information. You can access this page at *http://bit.ly/cassandra2e*.

To comment or ask technical questions about this book, send email to *bookquestions@oreilly.com*.

For more information about our books, courses, conferences, and news, see our website at *http://www.oreilly.com*.

Find us on Facebook: *http://facebook.com/oreilly*

Follow us on Twitter: *http://twitter.com/oreillymedia*

Watch us on YouTube: *http://www.youtube.com/oreillymedia*

Acknowledgments

There are many wonderful people to whom we are grateful for helping bring this book to life.

Thank you to our technical reviewers: Stu Hood, Robert Schneider, and Gary Dusbabek contributed thoughtful reviews to the first edition, while Andrew Baker, Ewan Elliot, Kirk Damron, Corey Cole, Jeff Jirsa, and Patrick McFadin reviewed the second edition. Chris Judson's feedback was key to the maturation of Chapter 14.

Thank you to Jonathan Ellis and Patrick McFadin for writing forewords for the first and second editions, respectively. Thanks also to Patrick for his contributions to the Spark integration section in Chapter 14.

Thanks to our editors, Mike Loukides and Marie Beaugureau, for their constant support and making this a better book.

Jeff would like to thank Eben for entrusting him with the opportunity to update such a well-regarded, foundational text, and for Eben's encouragement from start to finish.

Finally, we've been inspired by the many terrific developers who have contributed to Cassandra. Hats off for making such an elegant and powerful database.

## CHAPTER 1

Beyond Relational Databases

If at first the idea is not absurd, then there is no hope for it.
—Albert Einstein

Welcome to *Cassandra: The Definitive Guide*. The aim of this book is to help developers and database administrators understand this important database technology. During the course of this book, we will explore how Cassandra compares to traditional relational database management systems, and help you put it to work in your own environment.

What's Wrong with Relational Databases?

If I had asked people what they wanted, they would have said faster horses.
—Henry Ford

We ask you to consider a certain model for data, invented by a small team at a company with thousands of employees. It was accessible over a TCP/IP interface and was available from a variety of languages, including Java and web services. This model was difficult at first for all but the most advanced computer scientists to understand, until broader adoption helped make the concepts clearer. Using the database built around this model required learning new terms and thinking about data storage in a different way. But as products sprang up around it, more businesses and government agencies put it to use, in no small part because it was fast—capable of processing thousands of operations a second. The revenue it generated was tremendous.

And then a new model came along.

The new model was threatening, chiefly for two reasons. First, the new model was very different from the old model, which it pointedly controverted. It was threatening because it can be hard to understand something different and new. Ensuing debates can help entrench people stubbornly further in their views—views that might have been largely inherited from the climate in which they learned their craft and the circumstances in which they work. Second, and perhaps more importantly, as a barrier, the new model was threatening because businesses had made considerable investments in the old model and were making lots of money with it. Changing course seemed ridiculous, even impossible.

Of course, we are talking about the Information Management System (IMS) hierarchical database, invented in 1966 at IBM.

IMS was built for use in the Saturn V moon rocket. Its architect was Vern Watts, who dedicated his career to it. Many of us are familiar with IBM's database DB2. IBM's wildly popular DB2 database gets its name as the successor to DB1—the product built around the hierarchical data model IMS. IMS was released in 1968, and subsequently enjoyed success in Customer Information Control System (CICS) and other applications. It is still used today.

But in the years following the invention of IMS, the new model, the disruptive model, the threatening model, was the relational database.

In his 1970 paper "A Relational Model of Data for Large Shared Data Banks," Dr. Edgar F. Codd, also at advanced his theory of the relational model for data while working at IBM's San Jose research laboratory. This paper, still available at *http://www.seas.upenn.edu/~zives/03f/cis550/codd.pdf*, became the foundational work for relational database management systems.

Codd's work was antithetical to the hierarchical structure of IMS. Understanding and working with a relational database required learning new terms, including "relations," "tuples," and "normal form," all of which must have sounded very strange indeed to users of IMS. It presented certain key advantages over its predecessor, such as the ability to express complex relationships between multiple entities, well beyond what could be represented by hierarchical databases.

While these ideas and their application have evolved in four decades, the relational database still is clearly one of the most successful software applications in history. It's used in the form of Microsoft Access in sole proprietorships, and in giant multinational corporations with clusters of hundreds of finely tuned instances representing multi-terabyte data warehouses. Relational databases store invoices, customer records, product catalogues, accounting ledgers, user authentication schemes—the very world, it might appear. There is no question that the relational database is a key facet of the modern technology and business landscape, and one that will be with us in its various forms for many years to come, as will IMS in its various forms. The relational model presented an alternative to IMS, and each has its uses.

So the short answer to the question, "What's wrong with relational databases?" is "Nothing."

There is, however, a rather longer answer, which says that every once in a while an idea is born that ostensibly changes things, and engenders a revolution of sorts. And yet, in another way, such revolutions, viewed structurally, are simply history's business as usual. IMS, RDBMSs, NoSQL. The horse, the car, the plane. They each build on prior art, they each attempt to solve certain problems, and so they're each good at certain things—and less good at others. They each coexist, even now.

So let's examine for a moment why, at this point, we might consider an alternative to the relational database, just as Codd himself four decades ago looked at the Information Management System and thought that maybe it wasn't the only legitimate way of organizing information and solving data problems, and that maybe, for certain problems, it might prove fruitful to consider an alternative.

We encounter scalability problems when our relational applications become successful and usage goes up. Joins are inherent in any relatively normalized relational database of even modest size, and joins can be slow. The way that databases gain consistency is typically through the use of transactions, which require locking some portion of the database so it's not available to other clients. This can become untenable under very heavy loads, as the locks mean that competing users start queuing up, waiting for their turn to read or write the data.

We typically address these problems in one or more of the following ways, sometimes in this order:

- Throw hardware at the problem by adding more memory, adding faster processors, and upgrading disks. This is known as *vertical scaling*. This can relieve you for a time.

- When the problems arise again, the answer appears to be similar: now that one box is maxed out, you add hardware in the form of additional boxes in a database cluster. Now you have the problem of data replication and consistency during regular usage and in failover scenarios. You didn't have that problem before.

- Now we need to update the configuration of the database management system. This might mean optimizing the channels the database uses to write to the underlying filesystem. We turn off logging or journaling, which frequently is not a desirable (or, depending on your situation, legal) option.

- Having put what attention we could into the database system, we turn to our application. We try to improve our indexes. We optimize the queries. But presumably at this scale we weren't wholly ignorant of index and query optimization, and already had them in pretty good shape. So this becomes a painful process of picking through the data access code to find any opportunities for fine-tuning. This might include reducing or reorganizing joins, throwing out resource-intensive features such as XML processing within a stored procedure, and so forth. Of course, presumably we were doing that XML processing for a reason, so if we have to do it somewhere, we move that problem to the application layer, hoping to solve it there and crossing our fingers that we don't break something else in the meantime.

- We employ a caching layer. For larger systems, this might include distributed caches such as memcached, Redis, Riak, EHCache, or other related products. Now we have a consistency problem between updates in the cache and updates in the database, which is exacerbated over a cluster.

- We turn our attention to the database again and decide that, now that the application is built and we understand the primary query paths, we can duplicate some of the data to make it look more like the queries that access it. This process, called denormalization, is antithetical to the five normal forms that characterize the relational model, and violates Codd's 12 Rules for relational data. We remind ourselves that we live in this world, and not in some theoretical cloud, and then undertake to do what we must to make the application start responding at acceptable levels again, even if it's no longer "pure."

Codd's Twelve Rules

Codd provided a list of 12 rules (there are actually 13, numbered 0 to 12) formalizing his definition of the relational model as a response to the divergence of commercial databases from his original concepts. Codd introduced his rules in a pair of articles in *CompuWorld* magazine in October 1985, and formalized them in the second edition of his book *The Relational Model for Database Management*, which is now out of print.

This likely sounds familiar to you. At web scale, engineers may legitimately ponder whether this situation isn't similar to Henry Ford's assertion that at a certain point, it's not simply a faster horse that you want. And they've done some impressive, interesting work.

We must therefore begin here in recognition that the relational model is simply a model. That is, it's intended to be a useful way of looking at the world, applicable to certain problems. It does not purport to be exhaustive, closing the case on all other ways of representing data, never again to be examined, leaving no room for alternatives. If we take the long view of history, Dr. Codd's model was a rather disruptive one in its time. It was new, with strange new vocabulary and terms such as "tuples"— familiar words used in a new and different manner. The relational model was held up to suspicion, and doubtless suffered its vehement detractors. It encountered opposition even in the form of Dr. Codd's own employer, IBM, which had a very lucrative product set around IMS and didn't need a young upstart cutting into its pie.

But the relational model now arguably enjoys the best seat in the house within the data world. SQL is widely supported and well understood. It is taught in introductory university courses. There are open source databases that come installed and ready to use with a $4.95 monthly web hosting plan. Cloud-based Platform-as-a-Service (PaaS) providers such as Amazon Web Services, Google Cloud Platform, Rackspace, and Microsoft Azure provide relational database access as a service, including automated monitoring and maintenance features. Often the database we end up using is dictated to us by architectural standards within our organization. Even absent such standards, it's prudent to learn whatever your organization already has for a database platform. Our colleagues in development and infrastructure have considerable hard-won knowledge.

If by nothing more than osmosis (or inertia), we have learned over the years that a relational database is a one-size-fits-all solution.

So perhaps a better question is not, "What's wrong with relational databases?" but rather, "What problem do you have?"

That is, you want to ensure that your solution matches the problem that you have. There are certain problems that relational databases solve very well. But the explosion of the Web, and in particular social networks, means a corresponding explosion in the sheer volume of data we must deal with. When Tim Berners-Lee first worked on the Web in the early 1990s, it was for the purpose of exchanging scientific documents between PhDs at a physics laboratory. Now, of course, the Web has become so ubiquitous that it's used by everyone, from those same scientists to legions of five-year-olds exchanging emoticons about kittens. That means in part that it must support enormous volumes of data; the fact that it does stands as a monument to the ingenious architecture of the Web.

But some of this infrastructure is starting to bend under the weight.

A Quick Review of Relational Databases

Though you are likely familiar with them, let's briefly turn our attention to some of the foundational concepts in relational databases. This will give us a basis on which to consider more recent advances in thought around the trade-offs inherent in distributed data systems, especially very large distributed data systems, such as those that are required at web scale.

RDBMSs: The Awesome and the Not-So-Much

There are many reasons that the relational database has become so overwhelmingly popular over the last four decades. An important one is the Structured Query Language (SQL), which is feature-rich and uses a simple, declarative syntax. SQL was first officially adopted as an ANSI standard in 1986; since that time, it's gone through several revisions and has also been extended with vendor proprietary syntax such as Microsoft's T-SQL and Oracle's PL/SQL to provide additional implementation-specific features.

SQL is powerful for a variety of reasons. It allows the user to represent complex relationships with the data, using statements that form the Data Manipulation Language (DML) to insert, select, update, delete, truncate, and merge data. You can perform a rich variety of operations using functions based on relational algebra to find a maximum or minimum value in a set, for example, or to filter and order results. SQL statements support grouping aggregate values and executing summary functions. SQL provides a means of directly creating, altering, and dropping schema structures at runtime using Data Definition Language (DDL). SQL also allows you to grant and revoke rights for users and groups of users using the same syntax.

SQL is easy to use. The basic syntax can be learned quickly, and conceptually SQL and RDBMSs offer a low barrier to entry. Junior developers can become proficient readily, and as is often the case in an industry beset by rapid changes, tight deadlines, and exploding budgets, ease of use can be very important. And it's not just the syntax that's easy to use; there are many robust tools that include intuitive graphical interfaces for viewing and working with your database.

In part because it's a standard, SQL allows you to easily integrate your RDBMS with a wide variety of systems. All you need is a driver for your application language, and you're off to the races in a very portable way. If you decide to change your application implementation language (or your RDBMS vendor), you can often do that painlessly, assuming you haven't backed yourself into a corner using lots of proprietary extensions.

Transactions, ACID-ity, and two-phase commit

In addition to the features mentioned already, RDBMSs and SQL also support *transactions*. A key feature of transactions is that they execute virtually at first, allowing the programmer to undo (using rollback) any changes that may have gone awry during execution; if all has gone well, the transaction can be reliably committed. As Jim Gray puts it, a transaction is "a transformation of state" that has the ACID properties (see "The Transaction Concept: Virtues and Limitations" (*http://research.micro soft.com/en-us/um/people/gray/papers/theTransactionConcept.pdf*)).

ACID is an acronym for Atomic, Consistent, Isolated, Durable, which are the gauges we can use to assess that a transaction has executed properly and that it was successful:

Atomic
    Atomic means "all or nothing"; that is, when a statement is executed, every update within the transaction must succeed in order to be called successful.

There is no partial failure where one update was successful and another related update failed. The common example here is with monetary transfers at an ATM: the transfer requires subtracting money from one account and adding it to another account. This operation cannot be subdivided; they must both succeed.

Consistent

Consistent means that data moves from one correct state to another correct state, with no possibility that readers could view different values that don't make sense together. For example, if a transaction attempts to delete a customer and her order history, it cannot leave order rows that reference the deleted customer's primary key; this is an inconsistent state that would cause errors if someone tried to read those order records.

Isolated

Isolated means that transactions executing concurrently will not become entangled with each other; they each execute in their own space. That is, if two different transactions attempt to modify the same data at the same time, then one of them will have to wait for the other to complete.

Durable

Once a transaction has succeeded, the changes will not be lost. This doesn't imply another transaction won't later modify the same data; it just means that writers can be confident that the changes are available for the next transaction to work with as necessary.

The debate about support for transactions comes up very quickly as a sore spot in conversations around non-relational data stores, so let's take a moment to revisit what this really means. On the surface, ACID properties seem so obviously desirable as to not even merit conversation. Presumably no one who runs a database would suggest that data updates don't have to endure for some length of time; that's the very point of making updates—that they're there for others to read. However, a more subtle examination might lead us to want to find a way to tune these properties a bit and control them slightly. There is, as they say, no free lunch on the Internet, and once we see how we're paying for our transactions, we may start to wonder whether there's an alternative.

Transactions become difficult under heavy load. When you first attempt to horizontally scale a relational database, making it distributed, you must now account for *distributed transactions*, where the transaction isn't simply operating inside a single table or a single database, but is spread across multiple systems. In order to continue to honor the ACID properties of transactions, you now need a transaction manager to orchestrate across the multiple nodes.

In order to account for successful completion across multiple hosts, the idea of a two-phase commit (sometimes referred to as "2PC") is introduced. But then, because two-phase commit locks all associated resources, it is useful only for operations that can complete very quickly. Although it may often be the case that your distributed operations can complete in sub-second time, it is certainly not always the case. Some use cases require coordination between multiple hosts that you may not control yourself. Operations coordinating several different but related activities can take hours to update.

Two-phase commit *blocks*; that is, clients ("competing consumers") must wait for a prior transaction to finish before they can access the blocked resource. The protocol will wait for a node to respond, even if it has died. It's possible to avoid waiting forever in this event, because a timeout can be set that allows the transaction coordinator node to decide that the node isn't going to respond and that it should abort the transaction. However, an infinite loop is still possible with 2PC; that's because a node can send a message to the transaction coordinator node agreeing that it's OK for the coordinator to commit the entire transaction. The node will then wait for the coordinator to send a commit response (or a rollback response if, say, a different node can't commit); if the coordinator is down in this scenario, that node conceivably will wait forever.

So in order to account for these shortcomings in two-phase commit of distributed transactions, the database world turned to the idea of *compensation*. Compensation, often used in web services, means in simple terms that the operation is immediately committed, and then in the event that some error is reported, a new operation is invoked to restore proper state.

There are a few basic, well-known patterns for compensatory action that architects frequently have to consider as an alternative to two-phase commit. These include writing off the transaction if it fails, deciding to discard erroneous transactions and reconciling later. Another alternative is to retry failed operations later on notification. In a reservation system or a stock sales ticker, these are not likely to meet your requirements. For other kinds of applications, such as billing or ticketing applications, this can be acceptable.

The Problem with Two-Phase Commit

Gregor Hohpe, a Google architect, wrote a wonderful and often-cited blog entry called "Starbucks Does Not Use Two-Phase Commit" (*http://www.eaipatterns.com/ramblings/18_starbucks.html*). It shows in real-world terms how difficult it is to scale two-phase commit and highlights some of the alternatives that are mentioned here. It's an easy, fun, and enlightening read.

The problems that 2PC introduces for application developers include loss of availability and higher latency during partial failures. Neither of these is desirable. So once you've had the good fortune of being successful enough to necessitate scaling your database past a single machine, you now have to figure out how to handle transactions across multiple machines and still make the ACID properties apply. Whether you have 10 or 100 or 1,000 database machines, atomicity is still required in transactions as if you were working on a single node. But it's now a much, much bigger pill to swallow.

Schema

One often-lauded feature of relational database systems is the rich schemas they afford. You can represent your domain objects in a relational model. A whole industry has sprung up around (expensive) tools such as the CA ERWin Data Modeler to support this effort. In order to create a properly normalized schema, however, you are forced to create tables that don't exist as business objects in your domain. For example, a schema for a university database might require a "student" table and a "course" table. But because of the "many-to-many" relationship here (one student can take many courses at the same time, and one course has many students at the same time), you have to create a join table. This pollutes a pristine data model, where we'd prefer to just have students and courses. It also forces us to create more complex SQL statements to join these tables together. The join statements, in turn, can be slow.

Again, in a system of modest size, this isn't much of a problem. But complex queries and multiple joins can become burdensomely slow once you have a large number of rows in many tables to handle.

Finally, not all schemas map well to the relational model. One type of system that has risen in popularity in the last decade is the complex event processing system, which represents state changes in a very fast stream. It's often useful to contextualize events at runtime against other events that might be related in order to infer some conclusion to support business decision making. Although event streams could be represented in terms of a relational database, it is an uncomfortable stretch.

And if you're an application developer, you'll no doubt be familiar with the many object-relational mapping (ORM) frameworks that have sprung up in recent years to help ease the difficulty in mapping application objects to a relational model. Again, for small systems, ORM can be a relief. But it also introduces new problems of its own, such as extended memory requirements, and it often pollutes the application code with increasingly unwieldy mapping code. Here's an example of a Java method using Hibernate to "ease the burden" of having to write the SQL code:

```
@CollectionOfElements
@JoinTable(name="store_description",
  joinColumns = @JoinColumn(name="store_code"))
@MapKey(columns={@Column(name="for_store",length=3)})
@Column(name="description")
private Map<String, String> getMap() {
  return this.map;
```

```
}
//... etc.
```

Is it certain that we've done anything but move the problem here? Of course, with some systems, such as those that make extensive use of document exchange, as with services or XML-based applications, there are not always clear mappings to a relational database. This exacerbates the problem.

Sharding and shared-nothing architecture

> *If you can't split it, you can't scale it.*
> —Randy Shoup, Distinguished Architect, eBay

Another way to attempt to scale a relational database is to introduce *sharding* to your architecture. This has been used to good effect at large websites such as eBay, which supports billions of SQL queries a day, and in other modern web applications. The idea here is that you split the data so that instead of hosting all of it on a single server or replicating all of the data on all of the servers in a cluster, you divide up portions of the data horizontally and host them each separately.

For example, consider a large customer table in a relational database. The least disruptive thing (for the programming staff, anyway) is to vertically scale by adding CPU, adding memory, and getting faster hard drives, but if you continue to be successful and add more customers, at some point (perhaps into the tens of millions of rows), you'll likely have to start thinking about how you can add more machines. When you do so, do you just copy the data so that all of the machines have it? Or do you instead divide up that single customer table so that each database has only some of the records, with their order preserved? Then, when clients execute queries, they put load only on the machine that has the record they're looking for, with no load on the other machines.

It seems clear that in order to shard, you need to find a good key by which to order your records. For example, you could divide your customer records across 26 machines, one for each letter of the alphabet, with each hosting only the records for customers whose last names start with that particular letter. It's likely this is not a good strategy, however—there probably aren't many last names that begin with "Q" or "Z," so those machines will sit idle while the "J," "M," and "S" machines spike. You could shard according to something numeric, like phone number, "member since" date, or the name of the customer's state. It all depends on how your specific data is likely to be distributed.

There are three basic strategies for determining shard structure:

Feature-based shard or functional segmentation
This is the approach taken by Randy Shoup, Distinguished Architect at eBay, who in 2006 helped bring the site's architecture into maturity to support many billions of queries per day. Using this strategy, the data is split not by dividing records in a single table (as in the customer example discussed earlier), but rather by splitting into separate databases the features that don't overlap with each other very much. For example, at eBay, the users are in one shard, and the items for sale are in another. At Flixster, movie ratings are in one shard and comments are in another. This approach depends on understanding your domain so that you can segment data cleanly.

Key-based sharding
In this approach, you find a key in your data that will evenly distribute it across shards. So instead of simply storing one letter of the alphabet for each server as in the (naive and improper) earlier example, you use a one-way hash on a key data element and distribute data across machines according to the hash. It is common in this strategy to find time-based or numeric keys to hash on.

Lookup table
In this approach, one of the nodes in the cluster acts as a "yellow pages" directory and looks up which node has the data you're trying to access. This has two obvious disadvantages. The first is that you'll take a performance hit every time you have to go through the lookup table as an additional hop. The second is that the lookup table not only becomes a bottleneck, but a single point of failure.

Sharding can minimize contention depending on your strategy and allows you not just to scale horizontally, but then to scale more precisely, as you can add power to the particular shards that need it.

Sharding could be termed a kind of "shared-nothing" architecture that's specific to databases. A *shared-nothing* architecture is one in which there is no centralized (shared) state, but each node in a distributed system is independent, so there is no client contention for shared resources. The term was first coined by Michael Stonebraker at the University of California at Berkeley in his 1986 paper "The Case for Shared Nothing."

Shared-nothing architecture was more recently popularized by Google, which has written systems such as its Bigtable database and its MapReduce implementation that do not share state, and are therefore capable of near-infinite scaling. The Cassandra database is a shared-nothing architecture, as it has no central controller and no notion of master/slave; all of its nodes are the same.

More on Shared-Nothing Architecture

You can read the 1986 paper "The Case for Shared Nothing" online at *http://db.cs.berkeley.edu/papers/hpts85-nothing.pdf*. It's only a few pages. If you take a look, you'll see that many of the features of shared-nothing distributed data architecture, such as ease of high availability and the ability to scale to a very large number of machines, are the very things that Cassandra excels at.

MongoDB also provides auto-sharding capabilities to manage failover and node balancing. That many non-relational databases offer this automatically and out of the box is very handy; creating and maintaining custom data shards by hand is a wicked proposition. It's good to understand sharding in terms of data architecture in general, but especially in terms of Cassandra more specifically, as it can take an approach similar to key-based sharding to distribute data across nodes, but does so automatically.

Web Scale

In summary, relational databases are very good at solving certain data storage problems, but because of their focus, they also can create problems of their own when it's time to scale. Then, you often need to find a way to get rid of your joins, which means denormalizing the data, which means maintaining multiple copies of data and seriously disrupting your design, both in the database and in your application. Further, you almost certainly need to find a way around distributed transactions, which will quickly become a bottleneck. These compensatory actions are not directly supported in any but the most expensive RDBMSs. And even if you can write such a huge check, you still need to carefully choose partitioning keys to the point where you can never entirely ignore the limitation.

Perhaps more importantly, as we see some of the limitations of RDBMSs and consequently some of the strategies that architects have used to mitigate their scaling issues, a picture slowly starts to emerge. It's a picture that makes some NoSQL solutions seem perhaps less radical and less scary than we may have thought at first, and more like a natural expression and encapsulation of some of the work that was already being done to manage very large databases.

Because of some of the inherent design decisions in RDBMSs, it is not always as easy to scale as some other, more recent possibilities that take the structure of the Web into consideration. However, it's not only the structure of the Web we need to consider, but also its phenomenal growth, because as more and more data becomes available, we need architectures that allow our organizations to take advantage of this data in near real time to support decision making and to offer new and more powerful features and capabilities to our customers.

Data Scale, Then and Now

It has been said, though it is hard to verify, that the 17th-century English poet John Milton had actually read every published book on the face of the earth. Milton knew many languages (he was even learning Navajo at the time of his death), and given that the total number of published books at that time was in the thousands, this would have been possible. The size of the world's data stores have grown somewhat since then.

With the rapid growth in the Web, there is great variety to the kinds of data that need to be stored, processed, and queried, and some variety to the businesses that use such data. Consider not only customer data at familiar retailers or suppliers, and not only digital video content, but also the required move to digital television and the explosive growth of email, messaging, mobile phones, RFID, Voice Over IP (VoIP) usage, and the Internet of Things (IoT). As we have departed from physical consumer media storage, companies that provide content—and the third-party value-add businesses built around them—require very scalable data solutions. Consider too that as a typical business application developer or database administrator, we may be used to thinking of relational databases as the center of our universe. You might then be surprised to learn that within corporations, around 80% of data is unstructured.

The Rise of NoSQL

The recent interest in non-relational databases reflects the growing sense of need in the software development community for web scale data solutions. The term "NoSQL" began gaining popularity around 2009 as a shorthand way of describing these databases. The term has historically been the subject of much debate, but a consensus has emerged that the term refers to non-relational databases that support "not only SQL" semantics.

Various experts have attempted to organize these databases in a few broad categories; we'll examine a few of the most common:

Key-value stores

> In a key-value store, the data items are keys that have a set of attributes. All data relevant to a key is stored with the key; data is frequently duplicated. Popular key-value stores include Amazon's Dynamo DB, Riak, and Voldemort. Additionally, many popular caching technologies act as key-value stores, including Oracle Coherence, Redis, and MemcacheD.

Column stores

> Column stores are also frequently known as wide-column stores. Google's Bigtable served as the inspiration for implementations including Cassandra, Hypertable, and Apache Hadoop's HBase.

Document stores

The basic unit of storage in a document database is the complete document, often stored in a format such as JSON, XML, or YAML. Popular document stores include MongoDB and CouchDB.

Graph databases

Graph databases represent data as a graph—a network of nodes and edges that connect the nodes. Both nodes and edges can have properties. Because they give heightened importance to relationships, graph databases such as FlockDB, Neo4J, and Polyglot have proven popular for building social networking and semantic web applications.

Object databases

Object databases store data not in terms of relations and columns and rows, but in terms of the objects themselves, making it straightforward to use the database from an object-oriented application. Object databases such as db4o and InterSystems Caché allow you to avoid techniques like stored procedures and object-relational mapping (ORM) tools.

XML databases

XML databases are a special form of document databases, optimized specifically for working with XML. So-called "XML native" databases include Tamino from Software AG and eXist.

For a comprehensive list of NoSQL databases, see the site *http://nosql-database.org.*

There is wide variety in the goals and features of these databases, but they tend to share a set of common characteristics. The most obvious of these is implied by the name NoSQL—these databases support data models, data definition languages (DDLs), and interfaces beyond the standard SQL available in popular relational databases. In addition, these databases are typically distributed systems without centralized control. They emphasize horizontal scalability and high availability, in some cases at the cost of strong consistency and ACID semantics. They tend to support rapid development and deployment. They take flexible approaches to schema definition, in some cases not requiring any schema to be defined up front. They provide support for Big Data and analytics use cases.

Over the past several years, there have been a large number of open source and commercial offerings in the NoSQL space. The adoption and quality of these have varied widely, but leaders have emerged in the categories just discussed, and many have become mature technologies with large installation bases and commercial support. We're happy to report that Cassandra is one of those technologies, as we'll dig into more in the next chapter.

Summary

The relational model has served the software industry well over the past four decades, but the level of availability and scalability required for modern applications has stretched relational database technology to the breaking point.

The intention of this book is not to convince you by clever argument to adopt a non-relational database such as Apache Cassandra. It is only our intention to present what Cassandra can do and how it does it so that you can make an informed decision and get started working with it in practical ways if you find it applies.

Perhaps the ultimate question, then, is not "What's wrong with relational databases?" but rather, "What kinds of things would I do with data if it wasn't a problem?" In a world now working at web scale and looking to the future, Apache Cassandra might be one part of the answer.

## CHAPTER 2

Introducing Cassandra

An invention has to make sense in the world in which it is finished,
not the world in which it is started.
—Ray Kurzweil

In the previous chapter, we discussed the emergence of non-relational database technologies in order to meet the increasing demands of modern web scale applications.
In this chapter, we'll focus on Cassandra's value proposition and key tenets to show
how it rises to the challenge. You'll also learn about Cassandra's history and how you
can get involved in the open source community that maintains Cassandra.

The Cassandra Elevator Pitch

Hollywood screenwriters and software startups are often advised to have their "elevator pitch" ready. This is a summary of exactly what their product is all about—con-
cise, clear, and brief enough to deliver in just a minute or two, in the lucky event that
they find themselves sharing an elevator with an executive, agent, or investor who
might consider funding their project. Cassandra has a compelling story, so let's boil it
down to an elevator pitch that you can present to your manager or colleagues should
the occasion arise.

Cassandra in 50 Words or Less

"Apache Cassandra is an open source, distributed, decentralized, elastically scalable,
highly available, fault-tolerant, tuneably consistent, row-oriented database that bases
its distribution design on Amazon's Dynamo and its data model on Google's Bigtable.
Created at Facebook, it is now used at some of the most popular sites on the Web."
That's exactly 50 words.

Of course, if you were to recite that to your boss in the elevator, you'd probably get a blank look in return. So let's break down the key points in the following sections.

Distributed and Decentralized

Cassandra is *distributed*, which means that it is capable of running on multiple machines while appearing to users as a unified whole. In fact, there is little point in running a single Cassandra node. Although you can do it, and that's acceptable for getting up to speed on how it works, you quickly realize that you'll need multiple machines to really realize any benefit from running Cassandra. Much of its design and code base is specifically engineered toward not only making it work across many different machines, but also for optimizing performance across multiple data center racks, and even for a single Cassandra cluster running across geographically dispersed data centers. You can confidently write data to anywhere in the cluster and Cassandra will get it.

Once you start to scale many other data stores (MySQL, Bigtable), some nodes need to be set up as masters in order to organize other nodes, which are set up as slaves. Cassandra, however, is decentralized, meaning that every node is identical; no Cassandra node performs certain organizing operations distinct from any other node. Instead, Cassandra features a peer-to-peer protocol and uses gossip to maintain and keep in sync a list of nodes that are alive or dead.

The fact that Cassandra is *decentralized* means that there is no single point of failure. All of the nodes in a Cassandra cluster function exactly the same. This is sometimes referred to as "server symmetry." Because they are all doing the same thing, by definition there can't be a special host that is coordinating activities, as with the master/slave setup that you see in MySQL, Bigtable, and so many others.

In many distributed data solutions (such as RDBMS clusters), you set up multiple copies of data on different servers in a process called replication, which copies the data to multiple machines so that they can all serve simultaneous requests and improve performance. Typically this process is not decentralized, as in Cassandra, but is rather performed by defining a *master/slave relationship*. That is, all of the servers in this kind of cluster don't function in the same way. You configure your cluster by designating one server as the master and others as slaves. The master acts as the authoritative source of the data, and operates in a unidirectional relationship with the slave nodes, which must synchronize their copies. If the master node fails, the whole database is in jeopardy. The decentralized design is therefore one of the keys to Cassandra's high availability. Note that while we frequently understand master/slave replication in the RDBMS world, there are NoSQL databases such as MongoDB that follow the master/slave scheme as well.

Decentralization, therefore, has two key advantages: it's simpler to use than master/slave, and it helps you avoid outages. It can be easier to operate and maintain a decentralized store than a master/slave store because all nodes are the same. That means that you don't need any special knowledge to scale; setting up 50 nodes isn't much different from setting up one. There's next to no configuration required to support it. Moreover, in a master/slave setup, the master can become a single point of failure (SPOF). To avoid this, you often need to add some complexity to the environment in the form of multiple masters. Because all of the replicas in Cassandra are identical, failures of a node won't disrupt service.

In short, because Cassandra is distributed and decentralized, there is no single point of failure, which supports high availability.

Elastic Scalability

Scalability is an architectural feature of a system that can continue serving a greater number of requests with little degradation in performance. Vertical scaling—simply adding more hardware capacity and memory to your existing machine—is the easiest way to achieve this. Horizontal scaling means adding more machines that have all or some of the data on them so that no one machine has to bear the entire burden of serving requests. But then the software itself must have an internal mechanism for keeping its data in sync with the other nodes in the cluster.

Elastic scalability refers to a special property of horizontal scalability. It means that your cluster can seamlessly scale up and scale back down. To do this, the cluster must be able to accept new nodes that can begin participating by getting a copy of some or all of the data and start serving new user requests without major disruption or reconfiguration of the entire cluster. You don't have to restart your process. You don't have to change your application queries. You don't have to manually rebalance the data yourself. Just add another machine—Cassandra will find it and start sending it work.

Scaling down, of course, means removing some of the processing capacity from your cluster. You might do this for business reasons, such as adjusting to seasonal workloads in retail or travel applications. Or perhaps there will be technical reasons such as moving parts of your application to another platform. As much as we try to minimize these situations, they still happen. But when they do, you won't need to upset the entire apple cart to scale back.

High Availability and Fault Tolerance

In general architecture terms, the availability of a system is measured according to its ability to fulfill requests. But computers can experience all manner of failure, from hardware component failure to network disruption to corruption. Any computer is susceptible to these kinds of failure. There are of course very sophisticated (and often prohibitively expensive) computers that can themselves mitigate many of these circumstances, as they include internal hardware redundancies and facilities to send notification of failure events and hot swap components. But anyone can accidentally break an Ethernet cable, and catastrophic events can beset a single data center. So for a system to be highly available, it must typically include multiple networked computers, and the software they're running must then be capable of operating in a cluster and have some facility for recognizing node failures and failing over requests to another part of the system.

Cassandra is highly available. You can replace failed nodes in the cluster with no downtime, and you can replicate data to multiple data centers to offer improved local performance and prevent downtime if one data center experiences a catastrophe such as fire or flood.

Tuneable Consistency

Consistency essentially means that a read always returns the most recently written value. Consider two customers are attempting to put the same item into their shopping carts on an ecommerce site. If I place the last item in stock into my cart an instant after you do, you should get the item added to your cart, and I should be informed that the item is no longer available for purchase. This is guaranteed to happen when the state of a write is consistent among all nodes that have that data.

But as we'll see later, scaling data stores means making certain trade-offs between data consistency, node availability, and partition tolerance. Cassandra is frequently called "eventually consistent," which is a bit misleading. Out of the box, Cassandra trades some consistency in order to achieve total availability. But Cassandra is more accurately termed "tuneably consistent," which means it allows you to easily decide the level of consistency you require, in balance with the level of availability.

Let's take a moment to unpack this, as the term "eventual consistency" has caused some uproar in the industry. Some practitioners hesitate to use a system that is described as "eventually consistent."

For detractors of eventual consistency, the broad argument goes something like this: eventual consistency is maybe OK for social web applications where data doesn't *really* matter. After all, you're just posting to Mom what little Billy ate for breakfast, and if it gets lost, it doesn't really matter. But the data *I* have is actually really important, and it's ridiculous to think that I could allow eventual consistency in my model.

Set aside the fact that all of the most popular web applications (Amazon, Facebook, Google, Twitter) are using this model, and that perhaps there's something to it. Presumably such data is very important indeed to the companies running these applications, because that data is their primary product, and they are multibillion-dollar companies with billions of users to satisfy in a sharply competitive world. It may be possible to gain guaranteed, immediate, and perfect consistency throughout a highly trafficked system running in parallel on a variety of networks, but if you want clients to get their results sometime this year, it's a very tricky proposition.

The detractors claim that some Big Data databases such as Cassandra have merely eventual consistency, and that all other distributed systems have *strict* consistency. As with so many things in the world, however, the reality is not so black and white, and the binary opposition between consistent and not-consistent is not truly reflected in practice. There are instead *degrees* of consistency, and in the real world they are very susceptible to external circumstance.

Eventual consistency is one of several consistency models available to architects. Let's take a look at these models so we can understand the trade-offs:

Strict consistency
This is sometimes called sequential consistency, and is the most stringent level of consistency. It requires that any read will always return the most recently written value. That sounds perfect, and it's exactly what I'm looking for. I'll take it! However, upon closer examination, what do we find? What precisely is meant by "most recently written"? Most recently to whom? In one single-processor machine, this is no problem to observe, as the sequence of operations is known to the one clock. But in a system executing across a variety of geographically dispersed data centers, it becomes much more slippery. Achieving this implies some sort of global clock that is capable of timestamping all operations, regardless of the location of the data or the user requesting it or how many (possibly disparate) services are required to determine the response.

Causal consistency
This is a slightly weaker form of strict consistency. It does away with the fantasy of the single global clock that can magically synchronize all operations without creating an unbearable bottleneck. Instead of relying on timestamps, causal consistency instead takes a more semantic approach, attempting to determine the cause of events to create some consistency in their order. It means that writes that are potentially related must be read in sequence. If two different, unrelated operations suddenly write to the same field, then those writes are inferred not to be causally related. But if one write occurs after another, we might infer that they are causally related. Causal consistency dictates that causal writes must be read in sequence.

Weak (eventual) consistency
Eventual consistency means on the surface that all updates will propagate throughout all of the replicas in a distributed system, but that this may take some time. Eventually, all replicas will be consistent.

Eventual consistency becomes suddenly very attractive when you consider what is required to achieve stronger forms of consistency.

When considering consistency, availability, and partition tolerance, we can achieve only two of these goals in a given distributed system, a trade-off known as the CAP theorem (we explore this theorem in more depth in "Brewer's CAP Theorem" on page 23). At the center of the problem is data update replication. To achieve a strict consistency, all update operations will be performed synchronously, meaning that they must block, locking all replicas until the operation is complete, and forcing competing clients to wait. A side effect of such a design is that during a failure, some of the data will be entirely unavailable. As Amazon CTO Werner Vogels puts it, "rather than dealing with the uncertainty of the correctness of an answer, the data is made unavailable until it is absolutely certain that it is correct."[1]

We could alternatively take an optimistic approach to replication, propagating updates to all replicas in the background in order to avoid blowing up on the client. The difficulty this approach presents is that now we are forced into the situation of detecting and resolving conflicts. A design approach must decide whether to resolve these conflicts at one of two possible times: during reads or during writes. That is, a distributed database designer must choose to make the system either always readable or always writable.

Dynamo and Cassandra choose to be always writable, opting to defer the complexity of reconciliation to read operations, and realize tremendous performance gains. The alternative is to reject updates amidst network and server failures.

In Cassandra, consistency is not an all-or-nothing proposition. We might more accurately term it "tuneable consistency" because the client can control the number of replicas to block on for all updates. This is done by setting the consistency level against the replication factor.

The *replication factor* lets you decide how much you want to pay in performance to gain more consistency. You set the replication factor to the number of nodes in the cluster you want the updates to propagate to (remember that an update means any add, update, or delete operation).

The *consistency level* is a setting that clients must specify on every operation and that allows you to decide how many replicas in the cluster must acknowledge a write operation or respond to a read operation in order to be considered successful. That's the part where Cassandra has pushed the decision for determining consistency out to the client.

So if you like, you could set the consistency level to a number equal to the replication factor, and gain stronger consistency at the cost of synchronous blocking operations that wait for all nodes to be updated and declare success before returning. This is not

---

1 "Dynamo: Amazon's Highly Distributed Key-Value Store" (*http://www.allthingsdistributed.com/2007/10/amazons_dynamo.html*), 207.

often done in practice with Cassandra, however, for reasons that should be clear (it defeats the availability goal, would impact performance, and generally goes against the grain of why you'd want to use Cassandra in the first place). So if the client sets the consistency level to a value less than the replication factor, the update is considered successful even if some nodes are down.

Brewer's CAP Theorem

In order to understand Cassandra's design and its label as an "eventually consistent" database, we need to understand the CAP theorem. The CAP theorem is sometimes called Brewer's theorem after its author, Eric Brewer.

While working at the University of California at Berkeley, Eric Brewer posited his CAP theorem in 2000 at the ACM Symposium on the Principles of Distributed Computing. The theorem states that within a large-scale distributed data system, there are three requirements that have a relationship of sliding dependency:

Consistency
> All database clients will read the same value for the same query, even given concurrent updates.

Availability
> All database clients will always be able to read and write data.

Partition tolerance
> The database can be split into multiple machines; it can continue functioning in the face of network segmentation breaks.

Brewer's theorem is that in any given system, you can strongly support only two of the three. This is analogous to the saying you may have heard in software development: "You can have it good, you can have it fast, you can have it cheap: pick two."

We have to choose between them because of this sliding mutual dependency. The more consistency you demand from your system, for example, the less partition-tolerant you're likely to be able to make it, unless you make some concessions around availability.

The CAP theorem was formally proved to be true by Seth Gilbert and Nancy Lynch of MIT in 2002. In distributed systems, however, it is very likely that you will have network partitioning, and that at some point, machines will fail and cause others to become unreachable. Networking issues such as packet loss or high latency are nearly inevitable and have the potential to cause temporary partitions. This leads us to the conclusion that a distributed system must do its best to continue operating in the face of network partitions (to be partition tolerant), leaving us with only two real options to compromise on: availability and consistency.

Figure 2-1 illustrates visually that there is no overlapping segment where all three are obtainable.

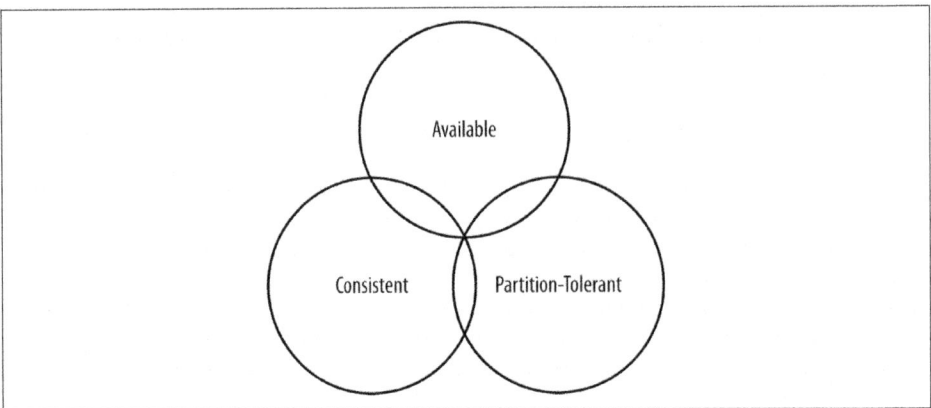

Figure 2-1. CAP theorem indicates that you can realize only two of these properties at once

It might prove useful at this point to see a graphical depiction of where each of the non-relational data stores we'll look at falls within the CAP spectrum. The graphic in Figure 2-2 was inspired by a slide in a 2009 talk given by Dwight Merriman, CEO and founder of MongoDB, to the MySQL User Group in New York City (*http://leadit.data basemonth.com/hands-on-tech/MongoDB-High-Performance-SQL-Free-Database*). However, we have modified the placement of some systems based on research.

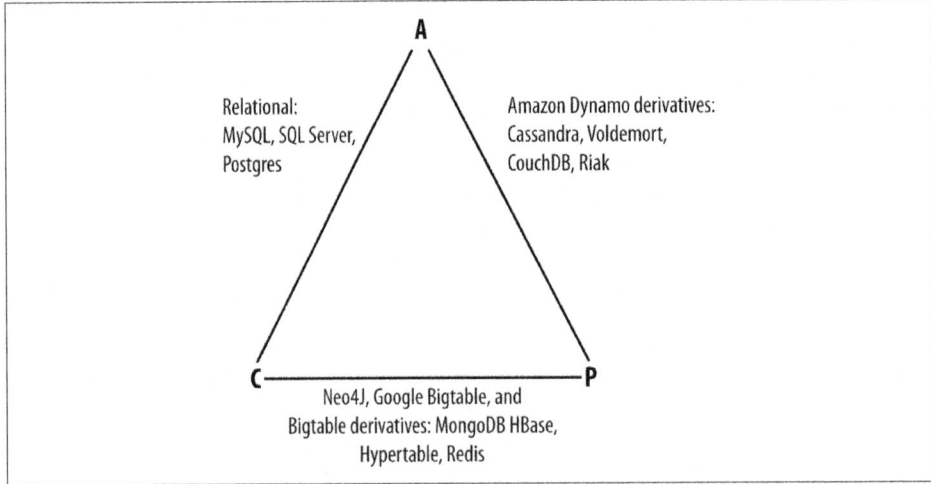

Figure 2-2. Where different databases appear on the CAP continuum

Figure 2-2 shows the general focus of some of the different databases we discuss in this chapter. Note that placement of the databases in this chart could change based on configuration. As Stu Hood points out, a distributed MySQL database can count as a consistent system only if you're using Google's synchronous replication patches; otherwise, it can only be available and partition tolerant (AP).

It's interesting to note that the design of the system around CAP placement is independent of the orientation of the data storage mechanism; for example, the CP edge is populated by graph databases and document-oriented databases alike.

In this depiction, relational databases are on the line between consistency and availability, which means that they can fail in the event of a network failure (including a cable breaking). This is typically achieved by defining a single master server, which could itself go down, or an array of servers that simply don't have sufficient mechanisms built in to continue functioning in the case of network partitions.

Graph databases such as Neo4J and the set of databases derived at least in part from the design of Google's Bigtable database (such as MongoDB, HBase, Hypertable, and Redis) all are focused slightly less on availability and more on ensuring consistency and partition tolerance.

Finally, the databases derived from Amazon's Dynamo design include Cassandra, Project Voldemort, CouchDB, and Riak. These are more focused on availability and partition tolerance. However, this does not mean that they dismiss consistency as unimportant, any more than Bigtable dismisses availability. According to the Bigtable paper, the average percentage of server hours that "some data" was unavailable is 0.0047% (section 4), so this is relative, as we're talking about very robust systems already. If you think of each of these letters (C, A, P) as knobs you can tune to arrive at the system you want, Dynamo derivatives are intended for employment in the many use cases where "eventual consistency" is tolerable and where "eventual" is a matter of milliseconds, read repairs mean that reads will return consistent values, and you can achieve strong consistency if you want to.

So what does it mean in practical terms to support only two of the three facets of CAP?

CA

To primarily support consistency and availability means that you're likely using two-phase commit for distributed transactions. It means that the system will block when a network partition occurs, so it may be that your system is limited to a single data center cluster in an attempt to mitigate this. If your application needs only this level of scale, this is easy to manage and allows you to rely on familiar, simple structures.

CP

To primarily support consistency and partition tolerance, you may try to advance your architecture by setting up data shards in order to scale. Your data will be consistent, but you still run the risk of some data becoming unavailable if nodes fail.

AP

To primarily support availability and partition tolerance, your system may return inaccurate data, but the system will always be available, even in the face of network partitioning. DNS is perhaps the most popular example of a system that is massively scalable, highly available, and partition tolerant.

Note that this depiction is intended to offer an overview that helps draw distinctions between the broader contours in these systems; it is not strictly precise. For example, it's not entirely clear where Google's Bigtable should be placed on such a continuum. The Google paper describes Bigtable as "highly available," but later goes on to say that if Chubby (the Bigtable persistent lock service) "becomes unavailable for an extended period of time [caused by Chubby outages or network issues], Bigtable becomes unavailable" (section 4). On the matter of data reads, the paper says that "we do not consider the possibility of multiple copies of the same data, possibly in alternate forms due to views or indices." Finally, the paper indicates that "centralized control and Byzantine fault tolerance are not Bigtable goals" (section 10). Given such variable information, you can see that determining where a database falls on this sliding scale is not an exact science.

An Updated Perspective on CAP

In February 2012, Eric Brewer provided an updated perspective on his CAP theorem in the article "CAP Twelve Years Later: How the 'Rules' Have Changed" (*http:// www.infoq.com/articles/cap-twelve-years-later-how-the-rules-have-changed*) in IEEE's *Computer*. Brewer now describes the "2 out of 3" axiom as somewhat misleading. He notes that designers only need sacrifice consistency or availability in the presence of partitions, and that advances in partition recovery techniques have made it possible for designers to achieve high levels of both consistency and availability.

These advances in partition recovery certainly would include Cassandra's usage of mechanisms such as hinted handoff and read repair. We'll explore these in Chapter 6. However, it is important to recognize that these partition recovery mechanisms are not infallible. There is still immense value in Cassandra's tuneable consistency, allowing Cassandra to function effectively in a diverse set of deployments in which it is not possible to completely prevent partitions.

Row-Oriented

Cassandra's data model can be described as a partitioned row store, in which data is stored in sparse multidimensional hashtables. "Sparse" means that for any given row you can have one or more columns, but each row doesn't need to have all the same columns as other rows like it (as in a relational model). "Partitioned" means that each row has a unique key which makes its data accessible, and the keys are used to distribute the rows across multiple data stores.

Row-Oriented Versus Column-Oriented

Cassandra has frequently been referred to as a "column-oriented" database, which has proved to be the source of some confusion. A column-oriented database is one in which the data is actually stored by columns, as opposed to relational databases, which store data in rows. Part of the confusion that occurs in classifying databases is that there can be a difference between the API exposed by the database and the underlying storage on disk. So Cassandra is not really column-oriented, in that its data store is not organized primarily around columns.

In the relational storage model, all of the columns for a table are defined beforehand and space is allocated for each column whether it is populated or not. In contrast, Cassandra stores data in a multidimensional, sorted hash table. As data is stored in each column, it is stored as a separate entry in the hash table. Column values are stored according to a consistent sort order, omitting columns that are not populated, which enables more efficient storage and query processing. We'll examine Cassandra's data model in more detail in Chapter 4.

Is Cassandra "Schema-Free"?

In its early versions. Cassandra was faithful to the original Bigtable whitepaper in supporting a "schema-free" data model in which new columns can be defined dynamically. Schema-free databases such as Bigtable and MongoDB have the advantage of being very extensible and highly performant in accessing large amounts of data. The major drawback of schema-free databases is the difficulty in determining the meaning and format of data, which limits the ability to perform complex queries. These disadvantages proved a barrier to adoption for many, especially as startup projects which benefitted from the initial flexibility matured into more complex enterprises involving multiple developers and administrators.

The solution for those users was the introduction of the Cassandra Query Language (CQL), which provides a way to define schema via a syntax similar to the Structured Query Language (SQL) familiar to those coming from a relational background. Initially, CQL was provided as another interface to Cassandra alongside the schema-free interface based on the Apache Thrift project. During this transitional phase, the term "Schema-optional" was used to describe that data models could be defined by schema using CQL, but could also be dynamically extended to add new columns via the Thrift API. During this period, the underlying data storage continued to be based on the Bigtable model.

Starting with the 3.0 release, the Thrift-based API that supported dynamic column creation has been deprecated, and Cassandra's underlying storage has been re-implemented to more closely align with CQL. Cassandra does not entirely limit the ability to dynamically extend the schema on the fly, but the way it works is significantly different. CQL collections such as lists, sets, and especially maps provide the ability to add content in a less structured form that can be leveraged to extend an existing schema. CQL also provides the ability to change the type of columns in certain instances, and facilities to support the storage of JSON-formatted text.

So perhaps the best way to describe Cassandra's current posture is that it supports "flexible schema."

High Performance

Cassandra was designed specifically from the ground up to take full advantage of multiprocessor/multi-core machines, and to run across many dozens of these machines housed in multiple data centers. It scales consistently and seamlessly to hundreds of terabytes. Cassandra has been shown to perform exceptionally well under heavy load. It consistently can show very fast throughput for writes per second on basic commodity computers, whether physical hardware or virtual machines. As you add more servers, you can maintain all of Cassandra's desirable properties without sacrificing performance.

Where Did Cassandra Come From?

The Cassandra data store is an open source Apache project (*http://cassandra.apache.org*). Cassandra originated at Facebook in 2007 to solve its inbox search problem—the company had to deal with large volumes of data in a way that was difficult to scale with traditional methods. Specifically, the team had requirements to handle huge volumes of data in the form of message copies, reverse indices of messages, and many random reads and many simultaneous random writes.

The team was led by Jeff Hammerbacher, with Avinash Lakshman, Karthik Ranganathan, and Facebook engineer on the Search Team Prashant Malik as key engineers. The code was released as an open source Google Code project in July 2008. During its tenure as a Google Code project in 2008, the code was updatable only by Facebook engineers, and little community was built around it as a result. So in March 2009, it was moved to an Apache Incubator project, and on February 17, 2010, it was voted into a top-level project. On the Apache Cassandra Wiki, you can find a list of the committers (*http://wiki.apache.org/cassandra/Committers*), many of whom have been with the project since 2010/2011. The committers represent companies including Twitter, LinkedIn, Apple, as well as independent developers.

The Paper that Introduced Cassandra to the World

"A Decentralized Structured Storage System" (*http://www.cs.cornell.edu/projects/ladis2009/papers/lakshman-ladis2009.pdf*) by Facebook's Lakshman and Malik was a central paper on Cassandra. An updated commentary (*http://docs.data stax.com/en/articles/cassandra/cassandrathenandnow.html*) on this paper was provided by Jonathan Ellis corresponding to the 2.0 release, noting changes to the technology since the transition to Apache. We'll unpack some of these changes in more detail in "Release History" on page 30.

How Did Cassandra Get Its Name?

In Greek mythology, Cassandra was the daughter of King Priam and Queen Hecuba of Troy. Cassandra was so beautiful that the god Apollo gave her the ability to see the future. But when she refused his amorous advances, he cursed her such that she would still be able to accurately predict everything that would happen—but no one would believe her. Cassandra foresaw the destruction of her city of Troy, but was powerless to stop it. The Cassandra distributed database is named for her. We speculate that it is also named as kind of a joke on the Oracle at Delphi, another seer for whom a database is named.

As commercial interest in Cassandra grew, the need for production support became apparent. Jonathan Ellis, the Apache Project Chair for Cassandra, and his colleague Matt Pfeil formed a services company called DataStax (originally known as Riptano) in April of 2010. DataStax has provided leadership and support for the Cassandra project, employing several Cassandra committers.

DataStax provides free products including Cassandra drivers for various languages and tools for development and administration of Cassandra. Paid product offerings include enterprise versions of the Cassandra server and tools, integrations with other data technologies, and product support. Unlike some other open source projects that have commercial backing, changes are added first to the Apache open source project, and then rolled into the commercial offering shortly after each Apache release.

DataStax also provides the Planet Cassandra website (*http://www.planetcassandra.org*) as a resource to the Cassandra community. This site is a great location to learn about the ever-growing list of companies and organizations that are using Cassandra in

industry and academia (*http://www.planetcassandra.org/companies*). Industries represented run the gamut: financial services, telecommunications, education, social
media, entertainment, marketing, retail, hospitality, transportation, healthcare,
energy, philanthropy, aerospace, defense, and technology. Chances are that you will
find a number of case studies here that are relevant to your needs.

Release History

Now that we've learned about the people and organizations that have shaped Cassandra, let's take a look at how Cassandra has matured through its various releases since
becoming an official Apache project. If you're new to Cassandra, don't worry if some
of these concepts and terms are new to you—we'll dive into them in more depth in
due time. You can return to this list later to get a sense of the trajectory of how Cassandra has matured over time and its future directions. If you've used Cassandra in
the past, this summary will give you a quick primer on what's changed.

Performance and Reliability Improvements

This list focuses primarily on features that have been added over
the course of Cassandra's lifespan. This is not to discount the steady
and substantial improvements in reliability and read/write performance.

Release 0.6

This was the first release after Cassandra graduated from the Apache Incubator
to a top-level project. Releases in this series ran from 0.6.0 in April 2010 through
0.6.13 in April 2011. Features in this series included:

- Integration with Apache Hadoop, allowing easy data retrieval from Cassandra via MapReduce
- Integrated row caching, which helped eliminate the need for applications to
  deploy other caching technologies alongside Cassandra

Release 0.7

Releases in this series ran from 0.7.0 in January 2011 through 0.7.10 in October
2011. Key features and improvements included:

- Secondary indexes—that is, indexes on non-primary columns
- Support for large rows, containing up to two billion columns
- Online schema changes, including adding, renaming, and removing keyspa-
  ces and column families in live clusters without a restart, via the Thrift API
- Expiring columns, via specification of a time-to-live (TTL) per column

- The NetworkTopologyStrategy was introduced to support multi-data center deployments, allowing a separate replication factor per data center, per keyspace
- Configuration files were converted from XML to the more readable YAML format

Release 0.8

This release began a major shift in Cassandra APIs with the introduction of CQL. Releases in this series ran from 0.8.0 in June 2011 through 0.8.10 in February 2012. Key features and improvements included:

- Distributed counters were added as a new data type that incrementally counts up or down
- The sstableloader tool was introduced to support bulk loading of data into Cassandra clusters
- An off-heap row cache was provided to allow usage of native memory instead of the JVM heap
- Concurrent compaction allowed for multi-threaded execution and throttling control of SSTable compaction
- Improved memory configuration parameters allowed more flexible control over the size of memtables

Release 1.0

In keeping with common version numbering practice, this is officially the first production release of Cassandra, although many companies were using Cassandra in production well before this point. Releases in this series ran from 1.0.0 in October 2011 through 1.0.12 in October 2012. In keeping with the focus on production readiness, improvements focused on performance and enhancements to existing features:

- CQL 2 added several improvements, including the ability to alter tables and columns, support for counters and TTL, and the ability to retrieve the count of items matching a query
- The leveled compaction strategy was introduced as an alternative to the original size-tiered compaction strategy, allowing for faster reads at the expense of more I/O on writes
- Compression of SSTable files, configurable on a per-table level

Release 1.1

Releases in this series ran from 1.1.0 in April 2011 through 1.1.12 in May 2013. Key features and improvements included:

- CQL 3 added the timeuuid type, and the ability to create tables with compound primary keys including clustering keys. Clustering keys support "order by" semantics to allow sorting. This was a much anticipated feature that allowed the creation of "wide rows" via CQL.

- Support for importing and exporting comma-separated values (CSV) files via `cqlsh`
- Flexible data storage settings allow the storage of data in SSDs or magnetic storage, selectable by table
- The schema update mechanism was reimplemented to allow concurrent changes and improve reliability. Schema are now stored in tables in the `system` keyspace.
- Caching was updated to provide more straightforward configuration of cache sizes
- A utility to leverage the bulk loader from Hadoop, allowing efficient export of data from Hadoop to Cassandra
- Row-level isolation was added to assure that when multiple columns are updated on a write, it is not possible for a read to get a mix of new and old column values

Release 1.2

Releases in this series ran from 1.2.0 in January 2013 through 1.2.19 in September 2014. Notable features and improvements included:

- CQL 3 added collection types (sets, lists, and maps), prepared statements, and a binary protocol as a replacement for Thrift
- Virtual nodes spread data more evenly across the nodes in a cluster, improving performance, especially when adding or replacing nodes
- Atomic batches ensure that all writes in a batch succeed or fail as a unit
- The `system` keyspace contains the `local` table containing information about the local node and the `peers` table describing other nodes in the cluster
- Request tracing can be enabled to allow clients to see the interactions between nodes for reads and writes. Tracing provides valuable insight into what is going on behind the scenes and can help developers understand the implications of various table design options.
- Most data structures were moved off of the JVM heap to native memory
- Disk failure policies allow flexible configuration of behaviors, including removing a node from the cluster on disk failure or making a best effort to access data from memory, even if stale

Release 2.0

The 2.0 release was an especially significant milestone in the history of Cassandra, as it marked the culmination of the CQL capability, as well as a new level of production maturity. This included significant performance improvements and cleanup of the codebase to pay down 5 years of accumulated technical debt.

Releases in this series ran from 2.0.0 in September 2013 through 2.0.16 in June 2015. Highlights included:

- Lightweight transactions were added using the Paxos consensus protocol
- CQL3 improvements included the addition of DROP semantics on the ALTER command, conditional schema modifications (IF EXISTS, IF NOT EXISTS), and the ability to create secondary indexes on primary key columns
- Native CQL protocol improvements began to make CQL demonstrably more performant than Thrift
- A prototype implementation of triggers was added, providing an extensible way to react to write operations. Triggers can be implemented in any JVM language.
- Java 7 was required for the first time
- Static columns were added in the 2.0.6 release

Release 2.1

Releases in this series ran from 2.1.0 in September 2014 through 2.1.8 in June 2015. Key features and improvements included:

- CQL3 added user-defined types (UDT), and the ability to create secondary indexes on collections
- Configuration options were added to move memtable data off heap to native memory
- Row caching was made more configurable to allow setting the number of cached rows per partition
- Counters were re-implemented to improve performance and reliability

Release 2.2

The original release plan outlined by the Cassandra developers did not contain a 2.2 release. The intent was to do some major "under the covers" rework for a 3.0 release to follow the 2.1 series. However, due to the amount and complexity of the changes involved, it was decided to release some of completed features separately in order to make them available while allowing some of the more complex changes time to mature. Release 2.2.0 became available in July 2015, and support releases are scheduled through fall 2016. Notable features and improvements in this series included:

- CQL3 improvements, including support for JSON-formatted input/output and user-defined functions
- With this release, Windows became a fully supported operating system. Although Cassandra still performs best on Linux systems, improvements in file I/O and scripting have made it much easier to run Cassandra on Windows.

- The Date Tiered Compaction Strategy (DTCS) was introduced to improve performance of time series data
- Role-based access control (RBAC) was introduced to allow more flexible management of authorization

---

Tick-Tock Releases

In June 2015, the Cassandra team announced plans to adopt a tick-tock release model as part of increased emphasis on improving agility and the quality of releases.

The tick-tock release model popularized by Intel was originally intended for chip design, and referred to changing chip architecture and production processes in alternate builds. You can read more about this approach at *http://www.intel.com/content/www/us/en/silicon-innovations/intel-tick-tock-model-general.html*.

The tick-tock approach has proven to be useful in software development as well. Starting with the Cassandra 3.0 release, even-numbered releases are feature releases with some bug fixes, while odd-numbered releases are focused on bug fixes, with the goal of releasing each month.

Release 3.0 (Feature release - November 2015)
- The underlying storage engine was rewritten to more closely match CQL constructs
- Support for materialized views (sometimes also called global indexes) was added
- Java 8 is now the supported version
- The Thrift-based command-line interface (CLI) was removed

Release 3.1 (Bug fix release - December 2015)

Release 3.2 (Feature release - January 2016)
- The way in which Cassandra allocates SSTable file storage across multiple disk in "just a bunch of disks" or JBOD configurations was reworked to improve reliability and performance and to enable backup and restore of individual disks
- The ability to compress and encrypt hints was added

Release 3.3 (Bug fix release - February 2016)

Release 3.4 (Feature release - March 2016)
- SSTableAttachedSecondaryIndex, or "SASI" for short, is an implementation of Cassandra's SecondaryIndex interface that can be used as an alternative to the existing implementations.

Release 3.5 (Bug fix release - April 2016)

The 4.0 release series is scheduled to begin in Fall 2016.

As you will have noticed, the trends in these releases include:

- Continuous improvement in the capabilities of CQL
- A growing list of clients for popular languages built on a common set of metaphors
- Exposure of configuration options to tune performance and optimize resource usage
- Performance and reliability improvements, and reduction of technical debt

Supported Releases

There are two officially supported releases of Cassandra at any one time: the latest stable release, which is considered appropriate for production, and the latest development release. You can see the officially supported versions on the project's download page (*http:// cassandra.apache.org/download*).

Users of Cassandra are strongly recommended to track the latest stable release in production. Anecdotally, a substantial majority of issues and questions posted to the Cassandra-users email list pertain to releases that are no longer supported. Cassandra experts are very gracious in answering questions and diagnosing issues with these unsupported releases, but more often than not the recommendation is to upgrade as soon as possible to a release that addresses the issue.

Is Cassandra a Good Fit for My Project?

We have now unpacked the elevator pitch and have an understanding of Cassandra's advantages. Despite Cassandra's sophisticated design and smart features, it is not the right tool for every job. So in this section, let's take a quick look at what kind of projects Cassandra is a good fit for.

Large Deployments

You probably don't drive a semitruck to pick up your dry cleaning; semis aren't well suited for that sort of task. Lots of careful engineering has gone into Cassandra's high availability, tuneable consistency, peer-to-peer protocol, and seamless scaling, which are its main selling points. None of these qualities is even meaningful in a single-node deployment, let alone allowed to realize its full potential.

There are, however, a wide variety of situations where a single-node relational database is all we may need. So do some measuring. Consider your expected traffic, throughput needs, and SLAs. There are no hard-and-fast rules here, but if you expect that you can reliably serve traffic with an acceptable level of performance with just a few relational databases, it might be a better choice to do so, simply because RDBMSs are easier to run on a single machine and are more familiar.

If you think you'll need at least several nodes to support your efforts, however, Cassandra might be a good fit. If your application is expected to require dozens of nodes, Cassandra might be a great fit.

Lots of Writes, Statistics, and Analysis

Consider your application from the perspective of the ratio of reads to writes. Cassandra is optimized for excellent throughput on writes.

Many of the early production deployments of Cassandra involve storing user activity updates, social network usage, recommendations/reviews, and application statistics. These are strong use cases for Cassandra because they involve lots of writing with less predictable read operations, and because updates can occur unevenly with sudden spikes. In fact, the ability to handle application workloads that require high performance at significant write volumes with many concurrent client threads is one of the primary features of Cassandra.

According to the project wiki, Cassandra has been used to create a variety of applications, including a windowed time-series store, an inverted index for document searching, and a distributed job priority queue.

Geographical Distribution

Cassandra has out-of-the-box support for geographical distribution of data. You can easily configure Cassandra to replicate data across multiple data centers. If you have a globally deployed application that could see a performance benefit from putting the data near the user, Cassandra could be a great fit.

Evolving Applications

If your application is evolving rapidly and you're in "startup mode," Cassandra might be a good fit given its support for flexible schemas. This makes it easy to keep your database in step with application changes as you rapidly deploy.

Getting Involved

The strength and relevance of any technology depend on the investment of individuals in a vibrant community environment. Thankfully, the Cassandra community is active and healthy, offering a number of ways for you to participate. We'll start with a few steps in Chapter 3 such as downloading Cassandra and building from the source. Here are a few other ways to get involved:

Chat

Many of the Cassandra developers and community members hang out in the #cassandra channel on *webchat.freenode.net*. This informal environment is a great place to get your questions answered or offer up some answers of your own.

Mailing lists

The Apache project hosts several mailing lists to which you can subscribe to learn about various topics of interest:

- *user@cassandra.apache.org* provides a general discussion list for users and is frequently used by new users or those needing assistance.
- *dev@cassandra.apache.org* is used by developers to discuss changes, prioritize work, and approve releases.
- *client-dev@cassandra.apache.org* is used for discussion specific to development of Cassandra clients for various programming languages.
- *commits@cassandra.apache.org* tracks Cassandra code commits. This is a fairly high volume list and is primarily of interest to committers.

Releases are typically announced to both the developer and user mailing lists.

Issues

If you encounter issues using Cassandra and feel you have discovered a defect, you should feel free to submit an issue to the Cassandra JIRA (*https:// issues.apache.org/jira/browse/cassandra*). In fact, users who identify defects on the *user@cassandra.apache.org* list are frequently encouraged to create JIRA issues.

Blogs

The DataStax developer blog (*http://www.datastax.com/dev/blog*) features posts on using Cassandra, announcements of Apache Cassandra and DataStax product releases, as well as occasional deep-dive technical articles on Cassandra implementation details and features under development. The Planet Cassandra blog (*http://www.planetcassandra.org/blog*) provides similar technical content, but has a greater focus on profiling companies using Cassandra.

The Apache Cassandra Wiki (*http://wiki.apache.org/cassandra*) provides helpful articles on getting started and configuration, but note that some content may not be fully up to date with current releases.

Meetups

A *meetup* group is a local community of people who meet face to face to discuss topics of common interest. These groups provide an excellent opportunity to network, learn, or share your knowledge by offering a presentation of your own. There are Cassandra meetups on every continent (*http://live-pc-*

development.pantheon.io/join-your-local-meetup), so you stand a good chance of being able to find one in your area.

Training and conferences

DataStax offers online training (*https://academy.datastax.com*), and in June 2015 announced a partnership with O'Reilly Media to produce Cassandra certifications. DataStax also hosts annual Cassandra Summits (*http://cassandrasummit-datastax.com*) in locations around the world.

A Marketable Skill

There continues to be increased demand for Cassandra developers and administrators. A 2015 Dice.com salary survey (*http://market ing.dice.com/pdf/Dice_TechSalarySurvey_2015.pdf*) placed Cassandra as the second most highly compensated skill set.

Summary

In this chapter, we've taken an introductory look at Cassandra's defining characteristics, history, and major features. We have learned about the Cassandra user community and how companies are using Cassandra. Now we're ready to start getting some hands-on experience.

## CHAPTER 3

Installing Cassandra

For those among us who like instant gratification, we'll start by installing Cassandra. Because Cassandra introduces a lot of new vocabulary, there might be some unfamiliar terms as we walk through this. That's OK; the idea here is to get set up quickly in a simple configuration to make sure everything is running properly. This will serve as an orientation. Then, we'll take a step back and understand Cassandra in its larger context.

Installing the Apache Distribution

Cassandra is available for download from the Web at *http://cassandra.apache.org*. Just click the link on the home page to download a version as a gzipped tarball. Typically two versions of Cassandra are provided. The *latest release* is recommended for those starting new projects not yet in production. The *most stable release* is the one recommended for production usage. For all releases, the prebuilt binary is named *apache-cassandra-x.x.x-bin.tar.gz*, where *x.x.x* represents the version number. The download is around 23MB.

Extracting the Download

The simplest way to get started is to download the prebuilt binary. You can unpack the compressed file using any regular ZIP utility. On Unix-based systems such as Linux or MacOS, GZip extraction utilities should be preinstalled; on Windows, you'll need to get a program such as WinZip, which is commercial, or something like 7-Zip (*http://www.7-zip.org*), which is freeware.

Open your extracting program. You might have to extract the ZIP file and the TAR file in separate steps. Once you have a folder on your filesystem called *apache-cassandra-x.x.x*, you're ready to run Cassandra.

What's In There?

Once you decompress the tarball, you'll see that the Cassandra binary distribution includes several files and directories.

The files include the *NEWS.txt* file, which includes the release notes describing features included in the current and prior releases, and the *CHANGES.txt*, which is similar but focuses on bug fixes. You'll want to make sure to review these files whenever you are upgrading to a new version so you know what changes to expect.

Let's take a moment to look around in the directories and see what we have.

bin

This directory contains the executables to run Cassandra as well as clients, including the query language shell (cqlsh) and the command-line interface (CLI) client. It also has scripts to run the nodetool, which is a utility for inspecting a cluster to determine whether it is properly configured, and to perform a variety of maintenance operations. We look at nodetool in depth later. The directory also contains several utilities for performing operations on SSTables, including listing the keys of an SSTable (sstablekeys), bulk extraction and restoration of SSTable contents (sstableloader), and upgrading SSTables to a new version of Cassandra (sstableupgrade).

conf

This directory contains the files for configuring your Cassandra instance. The required configuration files include: the *cassandra.yaml* file, which is the primary configuration for running Cassandra; and the *logback.xml* file, which lets you change the logging settings to suit your needs. Additional files can optionally be used to configure the network topology, archival and restore commands, and triggers. We see how to use these configuration files when we discuss configuration in Chapter 7.

interface

This directory contains a single file, called *cassandra.thrift*. This file defines a legacy Remote Procedure Call (RPC) API based on the Thrift syntax. The Thrift interface was used to create clients in Java, C++, PHP, Ruby, Python, Perl, and C# prior to the creation of CQL. The Thrift API has been officially marked as deprecated in the 3.2 release and will be deleted in the 4.0 release.

javadoc

This directory contains a documentation website generated using Java's JavaDoc tool. Note that JavaDoc reflects only the comments that are stored directly in the Java code, and as such does not represent comprehensive documentation. It's helpful if you want to see how the code is laid out. Moreover, Cassandra is a wonderful project, but the code contains relatively few comments, so you might find the JavaDoc's usefulness limited. It may be more fruitful to simply read the class files directly if you're familiar with Java. Nonetheless, to read the JavaDoc, open the *javadoc/index.html* file in a browser.

lib

This directory contains all of the external libraries that Cassandra needs to run. For example, it uses two different JSON serialization libraries, the Google collections project, and several Apache Commons libraries.

pylib

This directory contains Python libraries that are used by `cqlsh`.

tools

This directory contains tools that are used to maintain your Cassandra nodes. We'll look at these tools in Chapter 11.

Additional Directories

If you've already run Cassandra using the default configuration, you will notice two additional directories under the main Cassandra directory: *data* and *log*. We'll discuss the contents of these directories momentarily.

Building from Source

Cassandra uses Apache Ant for its build scripting language and Maven for dependency management.

Downloading Ant

You can download Ant from http://ant.apache.org. You don't need to download Maven separately just to build Cassandra.

Building from source requires a complete Java 7 or 8 JDK, not just the JRE. If you see a message about how Ant is missing *tools.jar*, either you don't have the full JDK or you're pointing to the wrong path in your environment variables. Maven downloads files from the Internet so if your connection is invalid or Maven cannot determine the proxy, the build will fail.

Downloading Development Builds

If you want to download the most cutting-edge builds, you can get the source from Jenkins, which the Cassandra project uses as its Continuous Integration tool. See *http://cassci.datastax.com* for the latest builds and test coverage information.

If you are a Git fan, you can get a read-only trunk version of the Cassandra source using this command:

```
$ git clone git://git.apache.org/cassandra.git
```

What Is Git?

Git is a source code management system created by Linus Torvalds to manage development of the Linux kernel. It's increasingly popular and is used by projects such as Android, Fedora, Ruby on Rails, Perl, and many Cassandra clients (as we'll see in Chapter 8). If you're on a Linux distribution such as Ubuntu, it couldn't be easier to get Git. At a console, just type >*apt-get install git* and it will be installed and ready for commands. For more information, visit *http://git-scm.com*.

Because Maven takes care of all the dependencies, it's easy to build Cassandra once you have the source. Just make sure you're in the root directory of your source download and execute the `ant` program, which will look for a file called *build.xml* in the current directory and execute the default build target. Ant and Maven take care of the rest. To execute the Ant program and start compiling the source, just type:

```
$ ant
```

That's it. Maven will retrieve all of the necessary dependencies, and Ant will build the hundreds of source files and execute the tests. If all went well, you should see a BUILD SUCCESSFUL message. If all did not go well, make sure that your path settings are all correct, that you have the most recent versions of the required programs, and that you downloaded a stable Cassandra build. You can check the Jenkins report to make sure that the source you downloaded actually can compile.

More Build Output

If you want to see detailed information on what is happening during the build, you can pass Ant the `-v` option to cause it to output verbose details regarding each operation it performs.

Additional Build Targets

To compile the server, you can simply execute *ant* as shown previously. This command executes the default target, *jar*. This target will perform a complete build including unit tests and output a file into the *build* directory called *apache-cassandra-x.x.x.jar*.

If you want to see a list of all of the targets supported by the build file, simply pass Ant the -p option to get a description of each target. Here are a few others you might be interested in:

test

Users will probably find this the most helpful, as it executes the battery of unit tests. You can also check out the unit test sources themselves for some useful examples of how to interact with Cassandra.

stress-build

This target builds the Cassandra stress tool, which we will try out in Chapter 12.

clean

This target removes locally created artifacts such as generated source files and classes and unit test results. The related target *realclean* performs a *clean* and additionally removes the Cassandra distribution JAR files and JAR files downloaded by Maven.

Running Cassandra

In earlier versions of Cassandra, before you could start the server there were some required steps to edit configuration files and set environment variables. But the developers have done a terrific job of making it very easy to start using Cassandra immediately. We'll note some of the available configuration options as we go.

Required Java Version

Cassandra requires a Java 7 or 8 JVM, preferably the latest stable version. It has been tested on both the Open JDK and Oracle's JDK. You can check your installed Java version by opening a command prompt and executing java -version. If you need a JDK, you can get one at *http://www.oracle.com/technetwork/java/javase/downloads/index.html*.

On Windows

Once you have the binary or the source downloaded and compiled, you're ready to start the database server.

Setting the `JAVA_HOME` environment variable is recommended. To do this on Windows 7, click the Start button and then right-click on Computer. Click Advanced System Settings, and then click the Environment Variables... button. Click New... to create a new system variable. In the Variable Name field, type `JAVA_HOME`. In the Variable Value field, type the path to your Java installation. This is probably something like *C:\Program Files\Java\jre7* if running Java 7 or *C:\Program Files\Java\jre1.8.0_25* if running Java 8.

Remember that if you create a new environment variable, you'll need to reopen any currently open terminals in order for the system to become aware of the new variable. To make sure your environment variable is set correctly and that Cassandra can subsequently find Java on Windows, execute this command in a new terminal: `echo %JAVA_HOME%`. This prints the value of your environment variable.

You can also define an environment variable called `CASSANDRA_HOME` that points to the top-level directory where you have placed or built Cassandra, so you don't have to pay as much attention to where you're starting Cassandra from. This is useful for other tools besides the database server, such as `nodetool` and `cqlsh`.

Once you've started the server for the first time, Cassandra will add directories to your system to store its data files. The default configuration creates these directories under the *CASSANDRA_HOME* directory.

data
> This directory is where Cassandra stores its data. By default, there are three subdirectories under the *data* directory, corresponding to the various data files Cassandra uses: *commitlog*, *data*, and *saved_caches*. We'll explore the significance of each of these data files in Chapter 6. If you've been trying different versions of the database and aren't worried about losing data, you can delete these directories and restart the server as a last resort.

logs
> This directory is where Cassandra stores its logs in a file called *system.log*. If you encounter any difficulties, consult the log to see what might have happened.

Data File Locations

The data file locations are configurable in the *cassandra.yaml* file, located in the *conf* directory. The properties are called data_file_directories, commit_log_directory, and saved_caches_directory. We'll discuss the recommended configuration of these directories in Chapter 7.

On Linux

The process on Linux and other *nix operating systems (including Mac OS) is similar to that on Windows. Make sure that your JAVA_HOME variable is properly set, according to the earlier description. Then, you need to extract the Cassandra gzipped tarball using *gunzip*. Many users prefer to use the */var/lib* directory for data storage. If you are changing this configuration, you will need to edit the *conf/cassandra.yaml* file and create the referenced directories for Cassandra to store its data and logs, making sure to configure write permissions for the user that will be running Cassandra:

```
$ sudo mkdir -p /var/lib/cassandra
$ sudo chown -R username /var/lib/cassandra
```

Instead of *username*, substitute your own username, of course.

Starting the Server

To start the Cassandra server on any OS, open a command prompt or terminal window, navigate to the *<cassandra-directory>/bin* where you unpacked Cassandra, and run the command cassandra -f to start your server.

Starting Cassandra in the Foreground

Using the -f switch tells Cassandra to stay in the foreground instead of running as a background process, so that all of the server logs will print to standard out and you can see them in your terminal window, which is useful for testing. In either case, the logs will append to the *system.log* file, described earlier.

In a clean installation, you should see quite a few log statements as the server gets running. The exact syntax of logging statements will vary depending on the release you're using, but there are a few highlights we can look for. If you search for "cassandra.yaml", you'll quickly run into the following:

```
DEBUG [main] 2015-12-08 06:02:38,677 YamlConfigurationLoader.java:104 -
  Loading settings from file:/.../conf/cassandra.yaml
INFO [main] 2015-12-08 06:02:38,781 YamlConfigurationLoader.java:179 -
  Node configuration:[authenticator=AllowAllAuthenticator;
```

```
authorizer=AllowAllAuthorizer; auto_bootstrap=false; auto_snapshot=true;
batch_size_fail_threshold_in_kb=50; ...
```

These log statements indicate the location of the *cassandra.yaml* file containing the configured settings. The Node configuration statement lists out the settings from the config file.

Now search for "JVM" and you'll find something like this:

```
INFO  [main] 2015-12-08 06:02:39,239 CassandraDaemon.java:436 -
JVM vendor/version: Java HotSpot(TM) 64-Bit Server VM/1.8.0_60
INFO  [main] 2015-12-08 06:02:39,239 CassandraDaemon.java:437 -
Heap size: 519045120/519045120
```

These log statements provide information describing the JVM being used, including memory settings.

Next, search for versions in use—"Cassandra version", "Thrift API Version", "CQL supported versions":

```
INFO  [main] 2015-12-08 06:02:43,931 StorageService.java:586 -
Cassandra version: 3.0.0
INFO  [main] 2015-12-08 06:02:43,932 StorageService.java:587 -
Thrift API version: 20.1.0
INFO  [main] 2015-12-08 06:02:43,932 StorageService.java:588 -
CQL supported versions: 3.3.1 (default: 3.3.1)
```

We can also find statements where Cassandra is initializing internal data structures such as caches:

```
INFO  [main] 2015-12-08 06:02:43,633 CacheService.java:115 -
Initializing key cache with capacity of 24 MBs.
INFO  [main] 2015-12-08 06:02:43,679 CacheService.java:137 -
Initializing row cache with capacity of 0 MBs
INFO  [main] 2015-12-08 06:02:43,686 CacheService.java:166 -
Initializing counter cache with capacity of 12 MBs
```

If we search for terms like "JMX", "gossip", and "clients", we can find statements like the following:

```
WARN  [main] 2015-12-08 06:08:06,078 StartupChecks.java:147 -
JMX is not enabled to receive remote connections.
Please see cassandra-env.sh for more info.
INFO  [main] 2015-12-08 06:08:18,463 StorageService.java:790 -
Starting up server gossip
INFO  [main] 2015-12-08 06:02:48,171 Server.java:162 -
Starting listening for CQL clients on /127.0.0.1:9042 (unencrypted)
```

These log statements indicate the server is beginning to initiate communications with other servers in the cluster and expose publicly available interfaces. By default, the management interface via the Java Management Extensions (JMX) is disabled for remote access. We'll explore the management interface in Chapter 10.

Finally, search for "state jump" and you'll see the following:

```
INFO [main] 2015-12-08 06:02:47,351 StorageService.java:1936 -
    Node /127.0.0.1 state jump to normal
```

Congratulations! Now your Cassandra server should be up and running with a new single node cluster called Test Cluster listening on port 9160. If you continue to monitor the output, you'll begin to see periodic output such as memtable flushing and compaction, which we'll learn about soon.

Starting Over

The committers work hard to ensure that data is readable from one minor dot release to the next and from one major version to the next. The commit log, however, needs to be completely cleared out from version to version (even minor versions).

If you have any previous versions of Cassandra installed, you may want to clear out the data directories for now, just to get up and running. If you've messed up your Cassandra installation and want to get started cleanly again, you can delete the data folders.

Stopping Cassandra

Now that we've successfully started a Cassandra server, you may be wondering how to stop it. You may have noticed the stop-server command in the *bin* directory. Let's try running that command. Here's what you'll see on Unix systems:

```
$ ./stop-server
please read the stop-server script before use
```

So you see that our server has not been stopped, but instead we are directed to read the script. Taking a look inside with our favorite code editor, you'll learn that the way to stop Cassandra is to kill the JVM process that is running Cassandra. The file suggests a couple of different techniques by which you can identify the JVM process and kill it.

The first technique is to start Cassandra using the -p option, which provides Cassandra with the name of a file to which it should write the process identifier (PID) upon starting up. This is arguably the most straightforward approach to making sure we kill the right process.

However, because we did not start Cassandra with the -p option, we'll need to find the process ourselves and kill it. The script suggests using pgrep to locate processes for the current user containing the term "cassandra":

```
user=`whoami`
pgrep -u $user -f cassandra | xargs kill -9
```

> **Stopping Cassandra on Windows**
>
> On Windows installations, you can find the JVM process and kill it using the Task Manager.

Other Cassandra Distributions

The instructions we just reviewed showed us how to install the Apache distribution of Cassandra. In addition to the Apache distribution, there are a couple of other ways to get Cassandra:

DataStax Community Edition
> This free distribution is provided by DataStax via the Planet Cassandra website. Installation options for various platforms include RPM and Debian (Linux), MSI (Windows), and a MacOS library. The community edition provides additional tools, including an integrated development environment (IDE) known as DevCenter, and the OpsCenter monitoring tool. Another useful feature is the ability to configure Cassandra as an OS-managed service on Windows. Releases of the community edition generally track the Apache releases, with availability soon after each Apache release.

DataStax Enterprise Edition
> DataStax also provides a fully supported version certified for production use. The product line provides an integrated database platform with support for complementary data technologies such as Hadoop and Apache Spark. We'll explore some of these integrations in Chapter 14.

Virtual machine images
> A frequent model for deployment of Cassandra is to package one of the preceding distributions in a virtual machine image. For example, multiple such images are available in the Amazon Web Services (AWS) Marketplace.

We'll take a deeper look at several options for deploying Cassandra in production environments, including cloud computing environments, in Chapter 14.

Selecting the right distribution will depend on your deployment environment; your needs for scale, stability, and support; and your development and maintenance budgets. Having both open source and commercial deployment options provides the flexibility to make the right choice for your organization.

Running the CQL Shell

Now that you have a Cassandra installation up and running, let's give it a quick try to make sure everything is set up properly. We'll use the CQL shell (`cqlsh`) to connect to our server and have a look around.

Deprecation of the CLI

If you've used Cassandra in releases prior to 3.0, you may also be familiar with the command-line client interface known as `cassandra-cli`. The CLI was removed in the 3.0 release because it depends on the legacy Thrift API.

To run the shell, create a new terminal window, change to the Cassandra home directory, and type the following command (you should see output similar to that shown here):

```
$ bin/cqlsh
Connected to Test Cluster at 127.0.0.1:9042.
[cqlsh 5.0.1 | Cassandra 3.0.0 | CQL spec 3.3.1 | Native protocol v4]
Use HELP for help.
cqlsh>
```

Because we did not specify a node to which we wanted to connect, the shell helpfully checks for a node running on the local host, and finds the node we started earlier. The shell also indicates that you're connected to a Cassandra server cluster called "Test Cluster". That's because this cluster of one node at `localhost` is set up for you by default.

Renaming the Default Cluster

In a production environment, be sure to change the cluster name to something more suitable to your application.

To connect to a specific node, specify the hostname and port on the command line. For example, the following will connect to our local node:

```
$ bin/cqlsh localhost 9042
```

Another alternative for configuring the `cqlsh` connection is to set the environment variables `$CQLSH_HOST` and `$CQLSH_PORT`. This approach is useful if you will be frequently connecting to a specific node on another host. The environment variables will be overriden if you specify the host and port on the command line.

Connection Errors

Have you run into an error like this while trying to connect to a server?

```
Exception connecting to localhost/9160. Reason:
    Connection refused.
```

If so, make sure that a Cassandra instance is started at that host and port, and that you can ping the host you're trying to reach. There may be firewall rules preventing you from connecting.

To see a complete list of the command-line options supported by cqlsh, type the command cqlsh -help.

Basic cqlsh Commands

Let's take a quick tour of cqlsh to learn what kinds of commands you can send to the server. We'll see how to use the basic environment commands and how to do a round-trip of inserting and retrieving some data.

Case in cqlsh

The cqlsh commands are all case insensitive. For our examples, we'll adopt the convention of uppercase to be consistent with the way the shell describes its own commands in help topics and output.

cqlsh Help

To get help for cqlsh, type HELP or ? to see the list of available commands:

```
cqlsh> HELP
Documented shell commands:
===========================
CAPTURE     COPY  DESCRIBE  EXPAND  PAGING  SOURCE
CONSISTENCY  DESC  EXIT      HELP    SHOW    TRACING

CQL help topics:
================
ALTER                CREATE_TABLE_TYPES  PERMISSIONS
ALTER_ADD            CREATE_USER         REVOKE
ALTER_ALTER          DATE_INPUT          REVOKE_ROLE
ALTER_DROP           DELETE              SELECT
ALTER_RENAME         DELETE_COLUMNS      SELECT_COLUMNFAMILY
ALTER_USER           DELETE_USING        SELECT_EXPR
ALTER_WITH           DELETE_WHERE        SELECT_LIMIT
APPLY                DROP                SELECT_TABLE
ASCII_OUTPUT         DROP_AGGREGATE      SELECT_WHERE
```

```
BEGIN                          DROP_COLUMNFAMILY      TEXT_OUTPUT
BLOB_INPUT                     DROP_FUNCTION          TIMESTAMP_INPUT
BOOLEAN_INPUT                  DROP_INDEX             TIMESTAMP_OUTPUT
COMPOUND_PRIMARY_KEYS          DROP_KEYSPACE          TIME_INPUT
CREATE                         DROP_ROLE              TRUNCATE
CREATE_AGGREGATE               DROP_TABLE             TYPES
CREATE_COLUMNFAMILY            DROP_USER              UPDATE
CREATE_COLUMNFAMILY_OPTIONS    GRANT                  UPDATE_COUNTERS
CREATE_COLUMNFAMILY_TYPES      GRANT_ROLE             UPDATE_SET
CREATE_FUNCTION                INSERT                 UPDATE_USING
CREATE_INDEX                   INT_INPUT              UPDATE_WHERE
CREATE_KEYSPACE                LIST                   USE
CREATE_ROLE                    LIST_PERMISSIONS       UUID_INPUT
CREATE_TABLE                   LIST_ROLES
CREATE_TABLE_OPTIONS           LIST_USERS
```

cqlsh Help Topics

You'll notice that the help topics listed differ slightly from the actual command syntax. The CREATE_TABLE help topic describes how to use the syntax > CREATE TABLE ..., for example.

To get additional documentation about a particular command, type HELP <command>. Many cqlsh commands may be used with no parameters, in which case they print out the current setting. Examples include CONSISTENCY, EXPAND, and PAGING.

Describing the Environment in cqlsh

After connecting to your Cassandra instance Test Cluster, if you're using the binary distribution, an empty *keyspace*, or Cassandra database, is set up for you to test with.

To learn about the current cluster you're working in, type:

```
cqlsh> DESCRIBE CLUSTER;
Cluster: Test Cluster
Partitioner: Murmur3Partitioner
...
```

For releases 3.0 and later, this command also prints out a list of token ranges owned by each node in the cluster, which have been omitted here for brevity.

To see which keyspaces are available in the cluster, issue this command:

```
cqlsh> DESCRIBE KEYSPACES;
system_auth    system_distributed  system_schema
system         system_traces
```

Initially this list will consist of several system keyspaces. Once you have created your own keyspaces, they will be shown as well. The system keyspaces are managed internally by Cassandra, and aren't for us to put data into. In this way, these keyspaces are similar to the master and temp databases in Microsoft SQL Server. Cassandra uses these keyspaces to store the schema, tracing, and security information. We'll learn more about these keyspaces in Chapter 6.

You can use the following command to learn the client, server, and protocol versions in use:

```
cqlsh> SHOW VERSION;
[cqlsh 5.0.1 | Cassandra 3.0.0 | CQL spec 3.3.1 | Native protocol v4]
```

You may have noticed that this version info is printed out when `cqlsh` starts. There are a variety of other commands with which you can experiment. For now, let's add some data to the database and get it back out again.

Creating a Keyspace and Table in cqlsh

A Cassandra keyspace is sort of like a relational database. It defines one or more tables or "column families." When you start `cqlsh` without specifying a keyspace, the prompt will look like this: `cqlsh>`, with no keyspace specified.

Let's create our own keyspace so we have something to write data to. In creating our keyspace, there are some required options. To walk through these options, we could use the command HELP CREATE_KEYSPACE, but instead we'll use the helpful command-completion features of `cqlsh`. Type the following and then hit the Tab key:

```
cqlsh> CREATE KEYSPACE my_keyspace WITH
```

When you hit the Tab key, `cqlsh` begins completing the syntax of our command:

```
cqlsh> CREATE KEYSPACE my_keyspace WITH replication = {'class': '
```

This is informing us that in order to specify a keyspace, we also need to specify a replication strategy. Let's Tab again to see what options we have:

```
cqlsh> CREATE KEYSPACE my_keyspace WITH replication = {'class': '
    NetworkTopologyStrategy      SimpleStrategy
    OldNetworkTopologyStrategy
```

Now `cqlsh` is giving us three strategies to choose from. We'll learn more about these strategies in Chapter 6. For now, we will choose the `SimpleStrategy` by typing the name. We'll indicate we're done with a closing quote and Tab again:

```
cqlsh> CREATE KEYSPACE my_keyspace WITH replication = {'class':
    'SimpleStrategy', 'replication_factor':
```

The next option we're presented with is a replication factor. For the simple strategy, this indicates how many nodes the data in this keyspace will be written to. For a production deployment, we'd want copies of our data stored on multiple nodes, but because we're just running a single node at the moment, we'll ask for a single copy. Let's specify a value of "1" and Tab again:

```
cqlsh> CREATE KEYSPACE my_keyspace WITH replication = {'class':
   'SimpleStrategy', 'replication_factor': 1};
```

We see that `cqlsh` has now added a closing bracket, indicating we've completed all of the required options. Let's complete our command with a semicolon and return, and our keyspace will be created.

 ### Keyspace Creation Options

For a production keyspace, we would probably never want to use a value of 1 for the replication factor. There are additional options on creating a keyspace depending on the replication strategy that is chosen. The command completion feature will walk through the different options.

Let's have a look at our keyspace using the`DESCRIBE KEYSPACE` command:

```
cqlsh> DESCRIBE KEYSPACE my_keyspace
CREATE KEYSPACE my_keyspace WITH replication = {'class':
   'SimpleStrategy', 'replication_factor': '1'} AND
   durable_writes = true;
```

We see that the table has been created with the `SimpleStrategy`, a `replication_fac` `tor` of one, and durable writes. Notice that our keyspace is described in much the same syntax that we used to create it, with one additional option that we did not specify: `durable_writes = true`. Don't worry about these settings now; we'll look at them in detail later.

After you have created your own keyspace, you can switch to it in the shell by typing:

```
cqlsh> USE my_keyspace;
cqlsh:my_keyspace>
```

Notice that the prompt has changed to indicate that we're using the keyspace.

Using Snake Case

You may have wondered why we chose to name our keyspace in "snake case" (`my_keyspace`) as opposed to "camel case" (`MyKeyspace`), which is familiar to developers using Java and other languages.

As it turns out, Cassandra naturally handles keyspace, table, and column names as lowercase. When you enter names in mixed case, Cassandra stores them as all lowercase.

This behavior can be overridden by enclosing your names in double quotes (e.g., `CREATE KEYSPACE "MyKeyspace"...`). However, it tends to be a lot simpler to use snake case than to go against the grain.

Now that we have a keyspace, we can create a table in our keyspace. To do this in cqlsh, use the following command:

```
cqlsh:my_keyspace> CREATE TABLE user ( first_name text ,
    last_name text, PRIMARY KEY (first_name)) ;
```

This creates a new table called "user" in our current keyspace with two columns to store first and last names, both of type text. The text and varchar types are synonymous and are used to store strings. We've specified the first_name column as our primary key and taken the defaults for other table options.

 **Using Keyspace Names in cqlsh**

We could have also created this table without switching to our keyspace by using the syntax CREATE TABLE my_keyspace.user (....

We can use cqlsh to get a description of a the table we just created using the DESCRIBE TABLE command:

```
cqlsh:my_keyspace> DESCRIBE TABLE user;
CREATE TABLE my_keyspace.user (
    first_name text PRIMARY KEY,
    last_name text
) WITH bloom_filter_fp_chance = 0.01
    AND caching = {'keys': 'ALL', 'rows_per_partition': 'NONE'}
    AND comment = ''
    AND compaction = {'class': 'org.apache.cassandra.db.compaction.
      SizeTieredCompactionStrategy', 'max_threshold': '32',
      'min_threshold': '4'}
    AND compression = {'chunk_length_in_kb': '64', 'class':
      'org.apache.cassandra.io.compress.LZ4Compressor'}
    AND crc_check_chance = 1.0
    AND dclocal_read_repair_chance = 0.1
    AND default_time_to_live = 0
    AND gc_grace_seconds = 864000
    AND max_index_interval = 2048
    AND memtable_flush_period_in_ms = 0
    AND min_index_interval = 128
    AND read_repair_chance = 0.0
    AND speculative_retry = '99PERCENTILE';
```

You'll notice that cqlsh prints a nicely formatted version of the CREATE TABLE command that we just typed in but also includes values for all of the available table options that we did not specify. These values are the defaults, as we did not specify them. We'll worry about these settings later. For now, we have enough to get started.

Writing and Reading Data in cqlsh

Now that we have a keyspace and a table, we'll write some data to the database and read it back out again. It's OK at this point not to know quite what's going on. We'll come to understand Cassandra's data model in depth later. For now, you have a keyspace (database), which has a table, which holds columns, the atomic unit of data storage.

To write a value, use the INSERT command:

```
cqlsh:my_keyspace> INSERT INTO user (first_name, last_name )
    VALUES ('Bill', 'Nguyen');
```

Here we have created a new row with two columns for the key Bill, to store a set of related values. The column names are first_name and last_name. We can use the SELECT COUNT command to make sure that the row was written:

```
cqlsh:my_keyspace> SELECT COUNT (*) FROM user;
 count
-------
     1

(1 rows)
```

Now that we know the data is there, let's read it, using the SELECT command:

```
cqlsh:my_keyspace> SELECT * FROM user WHERE first_name='Bill';

 first_name | last_name
------------+-----------
       Bill |    Nguyen

(1 rows)
```

In this command, we requested to return rows matching the primary key Bill including all columns. You can delete a column using the DELETE command. Here we will delete the last_name column for the Bill row key:

```
cqlsh:my_keyspace> DELETE last_name FROM USER WHERE
    first_name='Bill';
```

To make sure that it's removed, we can query again:

```
cqlsh:my_keyspace> SELECT * FROM user WHERE first_name='Bill';

 first_name | last_name
------------+-----------
       Bill |      null

(1 rows)
```

Now we'll clean up after ourselves by deleting the entire row. It's the same command, but we don't specify a column name:

```
cqlsh:my_keyspace> DELETE FROM USER WHERE first_name='Bill';
```

To make sure that it's removed, we can query again:

```
cqlsh:my_keyspace> SELECT * FROM user WHERE first_name='Bill';

 first_name | last_name
------------+-----------

(0 rows)
```

If we really want to clean up after ourselves, we can remove all data from the table using the TRUNCATE command, or even delete the table schema using the DROP TABLE command.

```
cqlsh:my_keyspace> TRUNCATE user;
cqlsh:my_keyspace> DROP TABLE user;
```

cqlsh Command History

Now that you've been using cqlsh for a while, you may have noticed that you can navigate through commands you've executed previously with the up and down arrow key. This history is stored in a file called *cqlsh_history*, which is located in a hidden directory called *.cassandra* within your home directory. This acts like your bash shell history, listing the commands in a plain-text file in the order Cassandra executed them. Nice!

Summary

Now you should have a Cassandra installation up and running. You've worked with the cqlsh client to insert and retrieve some data, and you're ready to take a step back and get the big picture on Cassandra before really diving into the details.

## CHAPTER 4

The Cassandra Query Language

In this chapter, you'll gain an understanding of Cassandra's data model and how that data model is implemented by the Cassandra Query Language (CQL). We'll show how CQL supports Cassandra's design goals and look at some general behavior characteristics.

For developers and administrators coming from the relational world, the Cassandra data model can be difficult to understand initially. Some terms, such as "keyspace," are completely new, and some, such as "column," exist in both worlds but have slightly different meanings. The syntax of CQL is similar in many ways to SQL, but with some important differences. For those familiar with NoSQL technologies such as Dynamo or Bigtable, it can also be confusing, because although Cassandra may be based on those technologies, its own data model is significantly different.

So in this chapter, we start from relational database terminology and introduce Cassandra's view of the world. Along the way we'll get more familiar with CQL and learn how it implements this data model.

The Relational Data Model

In a relational database, we have the database itself, which is the outermost container that might correspond to a single application. The database contains tables. Tables have names and contain one or more columns, which also have names. When we add data to a table, we specify a value for every column defined; if we don't have a value for a particular column, we use null. This new entry adds a row to the table, which we can later read if we know the row's unique identifier (primary key), or by using a SQL statement that expresses some criteria that row might meet. If we want to update values in the table, we can update all of the rows or just some of them, depending on the filter we use in a "where" clause of our SQL statement.

Now that we've had this review, we're in good shape to look at Cassandra's data model in terms of its similarities and differences.

Cassandra's Data Model

In this section, we'll take a bottom-up approach to understanding Cassandra's data model.

The simplest data store you would conceivably want to work with might be an array or list. It would look like Figure 4-1.

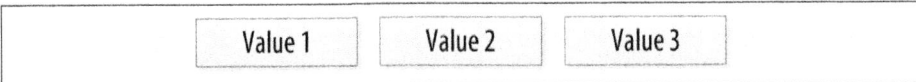

Figure 4-1. A list of values

If you persisted this list, you could query it later, but you would have to either examine each value in order to know what it represented, or always store each value in the same place in the list and then externally maintain documentation about which cell in the array holds which values. That would mean you might have to supply empty placeholder values (nulls) in order to keep the predetermined size of the array in case you didn't have a value for an optional attribute (such as a fax number or apartment number). An array is a clearly useful data structure, but not semantically rich.

So we'd like to add a second dimension to this list: names to match the values. We'll give names to each cell, and now we have a map structure, as shown in Figure 4-2.

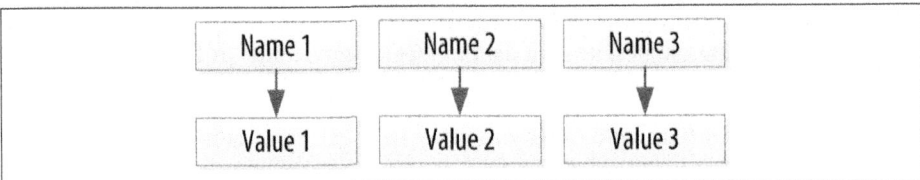

Figure 4-2. A map of name/value pairs

This is an improvement because we can know the names of our values. So if we decided that our map would hold User information, we could have column names like first_name, last_name, phone, email, and so on. This is a somewhat richer structure to work with.

But the structure we've built so far works only if we have one instance of a given entity, such as a single person, user, hotel, or tweet. It doesn't give us much if we want to store multiple entities with the same structure, which is certainly what we want to do. There's nothing to unify some collection of name/value pairs, and no way to repeat the same column names. So we need something that will group some of the column values together in a distinctly addressable group. We need a key to reference a group of columns that should be treated together as a set. We need rows. Then, if we get a single row, we can get all of the name/value pairs for a single entity at once, or just get the values for the names we're interested in. We could call these name/value pairs *columns*. We could call each separate entity that holds some set of columns *rows*. And the unique identifier for each row could be called a *row key* or *primary key*. Figure 4-3 shows the contents of a simple row: a primary key, which is itself one or more columns, and additional columns.

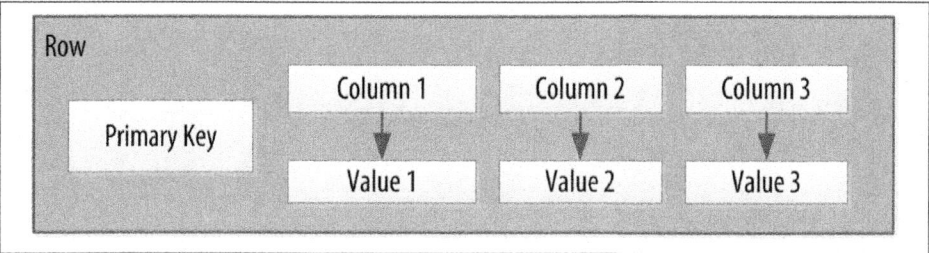

Figure 4-3. A Cassandra row

Cassandra defines a *table* to be a logical division that associates similar data. For example, we might have a user table, a hotel table, an address book table, and so on. In this way, a Cassandra table is analogous to a table in the relational world.

Now we don't need to store a value for every column every time we store a new entity. Maybe we don't know the values for every column for a given entity. For example, some people have a second phone number and some don't, and in an online form backed by Cassandra, there may be some fields that are optional and some that are required. That's OK. Instead of storing null for those values we don't know, which would waste space, we just won't store that column at all for that row. So now we have a sparse, multidimensional array structure that looks like Figure 4-4.

When designing a table in a traditional relational database, you're typically dealing with "entities," or the set of attributes that describe a particular noun (hotel, user, product, etc.). Not much thought is given to the size of the rows themselves, because row size isn't negotiable once you've decided what noun your table represents. However, when you're working with Cassandra, you actually have a decision to make about the size of your rows: they can be wide or skinny, depending on the number of columns the row contains.

A wide row means a row that has lots and lots (perhaps tens of thousands or even millions) of columns. Typically there is a smaller number of rows that go along with so many columns. Conversely, you could have something closer to a relational model, where you define a smaller number of columns and use many different rows—that's the skinny model. We've already seen a skinny model in Figure 4-4.

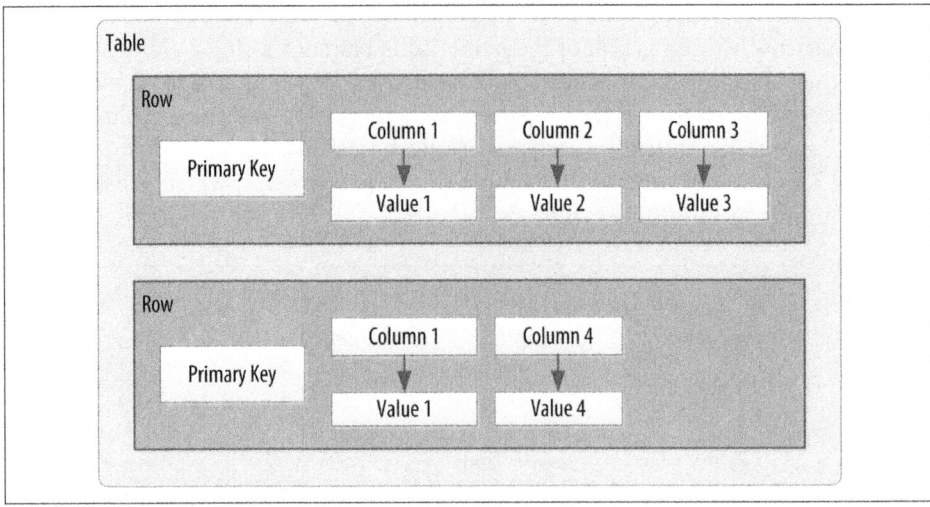

Figure 4-4. A Cassandra table

Cassandra uses a special primary key called a *composite key* (or compound key) to represent wide rows, also called *partitions*. The composite key consists of a *partition key*, plus an optional set of *clustering columns*. The partition key is used to determine the nodes on which rows are stored and can itself consist of multiple columns. The clustering columns are used to control how data is sorted for storage within a partition. Cassandra also supports an additional construct called a *static column*, which is for storing data that is not part of the primary key but is shared by every row in a partition.

Figure 4-5 shows how each partition is uniquely identified by a partition key, and how the clustering keys are used to uniquely identify the rows within a partition.

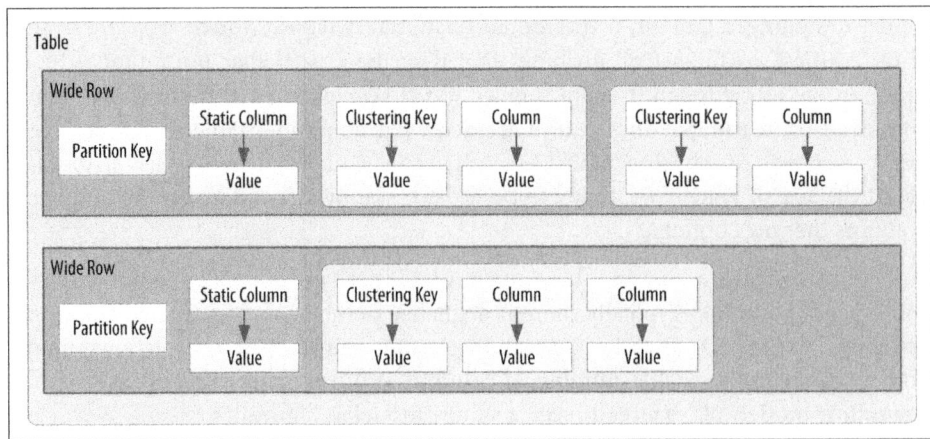

Figure 4-5. A Cassandra wide row

For this chapter, we will concern ourselves with simple primary keys consisting of a single column. In these cases, the primary key and the partition key are the same, because we have no clustering columns. We'll examine more complex primary keys in Chapter 5.

Putting this all together, we have the basic Cassandra data structures:

- The *column*, which is a name/value pair
- The *row*, which is a container for columns referenced by a primary key
- The *table*, which is a container for rows
- The *keyspace*, which is a container for tables
- The *cluster*, which is a container for keyspaces that spans one or more nodes

So that's the bottom-up approach to looking at Cassandra's data model. Now that we know the basic terminology, let's examine each structure in more detail.

Clusters

As previously mentioned, the Cassandra database is specifically designed to be distributed over several machines operating together that appear as a single instance to the end user. So the outermost structure in Cassandra is the *cluster*, sometimes called the *ring*, because Cassandra assigns data to nodes in the cluster by arranging them in a ring.

Keyspaces

A cluster is a container for keyspaces. A *keyspace* is the outermost container for data in Cassandra, corresponding closely to a relational database. In the same way that a database is a container for tables in the relational model, a keyspace is a container for tables in the Cassandra data model. Like a relational database, a keyspace has a name and a set of attributes that define keyspace-wide behavior.

Because we're currently focusing on the data model, we'll leave questions about setting up and configuring clusters and keyspaces until later. We'll examine these topics in Chapter 7.

Tables

A *table* is a container for an ordered collection of rows, each of which is itself an ordered collection of columns. The ordering is determined by the columns, which are identified as keys. We'll soon see how Cassandra uses additional keys beyond the primary key.

When you write data to a table in Cassandra, you specify values for one or more columns. That collection of values is called a *row*. At least one of the values you specify must be a *primary key* that serves as the unique identifier for that row.

Let's go back to the user table we created in the previous chapter. Remember how we wrote a row of data and then read it using the SELECT command in cqlsh:

```
cqlsh:my_keyspace> SELECT * FROM user WHERE first_name='Bill';

 first_name | last_name
------------+-----------
       Bill |    Nguyen

(1 rows)
```

You'll notice in the last row that the shell tells us that one row was returned. It turns out to be the row identified by the first_name "Bill". This is the primary key that identifies this row.

Data Access Requires a Primary Key

This is an important detail—the SELECT, INSERT, UPDATE, and DELETE commands in CQL all operate in terms of rows.

As we stated earlier, we don't need to include a value for every column when we add a new row to the table. Let's test this out with our user table using the ALTER TABLE command and then view the results using the DESCRIBE TABLE command:

```
cqlsh:my_keyspace> ALTER TABLE user ADD title text;
cqlsh:my_keyspace> DESCRIBE TABLE user;

CREATE TABLE my_keyspace.user (
    first_name text PRIMARY KEY,
    last_name text,
    title text
) ...
```

We see that the title column has been added. Note that we've shortened the output to omit the various table settings. You'll learn more about these settings and how to configure them in Chapter 7.

Now, let's write a couple of rows, populate different columns for each, and view the results:

```
cqlsh:my_keyspace> INSERT INTO user (first_name, last_name, title)
    VALUES ('Bill', 'Nguyen', 'Mr.');
cqlsh:my_keyspace> INSERT INTO user (first_name, last_name) VALUES
    ('Mary', 'Rodriguez');
cqlsh:my_keyspace> SELECT * FROM user;

 first_name | last_name | title
------------+-----------+-------
       Mary | Rodriguez |  null
       Bill |    Nguyen |   Mr.
```

```
(2 rows)
```

Now that we've learned more about the structure of a table and done some data modeling, let's dive deeper into columns.

Columns

A *column* is the most basic unit of data structure in the Cassandra data model. So far we've seen that a column contains a name and a value. We constrain each of the values to be of a particular type when we define the column. We'll want to dig into the various types that are available for each column, but first let's take a look into some other attributes of a column that we haven't discussed yet: timestamps and time to live. These attributes are key to understanding how Cassandra uses time to keep data current.

Timestamps

Each time you write data into Cassandra, a timestamp is generated for each column value that is updated. Internally, Cassandra uses these timestamps for resolving any conflicting changes that are made to the same value. Generally, the last timestamp wins.

Let's view the timestamps that were generated for our previous writes by adding the `writetime()` function to our `SELECT` command. We'll do this on the `lastname` column and include a couple of other values for context:

```
cqlsh:my_keyspace> SELECT first_name, last_name,
  writetime(last_name) FROM user;

 first_name | last_name | writetime(last_name)
------------+-----------+----------------------
       Mary | Rodriguez |     1434591198790252
       Bill |    Nguyen |     1434591198798235

(2 rows)
```

We might expect that if we ask for the timestamp on `first_name` we'd get a similar result. However, it turns out we're not allowed to ask for the timestamp on primary key columns:

```
cqlsh:my_keyspace> SELECT WRITETIME(first_name) FROM user;
InvalidRequest: code=2200 [Invalid query] message="Cannot use
  selection function writeTime on PRIMARY KEY part first_name"
```

Cassandra also allows us to specify a timestamp we want to use when performing writes. To do this, we'll use the CQL UPDATE command for the first time, using the optional USING TIMESTAMP option:

```
cqlsh:my_keyspace> UPDATE user USING TIMESTAMP 1434373756626000
  SET last_name = 'Boateng' WHERE first_name = 'Mary' ;
cqlsh:my_keyspace> SELECT first_name, last_name,
  WRITETIME(last_name) FROM user WHERE first_name = 'Mary';

 first_name | last_name  | writetime(last_name)
------------+------------+---------------------
    Mary    | Boateng    | 1434373756626000

(1 rows)
```

This statement has the effect of adding the last name column to the row identified by the primary key "Mary", and setting the timestamp to the value we provided.

Working with Timestamps

Setting the timestamp is not required for writes. This functionality is typically used for writes in which there is a concern that some of the writes may cause fresh data to be overwritten with stale data. This is advanced behavior and should be used with caution.

There is currently not a way to convert timestamps produced by writetime() into a more friendly format in cqlsh.

Time to live (TTL)

One very powerful feature that Cassandra provides is the ability to expire data that is no longer needed. This expiration is very flexible and works at the level of individual column values. The time to live (or TTL) is a value that Cassandra stores for each column value to indicate how long to keep the value.

The TTL value defaults to null, meaning that data that is written will not expire. Let's show this by adding the TTL() function to a SELECT command in cqlsh to see the TTL value for Mary's last name:

```
cqlsh:my_keyspace> SELECT first_name, last_name, TTL(last_name)
  FROM user WHERE first_name = 'Mary';

 first_name | last_name | ttl(last_name)
------------+-----------+----------------
    Mary    |  Boateng  |          null

(1 rows)
```

Now let's set the TTL on the last name column to an hour (3,600 seconds) by adding the USING TTL option to our UPDATE command:

```
cqlsh:my_keyspace> UPDATE user USING TTL 3600 SET last_name =
  'McDonald' WHERE first_name = 'Mary' ;
cqlsh:my_keyspace> SELECT first_name, last_name, TTL(last_name)
  FROM user WHERE first_name = 'Mary';

 first_name | last_name   | ttl(last_name)
------------+-------------+---------------
    Mary    |  McDonald   |           3588

(1 rows)
```

As you can see, the clock is already counting down our TTL, reflecting the several seconds it took to type the second command. If we run this command again in an hour, Mary's last_name will be set to null. We can also set TTL on INSERTS using the same USING TTL option.

 **Using TTL**

Remember that TTL is stored on a per-column level. There is currently no mechanism for setting TTL at a row level directly. As with the timestamp, there is no way to obtain or set the TTL value of a *primary key* column, and the TTL can only be set for a column when we provide a value for the column.

If we want to set TTL across an entire row, we must provide a value for every non-primary key column in our INSERT or UPDATE command.

CQL Types

Now that we've taken a deeper dive into how Cassandra represents columns including time-based metadata, let's look at the various types that are available to us for our values.

As we've seen in our exploration so far, each column in our table is of a specified type. Up until this point, we've only used the varchar type, but there are plenty of other options available to us in CQL, so let's explore them.

CQL supports a flexible set of data types, including simple character and numeric types, collections, and user-defined types. We'll describe these data types and provide some examples of how they might be used to help you learn to make the right choice for your data model.

Numeric Data Types

CQL supports the numeric types you'd expect, including integer and floating-point numbers. These types are similar to standard types in Java and other languages:

`int`
: A 32-bit signed integer (as in Java)

`bigint`
: A 64-bit signed long integer (equivalent to a Java `long`)

`smallint`
: A 16-bit signed integer (equivalent to a Java `short`)

`tinyint`
: An 8-bit signed integer (as in Java)

`varint`
: A variable precision signed integer (equivalent to `java.math.BigInteger`)

`float`
: A 32-bit IEEE-754 floating point (as in Java)

`double`
: A 64-bit IEEE-754 floating point (as in Java)

`decimal`
: A variable precision decimal (equivalent to `java.math.BigDecimal`)

Additional Integer Types

The `smallint` and `tinyint` types were added in the Cassandra 2.2 release.

While enumerated types are common in many languages, there is no direct equivalent in CQL. A common practice is to store enumerated values as strings. For example, using the `Enum.name()` method to convert an enumerated value to a String for writing to Cassandra as text, and the `Enum.valueOf()` method to convert from text back to the enumerated value.

Textual Data Types

CQL provides two data types for representing text, one of which we've made quite a bit of use of already (text):

text, varchar
Synonyms for a UTF-8 character string

ascii
An ASCII character string

UTF-8 is the more recent and widely used text standard and supports internationalization, so we recommend using text over ascii when building tables for new data. The ascii type is most useful if you are dealing with legacy data that is in ASCII format.

Setting the Locale in cqlsh

By default, cqlsh prints out control and other unprintable characters using a backslash escape. You can control how cqlsh displays non-ASCII characters by setting the locale via the $LANG environment variable before running the tool. See the cqlsh command HELP TEXT_OUTPUT for more information.

Time and Identity Data Types

The identity of data elements such as rows and partitions is important in any data model in order to be able to access the data. Cassandra provides several types which prove quite useful in defining unique partition keys. Let's take some time (pun intended) to dig into these:

timestamp
While we noted earlier that each column has a timestamp indicating when it was last modified, you can also use a timestamp as the value of a column itself. The time can be encoded as a 64-bit signed integer, but it is typically much more useful to input a timestamp using one of several supported ISO 8601 date formats. For example:

```
2015-06-15 20:05-0700
2015-06-15 20:05:07-0700
2015-06-15 20:05:07.013-0700
2015-06-15T20:05-0700
2015-06-15T20:05:07-0700
2015-06-15T20:05:07.013+-0700
```

The best practice is to always provide time zones rather than relying on the operating system time zone configuration.

date, time

Releases through Cassandra 2.1 only had the timestamp type to represent times, which included both a date and a time of day. The 2.2 release introduced date and time types that allowed these to be represented independently; that is, a date without a time, and a time of day without reference to a specific date. As with timestamp, these types support ISO 8601 formats.

Although there are new java.time types available in Java 8, the date type maps to a custom type in Cassandra in order to preserve compatibility with older JDKs. The time type maps to a Java long representing the number of nanoseconds since midnight.

uuid

A *universally unique identifier* (UUID) is a 128-bit value in which the bits conform to one of several types, of which the most commonly used are known as Type 1 and Type 4. The CQL uuid type is a Type 4 UUID, which is based entirely on random numbers. UUIDs are typically represented as dash-separated sequences of hex digits. For example:

```
1a6300ca-0572-4736-a393-c0b7229e193e
```

The uuid type is often used as a surrogate key, either by itself or in combination with other values.

Because UUIDs are of a finite length, they are not absolutely guaranteed to be unique. However, most operating systems and programming languages provide utilities to generate IDs that provide adequate uniqueness, and cqlsh does as well. You can obtain a Type 4 UUID value via the uuid() function and use this value in an INSERT or UPDATE.

timeuuid

This is a Type 1 UUID, which is based on the MAC address of the computer, the system time, and a sequence number used to prevent duplicates. This type is frequently used as a conflict-free timestamp. cqlsh provides several convenience functions for interacting with the timeuuid type: now(), dateOf() and unixTimestampOf().

The availability of these convenience functions is one reason why timeuuid tends to be used more frequently than uuid.

Building on our previous examples, we might determine that we'd like to assign a unique ID to each user, as first_name is perhaps not a sufficiently unique key for our user table. After all, it's very likely that we'll run into users with the same first name at some point. If we were starting from scratch, we might have chosen to make this identifier our primary key, but for now we'll add it as another column.

 **Primary Keys Are Forever**

After you create a table, there is no way to modify the primary key, because this controls how data is distributed within the cluster, and even more importantly, how it is stored on disk.

Let's add the identifier using a uuid :

```
cqlsh:my_keyspace> ALTER TABLE user ADD id uuid;
```

Next, we'll insert an ID for Mary using the uuid() function and then view the results:

```
cqlsh:my_keyspace> UPDATE user SET id = uuid() WHERE first_name =
  'Mary';
cqlsh:my_keyspace> SELECT first_name, id FROM user WHERE
  first_name = 'Mary';

 first_name | id
------------+--------------------------------------
       Mary | e43abc5d-6650-4d13-867a-70cbad7feda9

(1 rows)
```

Notice that the id is in UUID format.

Now we have a more robust table design, which we can extend with even more columns as we learn about more types.

Other Simple Data Types

CQL provides several other simple data types that don't fall nicely into one of the categories we've looked at already:

boolean
> This is a simple true/false value. The cqlsh is case insensitive in accepting these values but outputs True or False.

blob
> A *binary large object* (blob) is a colloquial computing term for an arbitrary array of bytes. The CQL blob type is useful for storing media or other binary file types. Cassandra does not validate or examine the bytes in a blob. CQL represents the data as hexadecimal digits—for example, 0x00000ab83cf0. If you want to encode

arbitrary textual data into the blob you can use the `textAsBlob()` function in order to specify values for entry. See the `cqlsh` help function `HELP BLOB_INPUT` for more information.

`inet`

This type represents IPv4 or IPv6 Internet addresses. `cqlsh` accepts any legal format for defining IPv4 addresses, including dotted or non-dotted representations containing decimal, octal, or hexadecimal values. However, the values are represented using the dotted decimal format in `cqlsh` output—for example, `192.0.2.235`.

IPv6 addresses are represented as eight groups of four hexadecimal digits, separated by colons—for example, `2001:0db8:85a3:0000:0000:8a2e:0370:7334`. The IPv6 specification allows the collapsing of consecutive zero hex values, so the preceding value is rendered as follows when read using `SELECT`: `2001:db8:85a3:a::8a2e:370:7334`.

`counter`

The counter data type provides 64-bit signed integer, whose value cannot be set directly, but only incremented or decremented. Cassandra is one of the few databases that provides race-free increments across data centers. Counters are frequently used for tracking statistics such as numbers of page views, tweets, log messages, and so on. The `counter` type has some special restrictions. It cannot be used as part of a primary key. If a counter is used, all of the columns other than primary key columns must be counters.

A Warning About Counters

Remember: the increment and decrement operators are not idempotent. There is no operation to reset a counter directly, but you can approximate a reset by reading the counter value and decrementing by that value. Unfortunately, this is not guaranteed to work perfectly, as the counter may have been changed elsewhere in between reading and writing.

Collections

Let's say we wanted to extend our `user` table to support multiple email addresses. One way to do this would be to create additional columns such as email2, email3, and so on. While this is an approach that will work, it does not scale very well and might cause a lot of rework. It is much simpler to deal with the email addresses as a group or "collection." CQL provides three collection types to help us out with these situations: sets, lists, and maps. Let's now take a look at each of them:

set

The set data type stores a collection of elements. The elements are unordered, but cqlsh returns the elements in sorted order. For example, text values are returned in alphabetical order. Sets can contain the simple types we reviewed earlier as well as user-defined types (which we'll discuss momentarily) and even other collections. One advantage of using set is the ability to insert additional items without having to read the contents first.

Let's modify our user table to add a set of email addresses:

```
cqlsh:my_keyspace> ALTER TABLE user ADD emails set<text>;
```

Then we'll add an email address for Mary and check that it was added successfully:

```
cqlsh:my_keyspace> UPDATE user SET emails = {
  'mary@example.com' } WHERE first_name = 'Mary';
cqlsh:my_keyspace> SELECT emails FROM user WHERE first_name =
  'Mary';

 emails
---------------------
 {'mary@example.com'}

(1 rows)
```

Note that in adding that first email address, we replaced the previous contents of the set, which in this case was null. We can add another email address later without replacing the whole set by using concatenation:

```
cqlsh:my_keyspace> UPDATE user SET emails = emails + {
  'mary.mcdonald.AZ@gmail.com' } WHERE first_name = 'Mary';
cqlsh:my_keyspace> SELECT emails FROM user WHERE first_name =
  'Mary';

 emails
----------------------------------------------------------
 {'mary.mcdonald.AZ@gmail.com', 'mary@example.com'}

(1 rows)
```

Other Set Operations

We can also clear items from the set by using the subtraction operator: SET emails = emails - {'mary@example.com'}.

Alternatively, we could clear out the entire set by using the empty set notation: SET emails = {}.

list

The list data type contains an ordered list of elements. By default, the values are stored in order of insertion. Let's modify our user table to add a list of phone numbers:

```
cqlsh:my_keyspace> ALTER TABLE user ADD
  phone_numbers list<text>;
```

Then we'll add a phone number for Mary and check that it was added successfully:

```
cqlsh:my_keyspace> UPDATE user SET phone_numbers = [
  '1-800-999-9999' ] WHERE first_name = 'Mary';
cqlsh:my_keyspace> SELECT phone_numbers FROM user WHERE
  first_name = 'Mary';

 phone_numbers
--------------------
 ['1-800-999-9999']

(1 rows)
```

Let's add a second number by appending it:

```
cqlsh:my_keyspace> UPDATE user SET phone_numbers =
  phone_numbers + [ '480-111-1111' ] WHERE first_name = 'Mary';
cqlsh:my_keyspace> SELECT phone_numbers FROM user WHERE
  first_name = 'Mary';

 phone_numbers
-----------------------------------
 ['1-800-999-9999', '480-111-1111']

(1 rows)
```

The second number we added now appears at the end of the list.

 We could also have prepended the number to the front of the list by reversing the order of our values: SET phone_numbers = ['4801234567'] + phone_numbers.

We can replace an individual item in the list when we reference it by its index:

```
cqlsh:my_keyspace> UPDATE user SET phone_numbers[1] =
  '480-111-1111' WHERE first_name = 'Mary';
```

As with sets, we can also use the subtraction operator to remove items that match a specified value:

```
cqlsh:my_keyspace> UPDATE user SET phone_numbers =
    phone_numbers - [ '480-111-1111' ] WHERE first_name = 'Mary';
```

Finally, we can delete a specific item directly using its index:

```
cqlsh:my_keyspace> DELETE phone_numbers[0] from user WHERE
    first_name = 'Mary';
```

map

The map data type contains a collection of key/value pairs. The keys and the values can be of any type except counter. Let's try this out by using a map to store information about user logins. We'll create a column to track login session time in seconds, with a timeuuid as the key:

```
cqlsh:my_keyspace> ALTER TABLE user ADD
    login_sessions map<timeuuid, int>;
```

Then we'll add a couple of login sessions for Mary and see the results:

```
cqlsh:my_keyspace> UPDATE user SET login_sessions =
    { now(): 13, now(): 18} WHERE first_name = 'Mary';
cqlsh:my_keyspace> SELECT login_sessions FROM user WHERE
    first_name = 'Mary';

 login_sessions
---------------------------------------------
 {6061b850-14f8-11e5-899a-a9fac1d00bce: 13,
  6061b851-14f8-11e5-899a-a9fac1d00bce: 18}

(1 rows)
```

We can also reference an individual item in the map by using its key.

Collection types are very useful in cases where we need to store a variable number of elements within a single column.

User-Defined Types

Now we might decide that we need to keep track of physical addresses for our users. We could just use a single text column to store these values, but that would put the burden of parsing the various components of the address on the application. It would be better if we could define a structure in which to store the addresses to maintain the integrity of the different components.

Fortunately, Cassandra gives us a way to define our own types. We can then create columns of these user-defined types (UDTs). Let's create our own address type, inserting some line breaks in our command for readability:

```
cqlsh:my_keyspace> CREATE TYPE address (
              ...     street text,
              ...     city text,
              ...     state text,
              ...     zip_code int);
```

A UDT is scoped by the keyspace in which it is defined. We could have written `CREATE TYPE my_keyspace.address`. If you run the command `DESCRIBE KEYSPACE my_keyspace`, you'll see that the address type is part of the keyspace definition.

Now that we have defined our address type, we'll try to use it in our user table, but if you're using Cassandra 2.1 or earlier, you'll run into a problem:

```
cqlsh:my_keyspace> ALTER TABLE user ADD
    addresses map<text, address>;
InvalidRequest: code=2200 [Invalid query] message="Non-frozen
    collections are not allowed inside collections: map<text,
    address>"
```

What is going on here? It turns out that a user-defined data type is considered a collection, as its implementation is similar to a `set`, `list`, or `map`.

Freezing Collections

Cassandra releases prior to 2.2 do not fully support the nesting of collections. Specifically, the ability to access individual attributes of a nested collection is not yet supported, because the nested collection is serialized as a single object by the implementation.

Freezing is a concept that the Cassandra community has introduced as a forward compatibility mechanism. For now, you can nest a collection within another collection by marking it as `frozen`. In the future, when nested collections are fully supported, there will be a mechanism to "unfreeze" the nested collections, allowing the individual attributes to be accessed.

You can also use a collection as a primary key if it is frozen.

Now that we've taken a short detour to discuss freezing and nested tables, let's get back to modifying our table, this time marking the address as frozen:

```
cqlsh:my_keyspace> ALTER TABLE user ADD addresses map<text,
    frozen<address>>;
```

Now let's add a home address for Mary:

```
cqlsh:my_keyspace> UPDATE user SET addresses = addresses +
  {'home': { street: '7712 E. Broadway', city: 'Tucson',
  state: 'AZ', zip_code: 85715} } WHERE first_name = 'Mary';
```

Now that we've finished learning about the various types, let's take a step back and look at the tables we've created so far by describing my_keyspace:

```
cqlsh:my_keyspace> DESCRIBE KEYSPACE my_keyspace ;

CREATE KEYSPACE my_keyspace WITH replication = {'class':
  'SimpleStrategy', 'replication_factor': '1'} AND
  durable_writes = true;

CREATE TYPE my_keyspace.address (
    street text,
    city text,
    state text,
    zip_code int
);

CREATE TABLE my_keyspace.user (
    first_name text PRIMARY KEY,
    addresses map<text, frozen<address>>,
    emails set<text>,
    id uuid,
    last_name text,
    login_sessions map<timeuuid, int>,
    phone_numbers list<text>,
    title text
) WITH bloom_filter_fp_chance = 0.01
    AND caching = '{"keys":"ALL", "rows_per_partition":"NONE"}'
    AND comment = ''
    AND compaction = {'min_threshold': '4', 'class':
      'org.apache.cassandra.db.compaction.
      SizeTieredCompactionStrategy', 'max_threshold': '32'}
    AND compression = {'sstable_compression':
      'org.apache.cassandra.io.compress.LZ4Compressor'}
    AND dclocal_read_repair_chance = 0.1
    AND default_time_to_live = 0
    AND gc_grace_seconds = 864000
    AND max_index_interval = 2048
    AND memtable_flush_period_in_ms = 0
    AND min_index_interval = 128
    AND read_repair_chance = 0.0
    AND speculative_retry = '99.0PERCENTILE';
```

Secondary Indexes

If you try to query on column in a Cassandra table that is not part of the primary key, you'll soon realize that this is not allowed. For example, consider our user table from the previous chapter, which uses first_name as the primary key. Attempting to query by last_name results in the following output:

```
cqlsh:my_keyspace> SELECT * FROM user WHERE last_name = 'Nguyen';
InvalidRequest: code=2200 [Invalid query] message="No supported
    secondary index found for the non primary key columns restrictions"
```

As the error message instructs us, we need to create a *secondary index* for the last_name column. A secondary index is an index on a column that is not part of the primary key:

```
cqlsh:my_keyspace> CREATE INDEX ON user ( last_name );
```

We can also give an optional name to the index with the syntax CREATE INDEX <name> ON.... If you don't specify a name, cqlsh creates a name automatically according to the form *<table name>_<column name>_idx*. For example, we can learn the name of the index we just created using DESCRIBE KEYSPACE:

```
cqlsh:my_keyspace> DESCRIBE KEYSPACE;
...
CREATE INDEX user_last_name_idx ON my_keyspace.user (last_name);
```

Now that we've created the index, our query will work as expected:

```
cqlsh:my_keyspace> SELECT * FROM user WHERE last_name = 'Nguyen';

 first_name | last_name
------------+-----------
       Bill |    Nguyen

(1 rows)
```

We're not limited just to indexes based only on simple type columns. It's also possible to create indexes that are based on values in collections. For example, we might wish to be able to search based on user addresses, emails, or phone numbers, which we have implemented using map, set, and list, respectively:

```
cqlsh:my_keyspace> CREATE INDEX ON user ( addresses );
cqlsh:my_keyspace> CREATE INDEX ON user ( emails );
cqlsh:my_keyspace> CREATE INDEX ON user ( phone_numbers );
```

Note that for maps in particular, we have the option of indexing either the keys, via the syntax KEYS(addresses), or the values, which is the default. You may not create indexes on both the keys and values of a map.

Finally, we can use the DROP INDEX command to remove an index:

```
cqlsh:my_keyspace> DROP INDEX user_last_name_idx;
```

Secondary Index Pitfalls

Because Cassandra partitions data across multiple nodes, each node must maintain its own copy of a secondary index based on the data stored in partitions it owns. For this reason, queries involving a secondary index typically involve more nodes, making them significantly more expensive.

Secondary indexes are not recommended for several specific cases:

- Columns with high cardinality. For example, indexing on the user.addresses column could be very expensive, as the vast majority of addresses are unique.
- Columns with very low data cardinality. For example, it would make little sense to index on the user.title column in order to support a query for every "Mrs." in the user table, as this would result in a massive row in the index.
- Columns that are frequently updated or deleted. Indexes built on these columns can generate errors if the amount of deleted data (tombstones) builds up more quickly than the compaction process can handle.

For optimal read performance, denormalized table designs or materialized views are generally preferred to using secondary indexes. We'll learn more about these in Chapter 5. However, secondary indexes can be a useful way of supporting queries that were not considered in the initial data model design.

SASI: A New Secondary Index Implementation

The Cassandra 3.4 release included an alternative implementation of secondary indexes known as the SSTable Attached Secondary Index (SASI). SASI was developed by Apple and released as an open source implementation of Cassandra's secondary index API. As the name implies, SASI indexes are calculated and stored as part of each SSTable file, differing from the original Cassandra implementation, which stores indexes in separate, "hidden" tables.

The SASI implementation exists alongside traditional secondary indexes, and you can create a SASI index with the CQL CREATE CUSTOM INDEX command:

```
CREATE CUSTOM INDEX user_last_name_sasi_idx ON user (last_name)
    USING 'org.apache.cassandra.index.sasi.SASIIndex';
```

SASI indexes do offer functionality beyond the traditional secondary index implementation, such as the ability to do inequality (greater than or less than) searches on indexed columns. You can also use the new CQL LIKE keyword to do text searches against indexed columns. For example, you could use the following query to find users whose last name begins with "N":

```
SELECT * FROM user WHERE last_name LIKE 'N%';
```

While SASI indexes do perform better than traditional indexes by eliminating the need to read from additional tables, they still require reads from a greater number of nodes than a denormalized design.

Summary

In this chapter, we took a quick tour of Cassandra's data model of clusters, keyspaces, tables, keys, rows, and columns. In the process, we learned a lot of CQL syntax and gained more experience working with tables and columns in cqlsh. If you're interested in diving deeper on CQL, you can read the full language specification (*https://cassandra.apache.org/doc/cql3/CQL.html*).

Data Modeling

In this chapter, you'll learn how to design data models for Cassandra, including a data modeling process and notation. To apply this knowledge, we'll design the data model for a sample application, which we'll build over the next several chapters. This will help show how all the parts fit together. Along the way, we'll use a tool to help us manage our CQL scripts.

Conceptual Data Modeling

First, let's create a simple domain model that is easy to understand in the relational world, and then see how we might map it from a relational to a distributed hashtable model in Cassandra.

To create the example, we want to use something that is complex enough to show the various data structures and design patterns, but not something that will bog you down with details. Also, a domain that's familiar to everyone will allow you to concentrate on how to work with Cassandra, not on what the application domain is all about.

For our example, we'll use a domain that is easily understood and that everyone can relate to: making hotel reservations.

Our conceptual domain includes hotels, guests that stay in the hotels, a collection of rooms for each hotel, the rates and availability of those rooms, and a record of reservations booked for guests. Hotels typically also maintain a collection of "points of interest," which are parks, museums, shopping galleries, monuments, or other places near the hotel that guests might want to visit during their stay. Both hotels and points of interest need to maintain geolocation data so that they can be found on maps for mashups, and to calculate distances.

We depict our conceptual domain in Figure 5-1 using the entity–relationship model popularized by Peter Chen. This simple diagram represents the entities in our domain with rectangles, and attributes of those entities with ovals. Attributes that represent unique identifiers for items are underlined. Relationships between entities are represented as diamonds, and the connectors between the relationship and each entity show the multiplicity of the connection.

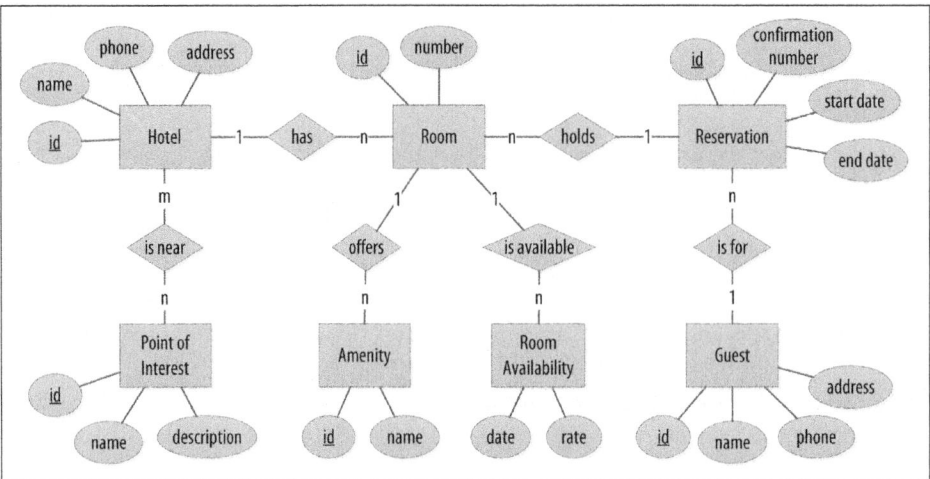

Figure 5-1. Hotel domain entity–relationship diagram

Obviously, in the real world, there would be many more considerations and much more complexity. For example, hotel rates are notoriously dynamic, and calculating them involves a wide array of factors. Here we're defining something complex enough to be interesting and touch on the important points, but simple enough to maintain the focus on learning Cassandra.

RDBMS Design

When you set out to build a new data-driven application that will use a relational database, you might start by modeling the domain as a set of properly normalized tables and use foreign keys to reference related data in other tables.

Figure 5-2 shows how we might represent the data storage for our application using a relational database model. The relational model includes a couple of "join" tables in order to realize the many-to-many relationships from our conceptual model of hotels-to-points of interest, rooms-to-amenities, rooms-to-availability, and guests-to-rooms (via a reservation).

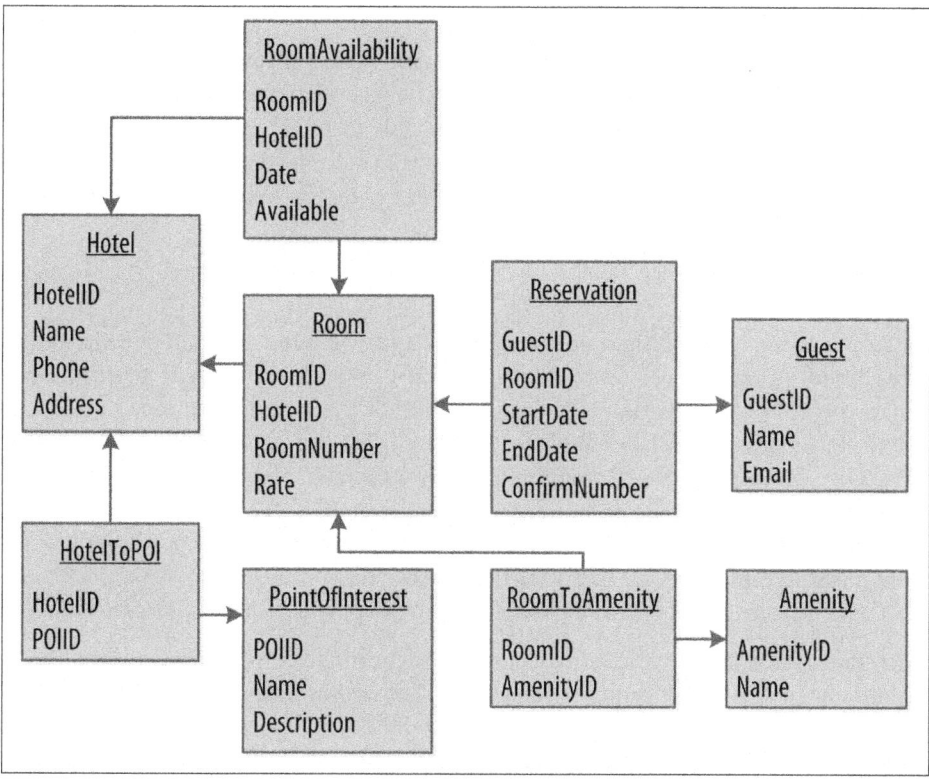

Figure 5-2. A simple hotel search system using RDBMS

Design Differences Between RDBMS and Cassandra

Of course, because this is a Cassandra book, what we really want is to model our data so we can store it in Cassandra. Before we start creating our Cassandra data model, let's take a minute to highlight some of the key differences in doing data modeling for Cassandra versus a relational database.

No joins

You cannot perform joins in Cassandra. If you have designed a data model and find that you need something like a join, you'll have to either do the work on the client side, or create a denormalized second table that represents the join results for you. This latter option is preferred in Cassandra data modeling. Performing joins on the client should be a very rare case; you really want to duplicate (denormalize) the data instead.

No referential integrity

Although Cassandra supports features such as lightweight transactions and batches, Cassandra itself has no concept of referential integrity across tables. In a relational database, you could specify foreign keys in a table to reference the primary key of a record in another table. But Cassandra does not enforce this. It is still a common design requirement to store IDs related to other entities in your tables, but operations such as cascading deletes are not available.

Denormalization

In relational database design, we are often taught the importance of normalization. This is not an advantage when working with Cassandra because it performs best when the data model is denormalized. It is often the case that companies end up denormalizing data in relational databases as well. There are two common reasons for this. One is performance. Companies simply can't get the performance they need when they have to do so many joins on years' worth of data, so they denormalize along the lines of known queries. This ends up working, but goes against the grain of how relational databases are intended to be designed, and ultimately makes one question whether using a relational database is the best approach in these circumstances.

A second reason that relational databases get denormalized on purpose is a business document structure that requires retention. That is, you have an enclosing table that refers to a lot of external tables whose data could change over time, but you need to preserve the enclosing document as a snapshot in history. The common example here is with invoices. You already have customer and product tables, and you'd think that you could just make an invoice that refers to those tables. But this should never be done in practice. Customer or price information could change, and then you would lose the integrity of the invoice document as it was on the invoice date, which could violate audits, reports, or laws, and cause other problems.

In the relational world, denormalization violates Codd's normal forms, and we try to avoid it. But in Cassandra, denormalization is, well, perfectly normal. It's not required if your data model is simple. But don't be afraid of it.

Server-Side Denormalization with Materialized Views

Historically, denormalization in Cassandra has required designing and managing multiple tables using techniques we will introduce momentarily. Beginning with the 3.0 release, Cassandra provides a feature known as *materialized views* which allows us to create multiple denormalized views of data based on a base table design. Cassandra manages materialized views on the server, including the work of keeping the views in sync with the table. In this chapter, we'll see examples of both classic denormalization and materialized views.

Query-first design

Relational modeling, in simple terms, means that you start from the conceptual domain and then represent the nouns in the domain in tables. You then assign primary keys and foreign keys to model relationships. When you have a many-to-many relationship, you create the join tables that represent just those keys. The join tables don't exist in the real world, and are a necessary side effect of the way relational models work. After you have all your tables laid out, you can start writing queries that pull together disparate data using the relationships defined by the keys. The queries in the relational world are very much secondary. It is assumed that you can always get the data you want as long as you have your tables modeled properly. Even if you have to use several complex subqueries or join statements, this is usually true.

By contrast, in Cassandra you don't start with the data model; you start with the query model. Instead of modeling the data first and then writing queries, with Cassandra you model the queries and let the data be organized around them. Think of the most common query paths your application will use, and then create the tables that you need to support them.

Detractors have suggested that designing the queries first is overly constraining on application design, not to mention database modeling. But it is perfectly reasonable to expect that you should think hard about the queries in your application, just as you would, presumably, think hard about your relational domain. You may get it wrong, and then you'll have problems in either world. Or your query needs might change over time, and then you'll have to work to update your data set. But this is no different from defining the wrong tables, or needing additional tables, in an RDBMS.

Designing for optimal storage

In a relational database, it is frequently transparent to the user how tables are stored on disk, and it is rare to hear of recommendations about data modeling based on how the RDBMS might store tables on disk. However, that is an important consideration in Cassandra. Because Cassandra tables are each stored in separate files on disk, it's important to keep related columns defined together in the same table.

A key goal that we will see as we begin creating data models in Cassandra is to minimize the number of partitions that must be searched in order to satisfy a given query. Because the partition is a unit of storage that does not get divided across nodes, a query that searches a single partition will typically yield the best performance.

Sorting is a design decision

In an RDBMS, you can easily change the order in which records are returned to you by using ORDER BY in your query. The default sort order is not configurable; by default, records are returned in the order in which they are written. If you want to

---

change the order, you just modify your query, and you can sort by any list of columns.

In Cassandra, however, sorting is treated differently; it is a design decision. The sort order available on queries is fixed, and is determined entirely by the selection of clustering columns you supply in the CREATE TABLE command. The CQL SELECT statement does support ORDER BY semantics, but only in the order specified by the clustering columns.

Defining Application Queries

Let's try the query-first approach to start designing the data model for our hotel application. The user interface design for the application is often a great artifact to use to begin identifying queries. Let's assume that we've talked with the project stakeholders and our UX designers have produced user interface designs or wireframes for the key use cases. We'll likely have a list of shopping queries like the following:

- Q1. Find hotels near a given point of interest.
- Q2. Find information about a given hotel, such as its name and location.
- Q3. Find points of interest near a given hotel.
- Q4. Find an available room in a given date range.
- Q5. Find the rate and amenities for a room.

Number Your Queries

It is often helpful to be able to refer to queries by a shorthand number rather that explaining them in full. The queries listed here are numbered Q1, Q2, and so on, which is how we will reference them in diagrams as we move throughout our example.

Now if our application is to be a success, we'll certainly want our customers to be able to book reservations at our hotels. This includes steps such as selecting an available room and entering their guest information. So clearly we will also need some queries that address the reservation and guest entities from our conceptual data model. Even here, however, we'll want to think not only from the customer perspective in terms of how the data is written, but also in terms of how the data will be queried by downstream use cases.

Our natural tendency as data modelers would be to focus first on designing the tables to store reservation and guest records, and only then start thinking about the queries that would access them. You may have felt a similar tension already when we began discussing the shopping queries before, thinking "but where did the hotel and point of interest data come from?" Don't worry, we will get to this soon enough. Here are some queries that describe how our users will access reservations:

- Q6. Lookup a reservation by confirmation number.
- Q7. Lookup a reservation by hotel, date, and guest name.
- Q8. Lookup all reservations by guest name.
- Q9. View guest details.

We show all of our queries in the context of the workflow of our application in Figure 5-3. Each box on the diagram represents a step in the application workflow, with arrows indicating the flows between steps and the associated query. If we've modeled our application well, each step of the workflow accomplishes a task that "unlocks" subsequent steps. For example, the "View hotels near POI" task helps the application learn about several hotels, including their unique keys. The key for a selected hotel may be used as part of Q2, in order to obtain detailed description of the hotel. The act of booking a room creates a reservation record that may be accessed by the guest and hotel staff at a later time through various additional queries.

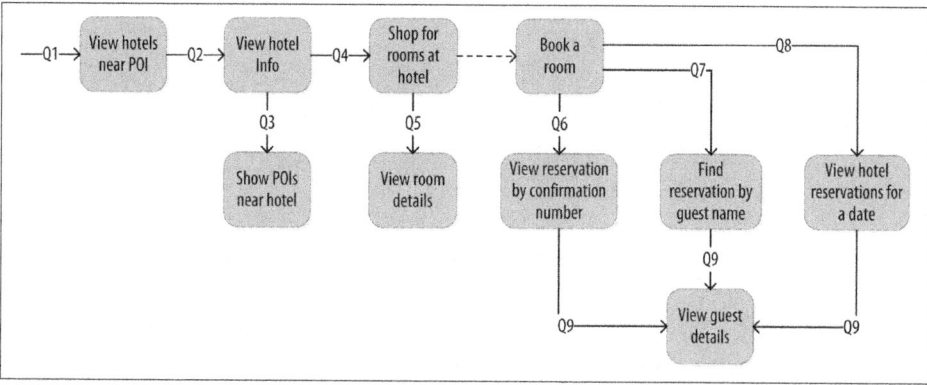

Figure 5-3. Hotel application queries

Logical Data Modeling

Now that we have defined our queries, we're ready to begin designing our Cassandra tables. First, we'll create a logical model containing a table for each query, capturing entities and relationships from the conceptual model.

To name each table, we'll identify the primary entity type for which we are querying and use that to start the entity name. If we are querying by attributes of other related entities, we append those to the table name, separated with _by_. For example, hotels_by_poi.

Next, we identify the primary key for the table, adding partition key columns based on the required query attributes, and clustering columns in order to guarantee uniqueness and support desired sort ordering.

We complete each table by adding any additional attributes identified by the query. If any of these additional attributes are the same for every instance of the partition key, we mark the column as static.

Now that was a pretty quick description of a fairly involved process, so it will be worth our time to work through a detailed example. First, let's introduce a notation that we can use to represent our logical models.

Introducing Chebotko Diagrams

Several individuals within the Cassandra community have proposed notations for capturing data models in diagrammatic form. We've elected to use a notation popularized by Artem Chebotko which provides a simple, informative way to visualize the relationships between queries and tables in our designs. Figure 5-4 shows the Chebotko notation for a logical data model.

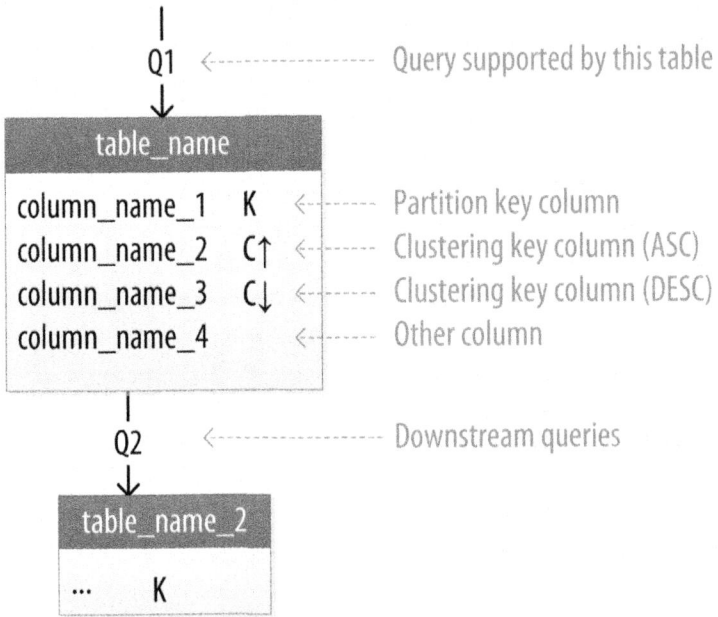

Figure 5-4. A Chebotko logical diagram

Each table is shown with its title and a list of columns. Primary key columns are identified via symbols such as **K** for partition key columns and **C↑** or **C↓** to represent clustering columns. Lines are shown entering tables or between tables to indicate the queries that each table is designed to support.

Hotel Logical Data Model

Figure 5-5 shows a Chebotko logical data model for the queries involving hotels, points of interest, rooms, and amenities. One thing we notice immediately is that our Cassandra design doesn't include dedicated tables for rooms or amenities, as we had in the relational design. This is because our workflow didn't identify any queries requiring this direct access.

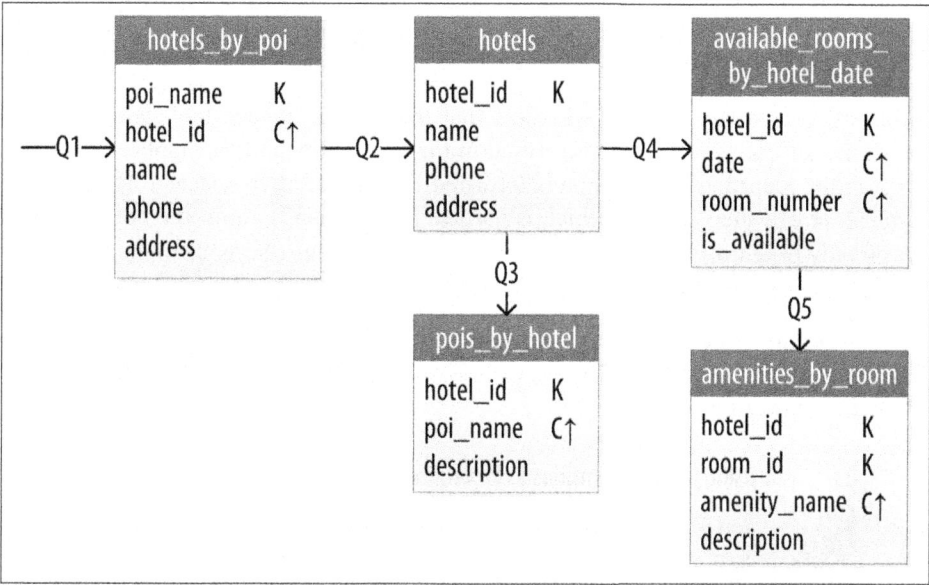

Figure 5-5. Hotel domain logical model

Let's explore the details of each of these tables.

Our first query Q1 is to find hotels near a point of interest, so we'll call our table `hotels_by_poi`. We're searching by a named point of interest, so that is a clue that the point of interest should be a part of our primary key. Let's reference the point of interest by name, because according to our workflow that is how our users will start their search.

You'll note that we certainly could have more than one hotel near a given point of interest, so we'll need another component in our primary key in order to make sure we have a unique partition for each hotel. So we add the hotel key as a clustering column.

Make Your Primary Keys Unique

An important consideration in designing your table's primary key is making sure that it defines a unique data element. Otherwise you run the risk of accidentally overwriting data.

Now for our second query (Q2), we'll need a table to get information about a specific hotel. One approach would have been to put all of the attributes of a hotel in the `hotels_by_poi` table, but we chose to add only those attributes that were required by our application workflow.

From our workflow diagram, we know that the `hotels_by_poi` table is used to display a list of hotels with basic information on each hotel, and the application knows the unique identifiers of the hotels returned. When the user selects a hotel to view details, we can then use Q2, which is used to obtain details about the hotel. Because we already have the `hotel_id` from Q1, we use that as our reference to the hotel we're looking for. Therefore our second table is just called `hotels`.

Another option would have been to store a set of `poi_names` in the hotels table. This is an equally valid approach. You'll learn through experience which approach is best for your application.

Using Unique Identifiers as References

You'll find that it's often helpful to use unique IDs to uniquely reference elements, and to use these `uuids` as references in tables representing other entities. This helps to minimize coupling between different entity types. This may prove especially helpful if you are using a microservice architectural style for your application, in which there are separate services responsible for each entity type.

For the purposes of this book, however, we'll use mostly `text` attributes as identifiers, to keep our samples simple and readable. For example, a common convention in the hospitality industry is to reference properties by short codes like "AZ123" or "NY229". We'll use these values for our `hotel_ids`, while acknowledging they are not necessarily globally unique.

Q3 is just a reverse of Q1—looking for points of interest near a hotel, rather than hotels near a point of interest. This time, however, we need to access the details of each point of interest, as represented by the `pois_by_hotel` table. As we have done previously, we add the point of interest name as a clustering key to guarantee uniqueness.

At this point, let's now consider how to support query Q4 to help our user find available rooms at a selected hotel for the nights they are interested in staying. Note that this query involves both a start date and an end date. Because we're querying over a range instead of a single date, we know that we'll need to use the date as a clustering key. We use the `hotel_id` as a primary key to group room data for each hotel on a single partition, which should help our search be super fast. Let's call this the `available_rooms_by_hotel_date` table.

Searching Over a Range

Use clustering columns to store attributes that you need to access in a range query. Remember that the order of the clustering columns is important. We'll learn more about range queries in Chapter 9.

In order to round out the shopping portion of our data model, we add the `amenities_by_room` table to support Q5. This will allow our user to view the amenities of one of the rooms that is available for the desired stay dates.

Reservation Logical Data Model

Now we switch gears to look at the reservation queries. Figure 5-6 shows a logical data model for reservations. You'll notice that these tables represent a denormalized design; the same data appears in multiple tables, with differing keys.

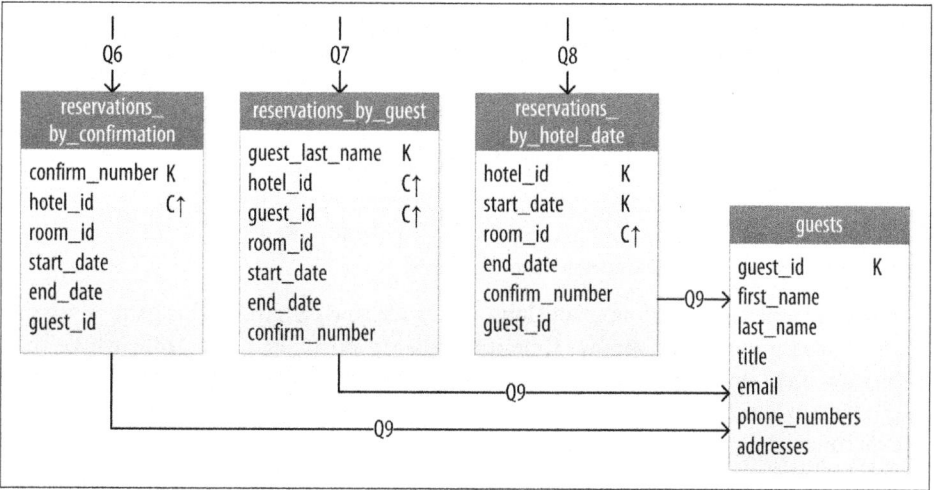

Figure 5-6. A denormalized logical model for reservations

In order to satisfy Q6, the `reservations_by_confirmation` table supports the look up of reservations by a unique confirmation number provided to the customer at the time of booking.

If the guest doesn't have the confirmation number, the `reservations_by_guest` table can be used to look up the reservation by guest name. We could envision query Q7 being used on behalf of a guest on a self-serve website or a call center agent trying to assist the guest. Because the guest name might not be unique, we include the guest ID here as a clustering column as well.

The hotel staff might wish to see a record of upcoming reservations by date in order to get insight into how the hotel is performing, such as what dates the hotel is sold out or undersold. Q8 supports the retrieval of reservations for a given hotel by date.

Finally, we create a `guests` table. You'll notice that it has similar attributes to our `user` table from Chapter 4. This provides a single location that we can use to store our guests. In this case, we specify a separate unique identifier for our guest records, as it is not uncommon for guests to have the same name. In many organizations, a customer database such as our `guests` table would be part of a separate customer management application, which is why we've omitted other guest access patterns from our example.

Design Queries for All Stakeholders

Q8 and Q9 in particular help to remind us that we need to create queries that support various stakeholders of our application, not just customers but staff as well, and perhaps even the analytics team, suppliers, and so on.

Patterns and Anti-Patterns

As with other types of software design, there are some well-known patterns and anti-patterns for data modeling in Cassandra. We've already used one of the most common patterns in our hotel model—the wide row.

The time series pattern is an extension of the wide row pattern. In this pattern, a series of measurements at specific time intervals are stored in a wide row, where the measurement time is used as part of the partition key. This pattern is frequently used in domains including business analysis, sensor data management, and scientific experiments.

The time series pattern is also useful for data other than measurements. Consider the example of a banking application. We could store each customer's balance in a row, but that might lead to a lot of read and write contention as various customers check their balance or make transactions. We'd probably be tempted to wrap a transaction around our writes just to protect the balance from being updated in error. In contrast, a time series–style design would store each transaction as a timestamped row and leave the work of calculating the current balance to the application.

One design trap that many new users fall into is attempting to use Cassandra as a queue. Each item in the queue is stored with a timestamp in a wide row. Items are appended to the end of the queue and read from the front, being deleted after they are read. This is a design that seems attractive, especially given its apparent similarity to the time series pattern. The problem with this approach is that the deleted items are now tombstones that Cassandra must scan past in order to read from the front of the queue. Over time, a growing number of tombstones begins to degrade read performance.

The queue anti-pattern serves as a reminder that any design that relies on the deletion of data is potentially a poorly performing design.

Physical Data Modeling

Once we have a logical data model defined, creating the physical model is a relatively simple process.

We walk through each of our logical model tables, assigning types to each item. We can use any of the types we covered in Chapter 4, including the basic types, collections, and user-defined types. We may identify additional user-defined types that can be created to simplify our design.

After we've assigned our data types, we analyze our model by performing size calculations and testing out how the model works. We may make some adjustments based on our findings. Once again we'll cover the data modeling process in more detail by working through our example.

Before we get started, let's look at a few additions to the Chebotko notation for physical data models.

Chebotko Physical Diagrams

To draw physical models, we need to be able to add the typing information for each column. Figure 5-7 shows the addition of a type for each column in a sample table.

The figure includes a designation of the keyspace containing each table and visual cues for columns represented using collections and user-defined types. We also note the designation of static columns and secondary index columns. There is no restriction on assigning these as part of a logical model, but they are typically more of a physical data modeling concern.

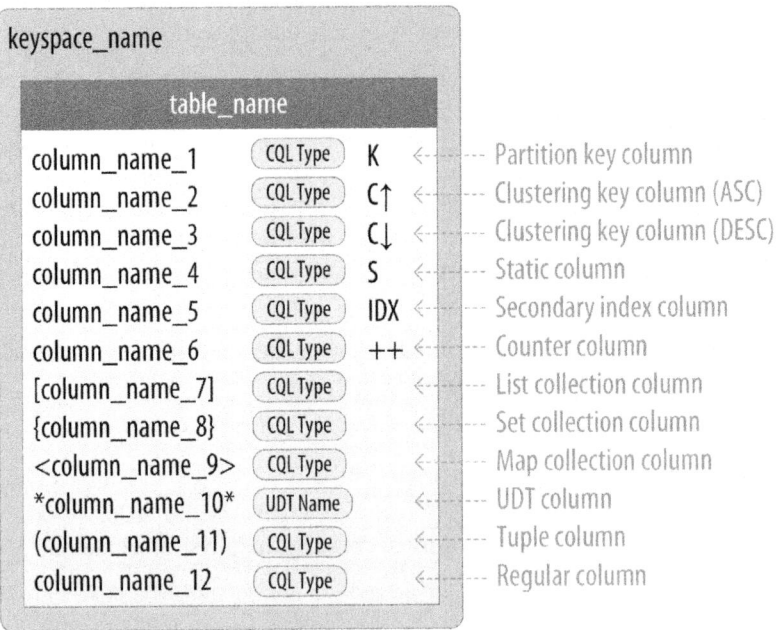

keyspace_name

table_name			
column_name_1	CQL Type	K	←---- Partition key column
column_name_2	CQL Type	C↑	←---- Clustering key column (ASC)
column_name_3	CQL Type	C↓	←---- Clustering key column (DESC)
column_name_4	CQL Type	S	←---- Static column
column_name_5	CQL Type	IDX	←---- Secondary index column
column_name_6	CQL Type	++	←---- Counter column
[column_name_7]	CQL Type		←---- List collection column
{column_name_8}	CQL Type		←---- Set collection column
<column_name_9>	CQL Type		←---- Map collection column
column_name_10	UDT Name		←---- UDT column
(column_name_11)	CQL Type		←---- Tuple column
column_name_12	CQL Type		←---- Regular column

Figure 5-7. Extending the Chebotko notation for physical data models

Hotel Physical Data Model

Now let's get to work on our physical model. First, we need keyspaces for our tables. To keep the design relatively simple, we'll create a `hotel` keyspace to contain our tables for hotel and availability data, and a `reservation` keyspace to contain tables for reservation and guest data. In a real system, we might divide the tables across even more keyspaces in order to separate concerns.

For our `hotels` table, we'll use Cassandra's `text` type to represent the hotel's id. For the address, we'll use the `address` type that we created in Chapter 4. We use the `text` type to represent the phone number, as there is considerable variance in the formatting of numbers between countries.

As we work to create physical representations of various tables in our logical hotel data model, we use the same approach. The resulting design is shown in Figure 5-8.

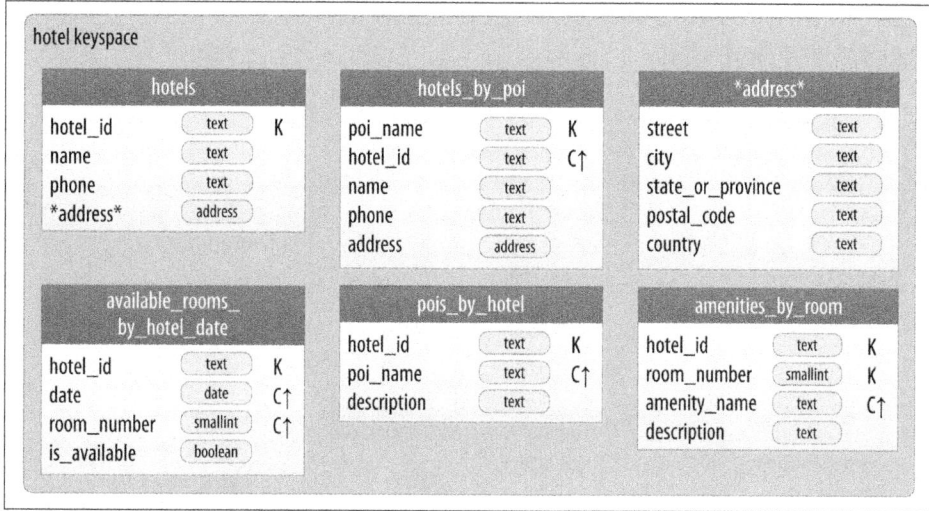

Figure 5-8. Hotel physical model

Note that we have also included the `address` type in our design. It is designated with an asterisk to denote that it is a user-defined type, and has no primary key columns identified. We make use of this type in the `hotels` and `hotels_by_poi` tables.

Taking Advantage of User-Defined Types

It is often helpful to make use of user-defined types to help reduce duplication of non-primary key columns, as we have done with the `address` user-defined type. This can reduce complexity in the design.

Remember that the scope of a UDT is the keyspace in which it is defined. To use `address` in the `reservation` keyspace we're about to design, we'll have to declare it again. This is just one of the many trade-offs we have to make in data model design.

Reservation Physical Data Model

Now, let's turn our attention to the reservation tables in our design. Remember that our logical model contained three denormalized tables to support queries for reservations by confirmation number, guest, and hotel and date. As we work to implement these different designs, we'll want to consider whether to manage the denormalization manually or use Cassandra's materialized view capability.

The design shown for the `reservation` keyspace in Figure 5-9 uses both approaches. We chose to implement `reservations_by_hotel_date` and `reservations_by_guest` as regular tables, and `reservations_by_confirmation` as a materialized view on the `reservations_by_hotel_date` table. We'll discuss the reasoning behind this design choice momentarily.

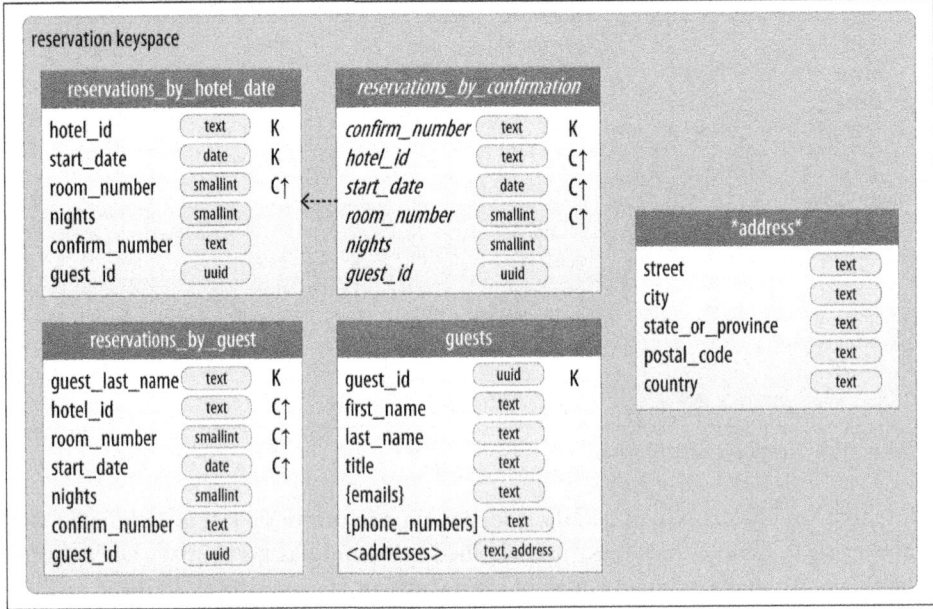

Figure 5-9. Reservation physical model

Note that we have reproduced the `address` type in this keyspace and modeled the `guest_id` as a `uuid` type in all of our tables.

Materialized Views

Materialized views were introduced to help address some of the shortcomings of secondary indexes, which we discussed in Chapter 4. Creating indexes on columns with high cardinality tends to result in poor performance, because most or all of the nodes in the ring need are queried.

Materialized views address this problem by storing preconfigured views that support queries on additional columns which are not part of the original clustering key. Materialized views simplify application development: instead of the application having to keep multiple denormalized tables in sync, Cassandra takes on the responsibility of updating views in order to keep them consistent with the base table.

Materialized views incur a small performance impact on writes in order to maintain this consistency. However, materialized views demonstrate more efficient performance compared to managing denormalized tables in application clients. Internally, materialized view updates are implemented using batching, which we will discuss in Chapter 9.

Similar to secondary indexes, materialized views can be created on existing tables.

To understand the syntax and constraints associated with materialized views, we'll take a look at the CQL command that creates the `reservations_by_confirmation` table from the reservation physical model:

```
cqlsh> CREATE MATERIALIZED VIEW reservation.reservations_by_confirmation
  AS SELECT *
  FROM reservation.reservations_by_hotel_date
  WHERE confirm_number IS NOT NULL and hotel_id IS NOT NULL and
    start_date IS NOT NULL and room_number IS NOT NULL
  PRIMARY KEY (confirm_number, hotel_id, start_date, room_number);
```

The order of the clauses in the CREATE MATERIALIZED VIEW command can appear somewhat inverted, so we'll walk through these clauses in an order that is a bit easier to process.

The first parameter after the command is the name of the materialized view—in this case, `reservations_by_confirmation`. The FROM clause identifies the base table for the materialized view, `reservations_by_hotel_date`.

The PRIMARY KEY clause identifies the primary key for the materialized view, which must include all of the columns in the primary key of the base table. This restriction keeps Cassandra from collapsing multiple rows in the base table into a single row in the materialized view, which would greatly increase the complexity of managing updates.

The grouping of the primary key columns uses the same syntax as an ordinary table. The most common usage is to place the additional column first as the partition key, followed by the base table primary key columns, used as clustering columns for purposes of the materialized view.

The WHERE clause provides support for filtering.Note that a filter must be specified for every primary key column of the materialized view, even if it is as simple as designating that the value IS NOT NULL.

The AS SELECT clause identifies the columns from the base table that we want our materialized view to contain. We can reference individual columns, but in this case have chosen for all columns to be part of the view by using the wildcard *.

Enhanced Materialized View Capabilities

The initial implementation of materialized views in the 3.0 release has some limitations on the selection of primary key columns and filters. There are several JIRA issues in progress to add capabilities such as multiple non-primary key columns in materialized view primary keys CASSANDRA-9928 (*https://issues.apache.org/jira/browse/CASSANDRA-9928*) or using aggregates in materialized views CASSANDRA-9778 (*https://issues.apache.org/jira/browse/CASSANDRA-9778*). If you're interested in these features, track the JIRA issues to see when they will be included in a release.

Now that we have a better understanding of the design and use of materialized views, we can revisit the prior decision made for the reservation physical design. Specifically, `reservations_by_confirmation` is a good candidate for implementation as a materialized view due to the high cardinality of the confirmation numbers—after all, you can't get any higher cardinality than a unique value per reservation.

An alternate design would have been to use `reservations_by_confirmation` as the base table and `reservations_by_hotel_date` as a materialized view. However, because we cannot (at least in early 3.X releases) create a materialized view with multiple non-primary key column from the base table, this would have required us to designate either `hotel_id` or `date` as a clustering column in `reservations_by_con` `firmation`. Both designs are acceptable, but this should give some insight into the trade-offs you'll want to consider in selecting which of several denormalized table designs to use as the base table.

Evaluating and Refining

Once we've created our physical model, there are some steps we'll want to take to evaluate and refine our table designs to help ensure optimal performance.

Calculating Partition Size

The first thing that we want to look for is whether our tables will have partitions that will be overly large, or to put it another way, wide rows that are too wide. Partition size is measured by the number of cells (values) that are stored in the partition. Cassandra's hard limit is 2 billion cells per partition, but we'll likely run into performance issues before reaching that limit.

In order to calculate the size of our partitions, we use the following formula:

$$N_v = N_r\left(N_c - N_{pk} - N_s\right) + N_s$$

The number of values (or cells) in the partition (N_v) is equal to the number of static columns (N_s) plus the product of the number of rows (N_r) and the number of of values per row. The number of values per row is defined as the number of columns (N_c) minus the number of primary key columns (N_{pk}) and static columns (N_s).

The number of columns tends to be relatively static, although as we have seen it is quite possible to alter tables at runtime. For this reason, a primary driver of partition size is the number of rows in the partition. This is a key factor that you must consider in determining whether a partition has the potential to get too large. Two billion values sounds like a lot, but in a sensor system where tens or hundreds of values are measured every millisecond, the number of values starts to add up pretty fast.

Let's take a look at one of our tables to analyze the partition size. Because it has a wide row design with a partition per hotel, we'll choose the `available_rooms_by_hotel_date` table. The table has four columns total ($N_c = 4$), including three primary key columns ($N_{pk} = 3$) and no static columns ($N_s = 0$). Plugging these values into our formula, we get:

$$N_v = N_r(4 - 3 - 0) + 0 = 1N_r$$

So the number of values for the table is equal to the number of rows. We still need to determine a number of rows. To do this, we make some estimates based on the application we're designing. Our table is storing a record for each room, in each of our hotels, for every night. Let's assume that our system will be used to store two years of inventory at a time, and there are 5,000 hotels in our system, with an average of 100 rooms in each hotel.

This leads an estimated number of rows as follows:

$$N_r = 5,000 \text{ hotels} \times 100 \text{ rooms/hotel} \times 730 \text{ days} = 365,000,000$$

So 365 million rows is not going to get us in too much trouble, but if we start adding a lot of hotels or don't manage the size of our inventory well using TTL, we could start having issues. We still might want to look at breaking up this large partition, which we'll do shortly.

Estimate for the Worst Case

When performing sizing calculations, it is tempting to assume the nominal or average case for variables such as the number of rows. Consider calculating the worst case as well, as these sorts of predictions have a way of coming true in successful systems.

Calculating Size on Disk

In addition to calculating the size of our partition, it is also an excellent idea for us to estimate the amount of disk space that will be required for each table we plan to store in the cluster. In order to determine the size, we use the following formula to determine the size S_t of a table:

$$S_t = \sum_i sizeOf\left(c_{k_i}\right) + \sum_j sizeOf\left(c_{s_j}\right) + N_r \times \sum_k \left(sizeOf\left(c_{r_k}\right) + \sum_l sizeOf\left(c_{c_l}\right)\right) + 8 \times N_v$$

This is a bit more complex than our previous formula, but we'll break it down a bit at a time. Let's take a look at the notation first:

- In this formula, c_k refers to partition key columns, c_s to static columns, c_r to regular columns, and c_c to clustering columns.
- We recognize the number of rows N_r and number of values N_v from our previous calculations.
- The *sizeOf()* function refers to the size in bytes of the CQL data type of each referenced column.

The first term asks us to sum the size of the partition key columns. For our example, the `available_rooms_by_hotel_date` table has a single partition key column, the `hotel_id`, which we chose to make of type `text`. Assuming our hotel identifiers are simple 5-character codes, we have a 5-byte value, so the sum of our partition key column sizes is 5 bytes.

The second term asks us to sum the size of our static columns. Our table has no static columns, so in our case this is 0 bytes.

The third term is the most involved, and for good reason—it is calculating the size of the cells in the partition. We sum the size of the clustering columns and add that value to the size of each regular column, summing those together (such that the size of the clustering columns is counted once for each regular column). Our two clustering columns are the `date`, which we assume is 4 bytes, and the `room_number`, which is a 2-byte short integer, giving us a sum of 6 bytes. There is only a single regular column, the boolean `is_available`, which is 1 byte in size. Summing the regular column size (1 byte) plus the clustering column size (6 bytes) for each regular column gives us a total of 7 bytes. To finish up the term, we multiply this value by the number of rows (365,000,000), giving us 2,555,000,000 bytes (2.56 GB).

The fourth term is simply counting the timestamps that that Cassandra stores for each cell. For our table, we reuse the number of values from our previous calculation and multiply by 8, which gives us 2.92 GB.

Adding these terms together, we get our final estimate:

Partition size = 16 bytes + 0 bytes + 2.56 GB + 2.92 GB = 5.48 GB

This formula is an approximation of the actual size of a partition on disk, but is accurate enough to be quite useful. Remembering that the partition must be able to fit on a single node, it looks like our table design is going to put a lot of strain on our disk storage.

Keep in mind also that this estimate only counts a single replica of our data. We will need to multiply the value obtained here by the number of replicas specified by the keyspace's replication strategy in order to determine the total required total capacity for each table. This will come in handy when we discuss how to plan our clusters in Chapter 14.

Breaking Up Large Partitions

As discussed previously, our goal is to design tables that can provide the data we need with queries that touch a single partition, or failing that, the minimum possible number of partitions. However, as we have seen in our examples, it is quite possible to design wide row-style tables that approach Cassandra's built-in limits. Performing sizing analysis on tables may reveal partitions that are potentially too large, either in number of values, size on disk, or both.

The technique for splitting a large partition is straightforward: add an additional column to the partition key. In most cases, moving one of the existing columns into the partition key will be sufficient. Another option is to introduce an additional column to the table to act as a sharding key, but this requires additional application logic.

Continuing to examine our available rooms example, if we add the `date` column to the partition key for the `available_rooms_by_hotel_date` table, each partition would then represent the availability of rooms at a specific hotel on a specific date. This will certainly yield partitions that are significantly smaller, perhaps too small, as the data for consecutive days will likely be on separate nodes.

Another technique known as *bucketing* is often used to break the data into moderate-size partitions. For example, we could bucketize our `available_rooms_by_hotel_date` table by adding a `month` column to the partition key. While this column is partially duplicative of the `date`, it provides a nice way of grouping related data in a partition that will not get too large.

If we really felt strongly about preserving a wide row design, we could instead add the `room_id` to the partition key, so that each partition would represent the availability of the room across all dates. Because we haven't identified a query that involves searching availability of a specific room, the first or second design approach is most suitable to our application needs.

Defining Database Schema

Once we have finished evaluating and refining our physical model, we're ready to implement the schema in CQL. Here is the schema for the hotel keyspace, using CQL's comment feature to document the query pattern supported by each table:

```
CREATE KEYSPACE hotel
    WITH replication = {'class': 'SimpleStrategy', 'replication_factor' : 3};

CREATE TYPE hotel.address (
    street text,
    city text,
    state_or_province text,
    postal_code text,
    country text
);

CREATE TABLE hotel.hotels_by_poi (
    poi_name text,
    hotel_id text,
    name text,
    phone text,
    address frozen<address>,
    PRIMARY KEY ((poi_name), hotel_id)
) WITH comment = 'Q1. Find hotels near given poi'
AND CLUSTERING ORDER BY (hotel_id ASC) ;

CREATE TABLE hotel.hotels (
    id text PRIMARY KEY,
    name text,
    phone text,
    address frozen<address>,
    pois set<text>
) WITH comment = 'Q2. Find information about a hotel';

CREATE TABLE hotel.pois_by_hotel (
    poi_name text,
    hotel_id text,
    description text,
    PRIMARY KEY ((hotel_id), poi_name)
) WITH comment = 'Q3. Find pois near a hotel';

CREATE TABLE hotel.available_rooms_by_hotel_date (
    hotel_id text,
    date date,
    room_number smallint,
    is_available boolean,
    PRIMARY KEY ((hotel_id), date, room_number)
) WITH comment = 'Q4. Find available rooms by hotel / date';

CREATE TABLE hotel.amenities_by_room (
    hotel_id text,
```

```
    room_number smallint,
    amenity_name text,
    description text,
    PRIMARY KEY ((hotel_id, room_number), amenity_name)
) WITH comment = 'Q5. Find amenities for a room';
```

Identify Partition Keys Explicitly

We chose to represent our tables by surrounding the elements of
our partition key with parentheses, even though the partition key
consists of the single column poi_name. This is a best practice that
makes our selection of partition key more explicit to others reading
our CQL.

Similarly, here is the schema for the reservation keyspace:

```
CREATE KEYSPACE reservation
    WITH replication = {'class': 'SimpleStrategy', 'replication_factor' : 3};

CREATE TYPE reservation.address (
    street text,
    city text,
    state_or_province text,
    postal_code text,
    country text
);

CREATE TABLE reservation.reservations_by_hotel_date (
    hotel_id text,
    start_date date,
    end_date date,
    room_number smallint,
    confirm_number text,
    guest_id uuid,
    PRIMARY KEY ((hotel_id, start_date), room_number)
) WITH comment = 'Q7. Find reservations by hotel and date';

CREATE MATERIALIZED VIEW reservation.reservations_by_confirmation AS
    SELECT * FROM reservation.reservations_by_hotel_date
    WHERE confirm_number IS NOT NULL and hotel_id IS NOT NULL and
        start_date IS NOT NULL and room_number IS NOT NULL
    PRIMARY KEY (confirm_number, hotel_id, start_date, room_number);

CREATE TABLE reservation.reservations_by_guest (
    guest_last_name text,
    hotel_id text,
    start_date date,
    end_date date,
    room_number smallint,
    confirm_number text,
    guest_id uuid,
```

```
    PRIMARY KEY ((guest_last_name), hotel_id)
) WITH comment = 'Q8. Find reservations by guest name';

CREATE TABLE reservation.guests (
    guest_id uuid PRIMARY KEY,
    first_name text,
    last_name text,
    title text,
    emails set<text>,
    phone_numbers list<text>,
    addresses map<text, frozen<address>>,
    confirm_number text
) WITH comment = 'Q9. Find guest by ID';
```

DataStax DevCenter

We've already had quite a bit of practice creating schema using `cqlsh`, but now that we're starting to create an application data model with more tables, it starts to be more of a challenge to keep track of all of that CQL.

Thankfully, there is a great development tool provided by DataStax called DevCenter. This tool is available as a free download from the DataStax Academy (*https://acad emy.datastax.com/downloads*). Figure 5-10 shows the hotel schema being edited in DevCenter.

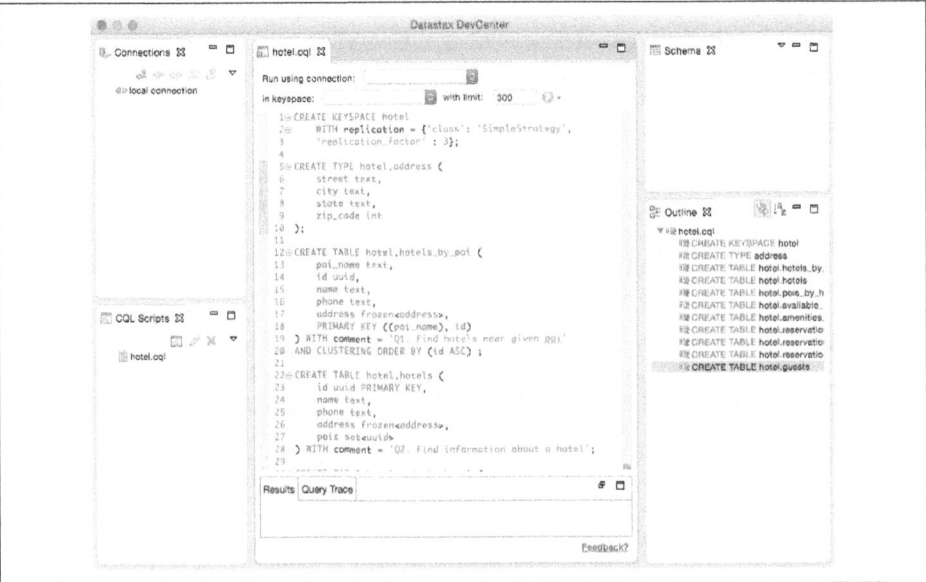

Figure 5-10. Editing the Hotel schema in DataStax DevCenter

The middle pane shows the currently selected CQL file, featuring syntax highlighting for CQL commands, CQL types, and name literals. DevCenter provides command completion as you type out CQL commands and interprets the commands you type, highlighting any errors you make. The tool provides panes for managing multiple CQL scripts and connections to multiple clusters. The connections are used to run CQL commands against live clusters and view the results.

Summary

In this chapter, we saw how to create a complete, working Cassandra data model and compared it with an equivalent relational model. We represented our data model in both logical and physical forms and learned a new tool for realizing our data models in CQL. Now that we have a working data model, we'll continue building our hotel application in the coming chapters.

The Cassandra Architecture

3.2 Architecture - fundamental concepts or properties of a system in its environment embod-
ied in its elements, relationships, and in the principles of its design and evolution.
—ISO/IEC/IEEE 42010

In this chapter, we examine several aspects of Cassandra's architecture in order to understand how it does its job. We'll explain the topology of a cluster, and how nodes interact in a peer-to-peer design to maintain the health of the cluster and exchange data, using techniques like gossip, anti-entropy, and hinted handoff. Looking inside the design of a node, we examine architecture techniques Cassandra uses to support reading, writing, and deleting data, and examine how these choices affect architectural considerations such as scalability, durability, availability, manageability, and more. We also discuss Cassandra's adoption of a Staged Event-Driven Architecture, which acts as the platform for request delegation.

As we introduce these topics, we also provide references to where you can find their implementations in the Cassandra source code.

Data Centers and Racks

Cassandra is frequently used in systems spanning physically separate locations. Cassandra provides two levels of grouping that are used to describe the topology of a cluster: data center and rack. A *rack* is a logical set of nodes in close proximity to each other, perhaps on physical machines in a single rack of equipment. A *data center* is a logical set of racks, perhaps located in the same building and connected by reliable network. A sample topology with multiple data centers and racks is shown in Figure 6-1.

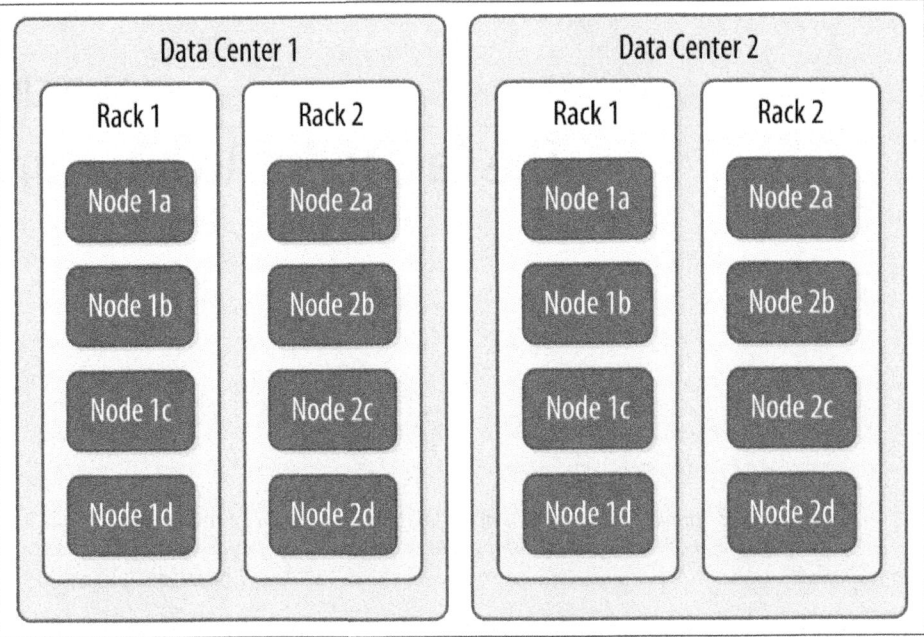

Figure 6-1. Topology of a sample cluster with data centers, racks, and nodes

Out of the box, Cassandra comes with a default configuration of a single data center ("DC1") containing a single rack ("RAC1"). We'll learn in Chapter 7 how to build a larger cluster and define its topology.

Cassandra leverages the information you provide about your cluster's topology to determine where to store data, and how to route queries efficiently. Cassandra tries to store copies of your data in multiple data centers to maximize availability and partition tolerance, while preferring to route queries to nodes in the local data center to maximize performance.

Gossip and Failure Detection

To support decentralization and partition tolerance, Cassandra uses a gossip protocol that allows each node to keep track of state information about the other nodes in the cluster. The gossiper runs every second on a timer.

Gossip protocols (sometimes called "epidemic protocols") generally assume a faulty network, are commonly employed in very large, decentralized network systems, and are often used as an automatic mechanism for replication in distributed databases. They take their name from the concept of human gossip, a form of communication in which peers can choose with whom they want to exchange information.

The Origin of "Gossip Protocol"

The term "gossip protocol" was originally coined in 1987 by Alan Demers, a researcher at Xerox's Palo Alto Research Center, who was studying ways to route information through unreliable networks.

The gossip protocol in Cassandra is primarily implemented by the `org.apache.cassandra.gms.Gossiper` class, which is responsible for managing gossip for the local node. When a server node is started, it registers itself with the gossiper to receive endpoint state information.

Because Cassandra gossip is used for failure detection, the `Gossiper` class maintains a list of nodes that are alive and dead.

Here is how the gossiper works:

1. Once per second, the gossiper will choose a random node in the cluster and initialize a gossip session with it. Each round of gossip requires three messages.

2. The gossip initiator sends its chosen friend a `GossipDigestSynMessage`.

3. When the friend receives this message, it returns a `GossipDigestAckMessage`.

4. When the initiator receives the `ack` message from the friend, it sends the friend a `GossipDigestAck2Message` to complete the round of gossip.

When the gossiper determines that another endpoint is dead, it "convicts" that endpoint by marking it as dead in its local list and logging that fact.

Cassandra has robust support for failure detection, as specified by a popular algorithm for distributed computing called Phi Accrual Failure Detection. This manner of failure detection originated at the Advanced Institute of Science and Technology in Japan in 2004.

Accrual failure detection is based on two primary ideas. The first general idea is that failure detection should be flexible, which is achieved by decoupling it from the application being monitored. The second and more novel idea challenges the notion of traditional failure detectors, which are implemented by simple "heartbeats" and decide whether a node is dead or not dead based on whether a heartbeat is received or not. But accrual failure detection decides that this approach is naive, and finds a place in between the extremes of dead and alive—a *suspicion level*.

Therefore, the failure monitoring system outputs a continuous level of "suspicion" regarding how confident it is that a node has failed. This is desirable because it can take into account fluctuations in the network environment. For example, just because one connection gets caught up doesn't necessarily mean that the whole node is dead. So suspicion offers a more fluid and proactive indication of the weaker or stronger possibility of failure based on interpretation (the sampling of heartbeats), as opposed to a simple binary assessment.

Phi Threshold and Accrual Failure Detectors

Accrual Failure Detectors output a value associated with each process (or node). This value is called Phi. The value is output in a manner that is designed from the ground up to be adaptive in the face of volatile network conditions, so it's not a binary condition that simply checks whether a server is up or down.

The Phi convict threshold in the configuration adjusts the sensitivity of the failure detector. Lower values increase the sensitivity and higher values decrease it, but not in a linear fashion.

The Phi value refers to a level of *suspicion* that a server might be down. Applications such as Cassandra that employ an AFD can specify variable conditions for the Phi value they emit. Cassandra can generally detect a failed node in about 10 seconds using this mechanism.

You can read the original Phi Accrual Failure Detection paper by Naohiro Hayashibara et al. at *http://www.jaist.ac.jp/~defago/files/pdf/IS_RR_2004_010.pdf.*

Failure detection is implemented in Cassandra by the `org.apache.cassandra.gms.FailureDetector` class, which implements the `org.apache.cassandra.gms.IFailureDetector` interface. Together, they allow operations including:

`isAlive(InetAddress)`
> What the detector will report about a given node's alive-ness.

`interpret(InetAddress)`
> Used by the gossiper to help it decide whether a node is alive or not based on suspicion level reached by calculating Phi (as described in the Hayashibara paper).

`report(InetAddress)`
> When a node receives a heartbeat, it invokes this method.

Snitches

The job of a snitch is to determine relative host proximity for each node in a cluster, which is used to determine which nodes to read and write from. Snitches gather information about your network topology so that Cassandra can efficiently route requests. The snitch will figure out where nodes are in relation to other nodes.

As an example, let's examine how the snitch participates in a read operation. When Cassandra performs a read, it must contact a number of replicas determined by the consistency level. In order to support the maximum speed for reads, Cassandra selects a single replica to query for the full object, and asks additional replicas for hash values in order to ensure the latest version of the requested data is returned. The role of the snitch is to help identify the replica that will return the fastest, and this is the replica which is queried for the full data.

The default snitch (the `SimpleSnitch`) is topology unaware; that is, it does not know about the racks and data centers in a cluster, which makes it unsuitable for multi-data center deployments. For this reason, Cassandra comes with several snitches for different cloud environments including Amazon EC2, Google Cloud, and Apache Cloudstack.

The snitches can be found in the package `org.apache.cassandra.locator`. Each snitch implements the `IEndpointSnitch` interface. We'll learn how to select and configure an appropriate snitch for your environment in Chapter 7.

While Cassandra provides a pluggable way to statically describe your cluster's topology, it also provides a feature called *dynamic snitching* that helps optimize the routing of reads and writes over time. Here's how it works. Your selected snitch is wrapped with another snitch called the `DynamicEndpointSnitch`. The dynamic snitch gets its basic understanding of the topology from the selected snitch. It then monitors the performance of requests to the other nodes, even keeping track of things like which nodes are performing compaction. The performance data is used to select the best replica for each query. This enables Cassandra to avoid routing requests to replicas that are performing poorly.

The dynamic snitching implementation uses a modified version of the Phi failure detection mechanism used by gossip. The "badness threshold" is a configurable parameter that determines how much worse a preferred node must perform than the best-performing node in order to lose its preferential status. The scores of each node are reset periodically in order to allow a poorly performing node to demonstrate that it has recovered and reclaim its preferred status.

Rings and Tokens

So far we've been focusing on how Cassandra keeps track of the physical layout of nodes in a cluster. Let's shift gears and look at how Cassandra distributes data across these nodes.

Cassandra represents the data managed by a cluster as a *ring*. Each node in the ring is assigned one or more ranges of data described by a *token*, which determines its position in the ring. A token is a 64-bit integer ID used to identify each partition. This gives a possible range for tokens from -2^{63} to $2^{63}-1$.

A node claims ownership of the range of values less than or equal to each token and greater than the token of the previous node. The node with lowest token owns the range less than or equal to its token and the range greater than the highest token, which is also known as the "wrapping range." In this way, the tokens specify a complete ring. Figure 6-2 shows a notional ring layout including the nodes in a single data center. This particular arrangement is structured such that consecutive token ranges are spread across nodes in different racks.

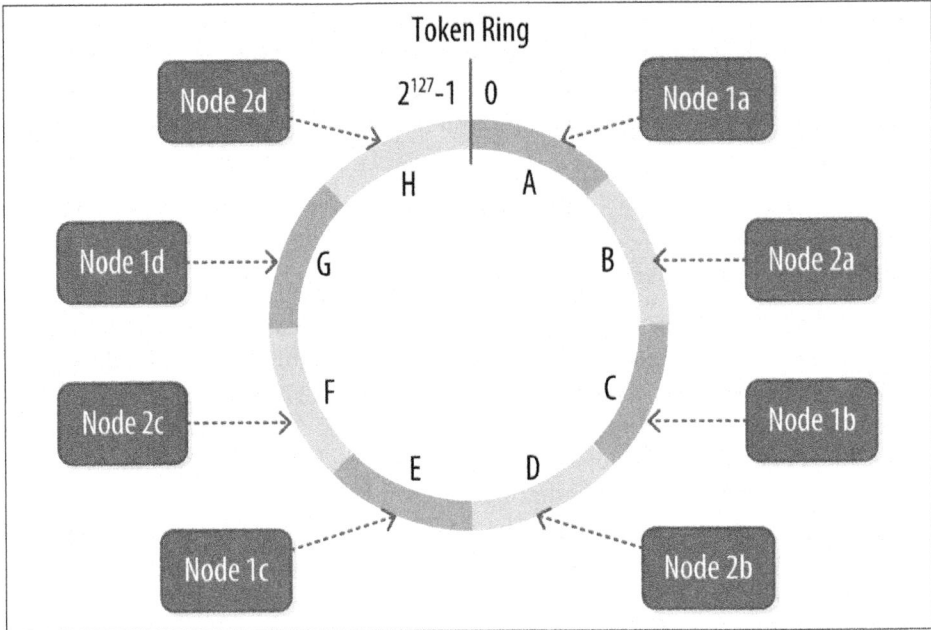

Figure 6-2. Example ring arrangement of nodes in a data center

Data is assigned to nodes by using a hash function to calculate a token for the partition key. This partition key token is compared to the token values for the various nodes to identify the range, and therefore the node, that owns the data.

Token ranges are represented by the `org.apache.cassandra.dht.Range` class.

Virtual Nodes

Early versions of Cassandra assigned a single token to each node, in a fairly static manner, requiring you to calculate tokens for each node. Although there are tools available to calculate tokens based on a given number of nodes, it was still a manual process to configure the `initial_token` property for each node in the *cassandra.yaml* file. This also made adding or replacing a node an expensive operation, as rebalancing the cluster required moving a lot of data.

Cassandra's 1.2 release introduced the concept of *virtual nodes*, also called *vnodes* for short. Instead of assigning a single token to a node, the token range is broken up into multiple smaller ranges. Each physical node is then assigned multiple tokens. By default, each node will be assigned 256 of these tokens, meaning that it contains 256 virtual nodes. Virtual nodes have been enabled by default since 2.0.

Vnodes make it easier to maintain a cluster containing heterogeneous machines. For nodes in your cluster that have more computing resources available to them, you can increase the number of vnodes by setting the num_tokens property in the *cassandra.yaml* file. Conversely, you might set num_tokens lower to decrease the number of vnodes for less capable machines.

Cassandra automatically handles the calculation of token ranges for each node in the cluster in proportion to their num_tokens value. Token assignments for vnodes are calculated by the org.apache.cassandra.dht.tokenallocator.ReplicationAware TokenAllocator class.

A further advantage of virtual nodes is that they speed up some of the more heavyweight Cassandra operations such as bootstrapping a new node, decommissioning a node, and repairing a node. This is because the load associated with operations on multiple smaller ranges is spread more evenly across the nodes in the cluster.

Partitioners

A *partitioner* determines how data is distributed across the nodes in the cluster. As we learned in Chapter 5, Cassandra stores data in wide rows, or "partitions." Each row has a partition key that is used to identify the partition. A partitioner, then, is a hash function for computing the token of a partition key. Each row of data is distributed within the ring according to the value of the partition key token.

Cassandra provides several different partitioners in the org.apache.cassandra.dht package (DHT stands for "distributed hash table"). The Murmur3Partitioner was added in 1.2 and has been the default partitioner since then; it is an efficient Java implementation on the murmur algorithm developed by Austin Appleby. It generates 64-bit hashes. The previous default was the RandomPartitioner.

Because of Cassandra's generally pluggable design, you can also create your own partitioner by implementing the org.apache.cassandra.dht.IPartitioner class and placing it on Cassandra's classpath.

Replication Strategies

A node serves as a *replica* for different ranges of data. If one node goes down, other replicas can respond to queries for that range of data. Cassandra replicates data across nodes in a manner transparent to the user, and the *replication factor* is the number of nodes in your cluster that will receive copies (replicas) of the same data. If your replication factor is 3, then three nodes in the ring will have copies of each row.

The first replica will always be the node that claims the range in which the token falls, but the remainder of the replicas are placed according to the *replication strategy* (sometimes also referred to as the *replica placement strategy*).

For determining replica placement, Cassandra implements the Gang of Four Strategy pattern, which is outlined in the common abstract class `org.apache.cassandra.loca` `tor.AbstractReplicationStrategy`, allowing different implementations of an algorithm (different strategies for accomplishing the same work). Each algorithm implementation is encapsulated inside a single class that extends the `AbstractRepli` `cationStrategy`.

Out of the box, Cassandra provides two primary implementations of this interface (extensions of the abstract class): `SimpleStrategy` and `NetworkTopologyStrategy`. The `SimpleStrategy` places replicas at consecutive nodes around the ring, starting with the node indicated by the partitioner. The `NetworkTopologyStrategy` allows you to specify a different replication factor for each data center. Within a data center, it allocates replicas to different racks in order to maximize availability.

Legacy Replication Strategies

A third strategy, `OldNetworkTopologyStrategy`, is provided for backward compatibility. It was previously known as the `RackAware` `Strategy`, while the `SimpleStrategy` was previously known as the `RackUnawareStrategy`. `NetworkTopologyStrategy` was previously known as `DataCenterShardStrategy`. These changes were effective in the 0.7 release.

The strategy is set independently for each keyspace and is a required option to create a keyspace, as we saw in Chapter 5.

Consistency Levels

In Chapter 2, we discussed Brewer's CAP theorem, in which consistency, availability, and partition tolerance are traded off against one another. Cassandra provides tuneable consistency levels that allow you to make these trade-offs at a fine-grained level. You specify a consistency level on each read or write query that indicates how much consistency you require. A higher consistency level means that more nodes need to respond to a read or write query, giving you more assurance that the values present on each replica are the same.

For read queries, the consistency level specifies how many replica nodes must respond to a read request before returning the data. For write operations, the consistency level specifies how many replica nodes must respond for the write to be reported as successful to the client. Because Cassandra is eventually consistent, updates to other replica nodes may continue in the background.

The available consistency levels include ONE, TWO, and THREE, each of which specify an absolute number of replica nodes that must respond to a request. The QUORUM consistency level requires a response from a majority of the replica nodes (sometimes expressed as "replication factor / 2 + 1"). The ALL consistency level requires a response from all of the replicas. We'll examine these consistency levels and others in more detail in Chapter 9.

For both reads and writes, the consistency levels of ANY, ONE, TWO, and THREE are considered weak, whereas QUORUM and ALL are considered strong. Consistency is tuneable in Cassandra because clients can specify the desired consistency level on both reads and writes. There is an equation that is popularly used to represent the way to achieve strong consistency in Cassandra: $R + W > N = strong\ consistency$. In this equation, R, W, and N are the read replica count, the write replica count, and the replication factor, respectively; all client reads will see the most recent write in this scenario, and you will have strong consistency.

Distinguishing Consistency Levels and Replication Factors

If you're new to Cassandra, the replication factor can sometimes be confused with the consistency level. The replication factor is set per keyspace. The consistency level is specified per query, by the client. The replication factor indicates how many nodes you want to use to store a value during each write operation. The consistency level specifies how many nodes the client has decided must respond in order to feel confident of a successful read or write operation. The confusion arises because the consistency level is based on the replication factor, not on the number of nodes in the system.

Queries and Coordinator Nodes

Let's bring these concepts together to discuss how Cassandra nodes interact to support reads and writes from client applications. Figure 6-3 shows the typical path of interactions with Cassandra.

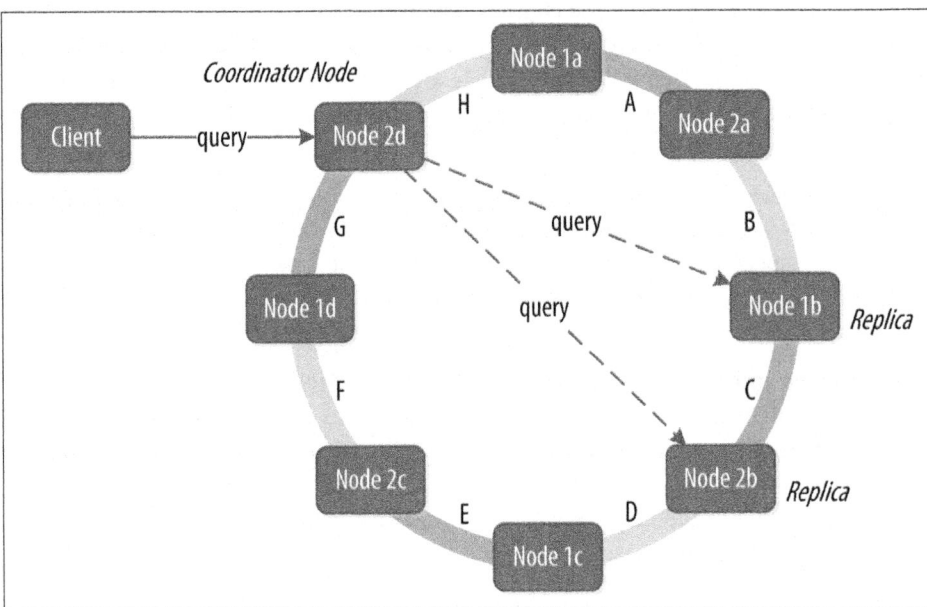

Figure 6-3. Clients, coordinator nodes, and replicas

A client may connect to any node in the cluster to initiate a read or write query. This node is known as the *coordinator node*. The coordinator identifies which nodes are replicas for the data that is being written or read and forwards the queries to them.

For a write, the coordinator node contacts all replicas, as determined by the consistency level and replication factor, and considers the write successful when a number of replicas commensurate with the consistency level acknowledge the write.

For a read, the coordinator contacts enough replicas to ensure the required consistency level is met, and returns the data to the client.

These, of course, are the "happy path" descriptions of how Cassandra works. We'll soon discuss some of Cassandra's high availability mechanisms, including hinted handoff.

Memtables, SSTables, and Commit Logs

Now let's take a look at some of Cassandra's internal data structures and files, summarized in Figure 6-4. Cassandra stores data both in memory and on disk to provide both high performance and durability. In this section, we'll focus on Cassandra's use of constructs called *memtables*, *SSTables*, and *commit logs* to support the writing and reading of data from tables.

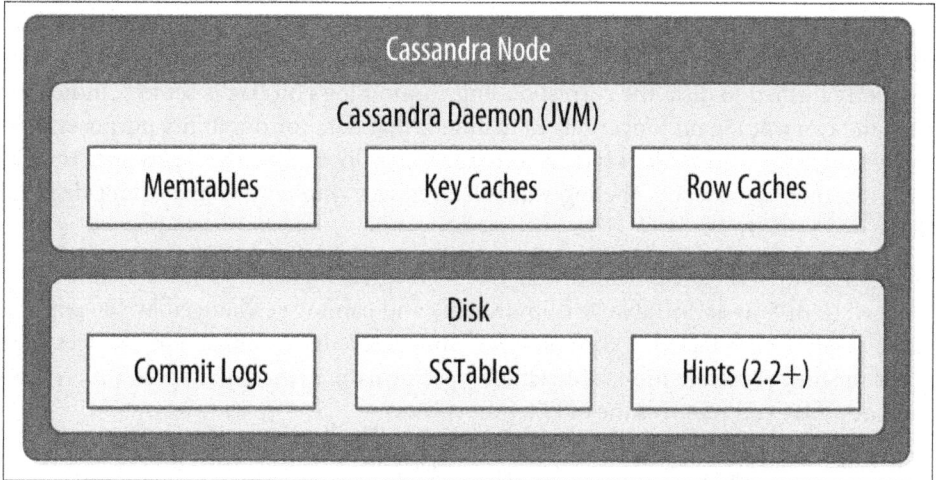

Figure 6-4. Internal data structures and files of a Cassandra node

When you perform a write operation, it's immediately written to a *commit log*. The commit log is a crash-recovery mechanism that supports Cassandra's durability goals. A write will not count as successful until it's written to the commit log, to ensure that if a write operation does not make it to the in-memory store (the memtable, discussed in a moment), it will still be possible to recover the data. If you shut down the database or it crashes unexpectedly, the commit log can ensure that data is not lost. That's because the next time you start the node, the commit log gets replayed. In fact, that's the only time the commit log is read; clients never read from it.

After it's written to the commit log, the value is written to a memory-resident data structure called the *memtable*. Each memtable contains data for a specific table. In early implementations of Cassandra, memtables were stored on the JVM heap, but improvements starting with the 2.1 release have moved the majority of memtable data to native memory. This makes Cassandra less susceptible to fluctuations in performance due to Java garbage collection.

When the number of objects stored in the memtable reaches a threshold, the contents of the memtable are flushed to disk in a file called an *SSTable*. A new memtable is then created. This flushing is a non-blocking operation; multiple memtables may exist for a single table, one current and the rest waiting to be flushed. They typically should not have to wait very long, as the node should flush them very quickly unless it is overloaded.

Each commit log maintains an internal bit flag to indicate whether it needs flushing. When a write operation is first received, it is written to the commit log and its bit flag is set to 1. There is only one bit flag per table, because only one commit log is ever being written to across the entire server. All writes to all tables will go into the same commit log, so the bit flag indicates whether a particular commit log contains anything that hasn't been flushed for a particular table. Once the memtable has been properly flushed to disk, the corresponding commit log's bit flag is set to 0, indicating that the commit log no longer has to maintain that data for durability purposes. Like regular logfiles, commit logs have a configurable rollover threshold, and once this file size threshold is reached, the log will roll over, carrying with it any extant dirty bit flags.

The SSTable is a concept borrowed from Google's Bigtable. Once a memtable is flushed to disk as an SSTable, it is immutable and cannot be changed by the application. Despite the fact that SSTables are compacted, this compaction changes only their on-disk representation; it essentially performs the "merge" step of a mergesort into new files and removes the old files on success.

Why Are They Called "SSTables"?

The idea that "SSTable" is a compaction of "Sorted String Table" is somewhat inaccurate for Cassandra, because the data is not stored as strings on disk.

Since the 1.0 release, Cassandra has supported the compression of SSTables in order to maximize use of the available storage. This compression is configurable per table. Each SSTable also has an associated Bloom filter, which is used as an additional performance enhancer (see "Bloom Filters" on page 120).

All writes are sequential, which is the primary reason that writes perform so well in Cassandra. No reads or seeks of any kind are required for writing a value to Cassandra because all writes are append operations. This makes one key limitation on performance the speed of your disk. Compaction is intended to amortize the reorganization of data, but it uses sequential I/O to do so. So the performance benefit is gained by splitting; the write operation is just an immediate append, and then compaction helps to organize for better future read performance. If Cassandra naively inserted values where they ultimately belonged, writing clients would pay for seeks up front.

On reads, Cassandra will read both SSTables and memtables to find data values, as the memtable may contain values that have not yet been flushed to disk. Memtables are implemented by the `org.apache.cassandra.db.Memtable` class.

Caching

As we saw in Figure 6-4, Cassandra provides three forms of caching:

- The *key cache* stores a map of partition keys to row index entries, facilitating faster read access into SSTables stored on disk. The key cache is stored on the JVM heap.
- The *row cache* caches entire rows and can greatly speed up read access for frequently accessed rows, at the cost of more memory usage. The row cache is stored in off-heap memory.
- The *counter cache* was added in the 2.1 release to improve counter performance by reducing lock contention for the most frequently accessed counters.

By default, key and counter caching are enabled, while row caching is disabled, as it requires more memory. Cassandra saves its caches to disk periodically in order to warm them up more quickly on a node restart. We'll investigate how to tune these caches in Chapter 12.

Hinted Handoff

Consider the following scenario: a write request is sent to Cassandra, but a replica node where the write properly belongs is not available due to network partition, hardware failure, or some other reason. In order to ensure general availability of the ring in such a situation, Cassandra implements a feature called *hinted handoff*. You might think of a *hint* as a little Post-it note that contains the information from the write request. If the replica node where the write belongs has failed, the coordinator will create a hint, which is a small reminder that says, "I have the write information that is intended for node B. I'm going to hang onto this write, and I'll notice when node B comes back online; when it does, I'll send it the write request." That is, once it detects via gossip that node B is back online, node A will "hand off" to node B the "hint" regarding the write. Cassandra holds a separate hint for each partition that is to be written.

This allows Cassandra to be always available for writes, and generally enables a cluster to sustain the same write load even when some of the nodes are down. It also reduces the time that a failed node will be inconsistent after it does come back online.

In general, hints do not count as writes for the purposes of consistency level. The exception is the consistency level ANY, which was added in 0.6. This consistency level means that a hinted handoff alone will count as sufficient toward the success of a write operation. That is, even if only a hint was able to be recorded, the write still counts as successful. Note that the write is considered durable, but the data may not be readable until the hint is delivered to the target replica.

Hinted Handoff and Guaranteed Delivery

Hinted handoff is used in Amazon's Dynamo and is familiar to those who are aware of the concept of guaranteed delivery in messaging systems such as the Java Message Service (JMS). In a durable guaranteed-delivery JMS queue, if a message cannot be delivered to a receiver, JMS will wait for a given interval and then resend the request until the message is received.

There is a practical problem with hinted handoffs (and guaranteed delivery approaches, for that matter): if a node is offline for some time, the hints can build up considerably on other nodes. Then, when the other nodes notice that the failed node has come back online, they tend to flood that node with requests, just at the moment it is most vulnerable (when it is struggling to come back into play after a failure). To address this problem, Cassandra limits the storage of hints to a configurable time window. It is also possible to disable hinted handoff entirely.

As its name suggests, `org.apache.cassandra.db.HintedHandOffManager` is the class that manages hinted handoffs internally.

Although hinted handoff helps increase Cassandra's availability, it does not fully replace the need for manual repair to ensure consistency.

Lightweight Transactions and Paxos

As we discussed in Chapter 2, Cassandra provides tuneable consistency, including the ability to achieve strong consistency by specifying sufficiently high consistency levels. However, strong consistency is not enough to prevent race conditions in cases where clients need to read, then write data.

To help explain this with an example, let's revisit our `my_keyspace.user` table from Chapter 5. Imagine we are building a client that wants to manage user records as part of an account management application. In creating a new user account, we'd like to make sure that the user record doesn't already exist, lest we unintentionally overwrite existing user data. So we do a read to see if the record exists first, and then only perform the create if the record doesn't exist.

The behavior we're looking for is called *linearizable consistency*, meaning that we'd like to guarantee that no other client can come in between our read and write queries with their own modification. Since the 2.0 release, Cassandra supports a *lightweight transaction* (or "LWT") mechanism that provides linearizable consistency.

Cassandra's LWT implementation is based on Paxos. Paxos is a consensus algorithm that allows distributed peer nodes to agree on a proposal, without requiring a master to coordinate a transaction. Paxos and other consensus algorithms emerged as alternatives to traditional two-phase commit based approaches to distributed transactions (reference the note on Two-Phase Commit in The Problem with Two-Phase Commit).

The basic Paxos algorithm consists of two stages: prepare/promise, and propose/accept. To modify data, a coordinator node can propose a new value to the replica nodes, taking on the role of leader. Other nodes may act as leaders simultaneously for other modifications. Each replica node checks the proposal, and if the proposal is the latest it has seen, it promises to not accept proposals associated with any prior proposals. Each replica node also returns the last proposal it received that is still in progress. If the proposal is approved by a majority of replicas, the leader commits the proposal, but with the caveat that it must first commit any in-progress proposals that preceded its own proposal.

The Cassandra implementation extends the basic Paxos algorithm in order to support the desired read-before-write semantics (also known as "check-and-set"), and to allow the state to be reset between transactions. It does this by inserting two additional phases into the algorithm, so that it works as follows:

1. Prepare/Promise
2. Read/Results
3. Propose/Accept
4. Commit/Ack

Thus, a successful transaction requires four round-trips between the coordinator node and replicas. This is more expensive than a regular write, which is why you should think carefully about your use case before using LWTs.

More on Paxos

Several papers have been written about the Paxos protocol. One of the best explanations available is Leslie Lamport's "Paxos Made Simple" (*http://www.cs.utexas.edu/users/lorenzo/corsi/cs380d/past/03F/notes/paxos-simple.pdf*).

Cassandra's lightweight transactions are limited to a single partition. Internally, Cassandra stores a Paxos state for each partition. This ensures that transactions on different partitions cannot interfere with each other.

You can find Cassandra's implementation of the Paxos algorithm in the package `org.apache.cassandra.service.paxos`. These classes are leveraged by the `Storage Service`, which we will learn about soon.

Tombstones

In the relational world, you might be accustomed to the idea of a "soft delete." Instead of actually executing a delete SQL statement, the application will issue an update statement that changes a value in a column called something like "deleted." Programmers sometimes do this to support audit trails, for example.

There's a similar concept in Cassandra called a *tombstone*. This is how all deletes work and is therefore automatically handled for you. When you execute a delete operation, the data is not immediately deleted. Instead, it's treated as an update operation that places a tombstone on the value. A tombstone is a deletion marker that is required to suppress older data in SSTables until compaction can run.

There's a related setting called Garbage Collection Grace Seconds. This is the amount of time that the server will wait to garbage-collect a tombstone. By default, it's set to 864,000 seconds, the equivalent of 10 days. Cassandra keeps track of tombstone age, and once a tombstone is older than GCGraceSeconds, it will be garbage-collected. The purpose of this delay is to give a node that is unavailable time to recover; if a node is down longer than this value, then it is treated as failed and replaced.

Bloom Filters

Bloom filters are used to boost the performance of reads. They are named for their inventor, Burton Bloom. Bloom filters are very fast, non-deterministic algorithms for testing whether an element is a member of a set. They are non-deterministic because it is possible to get a false-positive read from a Bloom filter, but not a false-negative. Bloom filters work by mapping the values in a data set into a bit array and condensing a larger data set into a digest string using a hash function. The digest, by definition, uses a much smaller amount of memory than the original data would. The filters are stored in memory and are used to improve performance by reducing the need for disk access on key lookups. Disk access is typically much slower than memory access. So, in a way, a Bloom filter is a special kind of cache. When a query is performed, the Bloom filter is checked first before accessing disk. Because false-negatives are not possible, if the filter indicates that the element does not exist in the set, it certainly doesn't; but if the filter thinks that the element is in the set, the disk is accessed to make sure.

Bloom filters are implemented by the org.apache.cassandra.utils.BloomFilter class. Cassandra provides the ability to increase Bloom filter accuracy (reducing the number of false positives) by increasing the filter size, at the cost of more memory. This false positive chance is tuneable per table.

Other Uses of Bloom Filters

Bloom filters are used in other distributed database and caching technologies, including Apache Hadoop, Google Bigtable, and Squid Proxy Cache.

Compaction

As we already discussed, SSTables are immutable, which helps Cassandra achieve such high write speeds. However, periodic compaction of these SSTables is important in order to support fast read performance and clean out stale data values. A compaction operation in Cassandra is performed in order to merge SSTables. During compaction, the data in SSTables is merged: the keys are merged, columns are combined, tombstones are discarded, and a new index is created.

Compaction is the process of freeing up space by merging large accumulated datafiles. This is roughly analogous to rebuilding a table in the relational world. But the primary difference in Cassandra is that it is intended as a transparent operation that is amortized across the life of the server.

On compaction, the merged data is sorted, a new index is created over the sorted data, and the freshly merged, sorted, and indexed data is written to a single new SSTable (each SSTable consists of multiple files including: *Data*, *Index*, and *Filter*). This process is managed by the class `org.apache.cassandra.db.compaction.CompactionManager`.

Another important function of compaction is to improve performance by reducing the number of required seeks. There are a bounded number of SSTables to inspect to find the column data for a given key. If a key is frequently mutated, it's very likely that the mutations will all end up in flushed SSTables. Compacting them prevents the database from having to perform a seek to pull the data from each SSTable in order to locate the current value of each column requested in a read request.

When compaction is performed, there is a temporary spike in disk I/O and the size of data on disk while old SSTables are read and new SSTables are being written.

Cassandra supports multiple algorithms for compaction via the strategy pattern. The compaction strategy is an option that is set for each table. The compaction strategy extends the `AbstractCompactionStrategy` class. The available strategies include:

- `SizeTieredCompactionStrategy` (STCS) is the default compaction strategy and is recommended for write-intensive tables
- `LeveledCompactionStrategy` (LCS) is recommended for read-intensive tables
- `DateTieredCompactionStrategy` (DTCS), which is intended for time series or otherwise date-based data.

We'll revisit these strategies in Chapter 12 to discuss selecting the best strategy for each table.

One interesting feature of compaction relates to its intersection with incremental repair. A feature called *anticompaction* was added in 2.1. As the name implies, anticompaction is somewhat of an opposite operation to regular compaction in that the result is the division of an SSTable into two SSTables, one containing repaired data, and the other containing unrepaired data.

The trade-off is that more complexity is introduced into the compaction strategies, which must handle repaired and unrepaired SSTables separately so that they are not merged together.

What About Major Compaction?

Users with prior experience may recall that Cassandra exposes an administrative operation called *major compaction* (also known as *full compaction*) that consolidates multiple SSTables into a single SSTable. While this feature is still available, the utility of performing a major compaction has been greatly reduced over time. In fact, usage is actually discouraged in production environments, as it tends to limit Cassandra's ability to remove stale data. We'll learn more about this and other administrative operations on SSTables available via `nodetool` in Chapter 11.

Anti-Entropy, Repair, and Merkle Trees

Cassandra uses an *anti-entropy* protocol, which is a type of gossip protocol for repairing replicated data. Anti-entropy protocols work by comparing replicas of data and reconciling differences observed between the replicas. Anti-entropy is used in Amazon's Dynamo, and Cassandra's implementation is modeled on that (see Section 4.7 of the Dynamo paper).

Anti-Entropy in Cassandra

In Cassandra, the term *anti-entropy* is often used in two slightly different contexts, with meanings that have some overlap:

- The term is often used as a shorthand for the replica synchronization mechanism for ensuring that data on different nodes is updated to the newest version.
- At other times, Cassandra is described as having an antientropy *capability* that includes replica synchronization as well as hinted handoff, which is a write-time anti-entropy mechanism we read about in "Hinted Handoff" on page 117.

Replica synchronization is supported via two different modes known as *read repair* and *anti-entropy repair*. Read repair refers to the synchronization of replicas as data is read. Cassandra reads data from multiple replicas in order to achieve the requested consistency level, and detects if any replicas have out of date values. If an insufficient number of nodes have the latest value, a read repair is performed immediately to update the out of date replicas. Otherwise, the repairs can be performed in the background after the read returns. This design is observed by Cassandra as well as by straight key/value stores such as Project Voldemort and Riak.

Anti-entropy repair (sometimes called *manual repair*) is a manually initiated operation performed on nodes as part of a regular maintenance process. This type of repair is executed by using a tool called *nodetool*, as we'll learn about in Chapter 11. Running `nodetool repair` causes Cassandra to execute a *major compaction* (see "Compaction" on page 121). During a major compaction, the server initiates a TreeRequest/TreeReponse conversation to exchange Merkle trees with neighboring nodes. The Merkle tree is a hash representing the data in that table. If the trees from the different nodes don't match, they have to be reconciled (or "repaired") to determine the latest data values they should all be set to. This tree comparison validation is the responsibility of the `org.apache.cassandra.service.AbstractReadExecutor` class.

What's a Merkle Tree?

A Merkle tree, named for its inventor, Ralph Merkle, is also known as a "hash tree." It's a data structure represented as a binary tree, and it's useful because it summarizes in short form the data in a larger data set. In a hash tree, the leaves are the data blocks (typically files on a filesystem) to be summarized. Every parent node in the tree is a hash of its direct child node, which tightly compacts the summary.

In Cassandra, the Merkle tree is implemented in the `org.apache.cassandra.utils .MerkleTree` class.

Merkle trees are used in Cassandra to ensure that the peer-to-peer network of nodes receives data blocks unaltered and unharmed. They are also used in cryptography to verify the contents of files and transmissions.

Both Cassandra and Dynamo use Merkle trees for anti-entropy, but their implementations are a little different. In Cassandra, each table has its own Merkle tree; the tree is created as a snapshot during a major compaction, and is kept only as long as is required to send it to the neighboring nodes on the ring. The advantage of this implementation is that it reduces network I/O.

Staged Event-Driven Architecture (SEDA)

Cassandra's design was influenced by Staged Event-Driven Architecture (SEDA). SEDA is a general architecture for highly concurrent Internet services, originally proposed in a 2001 paper called "SEDA: An Architecture for Well-Conditioned, Scalable Internet Services" by Matt Welsh, David Culler, and Eric Brewer (who you might recall from our discussion of the CAP theorem). You can read the original SEDA paper at *http://www.eecs.harvard.edu/~mdw/proj/seda* (*http://www.eecs.harvard.edu/%7Emdw/proj/seda*).

In a typical application, a single unit of work is often performed within the confines of a single thread. A write operation, for example, will start and end within the same thread. Cassandra, however, is different: its concurrency model is based on SEDA, so a single operation may start with one thread, which then hands off the work to another thread, which may hand it off to other threads. But it's not up to the current thread to hand off the work to another thread. Instead, work is subdivided into what are called *stages*, and the thread pool (really, a `java.util.concurrent.Execu torService`) associated with the stage determines execution.

A stage is a basic unit of work, and a single operation may internally state-transition from one stage to the next. Because each stage can be handled by a different thread pool, Cassandra experiences a massive performance improvement. This design also means that Cassandra is better able to manage its own resources internally because different operations might require disk I/O, or they might be CPU-bound, or they might be network operations, and so on, so the pools can manage their work according to the availability of these resources.

A stage consists of an incoming event queue, an event handler, and an associated thread pool. Stages are managed by a controller that determines scheduling and thread allocation; Cassandra implements this kind of concurrency model using the thread pool `java.util.concurrent.ExecutorService`. To see specifically how this works, check out the `org.apache.cassandra.concurrent.StageManager` class. The following operations are represented as stages in Cassandra, including many of the concepts we've discussed in this chapter:

- Read (local reads)
- Mutation (local writes)
- Gossip
- Request/response (interactions with other nodes)
- Anti-entropy (`nodetool` repair)
- Read repair
- Migration (making schema changes)
- Hinted handoff

You can observe the thread pools associated with each of these stages by using the `nodetool tpstats` command, which we'll learn about in Chapter 10.

A few additional operations are also implemented as stages, such as operations on memtables including flushing data out to SSTables and freeing memory. The stages implement the `IVerbHandler` interface to support the functionality for a given verb. Because the idea of mutation is represented as a stage, it can play a role in both insert and delete operations.

A Pragmatic Approach to SEDA

Over time, developers of Cassandra and other technologies based on the SEDA architecture article have encountered performance issues due to the inefficiencies of requiring separate thread pools for each stage and event queues between each stage, even for short-lived stages. These challenges were acknowledged by Matt Welsh in the follow-up blog post "A Retrospective on SEDA" (*http://matt-welsh.blogspot.com/2010/07/retrospective-on-seda.html*).

Over time, Cassandra's developers have relaxed the strict SEDA conventions, collapsing some stages into the same thread pool to improve throughput. However, the basic principles of separating work into stages and using queues and thread pools to manage these stages are still in evidence in the code.

Managers and Services

There is a set of classes that form Cassandra's basic internal control mechanisms. We've encountered a few of them already in this chapter, including the `HintedHandoffManager`, the `CompactionManager`, and the `StageManager`. We'll present a brief overview of a few other classes here so that you can become familiar with some of the more important ones. Many of these expose `MBeans` via the Java Management Extension (JMX) in order to report status and metrics, and in some cases to allow configuration and control of their activities. We'll learn more about interacting with these `MBeans` in Chapter 10.

Cassandra Daemon

The `org.apache.cassandra.service.CassandraDaemon` interface represents the life cycle of the Cassandra service running on a single node. It includes the typical life cycle operations that you might expect: `start`, `stop`, `activate`, `deactivate`, and `destroy`.

You can also create an in-memory Cassandra instance programmatically by using the class `org.apache.cassandra.service.EmbeddedCassandraService`. Creating an embedded instance can be useful for unit testing programs using Cassandra.

Storage Engine

Cassandra's core data storage functionality is commonly referred to as the storage engine, which consists primarily of classes in the `org.apache.cassandra.db` package. The main entry point is the `ColumnFamilyStore` class, which manages all aspects of table storage, including commit logs, memtables, SSTables, and indexes.

Major Changes to the Storage Engine

The storage engine was largely rewritten for the 3.0 release to bring Cassandra's in-memory and on-disk representations of data in alignment with the CQL. An excellent summary of the changes is provided in the CASSANDRA-8099 JIRA issue (*https://issues.apache.org/jira/browse/CASSANDRA-8099*).

The storage engine rewrite was a precursor for many other changes, most importantly, support for materialized views, which was implemented under CASSANDRA-6477 (*https://issues.apache.org/jira/browse/CASSANDRA-6477*). These two JIRA issues make for interesting reading if you want to better understand the changes required "under the hood" to enable these powerful new features.

Storage Service

Cassandra wraps the storage engine with a service represented by the `org.apache.cassandra.service.StorageService` class. The storage service contains the node's token, which is a marker indicating the range of data that the node is responsible for.

The server starts up with a call to the `initServer` method of this class, upon which the server registers the SEDA verb handlers, makes some determinations about its state (such as whether it was bootstrapped or not, and what its partitioner is), and registers an `MBean` with the JMX server.

Storage Proxy

The `org.apache.cassandra.service.StorageProxy` sits in front of the `StorageService` to handle the work of responding to client requests. It coordinates with other nodes to store and retrieve data, including storage of hints when needed. The `StorageProxy` also helps manage lightweight transaction processing.

Direct Invocation of the Storage Proxy

Although it is possible to invoke the StorageProxy programmatically, as an in-memory instance, note that this is not considered an officially supported API for Cassandra and therefore has undergone changes between releases.

Messaging Service

The purpose of org.apache.cassandra.net.MessagingService is to create socket listeners for message exchange; inbound and outbound messages from this node come through this service. The MessagingService.listen method creates a thread. Each incoming connection then dips into the ExecutorService thread pool using org.apache.cassandra.net.IncomingTcpConnection (a class that extends Thread) to deserialize the message. The message is validated, and then routed to the appropriate handler.

Because the MessagingService also makes heavy use of stages and the pool it maintains is wrapped with an MBean, you can find out a lot about how this service is working (whether reads are getting backed up and so forth) through JMX.

Stream Manager

Streaming is Cassandra's optimized way of sending sections of SSTable files from one node to another via a persistent TCP connection; all other communication between nodes occurs via serialized messages. The org.apache.cassandra.streaming. StreamManager handles these streaming messages, including connection management, message compression, progress tracking, and statistics.

CQL Native Transport Server

The CQL Native Protocol is the binary protocol used by clients to communicate with Cassandra. The org.apache.cassandra.transport package contains the classes that implement this protocol, including the Server. This native transport server manages client connections and routes incoming requests, delegating the work of performing queries to the StorageProxy.

There are several other classes that manage key features of Cassandra. Here are a few to investigate if you're interested:

Key feature	Class
Repair	org.apache.cassandra.service.ActiveRepairService
Caching	org.apache.cassandra.service.CachingService
Migration	org.apache.cassandra.service.MigrationManager

Key feature	Class
Materialized views	`org.apache.cassandra.db.view.MaterializedViewManager`
Secondary indexes	`org.apache.cassandra.db.index.SecondaryIndexManager`
Authorization	`org.apache.cassandra.auth.CassandraRoleManager`

System Keyspaces

In true "dogfooding" style, Cassandra makes use of its own storage to keep track of metadata about the cluster and local node. This is similar to the way in which Microsoft SQL Server maintains the meta-databases `master` and `tempdb`. The `master` is used to keep information about disk space, usage, system settings, and general server installation notes; the `tempdb` is used as a workspace to store intermediate results and perform general tasks. The Oracle database always has a tablespace called `SYSTEM`, used for similar purposes. The Cassandra `system` keyspaces are used much like these.

Let's go back to `cqlsh` to have a quick peek at the tables in Cassandra's `system` keyspace:

```
cqlsh> DESCRIBE TABLES;

Keyspace system_traces
----------------------
events sessions

Keyspace system_schema
----------------------
materialized_views  functions  aggregates  types          columns
tables              triggers   keyspaces   dropped_columns

Keyspace system_auth
--------------------
resource_role_permissons_index  role_permissions  role_members
roles

Keyspace system
---------------
available_ranges                      sstable_activity    local
range_xfers                           peer_events         hints
materialized_views_builds_in_progress paxos
"IndexInfo"                           batchlog
peers                                 size_estimates
built_materialized_views              compaction_history

Keyspace system_distributed
---------------------------
repair_history  parent_repair_history
```

Seeing Different System Keyspaces?

If you're using a version of Cassandra prior to 2.2, you may not see some of these keyspaces listed. While the basic system keyspace has been around since the beginning, the system_traces keyspace was added in 1.2 to support request tracing. The system_auth and system_distributed keyspaces were added in 2.2 to support role-based access control (RBAC) and persistence of repair data, respectively. Finally, tables related to schema definition were migrated from system to the system_schema keyspace in 3.0.

Looking over these tables, we see that many of them are related to the concepts discussed in this chapter:

- Information about the structure of the cluster communicated via gossip is stored in system.local and system.peers. These tables hold information about the local node and other nodes in the cluster including IP addresses, locations by data center and rack, CQL, and protocol versions.
- The system.range_xfers and system.available_ranges track token ranges managed by each node and any ranges needing allocation.
- The system_schema.keyspaces, system_schema.tables, and system_schema.columns store the definitions of the keyspaces, tables, and indexes defined for the cluster.
- The construction of materialized views is tracked in the system.materialized_views_builds_in_progress and system.built_materialized_views tables, resulting in the views available in system_schema.materialized_views.
- User-provided extensions such as system_schema.types for user-defined types, system_schema.triggers for triggers configured per table, system_schema.functions for user-defined functions, and system_schema.aggregates for user-defined aggregates.
- The system.paxos table stores the status of transactions in progress, while the system.batchlog table stores the status of atomic batches.
- The system.size_estimates stores the estimated number of partitions per table, which is used for Hadoop integration.

Removal of the system.hints Table

Hinted handoffs have traditionally been stored in the system.hints table. As thoughtful developers have noted, the fact that hints are really messages to be kept for a short time and deleted means this usage is really an instance of the well-known anti-pattern of using Cassandra as a queue, which we discussed in Chapter 5. Hint storage was moved to flat files in the 3.0 release.

Let's go back to `cqlsh` to have a quick peek at the attributes of Cassandra's `system` keyspace:

```
cqlsh> USE system;

cqlsh:system> DESCRIBE KEYSPACE;

CREATE KEYSPACE system WITH replication =
  {'class': 'LocalStrategy'} AND durable_writes = true;

...
```

We've truncated the output here because it lists the complete structure of each table. Looking at the first statement in the output, we see that the `system` keyspace is using the replication strategy `LocalStrategy`, meaning that this information is intended for internal use and not replicated to other nodes.

Immutability of the System Keyspace

Describing the `system` keyspaces produces similar output to describing any other keyspace, in that the tables are described using the `CREATE TABLE` command syntax. This may be somewhat misleading, as you cannot modify the schema of the `system` keyspaces.

Summary

In this chapter, we examined the main pillars of Cassandra's architecture, including gossip, snitches, partitioners, replication, consistency, anti-entropy, hinted handoff, and lightweight transactions, and how the use of a Staged Event-Driven Architecture maximizes performance. We also looked at some of Cassandra's internal data structures, including memtables, SSTables, and commit logs, and how it executes various operations, such as tombstones and compaction. Finally, we surveyed some of the major classes and interfaces, pointing out key points of interest in case you want to dive deeper into the code base.

Configuring Cassandra

In this chapter, we'll build our first cluster and look at the available options for configuring Cassandra. Out of the box, Cassandra works with no configuration at all; you can simply download and decompress, and then execute the program to start the server with its default configuration. However, one of the things that makes Cassandra such a powerful technology is its emphasis on configurability and customization. At the same time, the number of options may seem confusing at first.

We will focus on aspects of Cassandra that affect node behavior in a cluster and meta-operations such as partitioning, snitches, and replication. Performance tuning and security are additional configuration topics that get their own treatment in Chapters 12 and 13.

Cassandra Cluster Manager

In order to get practice in building and configuring a cluster, we'll take advantage of a tool called the Cassandra Cluster Manager or ccm. Built by Sylvain Lebresne and several other contributors, this tool is a set of Python scripts that allow you to run a multi-node cluster on a single machine. This allows you to quickly configure a cluster without having to provision additional hardware.

The tool is available on GitHub (*https://github.com/pcmanus/ccm*). A quick way to get started is to clone the repository using Git. We'll open a terminal window and navigate to a directory where we want to create our clone and run the following command:

```
$ git clone https://github.com/pcmanus/ccm.git
```

Then we can to run the installation script with administrative-level privileges:

```
$ sudo ./setup.py install
```

ccm Installation Updates

We've provide a simplified view of instructions here for getting started with ccm. You'll want to check the webpage for dependencies and special instructions for platforms such as Windows and MacOS X. Because ccm is an actively maintained tool, these details may change over time.

Once you've installed ccm, it should be on the system path. To get a list of supported commands, you can type ccm or ccm -help. If you need more information on the options for a specific cluster command, type ccm <command> -h. We'll use several of these commands in the following sections as we create and configure a cluster.

You can dig into the Python script files to learn more about what ccm is doing. You can also invoke the scripts directly from automated test suites.

Creating a Cluster

You can run Cassandra on a single machine, which is fine for getting started as you learn how to read and write data. But Cassandra is specifically engineered to be used in a cluster of many machines that can share the load in very high-volume situations. In this section, we'll learn about the configuration required to get multiple Cassandra instances to talk to each other in a ring. The key file for configuring each node in a cluster is the *cassandra.yaml* file, which you can find in the *conf* directory under your Cassandra installation.

The key values in configuring a cluster are the cluster name, the partitioner, the snitch, and the seed nodes. The cluster name, partitioner, and snitch must be the same in all of the nodes participating in the cluster. The seed nodes are not strictly required to be exactly the same for every node across the cluster, but it is a good idea to do so; we'll learn about the best practices for configuration momentarily.

Cassandra clusters are given names in order to prevent machines in one cluster from joining another that you don't want them to be a part of. The name of the default cluster in the *cassandra.yaml* file is "Test Cluster." You can change the name of the cluster by updating the cluster_name property—just make sure that you have done this on all nodes that you want to participate in this cluster.

Changing the Cluster Name

If you have written data to an existing Cassandra cluster and then change the cluster name, Cassandra will warn you with a cluster name mismatch error as it tries to read the datafiles on startup, and then it will shut down.

Let's try creating a cluster using ccm:

```
$ ccm create -v 3.0.0 -n 3 my_cluster --vnodes
Downloading http://archive.apache.org/dist/cassandra/3.0.0/
  apache-cassandra-3.0.0-src.tar.gz to
  /var/folders/63/6h7dm1k51bd6phvm7fbngskc0000gt/T/
    ccm-z2kHp0.tar.gz (22.934MB)
  24048379  [100.00%]
Extracting /var/folders/63/6h7dm1k51bd6phvm7fbngskc0000gt/T/
  ccm-z2kHp0.tar.gz as version 3.0.0 ...
Compiling Cassandra 3.0.0 ...
Current cluster is now: my_cluster
```

This command creates a cluster based on the version of Cassandra we selected—in this case, 3.0.0. The cluster is named my_cluster and has three nodes. We specify that we want to use virtual nodes, because ccm defaults to creating single token nodes. ccm designates our cluster as the current cluster that will be used for subsequent commands. You'll notice that ccm downloads the source for the version requested to run and compiles it. This is because ccm needs to make some minor modifications to the Cassandra source in order to support running multiple nodes on a single machine. We could also have used the copy of the source that we downloaded in Chapter 3. If you'd like to investigate additional options for creating a cluster, run the command ccm create -h.

Once we've created the cluster, we can see it is the only cluster in our list of clusters (and marked as the default), and we can learn about its status:

```
$ ccm list
 *my_cluster

$ ccm status
Cluster: 'my_cluster'
--------------------
node1: DOWN (Not initialized)
node3: DOWN (Not initialized)
node2: DOWN (Not initialized)
```

At this point, none of the nodes have been initialized. Let's start our cluster and then check status again:

```
$ ccm start

$ ccm status
Cluster: 'my_cluster'
--------------------
node1: UP
node3: UP
node2: UP
```

This is the equivalent of starting each individual node using the *bin/cassandra* script (or `service start cassandra` for package installations). To dig deeper on the status of an individual node, we'll enter the following command:

```
$ ccm node1 status

Datacenter: datacenter1
=======================
Status=Up/Down
|/ State=Normal/Leaving/Joining/Moving
--  Address    Load      Tokens  Owns  Host ID      Rack
UN  127.0.0.1  193.2 KB  256     ?     e5a6b739-... rack1
UN  127.0.0.2  68.45 KB  256     ?     48843ab4-... rack1
UN  127.0.0.3  68.5 KB   256     ?     dd728f0b-... rack1
```

This is equivalent to running the command `nodetool status` on the individual node. The output shows that all of the nodes are up and reporting normal status (UN). Each of the nodes has 256 tokens, and owns no data, as we haven't inserted any data yet. (We've shortened the host ID somewhat for brevity.)

We can run the `nodetool ring` command in order to get a list of the tokens owned by each node. To do this in `ccm`, we enter the command:

```
$ ccm node1 ring

Datacenter: datacenter1
==========
Address    Rack   Status  State   ...  Token
                                        9205346612887953633
127.0.0.1  rack1  Up      Normal  ...  -9211073930147845649
127.0.0.3  rack1  Up      Normal  ...  -9114803904447515108
127.0.0.3  rack1  Up      Normal  ...  -9091620194155459357
127.0.0.1  rack1  Up      Normal  ...  -9068215598443754923
127.0.0.2  rack1  Up      Normal  ...  -9063205907969085747
```

The command requires us to specify a node. This doesn't affect the output; it just indicates what node `nodetool` is connecting to in order to get the ring information. As you can see, the tokens are allocated randomly across our three nodes. (As before, we've abbreviated the output and omitted the Owns and Load columns for brevity.)

Seed Nodes

A new node in a cluster needs what's called a *seed node*. A seed node is used as a contact point for other nodes, so Cassandra can learn the topology of the cluster—that is, what hosts have what ranges. For example, if node A acts as a seed for node B, when node B comes online, it will use node A as a reference point from which to get data. This process is known as *bootstrapping* or sometimes *auto bootstrapping* because it is an operation that Cassandra performs automatically. Seed nodes do not auto bootstrap because it is assumed that they will be the first nodes in the cluster.

By default, the *cassandra.yaml* file will have only a single seed entry set to the localhost:

```
- seeds: "127.0.0.1"
```

To add more seed nodes to a cluster, we just add another seed element. We can set multiple servers to be seeds just by indicating the IP address or hostname of the node. For an example, if we look in the *cassandra.yaml* file for one of our ccm nodes, we'll find the following:

```
- seeds: 127.0.0.1, 127.0.0.2, 127.0.0.3
```

In a production cluster, these would be the IP addresses of other hosts rather than loopback addresses. To ensure high availability of Cassandra's bootstrapping process, it is considered a best practice to have at least two seed nodes per data center. This increases the likelihood of having at least one seed node available should one of the local seed nodes go down during a network partition between data centers.

As you may have noticed if you looked in the *cassandra.yaml* file, the list of seeds is actually part of a larger definition of the seed provider. The `org.apache.cassandra.locator.SeedProvider` interface specifies the contract that must be implemented. Cassandra provides the `SimpleSeedProvider` as the default implementation, which loads the IP addresses of the seed nodes from the *cassandra.yaml* file.

Partitioners

The purpose of the partitioner is to allow you to specify how partition keys should be sorted, which has a significant impact on how data will be distributed across your nodes. It also has an effect on the options available for querying ranges of rows. You set the partitioner by updating the value of the partitioner property in the *cassandra.yaml* file. There are a few different partitioners you can use, which we look at now.

Changing the Partitioner

You can't change the partitioner once you've inserted data into a cluster, so take care before deviating from the default!

Murmur3 Partitioner

The default partitioner is `org.apache.cassandra.dht.Murmur3Partitioner`. The `Murmur3Partitioner` uses the murmur hash algorithm to generate tokens. This has the advantage of spreading your keys evenly across your cluster, because the distribution is random. It has the disadvantage of causing inefficient range queries, because keys within a specified range might be placed in a variety of disparate locations in the ring, and key range queries will return data in an essentially random order.

In general, new clusters should always use the `Murmur3Partitioner`. However, Cassandra provides several older partitioners for backward compatibility.

Random Partitioner

The random partitioner is implemented by `org.apache.cassandra.dht.Ran domPartitioner` and is Cassandra's default. It uses a `BigIntegerToken` with an MD5 cryptographic hash applied to it to determine where to place the keys on the node ring. Although the `RandomPartitioner` and `Murmur3Partitioner` are both based on random hash functions, the cryptographic hash used by `RandomPartitioner` is considerably slower, which is why the `Murmur3Partitioner` replaced it as the default.

Order-Preserving Partitioner

The order-preserving partitioner is implemented by `org.apache.cassandra.dht. OrderPreservingPartitioner`. Using this type of partitioner, the token is a UTF-8 string, based on a key. Rows are therefore stored by key order, aligning the physical structure of the data with your sort order. Configuring your column family to use order-preserving partitioning (OPP) allows you to perform range slices.

It's worth noting that OPP isn't more efficient for range queries than random partitioning—it just provides ordering. It has the disadvantage of creating a ring that is potentially very lopsided, because real-world data typically is not written to evenly. As an example, consider the value assigned to letters in a Scrabble game. Q and Z are rarely used, so they get a high value. With OPP, you'll likely eventually end up with lots of data on some nodes and much less data on other nodes. The nodes on which lots of data is stored, making the ring lopsided, are often referred to as *hotspots*. Because of the ordering aspect, users are sometimes attracted to OPP. However, using OPP means in practice that your operations team needed to manually rebalance nodes more frequently using `nodetool loadbalance` or `move` operations. Because of these factors, usage of order preserving partitioners is discouraged. Instead, use indexes.

ByteOrderedPartitioner

The `ByteOrderedPartitioner` is an order-preserving partitioner that treats the data as raw bytes, instead of converting them to strings the way the order-preserving partitioner and collating order-preserving partitioner do. If you need an order-preserving partitioner that doesn't validate your keys as being strings, BOP is recommended for the performance improvement.

Avoiding Partition Hotspots

Although `Murmur3Partitioner` selects tokens randomly, it can still be susceptible to hotspots; however, the problem is significantly reduced compared to the order preserving partitioners. It turns out that in order to minimize hotspots, additional knowledge of the topology is required. An improvement to token selection was added in 3.0 to address this issue. Configuring the `allocate_tokens_keyspace` property in *cassandra.yaml* with the name of a specific keyspace instructs the partitioner to optimize token selection based on the replication strategy of that keyspace. This is most useful in cases where you have a single keyspace for the cluster or all of the keyspaces have the same replication strategy. As of the 3.0 release, this option is only available for the `Murmur3Partitioner`.

Snitches

The job of a snitch is simply to determine relative host proximity. Snitches gather some information about your network topology so that Cassandra can efficiently route requests. The snitch will figure out where nodes are in relation to other nodes. Inferring data centers is the job of the replication strategy. You configure the endpoint snitch implementation to use by updating the `endpoint_snitch` property in the *cassandra.yaml* file.

Simple Snitch

By default, Cassandra uses `org.apache.cassandra.locator.SimpleSnitch`. This snitch is not rack-aware (a term we'll explain in just a minute), which makes it unsuitable for multi-data center deployments. If you choose to use this snitch, you should also use the `SimpleStrategy` replication strategy for your keyspaces.

Property File Snitch

The `org.apache.cassandra.locator.PropertyFileSnitch` is what is known as a *rack-aware* snitch, meaning that it uses information you provide about the topology of your cluster in a standard Java key/value properties file called *cassandra-topology.properties*. The default configuration of *cassandra-topology.properties* looks like this:

```
# Cassandra Node IP=Data Center:Rack
192.168.1.100=DC1:RAC1
192.168.2.200=DC2:RAC2

10.0.0.10=DC1:RAC1
10.0.0.11=DC1:RAC1
10.0.0.12=DC1:RAC2
```

```
10.20.114.10=DC2:RAC1
10.20.114.11=DC2:RAC1

10.21.119.13=DC3:RAC1
10.21.119.10=DC3:RAC1

10.0.0.13=DC1:RAC2
10.21.119.14=DC3:RAC2
10.20.114.15=DC2:RAC2

# default for unknown nodes
default=DC1:r1
```

Here we see that there are three data centers (DC1, DC2, and DC3), each with two racks (RAC1 and RAC2). Any nodes that aren't identified here will be assumed to be in the default data center and rack (DC1, r1).

If you choose to use this snitch or one of the other rack-aware snitches, these are the same rack and data names that you will use in configuring the NetworkTopology Strategy settings per data center for your keyspace replication strategies.

Update the values in this file to record each node in your cluster to specify which rack contains the node with that IP and which data center it's in. Although this may seem difficult to maintain if you expect to add or remove nodes with some frequency, remember that it's one alternative, and it trades away a little flexibility and ease of maintenance in order to give you more control and better runtime performance, as Cassandra doesn't have to figure out where nodes are. Instead, you just tell it where they are.

Gossiping Property File Snitch

The org.apache.cassandra.locator.GossipingPropertyFileSnitch is another rack-aware snitch. The data exchanges information about its own rack and data center location with other nodes via gossip. The rack and data center locations are defined in the *cassandra-rackdc.properties* file. The GossipingPropertyFileSnitch also uses the *cassandra-topology.properties* file, if present.

Rack Inferring Snitch

The org.apache.cassandra.locator.RackInferringSnitch assumes that nodes in the cluster are laid out in a consistent network scheme. It operates by simply comparing different octets in the IP addresses of each node. If two hosts have the same value in the second octet of their IP addresses, then they are determined to be in the same data center. If two hosts have the same value in the third octet of their IP addresses, then they are determined to be in the same rack. "Determined to be" really means that Cassandra has to guess based on an assumption of how your servers are located in different VLANs or subnets.

Cloud Snitches

Cassandra comes with several snitches designed for use in cloud deployments:

- The `org.apache.cassandra.locator.Ec2Snitch` and `Ec2MultiRegionSnitch` are designed for use in Amazon's Elastic Compute Cloud (EC2), part of Amazon Web Services (AWS). The `Ec2Snitch` is useful for a deployment in a single AWS region or multi-region deployments in which the regions are on the same virtual network. The `Ec2MultiRegionSnitch` is designed for multi-region deployments in which the regions are connected via public Internet.
- The `org.apache.cassandra.locator.GoogleCloudSnitch` may be used across one region or multiple regions on the Google Cloud Platform.
- The `org.apache.cassandra.locator.CloudstackSnitch` is designed for use in public or private cloud deployments based on the Apache Cloudstack project.

The EC2 and Google Cloud snitches use the *cassandra-rackdc.properties* file, with rack and data center naming conventions that vary based on the environment. We'll revisit these snitches in Chapter 14.

Dynamic Snitch

As we discussed in Chapter 6, Cassandra wraps your selected snitch with a `org.apache.cassandra.locator.DynamicEndpointSnitch` in order to select the highest performing nodes for queries. The `dynamic_snitch_badness_threshold` property defines a threshold for changing the preferred node. The default value of 0.1 means that the preferred node must perform 10% worse than the fastest node in order to be lose its status. The dynamic snitch updates this status according to the `dynamic_snitch_update_interval_in_ms` property, and resets its calculations at the duration specified by the `dynamic_snitch_reset_interval_in_ms` property. The reset interval should be a much longer interval than the update interval because it is a more expensive operation, but it does allow a node to regain its preferred status without having to demonstrate performance superior to the badness threshold.

Node Configuration

Besides the cluster-related settings we discussed earlier, there are many other properties that can be set in the *cassandra.yaml* file. We'll look at a few highlights related to networking and disk usage in this chapter, and save some of the others for treatment in Chapters 12 and 13.

A Guided Tour of the cassandra.yaml File

We recommend checking the DataStax documentation for your release, which provides a helpful guide to configuring the various settings in the *cassandra.yaml* file (*http://docs.datastax.com/en/cassandra/3.0/cassandra/configuration/configCassandra_yaml.html*). This guide builds from the most commonly configured settings toward more advanced configuration options.

Tokens and Virtual Nodes

By default, Cassandra is configured to use virtual nodes (vnodes). The number of tokens that a given node will service is set by the num_tokens property. Generally this should be left at the default value (currently 256, but see the note that follows), but may be increased to allocate more tokens to more capable machines, or decreased to allocate fewer tokens to less capable machines.

How Many vnodes?

Many Cassandra experts have begun to recommend that the default num_tokens be changed from 256 to 32. They argue that having 32 tokens per node provides adequate balance between token ranges, while requiring significantly less bandwidth to maintain. Look for a possible change to this default in a future release.

To disable vnodes and configure the more traditional token ranges, you'll first need to set num_tokens to 1, or you may also comment out the property entirely. Then you'll also need to set the initial_token property to indicate the range of tokens that will be owned by the node. This will be a different value for each node in the cluster.

Cassandra releases prior to 3.0 provide a tool called token-generator that you can use to calculate initial token values for the nodes in the cluster. For example, let's run it for cluster consisting of a single data center of three nodes:

```
$ cd $CASSANDRA_HOME/tools/bin
$ ./token-generator 3
DC #1:
  Node #1:    -9223372036854775808
  Node #2:    -3074457345618258603
  Node #3:     3074457345618258602
```

For configurations with multiple data centers, just provide multiple integer values corresponding to the number of nodes in each data center. By default, token-generator generates initial tokens for the Murmur3Partitioner, but it can also generate tokens for the RandomPartitioner with the --random option. If you're determined to use initial tokens and the token-generator is not available in your release, there is a handy calculator available at *http://www.geroba.com/cassandra/cassandra-token-calculator*.

In general, it is highly recommended to use vnodes, due to the additional burden of calculating tokens and manual configuration steps required to rebalance the cluster when adding or deleting single-token nodes.

Network Interfaces

There are several properties in the *cassandra.yaml* file that relate to the networking of the node in terms of ports and protocols used for communications with clients and other nodes:

```
$ cd ~/.ccm
$ find . -name cassandra.yaml -exec grep -H 'listen_address' {} \;
./node1/conf/cassandra.yaml:listen_address: 127.0.0.1
./node2/conf/cassandra.yaml:listen_address: 127.0.0.2
./node3/conf/cassandra.yaml:listen_address: 127.0.0.3
```

If you'd prefer to bind via an interface name, you can use the `listen_interface` property instead of `listen_address`. For example, `listen_interface=eth0`. You may not set both of these properties.

The `storage_port` property designates the port used for inter-node communications, typically 7000. If you will be using Cassandra in a network environment that traverses public networks, or multiple regions in a cloud deployment, you should configure the `ssl_storage_port` (typically 7001). Configuring the secure port also requires the configuration of inter-node encryption options, which we'll discuss in Chapter 14.

Historically, Cassandra has supported two different client interfaces: the original Thrift API, also known as the Remote Procedure Call (RPC) interface, and the CQL interface first added in 0.8, also known as the *native transport*. For releases through 2.2, both interfaces were supported and enabled by default. Starting with the 3.0 release, Thrift is disabled by default and will be removed entirely in a future release.

The native transport is enabled or disabled by the `start_native_transport` property, which defaults to true. The native transport uses port 9042, as specified by the `native_transport_port` property.

The *cassandra.yaml* file contains a similar set of properties for configuring the RPC interface. RPC defaults to port 9160, as defined by the `rpc_port` property. If you have existing clients using Thrift, you may need to enable this interface. However, given that CQL has been available in its current form (CQL3) since 1.1, you should make every effort to upgrade clients to CQL.

There is one property, `rpc_keepalive`, which is used by both the RPC and native interfaces. The default value `true` means that Cassandra will allow clients to hold connections open across multiple requests. Other properties are available to limit the threads, connections, and frame size, which we'll examine in Chapter 12.

Data Storage

Cassandra allows you to configure how and where its various data files are stored on disk, including data files, commit logs, and saved caches. The default is the *data* directory under your Cassandra installation (*$CASSANDRA_HOME/data* or *%CAS-SANDRA_HOME%/data*). Older releases and some Linux package distributions use the directory */var/lib/cassandra/data*.

You'll remember from Chapter 6 that the *commit log* is used as short-term storage for incoming writes. As Cassandra receives updates, every write value is written immediately to the commit log in the form of raw sequential file appends. If you shut down the database or it crashes unexpectedly, the commit log can ensure that data is not lost. That's because the next time you start the node, the commit log gets replayed. In fact, that's the only time the commit log is read; clients never read from it. But the normal write operation to the commit log blocks, so it would damage performance to require clients to wait for the write to finish. Commit logs are stored in the location specified by the `commitlog_directory` property.

The *datafile* represents the Sorted String Tables (SSTables). Unlike the commit log, data is written to this file asynchronously. The SSTables are periodically merged during major compactions to free up space. To do this, Cassandra will merge keys, combine columns, and delete tombstones.

Data files are stored in the location specified by the `data_file_directories` property. You can specify multiple values if you wish, and Cassandra will spread the data files evenly across them. This is how Cassandra supports a "just a bunch of disks" or JBOD deployment, where each directory represents a different disk mount point.

Storage File Locations on Windows

You don't need to update the default storage file locations for Windows, because Windows will automatically adjust the path separator and place them under *C:*. Of course, in a real environment, it's a good idea to specify them separately, as indicated.

For testing, you might not see a need to change these locations. However, in production environments using spinning disks, it's recommended that you store the datafiles and the commit logs on separate disks for maximum performance and availability.

Cassandra is robust enough to handle loss of one or more disks without an entire node going down, but gives you several options to specify the desired behavior of nodes on disk failure. The behavior on disk failure impacting data files is specified by the `disk_failure_policy` property, while failure response for commit logs is specified by `commit_failure_policy`. The default behavior `stop` is to disable client interfaces while remaining alive for inspection via JMX. Other options include `die`, which stops the node entirely (JVM exit), and `ignore`, which means that filesystem errors are logged and ignored. Use of `ignore` is not recommended. An additional option `best_effort` is available for data files, allowing operations on SSTables stored on disks that are still available.

Startup and JVM Settings

We've spent most of our time in this chapter so far examining settings in the *cassandra.yaml* file, but there are other configuration files we should examine as well.

Cassandra's startup scripts embody a lot of hard-won logic to optimize configuration of the various JVM options. The key file to look at is the environment script *conf/cassandra.env.sh* (or *conf/cassandra.env.ps1* PowerShell script on Windows). This file contains settings to configure the JVM version (if multiple versions are available on your system), heap size, and other JVM options. Most of these options you'll rarely need to change from their default settings, with the possible exception of the JMX settings. The environment script allows you to set the JMX port and configure security settings for remote JMX access.

Cassandra's logging configuration is found in the *conf/logback.xml* file. This file includes settings such as the log level, message formatting, and log file settings including locations, maximum sizes, and rotation. Cassandra uses the Logback logging framework, which you can learn more about at *http://logback.qos.ch*. The logging implementation was changed from Log4J to Logback in the 2.1 release.

We'll examine logging and JMX configuration in more detail in Chapter 10 and JVM memory configuration in Chapter 12.

Adding Nodes to a Cluster

Now that you have an understanding of what goes into configuring each node of a Cassandra cluster, you're ready to learn how to add nodes. As we've already discussed, to add a new node manually, we need to configure the *cassandra.yaml* file for the new node to set the seed nodes, partitioner, snitch, and network ports. If you've elected to create single token nodes, you'll also need to calculate the token range for the new node and make adjustments to the ranges of other nodes.

Because we're using `ccm`, the process of adding a new node is quite simple. We run the following command:

```
$ ccm add node4 -i 127.0.0.4 -j 7400
```

This creates a new node, node4, with another loopback address and JMX port set to 7400. To see additional options for this command you can type ccm add -h. Now that we've added a node, let's check the status of our cluster:

```
$ ccm status
Cluster: 'my_cluster'
--------------------
node1: UP
node3: UP
node2: UP
node4: DOWN (Not initialized)
```

The new node has been added but has not been started yet. If you run the nodetool ring command again, you'll see that no changes have been made to the tokens. Now we're ready to start the new node by typing ccm node4 start (after double-checking that the additional loopback address is enabled). If you run the nodetool ring command once more, you'll see output similar to the following:

```
Datacenter: datacenter1
==========
Address     Rack      Status  State   ...  Token
                                           9218701579919475223
127.0.0.1   rack1     Up      Normal  ...  -9211073930147845649
127.0.0.4   rack1     Up      Normal  ...  -9190530381068170163
...
```

If you compare this with the previous output, you'll notice a couple of things. First, the tokens have been reallocated across all of the nodes, including our new node. Second, the token values have changed representing smaller ranges. In order to give our new node its 256 tokens (num_tokens), we now have 1,024 total tokens in the cluster.

We can observe what it looks like to other nodes when node4 starts up by examining the log file. On a standalone node, you might look at the *system.log* file in */var/log/ cassandra* (or *$CASSANDRA_HOME/logs)*, depending on your configuration. Because we're using ccm, there is a handy command that we can use to examine the log files from any node. We'll look at the node1 log using the command: ccm node1 showlog. This brings up a view similar to the standard unix more command that allows us to page through or search the log file contents. Searching for gossip-related statements in the log file near the end, we find the following:

```
INFO  [GossipStage:1] 2015-08-24 20:02:24,377 Gossiper.java:1005 -
  Node /127.0.0.4 is now part of the cluster
INFO  [HANDSHAKE-/127.0.0.4] 2015-08-24 20:02:24,380
  OutboundTcpConnection.java:494 - Handshaking version with /127.0.0.4
INFO  [SharedPool-Worker-1] 2015-08-24 20:02:24,383
  Gossiper.java:970 - InetAddress /127.0.0.4 is now UP
```

These statements show node1 successfully gossiping with node4 and that node4 is considered up and part of the cluster. At this point, the bootstrapping process begins to allocate tokens to node4 and stream any data associated with those tokens to node4.

Dynamic Ring Participation

Nodes in a Cassandra cluster can be brought down and brought back up without disruption to the rest of the cluster (assuming a reasonable replication factor and consistency level). Say that we have started a two-node cluster as described earlier in "Creating a Cluster" on page 132. We can cause an error to occur that will take down one of the nodes, and then make sure that the rest of the cluster is still OK.

We'll simulate this by taking one of our nodes down using the ccm node4 stop command. We can run the ccm status to verify the node is down, and then check a log file as we did earlier via the command ccm node1 showlog. Examining the log file we'll see some lines like the following:

```
INFO  [GossipStage:1] 2015-08-27 19:31:24,196 Gossiper.java:984 -
    InetAddress /127.0.0.4 is now DOWN
INFO  [HANDSHAKE-/127.0.0.4] 2015-08-27 19:31:24,745
    OutboundTcpConnection.java:494 - Handshaking version with /127.0.0.4
```

Now we bring node4 back up and recheck the logs at node1. Sure enough, Cassandra has automatically detected that the other participant has returned to the cluster and is again open for business:

```
INFO  [HANDSHAKE-/127.0.0.4] 2015-08-27 19:32:56,733 OutboundTcpConnection
    .java:494 - Handshaking version with /127.0.0.4
INFO  [GossipStage:1] 2015-08-27 19:32:57,574 Gossiper.java:1003 -
    Node /127.0.0.4 has restarted, now UP
INFO  [SharedPool-Worker-1] 2015-08-27 19:32:57,652 Gossiper.java:970 -
    InetAddress /127.0.0.4 is now UP
INFO  [GossipStage:1] 2015-08-27 19:32:58,115 StorageService.java:1886 -
    Node /127.0.0.4 state jump to normal
```

The state jump to normal for node4 indicates that it's part of the cluster again. As a final check, we run the status command again and see that the node is back up:

```
$ ccm status
Cluster: 'my_cluster'
--------------------
node1: UP
node2: UP
node3: UP
node4: UP
```

Replication Strategies

While we've spent a good amount of time learning about the various configuration options for our cluster and nodes, Cassandra also provides flexible configuration of keyspaces and tables. These values are accessed using cqlsh, or they may also be accessed via the client driver in use, which we'll learn about in Chapter 8.

```
cqlsh> DESCRIBE KEYSPACE my_keyspace ;

CREATE KEYSPACE my_keyspace WITH replication =
  {'class': 'SimpleStrategy',
   'replication_factor': '1'}  AND durable_writes = true;
```

What Are Durable Writes?

The durable_writes property allows you to bypass writing to the commit log for the keyspace. This value defaults to true, meaning that the commit log will be updated on modifications. Setting the value to false increases the speed of writes, but also has the risk of losing data if the node goes down before the data is flushed from memtables into SSTables.

Choosing the right replication strategy is important because the strategy determines which nodes are responsible for which key ranges. The implication is that you're also determining which nodes should receive which write operations, which can have a big impact on efficiency in different scenarios. If you set up your cluster such that all writes are going to two data centers—one in Australia and one in Reston, Virginia—you will see a matching performance degradation. The selection of pluggable strategies allows you greater flexibility, so that you can tune Cassandra according to your network topology and needs.

The first replica will always be the node that claims the range in which the token falls, but the remainder of the replicas are placed according to the replication strategy you use.

As we learned in Chapter 6, Cassandra provides two replication strategies, the SimpleStrategy and the NetworkTopologyStrategy.

SimpleStrategy

The SimpleStrategy places replicas in a single data center, in a manner that is not aware of their placement on a data center rack. This means that the implementation is theoretically fast, but not if the next node that has the given key is in a different rack than others. This is shown in Figure 7-1.

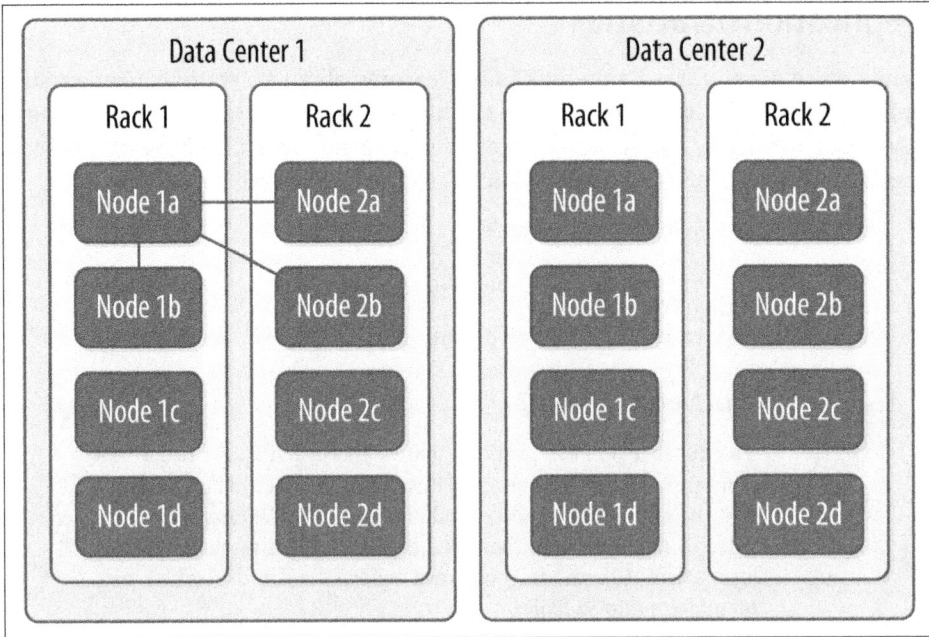

Figure 7-1. The SimpleStrategy places replicas in a single data center, without respect to topology

What's happening here is that the next N nodes on the ring are chosen to hold replicas, and the strategy has no notion of data centers. A second data center is shown in the diagram to highlight the fact that the strategy is unaware of it.

NetworkTopologyStrategy

Now let's say you want to spread replicas across multiple centers in case one of the data centers suffers some kind of catastrophic failure or network outage. The Network TopologyStrategy allows you to request that some replicas be placed in DC1, and some in DC2. Within each data center, the NetworkTopologyStrategy distributes replicas on distinct racks, as nodes in the same rack (or similar physical grouping) often fail at the same time due to power, cooling, or network issues.

The NetworkTopologyStrategy distributes the replicas as follows: the first replica is replaced according to the selected partitioner. Subsequent replicas are placed by traversing the nodes in the ring, skipping nodes in the same rack until a node in another rack is found. The process repeats for additional replicas, placing them on separate racks. Once a replica has been placed in each rack, the skipped nodes are used to place replicas until the replication factor has been met.

The NetworkTopologyStrategy allows you to specify a replication factor for each data center. Thus, the total number of replicas that will be stored is equal to the sum of the replication factors for each data center. The results of the NetworkTopology Strategy are depicted in Figure 7-2.

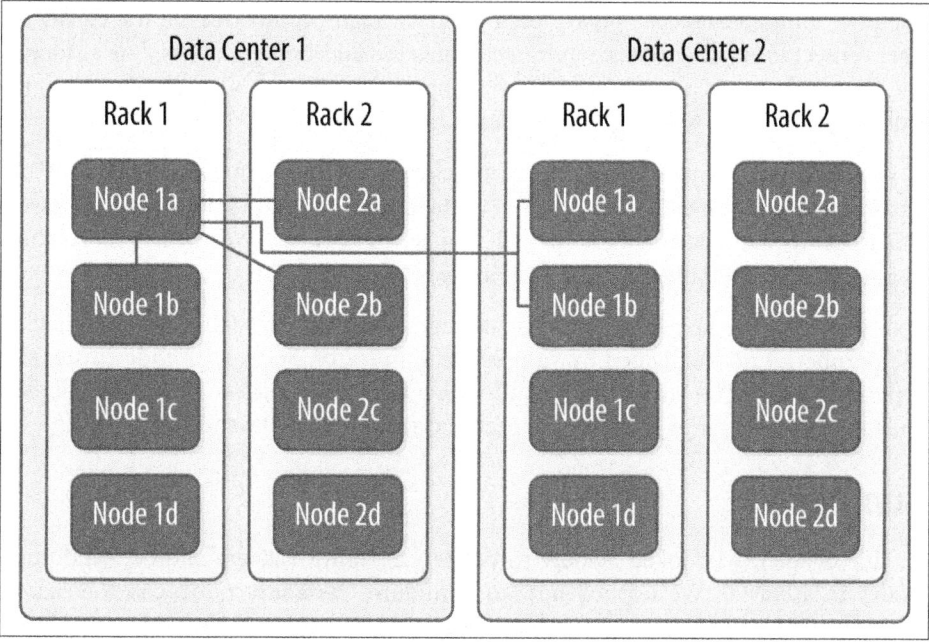

Figure 7-2. The NetworkTopologyStrategy places replicas in multiple data centers according to the specified replication factor per data center

Additional Replication Strategies

Careful observers will note that there are actually two additional replication strategies that ship with Cassandra: the OldNet workTopologyStrategy and the LocalStrategy.

The OldNetworkTopologyStrategy is similar to the NetworkTopol ogyStrategy in that it places replicas in multiple data centers, but its algorithm is less sophisticated. It places the second replica in a different data center from the first, the third replica in a different rack in the first data center, and any remaining replicas by traversing subsequent nodes on the ring.

The LocalStrategy is reserved for Cassandra's own internal use. As the name implies, the LocalStrategy keeps data only on the local node and does not replicate this data to other nodes. Cassandra uses this strategy for system keyspaces that store metadata about the local node and other nodes in the cluster.

Changing the Replication Factor

You can change the replication factor for an existing keyspace via `cqlsh` or another client. For the change to fully take effect, you'll need to run a `nodetool` command on each of the affected nodes. If you increase the replication factor for a cluster (or data center), run the `nodetool repair` command on each of the nodes in the cluster (or data center) to make sure Cassandra generates the additional replicas. For as long as the repair takes, it is possible that some clients will receive a notice that data does not exist if they connect to a replica that doesn't have the data yet.

If you decrease the replication factor for a cluster (or data center), run the `nodetool clean` command on each of the nodes in the cluster (or data center) so that Cassandra frees up the space associated with unneeded replicas. We'll learn more about `repair`, `clean`, and other `nodetool` commands in Chapter 11.

As a general guideline, you can anticipate that your write throughput capacity will be the number of nodes divided by your replication factor. So in a 10-node cluster that typically does 10,000 writes per second with a replication factor of 1, if you increase the replication factor to 2, you can expect to do around 5,000 writes per second.

Summary

In this chapter, we looked at how to create Cassandra clusters and add additional nodes to a cluster. We learned how to configure Cassandra nodes via the *cassandra.yaml* file, including setting the seed nodes, the partitioner, the snitch, and other settings. We also learned how to configure replication for a keyspace and how to select an appropriate replication strategy.

Clients

We're used to connecting to relational databases using drivers. For example, in Java, JDBC is an API that abstracts the vendor implementation of the relational database to present a consistent way of storing and retrieving data using Statements, Prepared Statements, ResultSets, and so forth. To interact with the database, you get a driver that works with the particular database you're using, such as Oracle, SQL Server, or MySQL; the implementation details of this interaction are hidden from the developer. Drivers are typically provided for a wide variety of programming languages to connect to a wide variety of databases.

There are a number of client drivers available for Cassandra as well, including support for most popular languages. There are benefits to these clients, in that you can easily embed them in your own applications (which we'll see how to do) and that they frequently offer more features than the CQL native interface does, including connection pooling and JMX integration and monitoring. In the following sections, we'll learn about the various clients available and the features they offer.

Hector, Astyanax, and Other Legacy Clients

In the early days of Cassandra, the community produced a number of client drivers for different languages. These contributions were a key enabler of Cassandra adoption. Some of the most notable early drivers included Hector and Astyanax.

Named after Cassandra's brother, a warrior of Troy in Greek mythology, Hector was one of the first Cassandra clients. Hector provided a simple Java interface that helped many early developers avoid the challenges of writing to the Thrift API, and served as the inspiration for several other drivers. The project is no longer active, but you can access it at *https://github.com/hector-client/hector*.

Astyanax was a Java client originally built by Netflix on top of the Thrift API as a logical successor to the Hector driver (Astyanax was Hector's son). Once the DataStax Java driver was introduced, Netflix adapted Astyanax to support the Java driver in addition to the original Thrift implementation. This helped many users transition from Thrift to CQL. However, as the Java driver gained prominence, activity on Astyanax slowed considerably, and the project was retired in February, 2016. You can still access the project at *https://github.com/Netflix/astyanax*.

Other clients included Pycassa for Python, Perlcassa for Perl, Helenus for Node.js, and Cassandra-Sharp for the Microsoft .NET framework and C#. Most of these clients are no longer actively maintained, as they were based on the now-deprecated Thrift interface. You can find a comprehensive list of both current and legacy drivers at *http://www.planetcassandra.org/client-drivers-tools*.

DataStax Java Driver

The introduction of CQL was the impetus for a major shift in the landscape of Cassandra client drivers. The simplicity and familiar syntax of CQL made the development of client programs similar to traditional relational database drivers. DataStax made a strategic investment of open source drivers for Java and several additional languages in order to continue to fuel Cassandra adoption. These drivers quickly became the de facto standard for new development projects. You can access the drivers as well as additional connectors and tools at *https://github.com/datastax*.

More Information on DataStax Drivers

Visit the driver matrix page (*http://docs.datastax.com/en/developer/ driver-matrix/doc/common/driverMatrix.html*) to access documentation and identify driver versions that are compatible with your server version.

The DataStax Java driver is the oldest and most mature of these drivers. For this reason, we'll focus on using the Java driver and use this as an opportunity to learn about the features that are provided by the DataStax drivers across multiple languages.

Development Environment Configuration

First, we'll need to access the driver in our development environment. We could download the driver directly from the URL listed before and manage the dependencies manually, but it is more typical in modern Java development to use a tool like Maven to manage dependencies. If you're using Maven, you'll need to add something like the following to your project *pom.xml* file:

```
<dependency>
  <groupId>com.datastax.cassandra</groupId>
```

```
  <artifactId>cassandra-driver-core</artifactId>
  <version>3.0.0</version>
</dependency>
```

You can find the Javadoc for the Java driver at *http://docs.datastax.com/en/drivers/java/3.0/index.html.* Alternatively, the Javadocs are also part of the source distribution.

All of the DataStax drivers are managed as open source projects on GitHub. If you're interested in seeing the Java driver source, you can get a read-only trunk version using this command:

```
$ git clone https://github.com/datastax/java-driver.git
```

Clusters and Contact Points

Once we've configured our environment, we're ready to start coding. We'll create a client application based on the hotel data model we created in Chapter 5. All of the source code used in this chapter and throughout the rest of the book is available at *https://github.com/jeffreyscarpenter/cassandra-guide.*

To start building our application, we'll use the driver's API to connect to our cluster. In the Java driver, this is represented by the com.datastax.driver.core.Cluster and Session classes.

The Cluster class is the main entry point of the driver. It supports a fluent-style API using the builder pattern. For example, the following lines create a connection to a node running on the local host:

```
Cluster cluster = Cluster.builder().
  addContactPoint("127.0.0.1").build();
```

This one statement represents the minimum required information to create a cluster: a single contact point. We can also specify multiple contact points. Contact points are similar to the concept seed nodes that a Cassandra node uses to connect to other nodes in the same cluster.

Creating a Custom Cluster Initializer

The Cluster.Builder class implements an interface called Cluster.Initializer. This allows us to plug in a different mechanism to initialize a Cluster using the static method Cluster.buildFrom(Initializer initializer). This could be useful if we wanted to load the connection information from a configuration file, for example.

There are several other options that we can configure on a Cluster, such as a metrics, default query options, and policies for reconnection, retry, and speculative execution.

We'll examine each of these options in later sections after we take a look at some other connection-related options: protocol version, compression, and authentication.

Protocol version

The driver supports multiple versions of the CQL native protocol. Cassandra 3.0 supports version 4, as we learned in our overview of Cassandra's release history in Chapter 2.

By default, the driver uses the protocol version supported by the first node it connects to. While in most cases this is sufficient, you may need to override this behavior if you're working with a cluster based on an older version of Cassandra. You can select your protocol version by passing the desired value from the `com.datastax.driver.core.ProtocolVersion` enumeration to the `Cluster.Builder.withProtocolVersion()` operation.

Compression

The driver provides the option of compressing messages between your client and Cassandra nodes, taking advantage of the compression options supported by the CQL native protocol. Enabling compression reduces network bandwidth consumed by the driver, at the cost of additional CPU usage for the client and server.

Currently there are two compression algorithms available, `LZ4` and `SNAPPY`, as defined by the `com.datastax.driver.core.ProtocolOptions.Compression` enumeration. The compression defaults to `NONE` but can be overridden by calling the `Cluster.Builder.withCompression()` operation.

Authentication and encryption

The driver provides a pluggable authentication mechanism that can be used to support a simple username/password login, or integration with other authentication systems. By default, no authentication is performed. You can select an authentication provider by passing an implementation of the `com.datastax.driver.core.AuthProvider` interface such as the `PlainTextAuthProvider` to the `Cluster.Builder.withAuthProvider()` operation.

The driver can also encrypt its communications with the server to ensure privacy. Client-server encryption options are specified by each node in its *cassandra.yaml* file. The driver complies with the encryption settings specified by each node.

We'll examine authentication, authorization, and encryption from both the client and server perspective in more detail in Chapter 13.

Sessions and Connection Pooling

After we create our `Cluster` instance, it is not connected to any Cassandra nodes until we initialize it by calling the `init()` method:

```
cluster.init();
```

When this method is invoked, the driver connects to one of the configured contact points in order to obtain metadata about the cluster. This operation will throw a `NoHostAvailableException` if none of the contact points is available, or an `Authenti cationException` if authentication fails. We'll discuss authentication in more detail in Chapter 13.

Once we have initialized our `Cluster` object, we need to establish a session in order to formulate our queries. We can obtain a `com.datastax.driver.core.Session` object by calling one of the `Cluster.connect()` operations. You can optionally provide the name of a keyspace to connect to, as we do in this example that connects to the hotel keyspace:

```
Session session = cluster.connect("hotel");
```

There is also a `connect()` operation with no parameters, which creates a `Session` that can be used with multiple keyspaces. If you choose this option, you'll have to qualify every table reference in your queries with the appropriate keyspace name. Note that it is not strictly required to call `Cluster.init()` explicitly, as it is also invoked behind the scenes when we call `connect()`.

Each `Session` manages connections to a Cassandra cluster, which are used to execute queries and control operations using the Cassandra native protocol. The session contains a pool of TCP connections for each host.

 **Sessions Are Expensive**

Because a session maintains connection pools for multiple nodes, it is a relatively heavyweight object. In most cases, you'll want to create a single `Session` and reuse it throughout your application, rather than continually building up and tearing down `Sessions`. Another acceptable option is to create a `Session` per keyspace, if your application is accessing multiple keyspaces.

Because the CQL native protocol is asynchronous, it allows multiple simultaneous requests per connection; the maximum is 128 simultaneous requests in protocol v2, while v3 and v4 allow up to 32,768 simultaneous requests. Because of this larger number of simultaneous requests, fewer connections per node are required. In fact, the default is a single connection per node.

The driver supports the ability to scale the number of connections up or down based on the number of requests per connection. These connection pool settings are configurable via the `PoolingOptions` class, which sets the maximum and minimum (or "core") number of connections to use for local and remote hosts. If the core and maximum values are different, the driver scales the size of the connection pool for each node up or down depending on the amount of requests made by the client. The settings of minimum and maximum thresholds of requests per connection are used to determine when new connections are created, and when underused connections can be reclaimed. There is also a buffer period to prevent the continual building up and tearing down of connections.

The `PoolingOptions` can be set when creating the `Cluster` using `ClusterBuilder.withPoolingOptions()`, or manipulated after the `Cluster` is created using `Cluster.getConfiguration().getPoolingOptions()`. Here is an example of creating a `Cluster` that limits the maximum number of connections to remote nodes to one:

```
PoolingOptions poolingOptions = new PoolingOptions().
    setMaxConnectionsPerHost(HostDistance.REMOTE, 1);

Cluster cluster = Cluster.builder().
    addContactPoint("127.0.0.1").
    withPoolingOptions(poolingOptions).build();
```

The driver provides a connection heartbeat which is used to make sure that connections are not closed prematurely by intervening network devices. This defaults to 30 seconds but can be overridden using the operation `PoolingOptions.setHeartbeatIntervalSeconds()`. However, this only applies to connections established after the value is set, so you'll most likely want to configure this when creating your `Cluster`.

Statements

Up until this point, we have only configured our connection to the cluster, and haven't yet performed any reads or writes. To begin doing some real application work, we'll create and execute statements using the `com.datastax.driver.core.Statement` class and its various subclasses. `Statement` is an abstract class with several implementations, including `SimpleStatement`, `PreparedStatement`, `BoundStatement`, `BatchStatement`, and `BuiltStatement`.

The simplest way to create and execute a statement is to call the `Session.execute()` operation with a string representing the statement. Here's an example of a statement that will return the entire contents of our hotels table:

```
session.execute("SELECT * from hotel.hotels");
```

This statement creates and executes a query in a single method call. In practice, this could turn out to be a very expensive query to execute in a large database, but it does serve as a useful example of a very simple query. Most queries we need to build will be more complex, as we'll have search criteria to specify or specific values to insert. We can certainly use Java's various string utilities to build up the syntax of our query by hand, but this of course is error prone. It may even expose our application to injection attacks, if we're not careful to sanitize strings that come from end users.

Simple statement

Thankfully, we needn't make things so hard on ourselves. The Java driver provides the `SimpleStatement` class to help construct parameterized statements. As it turns out, the `execute()` operation we saw before is actually a convenience method for creating a `SimpleStatement`.

Let's try building a query by asking our Session object to create a `SimpleStatement`. Here's an example of a statement that will insert a row in our `hotels` table, which we can then execute:

```
SimpleStatement hotelInsert = session.newSimpleStatement(
  "INSERT INTO hotels (hotel_id, name, phone) VALUES (?, ?, ?)",
  "AZ123", "Super Hotel at WestWorld", "1-888-999-9999");
session.execute(hotelInsert);
```

The first parameter to the call is the basic syntax of our query, indicating the table and columns we are interested in. The question marks are used to indicate values that we'll be providing in additional parameters. We use simple strings to hold the values of the hotel ID, name, and phone number.

If we've created our statement correctly, the insert will execute successfully (and silently). Now let's create another statement to read back the row we just inserted:

```
SimpleStatement hotelSelect = session.newSimpleStatement(
  "SELECT * FROM hotels WHERE id=?", "AZ123");
ResultSet hotelSelectResult = session.execute(hotelSelect);
```

Again, we make use of parameterization to provide the ID for our search. This time, when we execute the query, we make sure to receive the `ResultSet` which is returned from the `execute()` method. We can iterate through the rows returned by the `Result Set` as follows:

```
for (Row row : hotelSelectResult) {
  System.out.format("hotel_id: %s, name: %s, phone: %s\n",
  row.getString("hotel_id"), row.getString("name"), row.getString("phone"));
}
```

This code uses the `ResultSet.iterator()` option to get an `Iterator` over the rows in the result set and loop over each row, printing out the desired column values. Note that we use special accessors to obtain the value of each column depending on the desired type—in this case, `Row.getString()`. As we might expect, this will print out a result such as:

```
hotel_id: AZ123, name: Super Hotel at WestWorld, phone: 1-888-999-9999
```

Using a Custom Codec

As we already noted, we need to know the type of the columns we are requesting when interacting with the `Rows` in our `ResultSets`. If we were to request the `id` column using `Row.getString()`, we would receive a `CodecNotFoundException`, indicating that the driver does not know how to map the CQL type `uuid` to `java.lang.String`.

What is happening here is that the driver maintains a default list of mappings between Java and CQL types called a *codec*, which it uses to translate back and forth between your application and Cassandra. The driver provides a way to add additional mappings by extending the class `com.datastax.driver.core.TypeCodec<T>` and registering it with the `CodecRegistry` managed by the `Cluster`:

```
cluster.getConfiguration().getCodecRegistry().
  register(myCustomCodec)
```

The custom codec mechanism is very flexible, as demonstrated by the following use cases:

- Mapping to alternate date/time formats (e.g., Joda time for pre-Java 8 users)
- Mapping string data to/from formats such as XML and JSON
- Mapping lists, sets, and maps to various Java collection types

---

You can find code samples for working with `SimpleStatements` in the example `com.cassandraguide.clients.SimpleStatementExample`.

Asynchronous execution

The `Session.execute()` operation is synchronous, which means that it blocks until a result is obtained or an error occurs, such as a network timeout. The driver also provides the asynchronous `executeAsync()` operation to support non-blocking interactions with Cassandra. These non-blocking requests can make it simpler to send multiple queries in parallel to speed performance of your client application.

Let's take our operation from before and modify it to use the asynchronous operation:

```
ResultSetFuture result = session.executeAsync(statement);
```

The result is of the type `ResultSetFuture`, which is an implementation of the `java.util.concurrent.Future` interface. A `Future` is a Java generic type used to capture the result of an asynchronous operation. Each `Future` can be checked to see whether the operation has completed, and then queried for the result of the operation according to the bound type. There are also blocking `wait()` operations to wait for the result. A `Future` can also be cancelled if the caller is no longer interested in the result of the operation. The `Future` class is a useful tool for implementing asynchronous programming patterns, but requires either blocking or polling to wait for the operation to complete.

To address this drawback, the Java driver leverages the `ListenableFuture` interface from Google's Guava framework. The `ListenableFuture` interface extends `Future`, and adds an `addListener()` operation that allows the client to register a callback method that is invoked when the `Future` completes. The callback method is invoked in a thread managed by the driver, so it is important that the method complete quickly to avoid tying up driver resources. The `ResultSetFuture` is bound to the `ResultSet` type.

Additional Asynchronous Operations

In addition to the `Session.executeAsync()` operation, the driver supports several other asynchronous operations, including `Cluster.closeAsync()`, `Session.prepareAsync()`, and several operations on the object mapper.

Prepared statement

While `SimpleStatements` are quite useful for creating ad hoc queries, most applications tend to perform the same set of queries repeatedly. The `PreparedStatement` is designed to handle these queries more efficiently. The structure of the statement is sent to nodes a single time for preparation, and a handle for the statement is returned. To use the prepared statement, only the handle and the parameters need to be sent.

As you're building your application, you'll typically create `PreparedStatements` for reading data, corresponding to each access pattern you derive in your data model, plus others for writing data to your tables to support those access patterns.

Let's create some `PreparedStatements` to represent the same hotel queries as before, using the `Session.prepare()` operation:

```
PreparedStatement hotelInsertPrepared = session.prepare(
  "INSERT INTO hotels (hotel_id, name, phone) VALUES (?, ?, ?)");

PreparedStatement hotelSelectPrepared = session.prepare(
  "SELECT * FROM hotels WHERE hotel_id=?");
```

Note that the `PreparedStatement` uses the same parameterized syntax we used earlier for our `SimpleStatement`. A key difference, however, is that a `PreparedStatement` is not a subtype of `Statement`. This prevents the error of trying to pass an unbound `PreparedStatement` to the session to execute.

Before we get to that, however, let's take a step back and discuss what is happening behind the scenes of the `Session.prepare()` operation. The driver passes the contents of our `PreparedStatement` to a Cassandra node and gets back a unique identifier for the statement. This unique identifier is referenced when you create a `BoundStatement`. If you're curious, you can actually see this reference by calling `PreparedStatement.getPreparedID()`.

You can think of a `PreparedStatement` as a template for creating queries. In addition to specifying the form of our query, there are other attributes that we can set on a `PreparedStatement` that will be used as defaults for statements it is used to create, including a default consistency level, retry policy, and tracing.

In addition to improving efficiency, `PreparedStatements` also improve security by separating the query logic of CQL from the data. This provides protection against injection attacks, which attempt to embed commands into data fields in order to gain unauthorized access.

Bound statement

Now our `PreparedStatement` is available for us to use to create queries. In order to make use of a `PreparedStatement`, we bind it with actual values by calling the `bind()` operation. For example, we can bind the `SELECT` statement we created earlier as follows:

```
BoundStatement hotelSelectBound = hotelSelectPrepared.bind("AZ123");
```

The `bind()` operation we've used here allows us to provide values that match each variable in the `PreparedStatement`. It is possible to provide the first *n* bound values, in which case the remaining values must be bound separately before executing the statement. There is also a version of `bind()` which takes no parameters, in which case all of the parameters must be bound separately. There are several `set()` operations provided by `BoundStatement` that can be used to bind values of different types. For example, we can take our `INSERT` prepared statement from above and bind the name and phone values using the `setString()` operation:

```
BoundStatement hotelInsertBound = hotelInsertPrepared.bind("AZ123");
hotelInsertBound.setString("name", "Super Hotel at WestWorld");
hotelInsertBound.setString("phone", "1-888-999-9999");
```

Once we have bound all of the values, we execute a `BoundStatement` using `Session.execute()`. If we have failed to bind any of the values, they will be ignored on the server side, if protocol v4 (Cassandra 3.0 or later) is in use. The driver behavior for older protocol versions is to throw an `IllegalStateException` if there are any unbound values.

You can find code samples for working with `PreparedStatement` and `BoundStatement` in the example `com.cassandraguide.clients.PreparedStatementExample`.

Built statement and the Query Builder

The driver also provides the `com.datastax.driver.core.querybuilder.QueryBuilder` class, which provides a fluent-style API for building queries. This is suitable for cases where there is variation in the query structure (such as optional parameters) that would make using `PreparedStatements` difficult. Similar to `PreparedStatement`, it also provides some protection against injection attacks.

We construct a `QueryBuilder` using a simple constructor that takes our `Cluster` object:

```
QueryBuilder queryBuilder = new QueryBuilder(cluster);
```

The `QueryBuilder` produces queries that are represented using the `BuiltStatement` class and its subclasses. The methods on each class return instances of `BuiltStatement` that represent content added to a query as it is being built up. You'll likely find your IDE quite useful in helping to identify the allowed operations as you're building queries.

Let's reproduce the queries from before using the `QueryBuilder` to see how it works. First, we'll build a CQL INSERT query:

```
BuiltStatement hotelInsertBuilt =
  queryBuilder.insertInto("hotels")
  .value("hotel_id", "AZ123")
  .value("name", "Super Hotel at WestWorld")
  .value("phone", "1-888-999-9999");
```

The first operation calls the `QueryBuilder.insertInto()` operation to create an `Insert` statement for the hotels table. If desired, we could then add a CQL USING clause to our statement with `Insert.using()`, but instead we choose to start adding values to our query. The `Insert.value()` operation continues returning `Insert` statements as we add values. The resulting `Insert` can be executed like any other `Statement` using `Session.execute()` or `executeAsync()`.

The construction of the CQL SELECT command is similar:

```
BuiltStatement hotelSelectBuilt = queryBuilder.select()
  .all()
  .from("hotels")
  .where(eq("hotel_id", "AZ123"));
```

For this query, we call `QueryBuilder.select()` to create a `Select` statement. We use the `Select.all()` operation to select all columns, although we could also have used the `column()` operation to select specific columns. We add a CQL `WHERE` clause via the `Select.where()` operation, which accepts an instance of the `Clause` class. We create `Clauses` using static operations provided by the `QueryBuilder`. In this case, we use the `eq()` operation to check for equality with our ID.

To access these static operations, we need to add additional import statements to our Java source files such as:

```
import static com.datastax.driver.core.querybuilder.QueryBuilder.eq;
```

For a complete code sample using the `QueryBuilder` and `BuiltStatement`, see the class `com.cassandraguide.clients.QueryBuilderExample`.

Object mapper

We've explored several techniques for creating and executing query statements with the driver. There is one final technique that we'll look at that provides a bit more abstraction. The Java driver provides an object mapper that allows you to focus on developing and interacting with domain models (or data types used on APIs). The object mapper works off of annotations in source code that are used to map Java classes to tables or user-defined types (UDTs).

The object mapping API is provided as a separate library from the rest of the driver in the *cassandra-driver-mapping.jar* file, so you will need to include this additional Maven dependency in order to use Mapper in your project:

```
<dependency>
  <groupId>com.datastax.cassandra</groupId>
  <artifactId>cassandra-driver-mapping</artifactId>
  <version>3.0.0</version>
</dependency>
```

For example, let's create and annotate a `Hotel` domain model class corresponding to our `hotels` table:

```
import com.datastax.driver.mapping.annotations.Column;
import com.datastax.driver.mapping.annotations.PartitionKey;
import com.datastax.driver.mapping.annotations.Table;

@Table(keyspace = "hotel", name = "hotels")
public class Hotel {

    @PartitionKey
    private String id;

    @Column (name = "name")
    private String name;
```

```
@Column (name = "phone")
private String phone;

@Column (name = "address")
private String address;

@Column (name = "pois")
private Set<String> pointsOfInterest;

// constructors, get/set methods, hashcode, equals
}
```

Now we use the com.datastax.driver.mapping.MappingManager to attach to our Session and create a Mapper for our annotated domain model class:

```
MappingManager mappingManager = new MappingManager(session);
Mapper<Hotel> hotelMapper = MappingManager.mapper(Hotel.class);
```

Let's assume the Hotel class has a simple constructor that just takes a UUID, name, and phone number, which we'll use to create a simple hotel that we can save using the object mapper:

```
Hotel hotel = new Hotel("AZ123", "Super Hotel at WestWorld",
  "1-888-999-9999");
hotelMapper.save(hotel);
```

The Mapper.save() operation is all we need to execute to perform a CQL INSERT or UPDATE, as these are really the same operation to Cassandra. The Mapper builds and executes the statement on our behalf.

To retrieve an object, we use the Mapper.get() operation, passing in an argument list that matches the elements of the partition key:

```
Hotel retrievedHotel = hotelMapper.get(hotelId);
```

The syntax for deleting an object is similar:

```
hotelMapper.delete(hotelId);
```

As with the save() operation, get() and delete() completely handle the details of executing statements with the driver on our behalf. There are also saveAsync(), getAsync() and deleteAsync() operations that support asynchronous execution using the ListenableFuture interface we discussed earlier.

If you want to be able to configure the queries before they are executed, there are also operations on the Mapper that return Statements: saveQuery(), getQuery(), and deleteQuery().

The object mapper is a useful tool for abstracting some of the details of interacting with your code, especially if you have an existing domain model. If your domain model contains classes that reference other classes, you can annotate the referenced classes as user-defined types with the @UDT annotation. The object mapper processes objects recursively using your annotated types.

Achilles: An Advanced Object Mapper

DuyHai Doan has developed an advanced object mapper for Java called Achilles. Achilles provides support for more advanced functionality such as complex key mappings, lightweight transactions, user defined functions, and more. You can check it out at *https:// github.com/doanduyhai/Achilles*.

Policies

The Java driver provides several policy interfaces that can be used to tune the behavior of the driver. These include policies for load balancing, retrying requests, and managing connections to nodes in the cluster.

Load balancing policy

As we learned in Chapter 6, a query can be made to any node in a cluster, which is then known as the coordinator node for that query. Depending on the contents of the query, the coordinator may communicate with other nodes in order to satisfy the query. If a client were to direct all of its queries at the same node, this would produce an unbalanced load on the cluster, especially if other clients are doing the same.

To get around this issue, the driver provides a pluggable mechanism to balance the query load across multiple nodes. Load balancing is implemented by selecting an implementation of the `com.datastax.driver.core.policies.LoadBalancing Policy` interface.

Each `LoadBalancingPolicy` must provide a `distance()` operation to classify each node in the cluster as local, remote, or ignored, according to the `HostDistance` enumeration. The driver prefers interactions with local nodes and maintains more connections to local nodes than remote nodes. The other key operation is `newQueryPlan()`, which returns a list of nodes in the order they should be queried. The `LoadBalancingPolicy` interface also contains operations that are used to inform the policy when nodes are added or removed, or go up or down. These operations help the policy avoid including down or removed nodes in query plans.

The driver provides two basic load balancing implementations: the `RoundRobin Policy`, which is the default, and the `DCAwareRoundRobinPolicy`.

The `RoundRobinPolicy` allocates requests across the nodes in the cluster in a repeating pattern to spread the processing load. The `DCAwareRoundRobinPolicy` is similar, but focuses its query plans on nodes in the local data center. This policy can add a configurable number of nodes in remote data centers to query plans, but the remote nodes will always come after local nodes in priority. The local data center can be identified explicitly, or you can allow the driver to discover it automatically.

A second mode is token awareness, which uses the token value of the partition key in order to select a node which is a replica for the desired data, thus minimizing the number of nodes that must be queried. This is implemented by wrapping the selected policy with a `TokenAwarePolicy`.

The `LoadBalancingPolicy` is set on the `Cluster` when it is built. For example, the following statement will initialize a `Cluster` to have token awareness and to prefer nodes in the local data center:

```
Cluster.builder().withLoadBalancingPolicy(
    new TokenAwarePolicy(new DCAwareRoundRobinPolicy.Builder().build());
```

Retry policy

When Cassandra nodes fail or become unreachable, the driver automatically and transparently tries other nodes and schedules reconnection to the dead nodes in the background. Because temporary changes in network conditions can also make nodes appear offline, the driver also provides a mechanism to retry queries that fail due to network-related errors. This removes the need to write retry logic in client code.

The driver retries failed queries according to the provided implementation of the `com.datastax.driver.core.RetryPolicy` interface. The `onReadTimeout()`, `onWrite Timeout()`, and `onUnavailable()` operations define the behavior that should be taken when a query fails with the network-related exceptions `ReadTimeoutExcep tion`, `WriteTimeoutException`, or `UnavailableException`, respectively.

DataStax Java Driver Exceptions

The various exceptions and errors that can be generated by the Java driver are collected in the `com.datastax.driver.core.excep tions` package.

The `RetryPolicy` operations return a `RetryDecision`, which indicates whether the query should be retried, and if so, at what consistency level. If the exception is not retried, it can be rethrown, or ignored, in which case the query operation will return an empty `ResultSet`.

The Java driver provides several `RetryPolicy` implementations:

- The `DefaultRetryPolicy` is a conservative implementation that only retries queries under a narrow set of conditions.

- The `FallthroughRetryPolicy` never recommends a retry, always recommending that the exception be rethrown.
- The `DowngradingConsistencyRetryPolicy` is a more aggressive policy which downgrades the consistency level required, as an attempt to get the query to succeed.

A Word on DowngradingConsistencyRetryPolicy

This policy comes with a warning attached: if you are willing to accept a downgraded consistency level under some circumstances, do you really require a higher consistency level for the general case?

The `RetryPolicy` can be set on a `Cluster` when it is built, as shown by the following statement, which selects the `DowngradingConsistencyRetryPolicy` and wraps it with a `LoggingRetryPolicy` so that each retry attempt will be logged:

```
Cluster.builder().withRetryPolicy(new LoggingRetryPolicy(
    DowngradingConsistencyRetryPolicy.INSTANCE));
```

The `RetryPolicy` on a cluster will be used for all queries executed on that cluster, unless overridden on any individual query via the `Statement.setRetryPolicy()` operation.

Speculative execution policy

While it's great to have a retry mechanism that automates our response to network timeouts, we don't often have the luxury of being able to wait for timeouts or even long garbage collection pauses. To speed things up, the driver provides a speculative execution mechanism. If the original coordinator node for a query fails to respond in a predetermined interval, the driver preemptively starts an additional execution of the query against a different coordinator node. When one of the queries returns, the driver provides that response and cancels any other outstanding queries.

The speculative execution behavior is set on a `Cluster` by specifying an implementation of `com.datastax.driver.core.policies.SpeculativeExecutionPolicy`.

The default is the `NoSpeculativeExecutionPolicy`, which does not schedule any speculative executions. There is also a `ConstantSpeculativeExecutionPolicy`, which schedules up to a maximum number of retries with a fixed delay in milliseconds. The `PercentileSpeculativeExecutionPolicy` is a newer policy that is still considered a Beta as of the 3.0 driver release. It triggers speculative executions at a delay based on the observed latency to the original coordinator node.

The policy is set using the `Cluster.Builder`, for example:

```
Cluster.builder().withSpeculativeExecutionPolicy(
  new ConstantSpeculativeExecutionPolicy (
    200, // delay in ms
    3    // max number of speculative executions
);
```

This policy cannot be changed later, or overridden on individual `Statements`.

Address translator

In the examples we've seen so far, each node is identified by the IP address configured as the node's `rpc_address` in its *cassandra.yaml* file. In some deployments, that address may not be reachable by the client. To handle this case, the driver provides a pluggable capability to translate addresses via the `com.datastax.driver.core.policies.AddressTranslator` interface (in versions of the driver prior to 3.0, "translator" is misspelled as "translater" throughout the API).

For example, the Java driver comes with the `IdentityTranslator`, a default translator that leaves the IP address unchanged, and the `EC2MultiRegionAddressTranslator`, which is useful for Amazon EC2 environments. This translator is useful in cases where a client may need to access a node in another data center via a public IP address. We'll discuss EC2 deployments in more detail in Chapter 14.

Metadata

To access the cluster metadata, we invoke the `Cluster.getMetadata()` method. The `com.datastax.driver.core.Metadata` class provides information about the cluster including the cluster name, the schema including keyspaces and tables, and the known hosts in the cluster. We can obtain the name of the cluster via the following code:

```
Metadata metadata = cluster.getMetadata();
System.out.printf("Connected to cluster: %s\n",
  metadata.getClusterName(), cluster.getClusterName());
```

Assigning a Cluster Name

Somewhat confusingly, the `Cluster.Builder` class allows us to assign a name to the `Cluster` instance as it is being built. This name is really just a way for the client to keep track of multiple `Cluster` objects, and can be different than the name known by the nodes within the actual Cassandra cluster. This second cluster name is the one we obtain via the `Metadata` class.

If we do not specify a name for the `Cluster` on construction, it is assigned a default name such as "cluster1", "cluster2", and so on (if multiple clusters are created). You can see this value if you modify the example from before to change `metadata.getClusterName()` to `cluster.getClusterName()`.

Node discovery

A `Cluster` object maintains a permanent connection to one of the contact points, which it uses to maintain information on the state and topology of the cluster. Using this connection, the driver will discover all the nodes currently in the cluster. The driver uses the `com.datastax.driver.core.Host` class to represent each node. The following code shows an example of iterating over the hosts to print out their information:

```
for (Host host : cluster.getMetadata.getAllHosts())
{
  System.out.printf("Data Center: %s; Rack: %s; Host: %s\n",
  host.getDatacenter(), host.getRack(), host.getAddress());
}
```

You can find this code in the class `com.cassandraguide.clients.SimpleConnection Example`.

If we're running a multi-node cluster such as the one we created in Chapter 7 using the Cassandra Cluster Manager (`ccm`), the output of this program will look something like the following:

```
Connected to cluster: my_cluster
Data Center: datacenter1; Rack: rack1; Host: /127.0.0.1
Data Center: datacenter1; Rack: rack1; Host: /127.0.0.2
Data Center: datacenter1; Rack: rack1; Host: /127.0.0.3
```

Using the connection, the driver can also discover all the nodes currently in the cluster. The driver also can detect when new nodes are added to a cluster. You can register a listener to do this by implementing the `Host.StateListener` interface. This requires us to implement several operations such as `onAdd()` and `onRemove()`, which are called when nodes are added or removed from the cluster, as well as `onUp()` and `onDown()`, which indicate when nodes go up or down. Let's look at a portion of a sample class that registers a listener with the cluster:

```
public class ConnectionListenerExample implements Host.StateListener {

  public String getHostString(Host host) {
    return new StringBuilder("Data Center: " + host.getDatacenter() +
      " Rack: " + host.getRack() +
      " Host: " + host.getAddress().toString() +
      " Version: " + host.getCassandraVersion() +
      " State: " + host.getState());
  }

  public void onUp(Host host) {
    System.out.printf("Node is up: %s\n", getHostString(host));
  }

  public void onDown(Host host) {
    System.out.printf("Node is down: %s\n", getHostString(host));
  }

  // other required methods omitted...
  public static void main(String[] args) {

    List<Host.StateListener> list =
      ArrayList<Host.StateListener>();
    list.add(new ConnectionListenerExample());

    Cluster cluster = Cluster.builder().
      addContactPoint("127.0.0.1").
      withInitialListeners(list).
      build();

    cluster.init();
  }
}
```

This code simply prints out a status message when a node goes up or down. You'll note that we make use of a bit more information about each node than our previous example, including the Cassandra version in use by each of the nodes. You can find the full code listing in the class com.cassandraguide.clients.ConnectionListener Example.

Let's run this sample program. Because our listener was added before calling init(), we immediately get the following output:

```
Node added: Data Center: datacenter1 Rack: rack1
  Host: /127.0.0.1 Version: 3.0.0 State: UP
Node added: Data Center: datacenter1 Rack: rack1
  Host: /127.0.0.2 Version: 3.0.0 State: UP
Node added: Data Center: datacenter1 Rack: rack1
  Host: /127.0.0.3 Version: 3.0.0 State: UP
```

Now let's use the `ccm stop` command to shut down one of our nodes, and we'll see something like the following:

```
Node is down: Data Center: datacenter1 Rack: rack1
    Host: /127.0.0.1 Version: 3.0.0 State: DOWN
```

Similarly, if we bring the node back up, we'll see a notification that the node is back online:

```
Node is up: Data Center: datacenter1 Rack: rack1
    Host: /127.0.0.1 Version: 3.0.0 State: UP
```

Schema access

The `Metadata` class also allows the client to learn about the schema in a cluster. The `exportSchemaAsString()` operation creates a `String` describing all of the keyspaces and tables defined in the cluster, including the system keyspaces. This output is equivalent to the `cqlsh` command `DESCRIBE FULL SCHEMA`. Additional operations support browsing the contents of individual keyspaces and tables.

We've previously discussed Cassandra's support for eventual consistency at great length in Chapter 2. Because schema information is itself stored using Cassandra, it is also eventually consistent, and as a result it is possible for different nodes to have different versions of the schema. As of the 3.0 release, the Java driver does not expose the schema version directly, but you can see an example by running the `nodetool describecluster` command:

```
$ ccm node1 nodetool describecluster

Cluster Information:
    Name: test_cluster
    Snitch: org.apache.cassandra.locator.DynamicEndpointSnitch
    Partitioner: org.apache.cassandra.dht.Murmur3Partitioner
    Schema versions:
        ea46580a-4ab4-3e70-b68f-5e57da189ac5:
        [127.0.0.1, 127.0.0.2, 127.0.0.3]
```

This output shows us a couple of things. First, we see that the schema version is a UUID value. This value is calculated based on a hash of all of the keyspace and table definitions a node knows about. The fact that all three nodes share the same schema version means that they all have the same schema defined.

Of course, the schema version in use can change over time as keyspaces and tables are created, altered, and deleted. The driver provides a notification mechanism for clients to learn about these changes by registering a `com.datastax.driver.core.Schema ChangeListener` with the `Cluster`.

You can find an example of these calls by running the example `com.cassandra guide.clients.SimpleSchemaExample`.

In addition to the schema access we've just examined in the Metadata class, the Java driver also provides a facility for managing schema in the com.datastax. driver.core.schemabuilder package. The SchemaBuilder provides a fluent-style API for creating SchemaStatements representing operations such as CREATE, ALTER, and DROP operations on keyspaces, tables, indexes, and user-defined types (UDTs).

For example, the following code could be used to create our hotels keyspace:

```
SchemaStatement hotelSchemaStatement = SchemaBuilder.createTable("hotels").
  addPartitionKey("id", DataType.text()).
  addColumn("name", DataType.text()).
  addColumn("phone", DataType.text()).
  addColumn("address", DataType.text()).
  addColumn("pois", DataType.set(DataType.text()));

session.execute(hotelSchemaStatement);
```

We also import com.datastax.driver.core.DataType so that we can leverage its static operations to define the data types of each column.

Avoid Conflicts When Using Programmatic Schema Definition

Many developers have noted that this programmatic schema management capability can be used as a "lazy initialization" technique for simplified application deployment: if the schema our application uses doesn't exist, we can simply create it programmatically. However, this technique is not recommended when running multiple clients, even with IF NOT EXISTS semantics. CREATE TABLE or ALTER TABLE statements from multiple concurrent clients can result in inconsistent state between nodes, requiring manual repairs.

Debugging and Monitoring

The driver provides features for monitoring and debugging your client's use of Cassandra, including facilities for logging and metrics. There is also a query tracing capability, which we'll learn about in Chapter 12.

Logging

As we will learn in Chapter 10, Cassandra uses a logging API called Simple Logging Facade for Java (SLF4J). The Java driver uses the SLF4J API as well. In order to enable logging on your Java client application, you need to provide a compliant SLF4J implementation on the classpath.

Here's an example of a dependency we can add to our Maven POM file to select the Logback project as the implementation:

```
<dependency>
     <groupId>ch.qos.logback</groupId>
     <artifactId>logback-classic</artifactId>
     <version>1.1.3</version>
</dependency>
```

You can learn more about Logback at *http://logback.qos.ch/*.

By default, the Java driver is set to use the DEBUG logging level, which is fairly verbose. We can configure logging by taking advantage of Logback's configuration mechanism, which supports separate configuration for test and production environments. Logback inspects the classpath first for the file *logback-test.xml* representing the test configuration, and then if no test configuration is found, it searches for the file *logback.xml*.

For more detail on Logback configuration, including sample configuration files for test and production environments, see the configuration page (*http://logback.qos.ch/manual/configuration.html*).

Metrics

Sometimes it can be helpful to monitor the behavior of client applications over time in order to detect abnormal conditions and debug errors. The Java driver collects metrics on its activities and makes these available using the Dropwizard Metrics library (*https://github.com/dropwizard/metrics*). The driver reports metrics on connections, task queues, queries, and errors such as connection errors, read and write timeouts, retries, and speculative executions.

You can access the Java driver metrics locally via the Cluster.getMetrics() operation. The Metrics library also integrates with the Java Management Extensions (JMX) to allow remote monitoring of metrics. JMX reporting is enabled by default, but this can be overridden in the Configuration provided when building a Cluster.

DataStax Python Driver

The most popular early Python client was Pycassa, which was built on the Thrift interface. The Pycassa project is no longer maintained, however, and the recommendation is to use the DataStax Python Driver for all new development.

The first full version of the DataStax Python Driver was introduced January 2014 and provided session management, node discovery, connection pooling, synchronous/asynchronous queries, load balancing, query tracing, metrics (using the Scales library), logging, authentication and SSL. Features such as support for Cassandra 2.1 and later paging, lightweight transactions, and Python 3 support were added in the 2.0 release in May 2014. The Python Driver is compatible with Cassandra releases 1.2

and later and runs on Python 2.6, 2.7, 3.3, and 3.4. The driver runs on Linux, Mac OS, and Windows.

The official documentation for the driver is available at the DataStax website (*https://datastax.github.io/python-driver/index.html*), while the source driver is available on GitHub (*https://github.com/datastax/python-driver*). You can install the driver by running the Python installer *pip*:

```
$ pip install cassandra-driver
```

Installing Python and PIP

To use the example code, you'll need a compatible version of Python for your platform (as listed earlier), and `pip`. You can install `pip` by downloading the script *https://bootstrap.pypa.io/get-pip.py* and running the command `python get-pip.py`. You may need to run this command via `sudo` on Unix systems.

Here's a simple example of connecting to a cluster and inserting a row in the `hotels` table:

```
from cassandra.cluster import Cluster
cluster = Cluster(['127.0.0.1'])
session = cluster.connect('hotel')
session.execute("""
  insert into hotels (id, name, phone)
  values (%s, %s, %s)
  """
  ('AZ123', 'Super Hotel at WestWorld', '1-888-999-9999')
)
```

The Python driver includes an object mapper called *cqlengine*, which is accessed through the `cassandra.cqlengine.models.Model` class. The Python driver also makes use of third party libraries for performance, compression, and metrics. Some C extensions using Cython are used to speed up performance. The driver may also be run on PyPy, an alternative Python runtime that uses a JIT compiler. The reduced CPU consumption leads to improved throughput, up to two times better than regular Python. Compression requires installation of either the `lz4` or `python-snappy` libraries, depending on the desired algorithm.

DataStax Node.js Driver

The original Thrift-based client bindings for Node.js were provided by Helenus, and the *node-cassandra-cql* package by Jorge Bay subsequently provided a CQL native client.

The DataStax Node.js driver, which was officially available in October 2014, is based on *node-cassandra-cql*, adding in the standard features common across the other DataStax drivers for Apache Cassandra. You can access the driver at *https://github.com/datastax/nodejs-driver*.

The Node.js driver is installed via the node package manager (NPM):

```
$ npm install cassandra-driver
```

 **Installing the Node.js Runtime and Package Manager**

If you don't have experience using Node, you can get an installation for your platform at *https://nodejs.org* that includes both Node.js and NPM. These are typically installed at */usr/local/bin/node* and */usr/local/bin/npm* on Unix systems.

The syntax is a bit different, in that you access a `Client` object instead of a `Cluster` as in other language drivers. The other constructs are very similar:

```
var cassandra = require('cassandra-driver');
var client = new cassandra.Client({ contactPoints: ['127.0.0.1'],
  keyspace: 'hotel'});
```

Building and executing a parameterized query looks like this:

```
var query = 'SELECT * FROM hotels WHERE id=?';
client.execute(query, ['AZ123'], function(err, result) {
  assert.ifError(err);
  console.log('got hotel with name ' + result.rows[0].name);
});
```

DataStax Ruby Driver

Fauna was an early Thrift-based Ruby client created for Cassandra by Twitter. Starting in early 2013, Theo Hultberg led development of the `cql-rb` gem, which became the basis of the DataStax Ruby Driver released in November 2014. You can access the Ruby driver at *https://github.com/datastax/ruby-driver*.

You can install the driver using Ruby Gems:

```
$ gem install cassandra-driver
```

Here's an example of creating a cluster and session and executing a simple asynchronous query that iterates over the contents of our `hotels` table:

```
require 'cassandra'

cluster = Cassandra.cluster(hosts: ['127.0.0.1'])
session = cluster.connect('hotel')
```

```
future = session.execute_async('SELECT * FROM hotels')
future.on_success do |rows|
  rows.each do |row|
    puts "Hotel: #{row['id']} Name: #{row['name']}"
  end
end
future.join
```

The Ruby driver runs on standard Ruby, but can also be run on JRuby 1.7 or later for improved performance. The driver runs on Linux, Mac OS, but Windows is not supported.

DataStax C# Driver

First released in July 2013, the DataStax C# driver provides support for Windows clients using the .NET framework. For this reason, it is also frequently referred to as the ".NET Driver."

The C# Driver is available on NuGet, the package manager for the Microsoft development platform. Within PowerShell, run the following command at the Package Manager Console:

```
PM> Install-Package CassandraCSharpDriver
```

To use the driver, create a new project in Visual Studio and add a using directive that references the Cassandra namespace. The following example connects to our hotel keyspace and inserts a new record into the hotels table:

```
Cluster Cluster = Cluster.Builder()
  .AddContactPoint("127.0.0.1")  .Build();

ISession Session = Cluster.Connect("hotel");
Session.Execute(
  "INSERT INTO hotels (id, name, phone) " +
  "VALUES (" +
    "'AZ123'," +
    "'Super Hotel at WestWorld'," +
    "'1-888-999-9999'," +
    ";");
```

The C# driver integrates with Language Integrated Query (LINQ), a Microsoft .NET Framework component that adds query capabilities to .NET languages; there is a separate object mapper available as well.

A Sample Application: KillrVideo

Luke Tillman, Patrick McFadin, and others have created a video sharing application called KillrVideo (*http://www.killrvideo.com/*). KillrVideo is an open source .NET application built using the DataStax C# driver and deployed to Microsoft's Azure cloud. It also makes use of DataStax Enterprise features such as integration with Apache Spark and Apache SOLR. You can download the source on GitHub (*https://github.com/luketillman/killrvideo-csharp*).

DataStax C/C++ Driver

The DataStax C/C++ Driver was released in February 2014. You can access the driver at *https://github.com/datastax/cpp-driver*, and the documentation at *http://datastax.github.io/cpp-driver*.

The C/C++ Driver is a bit different than the other drivers in that its API focuses on asynchronous operations to the exclusion of synchronous operations. For example, creating a session is an asynchronous operation which returns a future:

```
#include <cassandra.h>
#include <stdio.h>

int main() {
  CassFuture* connect_future = NULL;
  CassCluster* cluster = cass_cluster_new();
  CassSession* session = cass_session_new();

  cass_cluster_set_contact_points(cluster, "127.0.0.1");

  connect_future = cass_session_connect(session, cluster);

  if (cass_future_error_code(connect_future) == CASS_OK) {
  /* proceed with processing... */
```

As shown in the example, however, synchronous semantics are easily supported by immediately blocking on the future. Building and executing a simple query looks like this:

```
CassStatement* select_statement
  = cass_statement_new("SELECT * "
                        "FROM hotel.hotels", 0);

CassFuture* hotel_select_future =
  cass_session_execute(session, select_statement);

if(cass_future_error_code(result_future) == CASS_OK) {

  const CassResult* result = cass_future_get_result(result_future);
```

```
    CassIterator* rows = cass_iterator_from_result(result);

    while(cass_iterator_next(rows)) {
      const CassRow* row = cass_iterator_get_row(rows);
      const CassValue* value =
        cass_row_get_column_by_name(row, "name");
      const char* name;
      size_t name_length;
      cass_value_get_string(value, &name, &name_length);
      printf("Hotel_name: '%.*s'\n", (int)name_length, name);
    }
  }
```

Remember that memory management is very important in C/C++ programs; we've omitted statements to free objects such as clusters, sessions, futures, and results for brevity.

The C/C++ driver uses the *libuv* library for asynchronous I/O operations, and optionally uses the OpenSSL library if needed for encrypted client-node connections. Instructions for compilation and linking vary by platform, so see the driver documentation for details.

DataStax PHP Driver

The DataStax PHP driver supports the PHP server side scripting language. Released in 2015, the driver wraps the DataStax C/C++ Driver and supports both Unix and Windows environments.

There are multiple installation options for the driver, but the simplest is to use the PECL repository:

```
pecl install cassandra
```

The following short example selects rows from the hotels table and prints out their values using the asynchronous API:

```
<?php

$keyspace  = 'hotel';
$session   = $cluster->connect($keyspace);
$statement = new Cassandra\SimpleStatement(
    'SELECT * FROM hotels'
);

$future    = $session->executeAsync($statement);
$result    = $future->get();
foreach ($result as $row) {
  printf("id: %s, name: %s, phone: %s\n",
    $row['id'], $row['name'], $row['phone']);
}
```

You can access the PHP driver documentation at *https://github.com/datastax/php-driver*, and the source code at *https://datastax.github.io/php-driver*.

Summary

You should now have an understanding of the various client interfaces available for Cassandra, the features they provide, and how to install and use them. We gave particular attention to the DataStax Java driver in order to get some hands-on experience, which should serve you well even if you choose to use one of the other DataStax drivers. We'll continue to use the DataStax Java driver in the coming chapters as we do more reading and writing.

Reading and Writing Data

Now that we understand the data model and how to use a simple client, we'll dig deeper into the different kinds of queries you can perform in Cassandra to read and write data. We'll also take a look behind the scenes to see how Cassandra handles your read and write queries.

As with the previous chapter, we've included code samples using the DataStax Java Driver to help illustrate how these concepts work in practice.

Writing

Let's start by noting some basic properties of writing data to Cassandra. First, writing data is very fast in Cassandra, because its design does not require performing disk reads or seeks. The memtables and SSTables save Cassandra from having to perform these operations on writes, which slow down many databases. All writes in Cassandra are append-only.

Because of the database commit log and hinted handoff design, the database is always writable, and within a column family, writes are always atomic.

Insert, Update, and Upsert

Because Cassandra uses an append model, there is no fundamental difference between the insert and update operations. If you insert a row that has the same primary key as an existing row, the row is replaced. If you update a row and the primary key does not exist, Cassandra creates it.

For this reason, it is often said that Cassandra supports *upsert*, meaning that inserts and updates are treated the same, with one minor exception which we'll see on lightweight transactions.

Write Consistency Levels

Cassandra's tuneable consistency levels mean that you can specify in your queries how much consistency you require on writes. A higher consistency level means that more replica nodes need to respond, indicating that the write has completed. Higher consistency levels also come with a reduction in availability, as more nodes must be operational for the write to succeed. The implications of using the different consistency levels on writes are shown in Table 9-1.

Table 9-1. Write consistency levels

Consistency level	Implication
ANY	Ensure that the value is written to a minimum of one replica node before returning to the client, allowing hints to count as a write.
ONE, TWO, THREE	Ensure that the value is written to the commit log and memtable of at least one, two, or three nodes before returning to the client.
LOCAL_ONE	Similar to ONE, with the additional requirement that the responding node is in the local data center.
QUORUM	Ensure that the write was received by at least a majority of replicas ((replication factor / 2) + 1).
LOCAL_QUORUM	Similar to QUORUM, where the responding nodes are in the local data center.
EACH_QUORUM	Ensure that a QUORUM of nodes respond in each data center.
ALL	Ensure that the number of nodes specified by replication factor received the write before returning to the client. If even one replica is unresponsive to the write operation, fail the operation.

The most notable consistency level for writes is the ANY level. This level means that the write is guaranteed to reach at least one node, but *it allows a hint to count as a successful write.* That is, if you perform a write operation and the node that the operation targets for that value is down, the server will make a note to itself, called a *hint*, which it will store until that node comes back up. Once the node is up, the server will detect this, look to see whether it has any writes that it saved for later in the form of a hint, and then write the value to the revived node. In many cases, the node that makes the hint actually *isn't* the node that stores it; instead, it sends it off to one of the non-replica neighbors of the node that is down.

Using the consistency level of ONE on writes means that the write operation will be written to both the commit log and the memtable. That means that writes at ONE are durable, so this level is the minimum level to use to achieve fast performance and durability. If this node goes down immediately after the write operation, the value will have been written to the commit log, which can be replayed when the server is brought back up to ensure that it still has the value.

The Cassandra Write Path

The *write path* describes how data modification queries initiated by clients are processed, eventually resulting in the data being stored on disk. We'll examine the write path both in terms of interactions between nodes, and the internal process of storing data on an individual node. An overview of the write path interactions between nodes in a multi-data center cluster is shown in Figure 9-1.

The write path begins when a client initiates a write query to a Cassandra node which serves as the coordinator for this request. The coordinator node uses the partitioner to identify which nodes in the cluster are replicas, according to the replication factor for the keyspace. The coordinator node may itself be a replica, especially if the client is using a token-aware driver. If the coordinator knows that there are not enough replicas up to satisfy the requested consistency level, it returns an error immediately.

Next, the coordinator node sends simultaneous write requests to all replicas for the data being written. This ensures that all nodes will get the write as long as they are up. Nodes that are down will not have consistent data, but they will be repaired via one of the anti-entropy mechanisms: hinted handoff, read repair, or anti-entropy repair.

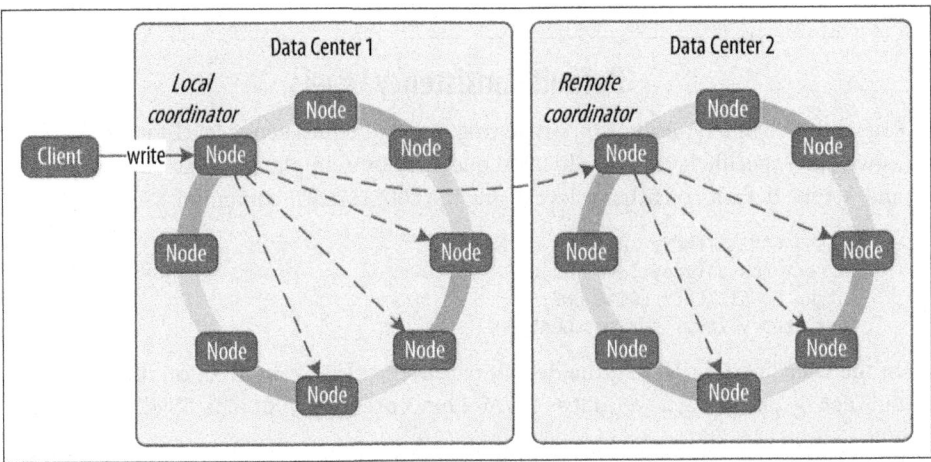

Figure 9-1. Interactions between nodes on the write path

If the cluster spans multiple data centers, the *local coordinator* node selects a *remote coordinator* in each of the other data centers to coordinate the write to the replicas in that data center. Each of the remote replicas responds directly to the original coordinator node.

The coordinator waits for the replicas to respond. Once a sufficient number of replicas have responded to satisfy the consistency level, the coordinator acknowledges the write to the client. If a replica doesn't respond within the timeout, it is presumed to be down, and a hint is stored for the write. A hint does not count as successful replica write unless the consistency level ANY is used.

Figure 9-2 depicts the interactions that take place within each replica node to process a write request.

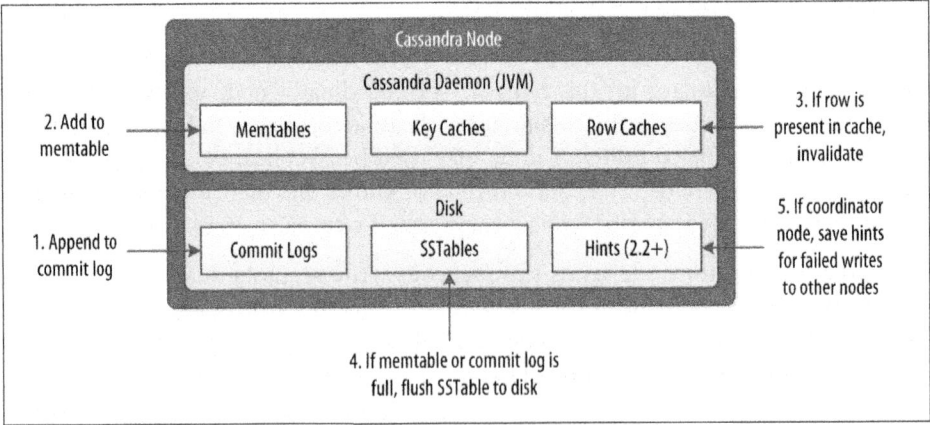

Figure 9-2. Interactions within a node on the write path

First, the replica node receives the write request and immediately writes the data to the commit log. Next, the replica node writes the data to a memtable. If row caching is used and the row is in the cache, the row is invalidated. We'll discuss caching in more detail under the read path.

If the write causes either the commit log or memtable to pass their maximum thresholds, a flush is scheduled to run. We'll learn how to tune these thresholds in Chapter 12.

At this point, the write is considered to have succeeded and the node can reply to the coordinator node or client.

After returning, the node executes a flush if one was scheduled. The contents of each memtable are stored as SSTables on disk and the commit log is cleared. After the flush completes, additional tasks are scheduled to check if compaction is needed and then a compaction is performed if necessary.

More Detail on the Write Path

Of course, this is a simple overview of the write path that doesn't take into account variants such as counter modifications and materialized views. Writes to tables with materialized views are more complex because partitions must be locked. Cassandra leverages logged batches internally in order to maintain materialized views.

For a more in-depth treatment of the write path, consult Michael Edge's excellent description on the Apache Cassandra Wiki at *https://wiki.apache.org/cassandra/WritePathForUsers*.

Writing Files to Disk

Let's examine a few more details on the files Cassandra writes to disk, including commit logs and SSTables.

Commit log files

Cassandra writes commit logs to the filesystem as binary files. The commit log files are found under the *$CASSANDRA_HOME/data/commitlog* directory.

Commit log files are named according to the pattern *CommitLog-<version>-<timestamp>.log*. For example: *CommitLog-6-1451831400468.log*. The *version* is an integer representing the commit log format. For example, the version for the 3.0 release is 6. You can find the versions in use by release in the org.apache.cassandra .db.commitlog.CommitLogDescriptor class.

SSTable files

When SSTables are written to the filesystem during a flush, there are actually several files that are written per SSTable. Let's take a look at the *$CASSANDRA_HOME/data/data* directory to see how the files are organized on disk.

Forcing SSTables to Disk

If you're following along with the exercises in this book on a real Cassandra node, you may want to execute the `nodetool flush` command at this point, as you may not have entered enough data yet for Cassandra to have flushed data to disk automatically. We'll learn more about this command in Chapter 11.

Looking in the *data* directory, you'll see a directory for each keyspace. These directories, in turn, contain a directory for each table, consisting of the table name plus a UUID. The purpose of the UUID is to distinguish between multiple schema versions, because the schema of a table can be altered over time.

Each of these directories contain SSTable files which contain the stored data. Here is an example directory path: *hotel/hotels-3677bbb0155811e5899aa9fac1d00bce*.

Each SSTable is represented by multiple files that share a common naming scheme. The files are named according to the pattern *<version>-<generation>-<implementation>-<component>.db*. The significance of the pattern is as follows:

- The *version* is a two-character sequence representing the major/minor version of the SSTable format. For example, the version for the 3.0 release is *ma*. You can learn more about various versions in the `org.apache.cassandra.io.sstable.Descriptor` class.
- The *generation* is an index number which is incremented every time a new SSTable is created for a table.
- The implementation is a reference to the implementation of the `org.apache.cassandra.io.sstable.format.SSTableWriter` interface in use. As of the 3.0 release the value is "big", which references the "Bigtable format" found in the `org.apache.cassandra.io.sstable.format.big.BigFormat` class.

Each SSTable is broken up into multiple files or *components*. These are the components as of the 3.0 release:

*-Data.db
These are the files that store the actual data and are the only files that are preserved by Cassandra's backup mechanisms, which we'll learn about in Chapter 11.

*-CompressionInfo.db
Provides metadata about the compression of the *Data.db* file.

*-Digest.adler32
Contains a checksum for the **-Data.db* file. (Releases prior to 3.0 use CRC 32 checksums and the *.crc32* extension.)

*-Filter.db
Contains the bloom filter for this SSTable.

*-Index.db
Provides row and column offsets within the corresponding **-Data.db* file.

Summary.db
A sample of the index for even faster reads.

Statistics.db
Stores statistics about the SSTable which are used by the `nodetool tablehisto grams` command.

TOC.txt
Lists the file components for this SSTable.

Older releases support different versions and filenames. Releases prior to 2.2 prepend the keyspace and table name to each file, while 2.2 and later leave these out because they can be inferred from the directory name.

We'll investigate some tools for working with SSTable files in Chapter 11.

Lightweight Transactions

As we've discussed previously in Chapter 1, Cassandra and many other NoSQL databases do not support transactions with full ACID semantics supported by relational databases. However, Cassandra does provide two mechanisms that offer some transactional behavior: *lightweight transactions* and *batches*.

Cassandra's lightweight transaction (LWT) mechanism uses the Paxos algorithm described in Chapter 6. LWTs were introduced in the 2.0 release. LWTs support the following semantics:

- The scope of each transaction is limited to a single partition.
- Each transaction consists of both a read and a write, also known as a "compare and set" operation. The set is only performed if the comparison is successful.
- If a transaction fails because the existing values did not match the one you expected, Cassandra will include the current ones so you can decide whether to retry or abort without needing to make an extra request.
- The USING TIMESTAMP option is not supported.

Let's say we wanted to create a record for a new hotel, using the data model we introduced in Chapter 5. We want to make sure that we're not overwriting a hotel with the same ID, so we add the IF NOT EXISTS syntax to our insert command:

```
cqlsh> INSERT INTO hotel.hotels (id, name, phone) VALUES (
  'AZ123', 'Super Hotel at WestWorld', '1-888-999-9999') IF NOT EXISTS;

 [applied]
-----------
    True
```

This command checks to see if there is a record with the partition key, which for this table consists of the hotel_id. So let's find out what happens when we execute this command a second time:

```
cqlsh> INSERT INTO hotel.hotels (id, name, phone) VALUES (
  'AZ123', 'Super Hotel at WestWorld', '1-888-999-9999') IF NOT EXISTS;

 [applied] | id    | address | name                     | phone           | pois
-----------+-------+---------+--------------------------+-----------------+------
    False | AZ123 |    null | Super Hotel at WestWorld | 1-888-999-9999 | null
```

In this case, the transaction fails, as there is already a hotel with the ID "AZ123", and cqlsh helpfully echoes back a row containing a failure indication and the values we tried to enter.

It works in a similar way for updates. For example, we might use the following statement to make sure we're changing the name for this hotel:

```
cqlsh> UPDATE hotel.hotels SET name='Super Hotel Suites at WestWorld'
... WHERE id='AZ123' IF name='Super Hotel at WestWorld';

 [applied]
-----------
    True

cqlsh> UPDATE hotel.hotels SET name='Super Hotel Suites at WestWorld'
... WHERE id='AZ123' IF name='Super Hotel at WestWorld';

 [applied] | name
-----------+-------------------------------------
    False | Super Hotel Suites at WestWorld
```

Similar to what we saw with multiple INSERT statements, entering the same UPDATE statement again fails because the value has already been set. Because of Cassandra's upsert model, the IF NOT EXISTS syntax available on INSERT and the IF x=y syntax on UPDATE represent the only semantic difference between these two operations.

Using Transactions on Schema Creation

CQL also supports the use of the IF NOT EXISTS option on the creation of keyspaces and tables. This is especially useful if you are scripting multiple schema updates.

Let's implement the hotel creation example from before using the DataStax Java Driver. When executing a conditional statement the ResultSet will contain a single Row with a column named applied of type boolean. This tells whether the conditional statement was successful or not. We can also use the wasApplied() operation on the statement:

```
SimpleStatement hotelInsert = session.newSimpleStatement(
  "INSERT INTO hotels (id, name, phone) VALUES (?, ?, ?) IF NOT EXISTS",
  "AZ123", "Super Hotel at WestWorld", "1-888-999-9999");

ResultSet hotelInsertResult = session.execute(hotelInsert);

boolean wasApplied = hotelInsertResult.wasApplied());

if (wasApplied) {
  Row row = hotelInsertResult.one();
  row.getBool("applied");
}
```

Conditional write statements can have a *serial consistency level* in addition to the regular consistency level. The serial consistency level determines the number of nodes that must reply in the Paxos phase of the write, when the participating nodes are negotiating about the proposed write. The two available options are shown in Table 9-2.

Table 9-2. Serial consistency levels

Consistency level	Implication
SERIAL	This is the default serial consistency level, indicating that a quorum of nodes must respond.
LOCAL_SERIAL	Similar to SERIAL, but indicates that the transaction will only involve nodes in the local data center.

The serial consistency level can apply on reads as well. If Cassandra detects that a query is reading data that is part of an uncommitted transaction, it commits the transaction as part of the read, according to the specified serial consistency level.

You can set a default serial consistency level for all statements in `cqlsh` using the `SERIAL CONSISTENCY` statement, or in the DataStax Java Driver using the `Query Options.setSerialConsistencyLevel()` operation.

Batches

While lightweight transactions are limited to a single partition, Cassandra provides a *batch* mechanism that allows you to group modifications to multiple partitions into a single statement.

The semantics of the batch operation are as follows:

- Only modification statements (`INSERT`, `UPDATE`, or `DELETE`) may be included in a batch.
- Batches are atomic—that is, if the batch is accepted, all of the statements in a batch will succeed eventually. This is why Cassandra's batches are sometimes referred to as *atomic batches* or *logged batches*.
- All updates in a batch belonging to a given partition key are performed in isolation, but there is no isolation guarantee across partitions. This means that modifications to different partitions may be read before the batch completes.
- Batches are not a transaction mechanism, but you can include lightweight transaction statements in a batch. Multiple lightweight transactions in a batch must apply to the same partition.
- Counter modifications are only allowed within a special form of batch known as a *counter batch*. A counter batch can only contain counter modifications.

Deprecation of Unlogged Batches

In releases prior to 3.0, Cassandra supported *unlogged batches*, or batches in which the steps involving the batchlog were skipped. The drawback of unlogged batches was that there was no guarantee that batches would complete successfully, which could leave the database in an inconsistent state.

Using a batch saves back and forth traffic between the client and the coordinator node, as the client is able to group multiple statements in a single query. However, the batch places additional work on the coordinator to orchestrate the execution of the various statements.

Cassandra's batches are a good fit for use cases such as making multiple updates to a single partition, or keeping multiple tables in sync. A good example is making modifications to denormalized tables that store the same data for different access patterns.

Batches Aren't for Bulk Loading

First time users often confuse batches for a way to get faster performance for bulk updates. This is definitely not the case—batches actually decrease performance and can cause garbage collection pressure.

Let's look at an example batch that we might use to insert a new hotel in our denormalized table design. We use the CQL BEGIN BATCH and APPLY BATCH keywords to surround the statements in our batch:

```
cqlsh> BEGIN BATCH
    INSERT INTO hotel.hotels (id, name, phone)
      VALUES ('AZ123', 'Super Hotel at WestWorld', '1-888-999-9999');
    INSERT INTO hotel.hotels_by_poi (poi_name, id, name, phone)
      VALUES ('West World', 'AZ123', 'Super Hotel at WestWorld',
      '1-888-999-9999');
APPLY BATCH;
```

The DataStax Java driver supports batches through the com.datastax. driver.core.BatchStatement class. Here's an example of what the same batch would look like in a Java client:

```
SimpleStatement hotelInsert = session.newSimpleStatement(
    "INSERT INTO hotels (id, name, phone) VALUES (?, ?, ?)",
    "AZ123", "Super Hotel at WestWorld", "1-888-999-9999");
SimpleStatement hotelsByPoiInsert = session.newSimpleStatement(
    "INSERT INTO hotels_by_poi (poi_name, id, name, phone)
    VALUES (?, ?, ?, ?)", "WestWorld", "AZ123",
    "Super Hotel at WestWorld", "1-888-999-9999");

BatchStatement hotelBatch = new BatchStatement();
hotelBatch.add(hotelsByPoiInsert);
hotelBatch.add(hotelInsert);

ResultSet hotelInsertResult = session.execute(hotelBatch);
```

You can also create batches using the QueryBuilder.batch() operation by passing other Statements. You can find code samples for working with BatchStatement and com.cassandraguide.readwrite.BatchStatementExample.

Creating Counter Batches in DataStax Drivers

The DataStax drivers do not provide separate mechanisms for counter batches. Instead, you must simply remember to create batches that include only counter modifications or only noncounter modifications.

Here's how a batch works under the covers: the coordinator sends a copy of the batch called a *batchlog* to two other nodes, where it is stored in the `system.batchlog` table. The coordinator then executes all of the statements in the batch, and deletes the batchlog from the other nodes after the statements are completed.

If the coordinator should fail to complete the batch, the other nodes have a copy in their batchlog and are therefore able to replay the batch. Each node checks its batchlog once a minute to see if there are any batches that should have completed. To give ample time for the coordinator to complete any in-progress batches, Cassandra uses a grace period from the timestamp on the batch statement equal to twice the value of the `write_request_timeout_in_ms` property. Any batches that are older than this grace period will be replayed and then deleted from the remaining node. The second batchlog node provides an additional layer of redundancy, ensuring high reliability of the batch mechanism.

Cassandra enforces limits on the size of batch statements to prevent them from becoming arbitrarily large and impacting the performance and stability of the cluster. The *cassandra.yaml* file contains two properties that control how this works: the `batch_size_warn_threshold_in_kb` property defines the level at which a node will log at the WARN log level that it has received a large batch, while any batch exceeding the value set `batch_size_fail_threshold_in_kb` will be rejected and result in error notification to the client. The batch size is measured in terms of the length of the CQL query statement. The warning threshold defaults to 5KB, while the fail threshold defaults to 50KB.

Reading

There are a few basic properties of Cassandra's read capability that are worth noting. First, it's easy to read data because clients can connect to any node in the cluster to perform reads, without having to know whether a particular node acts as a replica for that data. If a client connects to a node that doesn't have the data it's trying to read, the node it's connected to will act as coordinator node to read the data from a node that does have it, identified by token ranges.

In Cassandra, reads are generally slower than writes. To fulfill read operations, Cassandra typically has to perform seeks, but you may be able to keep more data in memory by adding nodes, using compute instances with more memory, and using Cassandra's caches. Cassandra also has to wait for responses synchronously on reads (based on consistency level and replication factor), and then perform read repairs as necessary.

Read Consistency Levels

The consistency levels for read operations are similar to the write consistency levels, but their meanings are slightly different. A higher consistency level means that more nodes need to respond to the query, giving you more assurance that the values present on each replica are the same. If two nodes respond with different timestamps, the newest value wins, and that's what will be returned to the client. In the background, Cassandra will then perform what's called a *read repair*: it takes notice of the fact that one or more replicas responded to a query with an outdated value, and updates those replicas with the most current value so that they are all consistent.

The possible consistency levels, and the implications of specifying each one for read queries, are shown in Table 9-3.

Table 9-3. Read consistency levels

Consistency level	Implication
ONE, TWO, THREE	Immediately return the record held by the first node(s) that respond to the query. A background thread is created to check that record against the same record on other replicas. If any are out of date, a *read repair* is then performed to sync them all to the most recent value.
LOCAL_ONE	Similar to ONE, with the additional requirement that the responding node is in the local data center.
QUORUM	Query all nodes. Once a majority of replicas ((replication factor / 2) + 1) respond, return to the client the value with the most recent timestamp. Then, if necessary, perform a read repair in the background on all remaining replicas.
LOCAL_QUORUM	Similar to QUORUM, where the responding nodes are in the local data center.
EACH_QUORUM	Ensure that a QUORUM of nodes respond in each data center.
ALL	Query all nodes. Wait for all nodes to respond, and return to the client the record with the most recent timestamp. Then, if necessary, perform a read repair in the background. If any nodes fail to respond, fail the read operation.

As you can see from the table, the ANY consistency level is not supported for read operations. Notice that the implication of consistency level ONE is that the first node to respond to the read operation is the value that the client will get—even if it is out of date. The read repair operation is performed after the record is returned, so any subsequent reads will all have a consistent value, regardless of the responding node.

Another item worth noting is in the case of consistency level ALL. If you specify ALL, then you're saying that you require all replicas to respond, so if any node with that record is down or otherwise fails to respond before the timeout, the read operation fails. A node is considered unresponsive if it does not respond to a query before the value specified by rpc_timeout_in_ms in the configuration file. The default is 10 seconds.

Aligning Read and Write Consistency Levels

The read and write consistency levels you choose to use in your applications are an example of the flexibility Cassandra provides us to make trade-offs between consistency, availability, and performance.

As we learned in Chapter 6, Cassandra can guarantee strong consistency on reads by using read and write consistency levels whose sum exceeds the replication factor. One simple way to achieve this is to require QUORUM for reads and writes. For example, on a keyspace with a replication factor of 3, QUORUM represents a response from 2 out of three nodes. Because 2 + 2 > 3, strong consistency is guaranteed.

If you are willing to sacrifice strong consistency in order to support increased throughput and more tolerance for downed nodes, you can use lesser consistency levels. For example, using QUORUM for writes and ONE for reads doesn't guarantee strong consistency, as 2 + 1 is merely equal to 3.

Thinking this through practically, if you are only guaranteed writes to two out of three replicas, there is certainly a chance that one of the replicas did not receive the write and has not yet been repaired, and a read at consistency level ONE could go to that very node.

The Cassandra Read Path

Now let's take a look at what happens when a client requests data. This is known as the *read path*. We'll describe the read path from the perspective of a query for a single partition key, starting with the interactions between nodes shown in Figure 9-3.

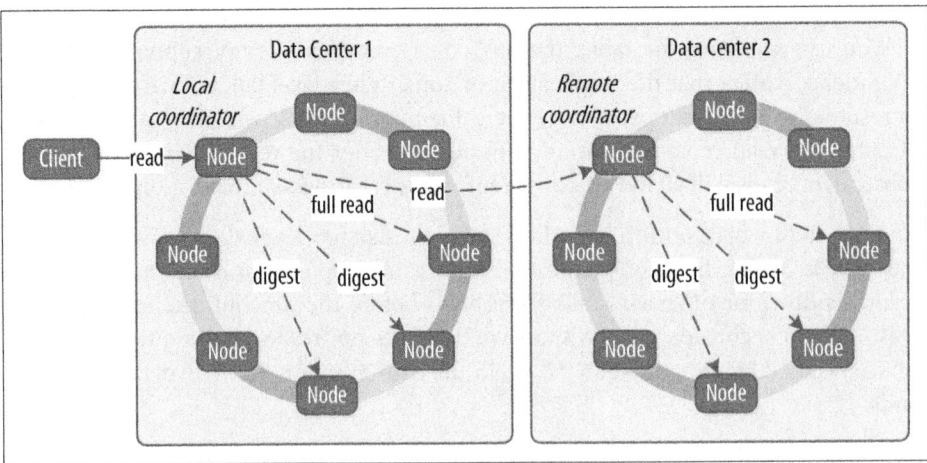

Figure 9-3. Interactions between nodes on the read path

The read path begins when a client initiates a read query to the coordinator node. As on the write path, the coordinator uses the partitioner to determine the replicas and checks that there are enough replicas up to satisfy the requested consistency level. Another similarity to the write path is that a remote coordinator is selected per data center for any read queries that involve multiple data centers.

If the coordinator is not itself a replica, the coordinator then sends a read request to the fastest replica, as determined by the dynamic snitch. The coordinator node also sends a *digest request* to the other replicas. A digest request is similar to a standard read request, except the replicas return a digest, or hash, of the requested data.

The coordinator calculates the digest hash for data returned from the fastest replica and compares it to the digests returned from the other replicas. If the digests are consistent, and the desired consistency level has been met, then the data from the fastest replica can be returned. If the digests are not consistent, then the coordinator must perform a read repair, as discussed in the following section.

Figure 9-4 shows the interactions that take place within each replica node to process read requests.

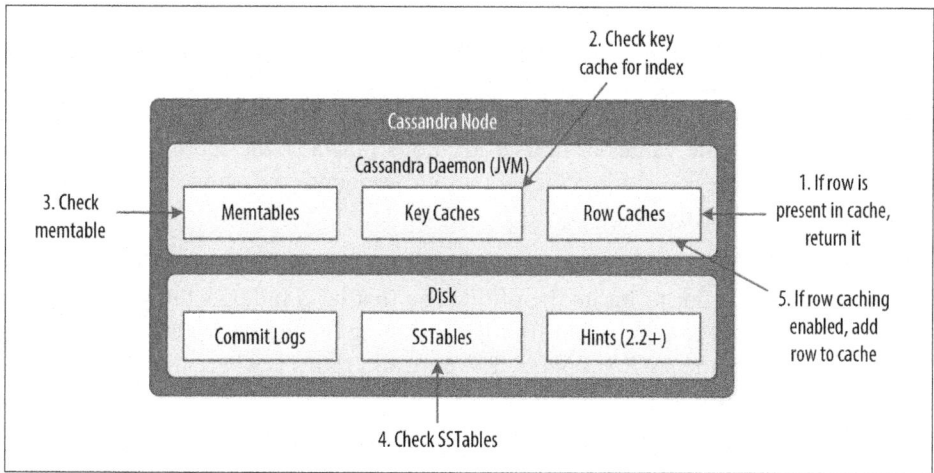

Figure 9-4. Interactions within a node on the read path

When the replica node receives the read request, it first checks the row cache. If the row cache contains the data, it can be returned immediately. The row cache helps speed read performance for rows that are accessed frequently. We'll discuss the pros and cons of row caching in Chapter 12.

If the data is not in the row cache, the replica node searches for the data in memtables and SSTables. There is only a single memtable for a given table, so that part of the search is straightforward. However, there are potentially many physical SSTables for a single Cassandra table, each of which may contain a portion of the requested data.

Cassandra implements several features to optimize the SSTable search: key caching, Bloom filters, SSTable indexes, and summary indexes.

The first step in searching SSTables on disk is to use a Bloom filter to determine whether requested partition does not exist in a given SSTable, which would make it unnecessary to search that SSTable.

Tuning Bloom Filters

Cassandra maintains a copy of Bloom filters in memory, although you may remember from our earlier discussion of files from above that the Bloom filters are stored in files alongside the SSTable data files so that they don't have to be recalculated if the node is restarted.

The Bloom filter does not guarantee that the SSTable contains the partition, only that it might contain it. You can set the `bloom_fil ter_fp_chance` property on each table to control the percentage of false positives that the Bloom filter reports. This increased accuracy comes at the cost of additional memory use.

If the SSTable passes the Bloom filter, Cassandra checks the key cache to see if it contains the offset of the partition key in the SSTable. The key cache is implemented as a map structure in which the keys are a combination of the SSTable file descriptor and partition key, and the values are offset locations into SSTable files. The key cache helps to eliminate seeks within SSTable files for frequently accessed data, because the data can be read directly.

If the offset is not obtained from the key cache, Cassandra uses a two-level index stored on disk in order to locate the offset. The first level index is the *partition summary*, which is used to obtain an offset for searching for the partition key within the second level index, the *partition index*. The partition index is where the offset into the SSTable for the partition key is stored.

If the offset for the partition key is found, Cassandra accesses the SSTable at the specified offset and starts reading data.

Once data has been obtained from all of the SSTables, Cassandra merges the SSTable data and memtable data by selecting the value with the latest timestamp for each requested column. Any tombstones encountered are ignored.

Finally, the merged data can be added to the row cache (if enabled) and returned to the client or coordinator node. A digest request is handled in much the same way as a regular read request, with the additional step that a digest is calculated on the result data and returned instead of the data itself.

More Detail on the Read Path

For more detail on the read path, consult the Apache Cassandra Wiki (*https://wiki.apache.org/cassandra/ReadPathForUsers*).

Read Repair

Here's how read repair works: the coordinator makes a full read request from all of the replica nodes. The coordinator node merges the data by selecting a value for each requested column. It compares the values returned from the replicas and returns the value that has the latest timestamp. If Cassandra finds different values stored with the same timestamp, it will compare the values lexicographically and choose the one that has the greater value. This case should be exceedingly rare. The merged data is the value that is returned to the client.

Asynchronously, the coordinator identifies any replicas that return obsolete data and issues a read-repair request to each of these replicas to update their data based on the merged data.

The read repair may be performed either before or after the return to the client. If you are using one of the two stronger consistency levels (QUORUM or ALL), then the read repair happens *before* data is returned to the client. If the client specifies a weak consistency level (such as ONE), then the read repair is optionally performed in the background after returning to the client. The percentage of reads that result in background repairs for a given table is determined by the read_repair_chance and dc_local_read_repair_chance options for the table.

Range Queries, Ordering and Filtering

So far in our travels we've confined our read queries to very simple examples. Let's take a look at more of the options that Cassandra provides on the SELECT command, such as the WHERE and ORDER BY clauses.

First, let's examine how to use the WHERE clause that Cassandra provides for reading ranges of data within a partition, sometimes called *slices*.

In order to do a range query, however, it will help to have some data to work with. Although we don't have a lot of data yet, we can quickly get some by using one of Cassandra's bulk loading tools.

Bulk Loading Options

In using Cassandra, you'll often find it useful to be able to load test or reference data into a cluster. Fortunately, there are a couple of easy ways to bulk load formatted data to and from Cassandra.

`cqlsh` supports loading and unloading of comma-separated variable (CSV) files via the `COPY` command.

For example, the following command could be used to save the contents of our hotels table to a file:

```
cqlsh:hotel> COPY hotels TO 'hotels.csv' WITH HEADER=TRUE;
```

The `TO` value specifies the file to write to, and the `HEADER` option to `TRUE` causes the column names to be printed in our output file. We could edit this file and read the contents back in with this command:

```
cqlsh:hotel> COPY hotels FROM 'hotels.csv' WITH HEADER=true;
```

The `COPY` command supports other options to configure how quotes, escapes, and times are represented.

Brian Hess has created a command-line tool called the Cassandra Loader (*https:// github.com/brianmhess/cassandra-loader*) that loads and unloads CSV files as well as other delimited files, and is flexible enough to handle using the comma as the decimal separator.

We can use `cqlsh` to load some sample hotel inventory data into our cluster. You can access a simple *.csv* file in the GitHub repository for this book (*https:// github.com/ jeffreyscarpenter/cassandra-guide*). The *available_rooms.csv* file contains a month's worth of inventory for two small hotels with five rooms each. Let's load the data into the cluster:

```
cqlsh:hotel> COPY available_rooms_by_hotel_date FROM
  'available_rooms.csv' WITH HEADER=true;

310 rows imported in 0.789 seconds.
```

If you do a quick query to read some of this data, you'll find that we have data for two hotels: "AZ123" and "NY229".

Now let's consider how to support the query we labeled "Q4. Find an available room in a given date range" from Chapter 5. Remember that we designed the `available_rooms_by_hotel_date` table to support this query, with the primary key:

```
PRIMARY KEY (hotel_id, date, room_number)
```

This means that the `hotel_id` is the partition key, while date and `room_number` are clustering columns.

Here's a CQL statement that allows us to search for hotel rooms for a specific hotel and date range:

```
cqlsh:hotel> SELECT * FROM available_rooms_by_hotel_date
   WHERE hotel_id='AZ123' and date>'2016-01-05' and date<'2016-01-12';

 hotel_id | date       | room_number | is_available
----------+------------+-------------+--------------
    AZ123 | 2016-01-06 |         101 |         True
    AZ123 | 2016-01-06 |         102 |         True
    AZ123 | 2016-01-06 |         103 |         True
    AZ123 | 2016-01-06 |         104 |         True
    AZ123 | 2016-01-06 |         105 |         True
 ...
(60 rows)
```

Note that this query involves the partition key `hotel_id` and a range of values representing the start and end of our search over the clustering key `date`.

If we wanted to try to find the records for room number 101 at hotel AZ123, we might attempt a query like the following:

```
cqlsh:hotel> SELECT * FROM available_rooms_by_hotel_date
   WHERE hotel_id='AZ123' and room_number=101;
InvalidRequest: code=2200 [Invalid query] message="PRIMARY KEY column
   "room_number" cannot be restricted as preceding column "date" is not
   restricted"
```

As you can see, this query results in an error, because we have attempted to restrict the value of the second clustering key while not limiting the value of the first clustering key.

The syntax of the WHERE clause involves the following rules:

- All elements of the partition key must be identified
- A given clustering key may only be restricted if all previous clustering keys are restricted

These restrictions are based on how Cassandra stores data on disk, which is based on the clustering columns and sort order specified on the CREATE TABLE command. The conditions on the clustering column are restricted to those that allow Cassandra to select a contiguous ordering of rows.

The exception to this rule is the ALLOW FILTERING keyword, which allows us to omit a partition key element. For example, we can search the room status across multiple hotels for rooms on a specific date with this query:

```
cqlsh:hotel> SELECT * FROM available_rooms_by_hotel_date
  WHERE date='2016-01-25' ALLOW FILTERING;

 hotel_id | date       | room_number | is_available
----------+------------+-------------+--------------
    AZ123 | 2016-01-25 |         101 |         True
    AZ123 | 2016-01-25 |         102 |         True
    AZ123 | 2016-01-25 |         103 |         True
    AZ123 | 2016-01-25 |         104 |         True
    AZ123 | 2016-01-25 |         105 |         True
    NY229 | 2016-01-25 |         101 |         True
    NY229 | 2016-01-25 |         102 |         True
    NY229 | 2016-01-25 |         103 |         True
    NY229 | 2016-01-25 |         104 |         True
    NY229 | 2016-01-25 |         105 |         True

(10 rows)
```

Usage of `ALLOW FILTERING` is not recommended, however, as it has the potential to result in very expensive queries. If you find yourself needing such a query, you will want to revisit your data model to make sure you have designed tables that support your queries.

The `IN` clause can be used to test equality with multiple possible values for a column. For example, we could use the following to find inventory on two dates a week apart with the command:

```
cqlsh:hotel> SELECT * FROM available_rooms_by_hotel_date
  WHERE hotel_id='AZ123' AND date IN ('2016-01-05', '2016-01-12');
```

Note that using the `IN` clause can result in slower performance on queries, as the specified column values may correspond to non-contiguous areas within the row.

Finally, the `SELECT` command allows us to override the sort order which has been specified on the columns when we created the table. For example, we could obtain the rooms in descending order by date for any of our previous queries using the `ORDER BY` syntax:

```
cqlsh:hotel> SELECT * FROM available_rooms_by_hotel_date
  WHERE hotel_id='AZ123' and date>'2016-01-05' and date<'2016-01-12'
  ORDER BY date DESC;
```

Functions and Aggregates

Cassandra 2.2 introduced two features that allow clients to shift some processing work to the coordinator node: user-defined functions (UDFs) and user-defined aggregates (UDAs). Using these features can improve performance in some situations by reducing the amount of data that has to be returned to the client and reducing processing load on the client, at the cost of additional processing on the server.

User-defined functions

UDFs are functions that are applied on Cassandra nodes to stored data as part of query processing. Before using UDFs in your cluster, they must be enabled in the *cassandra.yaml* file on each node:

```
enable_user_defined_functions: true
```

Here's a quick summary of how this works: we create a UDF using the CQL CREATE FUNCTION command, which causes the function to be propagated to every node in the cluster. When you execute a query that references the UDF, it is applied to each row of the query result.

Let's create an example UDF to count the number of available rooms in our `available_rooms_by_hotel_date` table:

```
cqlsh:hotel> CREATE FUNCTION count_if_true(input boolean)
  RETURNS NULL ON NULL INPUT
  RETURNS int
  LANGUAGE java AS 'if (input) return 1; else return 0;';
```

We'll dissect this command a bit at a time. We've created a UDF named `count_if_true` which operates on a `boolean` parameter and returns an integer. We've also included a null check to make sure the function works effectively just in case the value is not defined. Note that if a UDF fails, execution of the query is aborted, so this can be an important check.

 **UDF Security**

The 3.0 release added a security feature to run UDF code in a separate sandbox to limit the ability for a malicious function to gain unauthorized access to a node's Java runtime.

Next, note that we've declared this to be a Java implementation with the LANGUAGE clause. Cassandra natively supports functions and aggregates defined in Java and JavaScript. They can also be implemented using any language supported by the Java Scripting API specified in JSR 223, including Python, Ruby, and Scala. Functions defined in these languages require adding additional scripting engine JAR files to Cassandra's Java CLASSPATH.

Finally, we include the actual Java syntax of the function with the AS clause. Now this function is somewhat trivial by itself, because all we're doing is counting true values as 1. We'll do something more powerful with this UDF in a bit.

First, however, let's try our UDF out on our `available_rooms_by_hotel_date` table to see how it works:

```
cqlsh:hotel> SELECT room_number, count_if_true(is_available)
  FROM available_rooms_by_hotel_date
```

```
             WHERE hotel_id='AZ123' and date='2016-01-05';

   room_number | hotel.count_if_true(is_available)
  -------------+-----------------------------------
           101 |                                 1
           102 |                                 1
           103 |                                 1
           104 |                                 1
           105 |                                 1

   (5 rows)
```

As you can see, the column with our function result is qualified with the hotel key-space name. This is because each UDF is associated with a specific keyspace. If we were to execute a similar query in the DataStax Java Driver, we would find a `Column` in each `Row` with the name `hotel_count_if_true_is_available`.

User-defined aggregates

As we've just learned, user-defined functions operate on a single row. In order to perform operations across multiple rows, we create a user-defined aggregate. The UDA leverages two UDFs: a state function and an optional final function. A state function is executed against every row, while the final function, if present, operates on the results of the state function.

Let's look at a simple example to help investigate how this works. First, we'll need a state function. The `count_if_true` function is close to what we need, but we need to make a small change to allow the available count to be summed across multiple rows. Let's create a new function that allows a running total to be passed in, incremented and returned:

```
cqlsh:hotel> CREATE FUNCTION state_count_if_true(total int, input boolean)
   RETURNS NULL ON NULL INPUT
   RETURNS int
   LANGUAGE java AS 'if (input) return total+1; else return total;';
```

Note that the `total` parameter is passed as the first parameter, with its type matching the return type of the function (`int`). For a UDF to be used as a state function, the first parameter type and return types must match. The second parameter is the boolean which we had in our original `count_if_true` UDF.

Now we can create an aggregate that uses this state function:

```
cqlsh:hotel> CREATE AGGREGATE total_available (boolean)
   SFUNC state_count_if_true
   STYPE int
   INITCOND 0;
```

Let's break down this statement piece by piece: first, we've declared a UDA called `total_available`, which operates on columns of type boolean.

The SFUNC clause identifies the state function used by this query—in this case, state_count_if_true.

Next, we identify the type that is used to accumulate results from the state function by the STYPE clause. Cassandra maintains a value of this type, which it passes to the state function as it is called on each successive row. The STYPE must be the same as the first parameter and return type of the state function. The INITCOND clause allows us to set the initial value of the result; here, we set the initial count to zero.

In this case, we've chosen to omit the final function, but we could have included a function that took an argument of the STYPE and returned any other type, such as a function that accepts an integer argument and returns a boolean indicating if the inventory is at a low level that should generate an alert.

Now let's use our aggregate to get a count of available rooms returned by one of our previous queries. Note that our query must only include the UDA, with no other columns or functions:

```
cqlsh:hotel> SELECT total_available(is_available)
  FROM available_rooms_by_hotel_date
  WHERE hotel_id='AZ123' and date='2016-01-05';

 hotel.total_available(is_available)
-------------------------------------
                                   5

(1 rows)
```

As you can see, this query yields a result of five available rooms for the specified hotel and date.

Additional UDF/UDA Command Options

You can use the familiar IF NOT EXISTS syntax when creating UDFs and UDAs to avoid error messages for attempts to create functions and aggregates with duplicate signatures. Alternatively, you can use the CREATE OR REPLACE syntax when you can actually intend to override the current function or aggregate.

Use the DESCRIBE FUNCTIONS command or the DESCRIBE AGGREGATES command to learn which UDFs and UDAs have been defined already. This can be especially useful when there are functions with the same name but different signatures.

Finally, you can delete UDFs and UDAs using the DROP FUNCTION and DROP AGGREGATE commands.

Built-in functions and aggregates

In addition to user-defined functions and aggregates, Cassandra also provides some built-in, or *native* functions and aggregates that we can use:

COUNT

The COUNT function is used to count the number of rows returned by a query. For example, to count the number of hotels in our database:

```
SELECT COUNT(*) FROM hotel.hotels;
```

This command can also can be used to count the number of non-null values of a specified column. For example, the following could be used to count how many guests provided an email address:

```
SELECT COUNT(emails) FROM reservation.guests;
```

MIN *and* MAX

The MIN and MAX functions can be used to compute the minimum and maximum value returned by a query for a given column. For example, this query could be used to determine the minimum and maximum stay lengths (in nights) for reservations at a given hotel and arrival date:

```
SELECT MIN(nights), MAX(nights) FROM reservations_by_hotel_date
    WHERE hotel_id='AZ123' AND start_date='2016-09-09';
```

sum

The sum function can be used to sum up all the values returned by a query for a given column. We could sum the number of nights to be stayed across multiple reservations as follows:

```
SELECT SUM(nights) FROM reservations_by_hotel_date
    WHERE hotel_id='AZ123' AND start_date='2016-09-09';
```

avg

The avg function can be used to compute the average of all the values returned by a query for a given column. To get the average stay length in nights, we might execute a query like:

```
SELECT AVG(nights) FROM reservations_by_hotel_date
    WHERE hotel_id='AZ123' AND start_date='2016-09-09';
```

These built-in aggregates are technically part of the system keyspace. Therefore, the column name containing results of our last query would be system_avg_nights.

Paging

In early releases of Cassandra, clients had to make sure to carefully limit the amount of data requested at a time. For a large result set, it is possible to overwhelm both nodes and clients even to the point of running out of memory.

Thankfully, Cassandra provides a paging mechanism that allows retrieval of result sets incrementally. A simple example of this is shown by use of the CQL keyword LIMIT. For example, the following command will return no more than 100 hotels:

```
cqlsh> SELECT * FROM hotel.hotels LIMIT 100;
```

Of course, the limitation of the LIMIT keyword (pun intended) is that there's no way to obtain additional pages containing the additional rows beyond the requested quantity.

The 2.0 release of Cassandra introduced a feature known as *automatic paging*. Automatic paging allows clients to request a subset of the data that would be returned by a query. The server breaks the result into pages that are returned as the client requests them.

You can view paging status in cqlsh via the PAGING command. The following output shows a sequence of checking paging status, changing the fetch size (page size), and disabling paging:

```
cqlsh> PAGING;
Query paging is currently enabled. Use PAGING OFF to disable
Page size: 100
cqlsh> PAGING 1000;
Page size: 1000
cqlsh> PAGING OFF;
Disabled Query paging.
cqlsh> PAGING ON;
Now Query paging is enabled
```

Now let's see how paging works in the DataStax Java Driver. You can set a default fetch size globally for a Cluster instance:

```
Cluster cluster = Cluster.builder().addContactPoint("127.0.0.1").
    withQueryOptions(new QueryOptions().setFetchSize(2000)).build();
```

The fetch size can also be set on an individual statement, overriding the default value:

```
Statement statement = new SimpleStatement("...");
statement.setFetchSize(2000);
```

If the fetch size is set on a statement, it will take precedence; otherwise, the cluster-wide value (which defaults to 5,000) will be used. Note that setting a fetch size doesn't mean that Cassandra will always return the exact number of rows requested; it is possible that it returns slightly more or less results.

The driver handles automatic paging on our behalf, allowing us to iterate over a ResultSet without requiring knowledge of the paging mechanism. For example, consider the following code sample for iterating over a query for hotels:

```
SimpleStatement hotelSelect = session.newSimpleStatement(
    "SELECT * FROM hotels");
```

```
ResultSet resultSet = session.execute(hotelSelect);

for (Row row : resultSet) {
  // process the row
}
```

What happens behind the scenes is as follows: when our application invokes the `session.execute()` operation, the driver performs our query to Cassandra, requesting the first page of results. Our application iterates over the results as shown in the `for` loop, and when the driver detects that there are no more items remaining on the current page, it requests the next page.

It is possible that the small pause of requesting the next page would affect the performance and user experience of our application, so the `ResultSet` provides additional operations that allow more fine grained control over paging. Here's an example of how we could extend our application to do some pre-fetching of rows:

```
for (Row row : resultSet) {
  if (resultSet.getAvailableWithoutFetching() < 100 &&
      !resultSet.isFullyFetched())
        resultSet.fetchMoreResults();
  // process the row
}
```

This additional statement checks to see if there are less than 100 rows remaining on the current page using `getAvailableWithoutFetching()`. If there is another page to be retrieved, which we determine by checking `isFullyFetched()`, we initiate an asynchronous call to obtain the extra rows via `fetchMoreResults()`.

The driver also exposes the ability to access the paging state more directly so it can be saved and reused later. This could be useful if your application is a stateless web service that doesn't sustain a session across multiple invocations.

We can access the paging state through the `ExecutionInfo` of the `ResultSet`:

```
PagingState nextPage = resultSet.getExecutionInfo().getPagingState();
```

We can then save this state within our application, or return it to clients. The `Paging State` can be converted to a string using `toString()`, or a byte array using `toBytes()`.

Note that in either string or byte array form, the state is not something you should try to manipulate or reuse with a different statement. Doing so will result in a `Paging StateException`.

To resume a query from a given `PagingState`, we set it on the `Statement`:

```
SimpleStatement hotelSelect = session.newSimpleStatement(
  "SELECT * FROM hotels");
hotelSelect.setPagingState(pagingState);
```

Speculative Retry

We've previously discussed in Chapter 8 the `SpeculativeExecutionPolicy` provided by the DataStax Java Driver, which pre-emptively retries read queries using different nodes if the initial node does not respond in a configurable amount of time.

The same behavior is available for us to configure on each node so that when the node acts as a coordinator, it can initiate speculative requests to alternate nodes. This behavior is configurable on each table via the `speculative_retry` property, which allows the following values:

ALWAYS
> Retry reads of all replicas.

<X>PERCENTILE
> Initiate retries if a response isn't received within the Xth percentile response time.

<Y>ms
> Retry if no response is received in Y milliseconds.

NONE
> Do not retry reads.

The default value is `99.0PERCENTILE`. This achieves a good balance by speeding up the "outlier" slow performing requests without flooding the cluster with a large number of duplicate read requests.

This feature is also known as *rapid read protection*, and was introduced in release 2.0.2. Note that it has no effect for queries at consistency level `ALL`, as there are no additional nodes to retry.

Deleting

Deleting data is not the same in Cassandra as it is in a relational database. In an RDBMS, you simply issue a delete statement that identifies the row or rows you want to delete. In Cassandra, a delete does not actually remove the data immediately. There's a simple reason for this: Cassandra's durable, eventually consistent, distributed design. If Cassandra had a traditional design for deletes, any nodes that were down at the time of a delete would not receive the delete. Once one of these nodes came back online, it would mistakenly think that all of the nodes that had received the delete had actually missed a write (the data that it still has because it missed the delete), and it would start repairing all of the other nodes. So Cassandra needs a more sophisticated mechanism to support deletes. That mechanism is called a *tombstone*.

A tombstone is a special marker issued in a delete that overwrites the deleted values, acting as a placeholder. If any replica did not receive the delete operation, the tombstone can later be propagated to those replicas when they are available again. The net effect of this design is that your data store will not immediately shrink in size following a delete. Each node keeps track of the age of all its tombstones. Once they reach the age as configured in gc_grace_seconds (which is 10 days by default), then a compaction is run, the tombstones are garbage-collected, and the corresponding disk space is recovered.

Because SSTables are immutable, the data is not deleted from the SSTable. On compaction, tombstones are accounted for, merged data is sorted, a new index is created over the sorted data, and the freshly merged, sorted, and indexed data is written to a single new file. The assumption is that 10 days is plenty of time for you to bring a failed node back online before compaction runs. If you feel comfortable doing so, you can reduce that grace period to reclaim disk space more quickly.

A simple delete of an entire row in the DataStax Java Driver looks like this:

```
SimpleStatement hotelDelete = session.newSimpleStatement(
  "DELETE * FROM hotels WHERE id=?", "AZ123");

ResultSet hotelDeleteResult = session.execute(hotelDelete);
```

You can delete non-primary key columns by identifying them by name in the query.

You can also delete data using PreparedStatements, the QueryBuilder, and the MappingManager.

Here is an example of deleting an entire row using the QueryBuilder:

```
BuiltStatement hotelDeleteBuilt = queryBuilder.delete().all().
  from("hotels").where(eq("id", "AZ123"));

session.execute(hotelDeleteBuilt);
```

Consistency Levels for Deletion

Because a delete is a form of write, the consistency levels available for deletes are the same as those listed for writes.

Summary

In this chapter, we saw how to read, write, and delete data using both cqlsh and client drivers. We also took a peek behind the scenes to learn how Cassandra implements these operations, which should help us to make more informed decisions as we design, implement, deploy and maintain applications using Cassandra.

Monitoring

In this chapter, you'll learn how to use a variety of tools to monitor and understand important events in the life cycle of your Cassandra cluster. We'll look at some simple ways to see what's going on, such as changing the logging levels and understanding the output.

Cassandra also features built-in support for Java Management Extensions (JMX), which offers a rich way to monitor your Cassandra nodes and their underlying Java environment. Through JMX, we can see the health of the database and ongoing events, and even interact with it remotely to tune certain values. JMX is an important part of Cassandra, and we'll spend some time to make sure we know how it works and what exactly Cassandra makes available for monitoring and management with JMX. Let's get started!

Logging

The simplest way to get a picture of what's happening in your database is to just change the logging level to make the output more verbose. This is great for development and for learning what Cassandra is doing under the hood.

Cassandra uses the Simple Logging Facade for Java (SLF4J) API for logging, with Logback as the implementation. SLF4J provides a facade over various logging frameworks such as Logback, Log4J, and Java's built-in logger (java.util.logging). You can learn more about Logback at *http://logback.qos.ch/*.

By default, the Cassandra server log level is set at INFO, which doesn't give you much detail about what work Cassandra is doing at any given time. It just outputs basic status updates, such as the following:

```
INFO  [main] 2015-09-19 09:40:20,215 CassandraDaemon.java:149 -
   Hostname: Carp-iMac27.local
```

```
INFO  [main] 2015-09-19 09:40:20,233 YamlConfigurationLoader.java:92 -
  Loading settings from file:/Users/jeff/Cassandra/
  apache-cassandra-2.1.8/conf/cassandra.yaml
INFO  [main] 2015-09-19 09:40:20,333 YamlConfigurationLoader.java:135 -
  Node configuration
...
```

When you start Cassandra in a terminal, you keep this output running in the terminal window by passing the program the -f flag (to keep output visible in the foreground of the terminal window). But Cassandra is also writing these logs to physical files for you to examine later.

By changing the logging level to DEBUG, we can see much more clearly what activity the server is working on, instead of seeing only these stage updates.

To change the logging level, open the file *<cassandra-home>/conf/logback.xml* and find the section that looks like this:

```
<root level="INFO">
  <appender-ref ref="FILE" />
  <appender-ref ref="STDOUT" />
</root>
```

Change the first line so it looks like this:

```
<root level="DEBUG">
```

Once we have made this change and saved the file, Cassandra will shortly begin printing DEBUG-level logging statements. This is because the default logging is configured to scan the configuration file once a minute, as set by the line:

```
<configuration scan="true">
```

Now we can see a lot more activity as Cassandra does its work. This allows you to see exactly what Cassandra is doing and when, which is very helpful in troubleshooting. But it's also helpful in simply understanding what Cassandra does to maintain itself.

Tuning Logging in Production

Of course, in production you'll want to tune the logging level back up to WARN or ERROR, as the verbose output will slow things down considerably.

By default, Cassandra's log files are stored in the *logs* directory underneath the Cassandra installation directory.

If you want to change the location of the logs directory, just find the following entry in the *logback.xml* file and chose a different filename:

```
<file>${cassandra.logdir}/system.log</file>
```

Missing Log Files

If you don't see any logfiles in the location specified, make sure that you are the owner of the directories, or at least that proper read and write permissions are set. Cassandra won't tell you if it can't write the log; it just won't write. Same for the datafiles.

Other settings in the *logback.xml* file support rolling log files. By default, the *system.log* file is rolled to an archive once it reaches a size of 20 MB. Each log file archive is compressed in zip format and named according to the pattern *system.log.1.zip*, *system.log.2.zip*, and so on.

Tailing

You don't need to start Cassandra using the foreground switch in order to see the rolling log. You can also simply start it without the -f option and then tail the logs. Tailing is not specific to Cassandra; it's a small program available in Linux distributions to see new values printed to a console as they are appended to a file.

To tail the logs, start Cassandra like this:

```
$ bin/cassandra
```

Then open a second console, enter the `tail` command, and pass it the location of the particular file you want to tail, like this:

```
$ tail -f $CASSANDRA_HOME/logs/system.log
```

The -f option means "follow," and as Cassandra outputs information to the physical logfile, `tail` will output it to the screen. To stop tailing, just press Ctrl-C.

You can do the same thing if you're using Windows, but Windows doesn't include a tail program natively. So to achieve this, you'll need to download and install Cygwin (*http://www.cygwin.com*), which is a free and open source Bash shell emulator. Cygwin allows you to have a Linux-style interface and use a variety of Linux tools on Windows.

Then you can start Cassandra regularly and tail the logfile using this command:

```
$ tail -f %CASSANDRA_HOME%\\logs\\system.log
```

This will show the output in the console in the same way as if it were foregrounded.

Examining Log Files

Once you're running the server with debug logging enabled, you can see a lot more happening that can help during debugging. For example, here we can see the output when writing a simple value to the database using cqlsh:

```
cqlsh> INSERT INTO hotel.hotels (id, name, phone, address)
   ... VALUES ( 'AZ123', 'Comfort Suites Old Town Scottsdale',
   ... '(480) 946-1111', { street : '3275 N. Drinkwater Blvd.',
   ... city : 'Scottsdale', state : 'AZ', zip_code : 85251 });

DEBUG [SharedPool-Worker-1] 2015-09-30 06:21:41,410 Message.java:506 -
   Received: OPTIONS, v=4
DEBUG [SharedPool-Worker-1] 2015-09-30 06:21:41,410 Message.java:525 -
   Responding: SUPPORTED {COMPRESSION=[snappy, lz4],
   CQL_VERSION=[3.3.1]}, v=4
DEBUG [SharedPool-Worker-1] 2015-09-30 06:21:42,082 Message.java:506 -
   Received: QUERY INSERT INTO hotel.hotels (id, name, phone, address)
   VALUES ( 'AZ123', 'Comfort Suites Old Town Scottsdale',
   '(480) 946-1111', { street : '3275 N. Drinkwater Blvd.',
   city : 'Scottsdale', state : 'AZ', zip_code : 85251 });
   [pageSize = 100], v=4
DEBUG [SharedPool-Worker-1] 2015-09-30 06:21:42,086
   AbstractReplicationStrategy.java:87 - clearing cached endpoints
DEBUG [SharedPool-Worker-1] 2015-09-30 06:21:42,087 Tracing.java:155 -
request complete
DEBUG [SharedPool-Worker-1] 2015-09-30 06:21:42,087 Message.java:525 -
   Responding: EMPTY RESULT, v=4
```

This particular output is less expressive than it could otherwise be, given that it was run on a single node cluster.

If we then load the row via a simple query:

```
cqlsh> SELECT * from hotel.hotels;
```

The server log records this query as follows:

```
DEBUG [SharedPool-Worker-1] 2015-09-30 06:27:27,392 Message.java:506 -
   Received: QUERY SELECT * from hotel.hotels;[pageSize = 100], v=4
DEBUG [SharedPool-Worker-1] 2015-09-30 06:27:27,395
   StorageProxy.java:2021 - Estimated result rows per range: 0.0;
   requested rows: 100, ranges.size(): 257; concurrent range requests: 1
DEBUG [SharedPool-Worker-1] 2015-09-30 06:27:27,401
   ReadCallback.java:141 - Read: 0 ms.
DEBUG [SharedPool-Worker-1] 2015-09-30 06:27:27,401 Tracing.java:155 -
   request complete
DEBUG [SharedPool-Worker-1] 2015-09-30 06:27:27,401 Message.java:525 -
   Responding: ROWS [id(hotel, hotels),
   org.apache.cassandra.db.marshal.UUIDType][address(hotel, hotels),
   org.apache.cassandra.db.marshal.UserType(hotel,61646472657373,
   737472656574:org.apache.cassandra.db.marshal.UTF8Type,
```

```
63697479:org.apache.cassandra.db.marshal.UTF8Type,7374617465:
org.apache.cassandra.db.marshal.UTF8Type,7a69705f636f6465:
org.apache.cassandra.db.marshal.Int32Type)][name(hotel, hotels),
org.apache.cassandra.db.marshal.UTF8Type][phone(hotel, hotels),
org.apache.cassandra.db.marshal.UTF8Type][pois(hotel, hotels),
org.apache.cassandra.db.marshal.SetType(org.apache.cassandra.db.
marshal.UUIDType)]
| 452d27e1-804e-479b-aeaf-61d1fa31090f | 3275 N. Drinkwater Blvd.:
Scottsdale:AZ:85251 | Comfort Suites Old Town Scottsdale |
(480) 946-1111 | null
```

As you can see, the server loads each of the columns we requested via a class responsible for marshalling data from the on-disk format.

The DEBUG log level should give you enough information to follow along with what the server's doing as you work.

Monitoring Cassandra with JMX

In this section, we explore how Cassandra makes use of Java Management Extensions (JMX) to enable remote management of your servers. JMX started as Java Specification Request (JSR) 160 and has been a core part of Java since version 5.0.

More on JMX

You can read more about the JMX implementation in Java by examining the java.lang.management package.

JMX is a Java API that provides management of applications in two key ways. First, JMX allows you to understand your application's health and overall performance in terms of memory, threads, and CPU usage—things that are generally applicable to any Java application. Second, JMX allows you to work with specific aspects of your application that you have instrumented.

Instrumentation refers to putting a wrapper around application code that provides hooks from the application to the JVM in order to allow the JVM to gather data that external tools can use. Such tools include monitoring agents, data analysis tools, profilers, and more. JMX allows you not only to view such data but also, if the application enables it, to manage your application at runtime by updating values.

JMX is commonly used for a variety of application control operations, including:

- Low available memory detection, including the size of each generation space on the heap

- Thread information such as deadlock detection, peak number of threads, and current live threads

- Verbose classloader tracing
- Log level control
- General information such as application uptime and the active classpath

Many popular Java applications are instrumented using JMX, including the JVM itself, the Tomcat application server, and Cassandra. A depiction of the JMX architecture is shown in Figure 10-1.

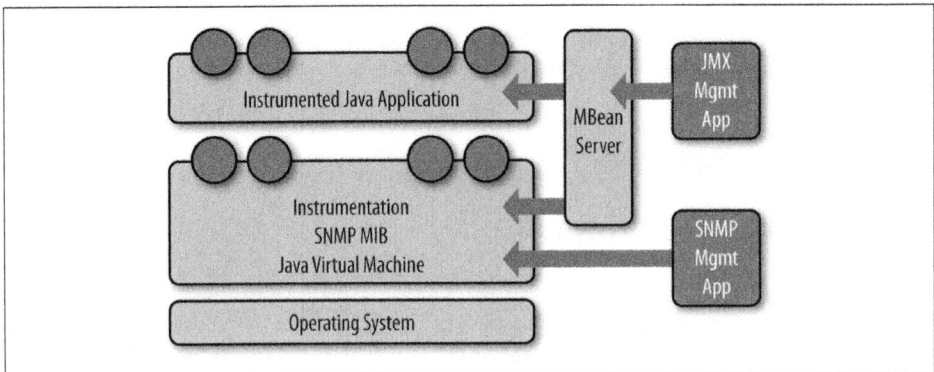

Figure 10-1. The JMX architecture

The JMX architecture is simple. The JVM collects information from the underlying operating system. The JVM itself is instrumented, so many of its features are exposed for management as described earlier. An instrumented Java application (such as Cassandra) runs on top of this, also exposing some of its features as manageable objects. The JDK includes an MBean server that makes the instrumented features available over a remote protocol to a JMX Management Application. The JVM also offers management capabilities via Simple Network Monitoring Protocol (SNMP), which may be useful if you are using SMTP monitoring tools such as Nagios or Zenoss.

But within a given application, you can manage only what the application developers have made available for you to manage. Luckily, the Cassandra developers have instrumented large parts of the database engine, making management via JMX fairly straightforward.

This instrumentation of a Java application is performed by wrapping the application code that you want JMX to hook into with managed beans.

Connecting to Cassandra via JConsole

The `jconsole` tool ships with the standard Java Development Kit. It provides a graphical user interface client for working with MBeans and can be used for local or remote management. Let's connect to Cassandra on its JMX port using JConsole. To do so, open a new terminal and type the following:

```
>jconsole
```

When you run `jconsole`, you'll see a login screen similar to that in Figure 10-2.

Figure 10-2. The jconsole login

From here, you can simply double-click on the value `org.apache.cassandra.service.CassandraDaemon` under the Local Process section if you're monitoring a node on the same machine. If you want to monitor a node on a different machine, check the Remote Process radio button, then enter the host and port you want to connect to. Cassandra JMX by default broadcasts on port 7199, so you can enter a value like the one shown here and then hit Connect:

```
>lucky:7199
```

Connecting Remotely via JMX

By default, Cassandra runs with JMX enabled for local access only. To enable remote access, edit the file *<cassandra-home>/cassandra-env.sh* (or *cassandra.ps1* on Windows). Search for "JMX" to find the section of the file with options to control the JMX port and other local/remote connection settings.

Once you've connected to a server, the default view includes four major categories about your server's state, which are updated constantly:

Heap memory usage
This shows the total memory available to the Cassandra program, as well as how much it's using right now.

Threads
This is the number of live threads Cassandra is using.

Classes
The number of classes that Cassandra has loaded. This number is relatively small for such a powerful program; Cassandra typically requires under 3,000 classes out of the box. Compare this to a program such as Oracle WebLogic, which typically loads around 24,000 classes.

CPU usage
This shows the percentage of the processor that the Cassandra program is currently using.

You can use the selector to adjust the time range shown in the charts.

If you want to see a more detailed view of how Cassandra is using the Java heap and non-heap memory, click the Memory tab. By changing the chart value in the drop-down, you can see in detail the graduations in which Cassandra is using its memory. You can also (try to) force a garbage collection if you think it's necessary.

You can connect to more than one JMX agent at once. Just choose File → New Connection... and repeat the steps to connect to another running Cassandra node to view multiple servers at once.

Other JMX Clients

JConsole is an easy choice when you're looking for a JMX client, because it's easy to use and ships with the JDK. But this is only one possible JMX client—there are plenty of others available. Here are a few examples of clients that might meet your needs:

Oracle Java Mission Control and Visual VM
These tools also ship with the Oracle JDK and provide more robust metrics, diagnostics, and visualizations for memory usage, threads, garbage collection, and others. The main comparison between the two is that Visual VM is an open source project available under the GNU license, while Mission Control provides a deeper level of integration with the Oracle JVM via a framework called Flight Control.

Java Mission Control can be run via the command `$JAVA_HOME/bin/jmc`, and Visual VM via the command `$JAVA_HOME/bin/jvisualvm`. Both are suitable for usage in both development and production environments.

MX4J
The Management Extensions for Java (MX4J) project provides an open source implementation of JMX, including tooling such as an embedded web interface to JMX using HTTP/HTML. This allows interactions with JMX via a standard web browser.

To integrate MX4J into a Cassandra installation, download the *mx4j_tools.jar* library (*http://mx4j.sourceforge.net*), save the JAR file in the *lib* directory of your Cassandra installation, and configure the `MX4J_ADDRESS` and `MX4J_PORT` options in *conf/cassandra-env.sh*.

Jmxterm
Jmxterm is a command-line JMX client that allows access to a JMX server without a graphical interface. This can be especially useful when working in cloud environments, as the graphical tools are typically more resource intensive.

Jmxterm is an open source Java project available from the Cyclops Group (*http://wiki.cyclopsgroup.org/jmxterm*).

IDE Integrations
You can also find JMX clients that integrate with popular IDEs; for example, eclipse-jmx (*https://code.google.com/p/eclipse-jmx*).

Overview of MBeans

A *managed bean*, or MBean, is a special type of Java bean that represents a single manageable resource inside the JVM. MBeans interact with an MBean server to make their functions remotely available.

A view of JConsole is provided in Figure 10-3.

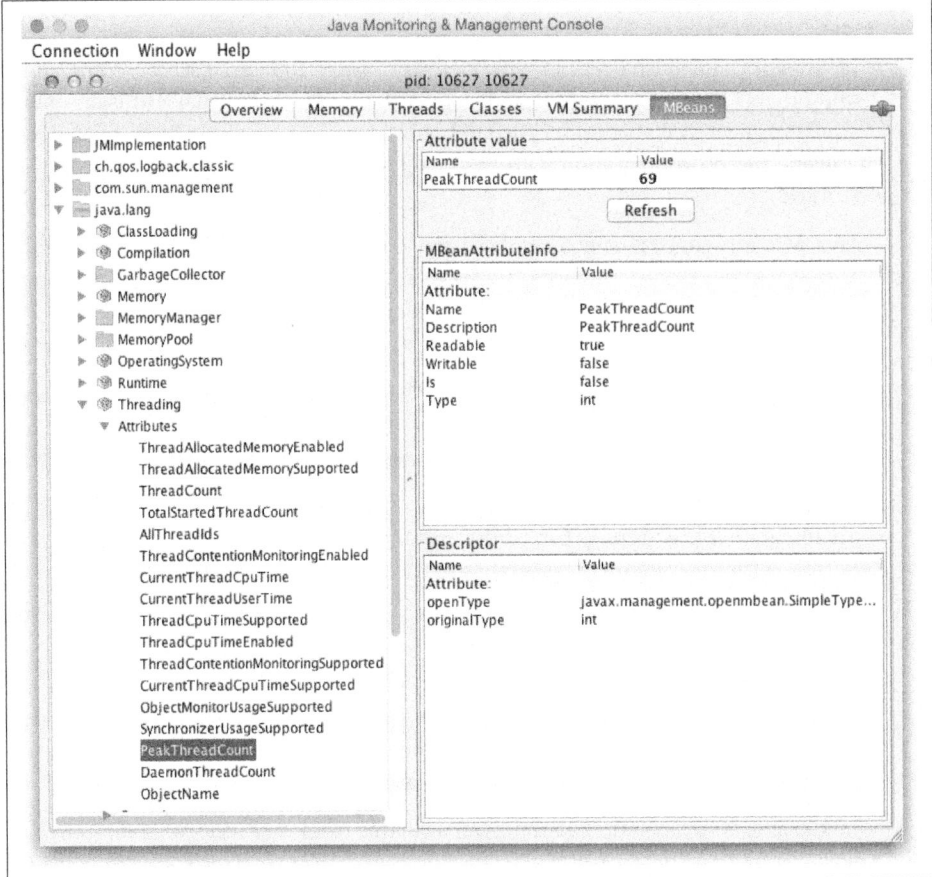

Figure 10-3. JConsole showing the peak thread count for a Cassandra daemon

In this figure, you can see tabbed windows that offer general views about threads, memory, and CPU that every application will have, and a more detailed MBeans tab that exposes the ability to interact in more detail with MBeans exposed by the application. For example, in the figure, we've selected to view the peak thread count value. You can see that many other instrumented aspects of the application are also available.

There are many aspects of an application or the JVM that can be instrumented but that may be disabled. Thread Contention is one example of a potentially useful MBean that is turned off by default in the JVM. These aspects can be very useful for debugging, so if you see an MBean that you think might help you hunt down a problem, go ahead and enable it. But keep in mind that nothing comes for free, and it's a good idea to read the JavaDoc on the MBean you want to enable in order to understand the potential impact on performance. For example, measuring CPU time per thread is an example of a useful, but expensive, MBean operation.

 **MBean Object Name Conventions**

When an MBean is registered with the MBean server, it specifies an object name that is used to identify the MBean to JMX clients. An object name consists of a domain followed by a list of key-value pairs, at least one of which must identify a type. The typical convention is to choose a domain name that is similar to the Java package name of the MBean, and to name the type after the MBean interface name (minus the "MBean"), but this is not strictly required.

For example, the threading attributes we looked at earlier appear under the `java.lang.Threading` heading in JConsole, and are exposed by a class implementing the `java.lang.management.ThreadMXBean` interface, which registers the MBean with the object name `java.lang.type=Threading`.

As we discuss various MBeans in this chapter, we'll identify both the MBean object name and the interface to help you navigate between JMX clients and the Cassandra source code.

Some simple values in the application are exposed as *attributes*. An example of this is `Threading > PeakThreadCount`, which just reports the value that the MBean has stored for the greatest number of threads the application used at a single point in time. You can refresh to see the most recent value, but that's pretty much all you can do with it. Because such a value is maintained internally in the JVM, it doesn't make sense to set it externally (it's derived from actual events, and not configurable).

But other MBeans are configurable. They make *operations* available to the JMX agent that let you get and set values. You can tell whether the MBean will let you set a value by looking at the value for `writable`. If it's false, you will see a label indicating the read-only value; if it's true, you will see a set of one or more fields to add your new value and a button to update it. An example of this is the `ch.qos.logback.classic.jmx.JMXConfigurator` bean, as shown in Figure 10-4.

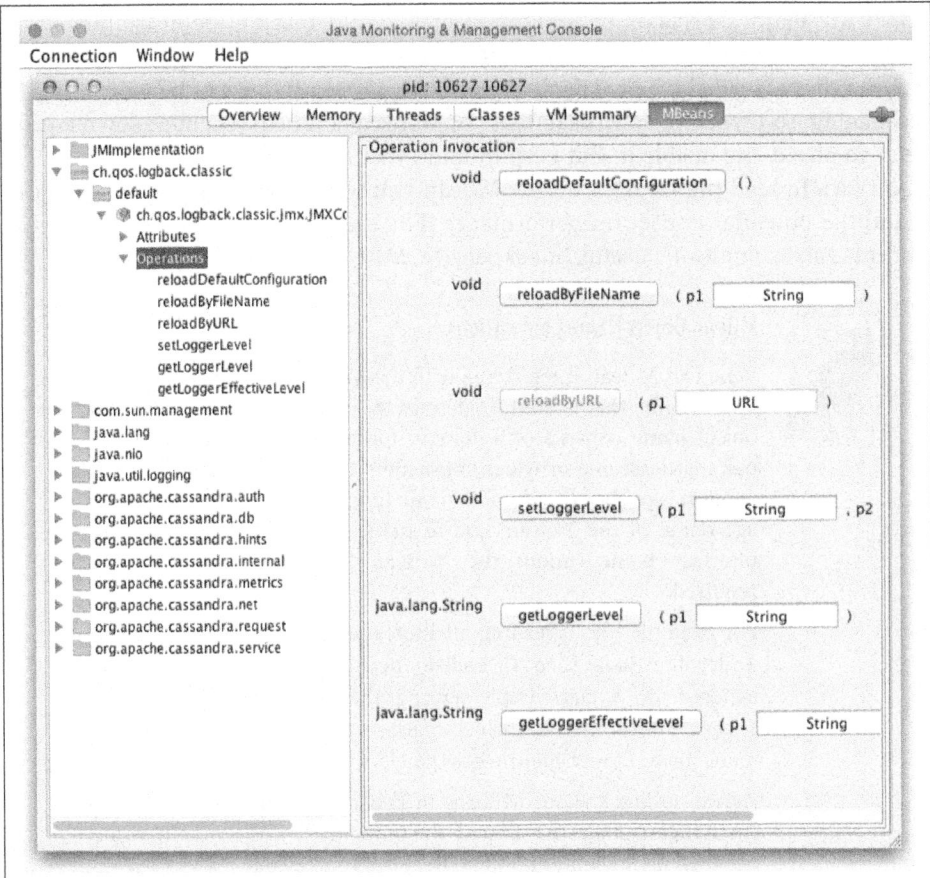

Figure 10-4. The JMXConfigurator MBean allows you to set a logger's log level

Note that the parameter names are not available to the JMX agent; they're just labeled as p0, p1, and so on. That's because the Java compiler "erased" the parameter names during compilation. So in order to know what parameters to set on an operation, you'll need to look at the JavaDoc for the particular MBean you're working with.

In the case of JMXConfigurator, this class implements an interface called JMXConfiguratorMBean, which wraps it for instrumentation. To find out what the right parameters are for the setLoggerLevel operation, we examine the JavaDoc for this interface, available at *http://logback.qos.ch/apidocs/ch/qos/logback/classic/jmx/ JMXConfiguratorMBean.html*. Looking at the documentation, you'll see that p0 represents the name of the logger you want to change, and p1 describes the logging level you want to set that logger to.

Some MBeans return an attribute value of javax.management.openmbean.Composite DataSupport. That means that these are not simple values that can be displayed in a single field, such as LoadedClassCount, but are instead multivalued. One example is Memory > HeapMemoryUsage, which offers several data points and therefore has its own view.

Another type of MBean operation is one that doesn't simply show a value or allow you to set a value, but instead lets you execute some useful action. dumpAllThreads and resetPeakThreadCount are two such operations.

Now we'll quickly get set up to start monitoring and managing Cassandra specifically.

Cassandra's MBeans

Once you've connected with a JMX agent such as JConsole, you can manage Cassandra using the MBeans it exposes. To do so, click the MBeans tab. Other than the standard Java items available to every agent, there are several Cassandra packages that contain manageable beans, organized by their package names, which start with org.apache.cassandra. We won't go into detail on all of them here, but there are several of interest that we'll take a look at.

Many classes in Cassandra are exposed as MBeans, which means in practical terms that they implement a custom interface that describes the operations that need to be implemented and for which the JMX agent will provide hooks. The steps are basically the same for getting any MBean to work. If you'd like to JMX-enable something that isn't already enabled, modify the source code following this general outline and you'll be in business.

For example, we look at Cassandra's CompactionManager from the org.apache. cassandra.db.compaction package and how it uses MBeans. Here's the definition of the CompactionManagerMBean class, with comments omitted for brevity:

```
public interface CompactionManagerMBean
{
    public List<Map<String, String>> getCompactions();
    public List<String> getCompactionSummary();
    public TabularData getCompactionHistory();

    public void forceUserDefinedCompaction(String dataFiles);
    public void stopCompaction(String type);
    public void stopCompactionById(String compactionId);

    public int getCoreCompactorThreads();
    public void setCoreCompactorThreads(int number);

    public int getMaximumCompactorThreads();
    public void setMaximumCompactorThreads(int number);
```

```
public int getCoreValidationThreads();
public void setCoreValidationThreads(int number);

public int getMaximumValidatorThreads();
public void setMaximumValidatorThreads(int number);
}
```

As you can see by this MBean interface definition, there's no magic going on. This is just a regular interface defining the set of operations that will be exposed to JMX that the CompactionManager implementation must support. This typically means maintaining additional metadata as the regular operations do their work.

The CompactionManager class implements this interface and must do the work of directly supporting JMX. The CompactionManager class itself registers and unregisters with the MBean server for the JMX properties that it maintains locally:

```
public static final String MBEAN_OBJECT_NAME =
    "org.apache.cassandra.db:type=CompactionManager";
// ...
static
{
    instance = new CompactionManager();
    MBeanServer mbs = ManagementFactory.getPlatformMBeanServer();
    try
    {
        mbs.registerMBean(instance,
            new ObjectName(MBEAN_OBJECT_NAME));
    }
    catch (Exception e)
    {
        throw new RuntimeException(e);
    }
}
```

Note that the MBean is registered in the domain org.apache.cassandra.db with a type of CompactionManager. The attributes and operations exposed by this MBean appear under org.apache.cassandra.db > CompactionManager in JMX clients. The implementation does all of the work that it is intended to do, and then has implementations of the methods that are only necessary for talking to the MBean server. For example, here is the CompactionManager implementation of the stopCompaction() operation:

```
public void stopCompaction(String type)
{
    OperationType operation = OperationType.valueOf(type);
    for (Holder holder : CompactionMetrics.getCompactions())
    {
        if (holder.getCompactionInfo().getTaskType() == operation)
            holder.stop();
```

```
        }
    }
```

The `CompactionManager` iterates through the compactions in progress, stopping each one that is of the specified type. The Javadoc lets us know that the valid types are `COMPACTION`, `VALIDATION`, `CLEANUP`, `SCRUB`, and `INDEX_BUILD`.

When we view the `CompactionManagerMBean` in JConsole we can select the operations and view the `stopCompaction()` operation, as shown in Figure 10-5. We can enter one of the preceding types and request that the compactions be stopped.

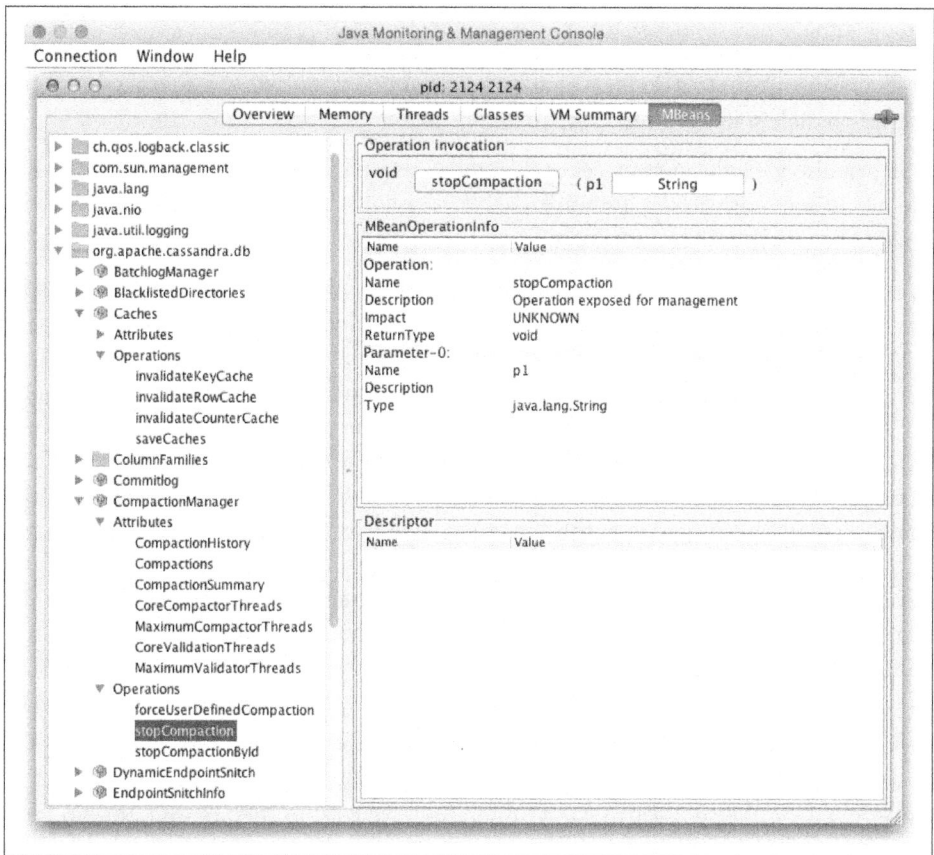

Figure 10-5. The CompactionManager stopCompaction() operation

In the following sections, we see what features are available for monitoring and management via JMX.

Database MBeans

These are the Cassandra classes related to the core database itself that are exposed to clients in the org.apache.cassandra.db domain. There are many MBeans in this domain, but we'll focus on a few key ones related to storage, caching, the commit log, and table stores.

Storage Service MBean

Because Cassandra is a database, it's essentially a very sophisticated storage program; therefore, one of the first places you'll want to look when you encounter problems is the org.apache.cassandra.service.StorageServiceMBean. This allows you to inspect your OperationMode, which reports normal if everything is going smoothly (other possible states are leaving, joining, decommissioned, and client).

You can also view the current set of live nodes, as well as the set of unreachable nodes in the cluster. If any nodes are unreachable, Cassandra will tell you their IP addresses in the UnreachableNodes attribute.

If you want to change Cassandra's log level at runtime without interrupting service (as we saw earlier in the general example), you can invoke the setLoggingLevel(String classQualifier, String level) method. For example, say that you have set Cassandra's log level to DEBUG because you're troubleshooting an issue. You can use some of the methods described here to try to help fix your problem, then you might want to change the log level to something less taxing on the system. To do this, navigate to the StorageService MBean in a JMX client such as JConsole. We'll change the value for a particularly chatty class: the Gossiper. The first parameter to this operation is the name of the class you want to set the log level for, and the second parameter is the level you want to set it to. Enter org.apache.cassandra.gms.Gossiper and INFO, and click the button labeled setLoggingLevel. You should see the following output in your logs (assuming your level was already debug):

```
INFO  03:08:20 set log level to INFO for classes under
   'org.apache.cassandra.gms.Gossiper' (if the level doesn't look
   like 'INFO' then the logger couldn't parse 'INFO')
```

After invoking the setLoggingLevel operation, we get the INFO output and no more DEBUG-level statements.

To get an understanding of how much data is stored on each node, you can use the getLoadMap() method, which will return to you a Java Map with keys of IP addresses with values of their corresponding storage loads. You can also use the effectiveOwnership(String keyspace) operation to access the percentage of the data in a keyspace owned by each node.

If you're looking for a certain key, you can use the getNaturalEndpoints(String table, byte[] key) operation. Pass it the table name and the key for which you want to find the endpoint value, and it will return a list of IP addresses that are responsible for storing this key.

You can also use the getRangeToEndpointMap operation to get a map of range to end points describing your ring topology.

If you're feeling brave, you can invoke the truncate() operation for a given table in a given keyspace. If all of the nodes are available, this operation will delete all data from the table but leave its definition intact.

There are many standard maintenance operations that the StorageServiceMBean affords you, including resumeBootstrap(), joinRing(), repairAsync(), drain(), removeNode(), decommission(), and operations to start and stop gossip, the native transport, and Thrift (until Thrift is finally removed). Understanding the available maintenance operations is important to keeping your cluster in good health, and we'll dig more into these in Chapter 11.

Storage Proxy MBean

As we learned in Chapter 6, the org.apache.cassandra.service.StorageProxy provides a layer on top of the StorageService to handle client requests and inter-node communications. The StorageProxyMBean provides the ability to check and set time-out values for various operations including read and write.

This MBean also provides access to hinted handoff settings such as the maximum time window for storing hints. Hinted handoff statistics include getTotalHints() and getHintsInProgress(). You can disable hints for a particular node with the dis ableHintsForDC() operation.

You can also turn this node's participation in hinted handoff on or off via setHinted HandoffEnabled(), or check the current status via getHintedHandoffEnabled(). These are used by nodetool's enablehandoff, disablehandoff, and statushandoff commands, respectively.

The reloadTriggerClasses() operation allows you to install a new trigger without having to restart a node.

ColumnFamilyStoreMBean

Cassandra registers an instance of the org.apache.cassandra.db.ColumnFamily StoreMBean for each table stored in the node under org.apache.cassandra.db > Tables (previously ColumnFamilies).

The `ColumnFamilyStoreMBean` provides access to the compaction and compression settings for each table. This allows you to temporarily override these settings on a specific node. The values will be reset to those configured on the table schema when the node is restarted.

The MBean also exposes a lot of information about the node's storage of data for this table on disk. The `getSSTableCountPerLevel()` operation provides a list of how many SStables are in each tier. The `estimateKeys()` operation provides an estimate of the number of partitions stored on this node. Taken together, this information can give you some insight as to whether invoking the `forceMajorCompaction()` operation for this table might help free space on this node and increase read performance.

There is also a `trueSnapshotsSize()` operation that allows you to determine the size of SSTable shapshots which are no longer active. A large value here indicates that you should consider deleting these snapshots, possibly after making an archive copy.

Because Cassandra stores indexes as tables, there is also a `ColumnFamilyStoreMBean` instance for each indexed column, available under `org.apache.cassandra.db > IndexTables` (previously `IndexColumnFamilies`), with the same attributes and operations.

CacheServiceMBean

The `org.apache.cassandra.service.CacheServiceMBean` provides access to Cassandra's key cache, row cache, and counter cache under the domain `org.apache.cassandra.db > Caches`. The information available for each cache includes the maximum size and time duration to cache items, and the ability to invalidate each cache.

CommitLogMBean

The `org.apache.cassandra.db.commitlog.CommitLogMBean` exposes attributes and operations that allow you to learn about the current state of commit logs. The `CommitLogMBean` also exposes the `recover()` operation which can be used to restore database state from archived commit log files.

The default settings that control commit log recovery are specified in the *conf/commitlog_archiving.properties* file, but can be overridden via the MBean. We'll learn more about data recovery in Chapter 11.

Compaction Manager MBean

We've already taken a peek inside the source of the `org.apache.cassandra.db.compaction.CompactionManagerMBean` to see how it interacts with JMX, but we didn't really talk about its purpose. This MBean allows us to get statistics about compactions performed in the past, and the ability to force compaction of specific SSTable files we identify by calling the forceUserDefinedCompaction method of the CompactionManager class. This MBean is leveraged by nodetool commands including compact, compactionhistory, and compactionstats.

Snitch MBeans

Cassandra provides two MBeans to monitor and configure behavior of the snitch. The org.apache.cassandra.locator.EndpointSnitchInfoMBean provides the name of the rack and data center for a given host, as well as the name of the snitch in use.

If you're using the DynamicEndpointSnitch, the org.apache.cassandra.locator.DynamicEndpointSnitchMBean is registered. This MBean exposes the ability to reset the badness threshold used by the snitch for marking nodes as offline, as well as allowing you to see the scores for various nodes.

HintedHandoffManagerMBean

In addition to the hinted handoff operations on the StorageServiceMBean mentioned earlier, Cassandra provides more fine grained control of hinted handoff via the org.apache.cassandra.db.HintedHandOffManagerMBean. The MBean exposes the ability to list nodes for which hints are stored by calling listEndpointsPendingHints(). You can then force delivery of hints to a node via scheduleHintDelivery(), or delete hints that are stored up for a specific node with deleteHintsForEndpoint().

Additionally, you can pause and resume hint delivery to all nodes with pauseHintDelivery() or delete stored hints for all nodes with the truncateAllHints() operation. These are used by nodetool's pausehandoff, resumehandoff, and truncate hints commands, respectively.

Duplicative Hinted Handoff Management

The org.apache.cassandra.hints.HintsService exposes the HintsServiceMBean under the domain org.apache.cassandra .hints > HintsService. This MBean provides operations to pause and resume hinted handoff, and to delete hints stored for all nodes, or for a specific node identified by IP address.

Because there is a lot of overlap between the StorageService MBean, HintedHandOffManagerMBean, and HintsServiceMBean, there is likely to be some consolidation of these operations in future releases.

Networking MBeans

The `org.apache.cassandra.net` domain contains MBeans to help manage Cassandra's network-related activities, including Phi failure detection and gossip, the Messaging Service, and Stream Manager.

FailureDetectorMBean

The `org.apache.cassandra.gms.FailureDetectorMBean` provides attributes describing the states and Phi scores of other nodes, as well as the Phi conviction threshold.

GossiperMBean

The `org.apache.cassandra.gms.GossiperMBean` provides access to the work of the `Gossiper`.

We've already discussed how the `StorageServiceMBean` reports which nodes are unreachable. Based on that list, you can call the `getEndpointDowntime()` operation on the `GossiperMBean` to determine how long a given node has been down. The downtime is measured from the perspective of the node whose MBean we're inspecting, and the value resets when the node comes back online. Cassandra uses this operation internally to know how long it can wait to discard hints.

The `getCurrentGenerationNumber()` operation returns the generation number associated with a specific node. The generation number is included in gossip messages exchanged between nodes and is used to distinguish the current state of a node from the state prior to a restart. The generation number remains the same while the node is alive and is incremented each time the node restarts. It's maintained by the `Gossiper` using a timestamp.

The `assassinateEndpoint()` operation attempts to remove a node from the ring by telling the other nodes that the node has been permanently removed, similar to the concept of "character assassination" in human gossip. Assassinating a node is a maintenance step of last resort when a node cannot be removed from the cluster normally. This operation is used by the `nodetool assassinate` command.

StreamManagerMBean

The `org.apache.cassandra.streaming.StreamManagerMBean` allows us to see the streaming activities that occur between a node and its peers. There are two basic ideas here: a stream source and a stream destination. Each node can stream its data to another node in order to perform load balancing, and the `StreamManager` class supports these operations. The `StreamManagerMBean` gives necessary view into the data that is moving between nodes in the cluster.

The `StreamManagerMBean` supports two modes of operation. The `getCurrent Streams()` operation provides a snapshot of the current incoming and outgoing streams, and the MBean also publishes notifications associated with stream state changes, such as initialization, completion or failure. You can subscribe to these notifications in your JMX client in order to watch the streaming operations as they occur.

So in conjunction with the `StorageServiceMBean`, if you're concerned that a node is not receiving data as it should, or that a node is unbalanced or even down, these two MBeans working together can give you very rich insight into exactly what's happening in your cluster.

Metrics MBeans

The ability to access metrics related to application performance, health, and key activities has become an essential tool for maintaining web-scale applications. Fortunately, Cassandra collects a wide range of metrics on its own activities to help us understand the behavior.

The metrics reported by Cassandra include the following:

- *Buffer pool metrics* describing Cassandra's use of memory.
- *CQL metrics* including the number of prepared and regular statement executions.
- *Cache metrics* for key, row, and counter caches such as the number of entries versus capacity, as well as hit and miss rates.
- *Client metrics* including the number of connected clients, and information about client requests such as latency, failures, and timeouts.
- *Commit log metrics* including the commit log size and statistics on pending and completed tasks.
- *Compaction metrics* including the total bytes compacted and statistics on pending and completed compactions.
- *Connection metrics* to each node in the cluster including gossip.
- *Dropped message metrics* which are used as part of `nodetool tpstats`.
- *Read repair metrics* describing the number of background versus blocking read repairs performed over time.
- *Storage metrics*, including counts of hints in progress and total hints.
- *Thread pool metrics*, including active, completed, and blocked tasks for each thread pool.
- *Table metrics*, including caches, memtables, SSTables, and Bloom filter usage and the latency of various read and write operations, reported at one, five, and fifteen minute intervals.
- *Keyspace metrics* that aggregate the metrics for the tables in each keyspace.

To make these metrics accessible via JMX, Cassandra uses the Dropwizard Metrics open source Java library (*http://metrics.dropwizard.io*). Cassandra registers its metrics with the Metrics library, which in turn exposes them as MBeans in the `org.apache.cassandra.metrics` domain.

Many of these metrics are used by `nodetool` commands such as `tpstats`, `tablehisto grams`, and `proxyhistograms`. For example, `tpstats` is simply a presentation of the thread pool and dropped message metrics.

Threading MBeans

The `org.apache.cassandra.internal` domain houses MBeans that allow you to configure the thread pools associated with each stage in Cassandra's Staged Event-Driven Architecture (SEDA). The stages include `AntiEntropyStage`, `GossipStage`, `InternalResponseStage`, `MigrationStage`, and others.

Read Repair MBean

For historical reasons, the `ReadRepairStage` MBean is located under the `org.apache.cassandra.request` domain instead of `org.apache.cassandra.internal`.

The thread pools are implemented via the `JMXEnabledThreadPoolExecutor` and `JMXEnabledScheduledThreadPoolExecutor` classes in the `org.apache.cassandra .concurrent` package. The MBeans for each stage implement the `JMXEnabledSchedu ledThreadPoolExecutorMBean` interface, which allows you to view and configure the number of core threads in each thread pool as well as the maximum number of threads.

Service MBeans

The `GCInspectorMXBean` exposes a single operation `getAndResetStats()` which retrieves and then resets garbage collection metrics that Cassandra collects on its JVM. This MBean appears in the `org.apache.cassandra.service` domain. This MBean is accessed by the `nodetool gcstats` command.

Security MBeans

The `org.apache.cassandra.auth` domain contains security-related MBeans that are grouped according to the same Java package name. As of the 3.0 release, this consists of a single MBean, the `PermissionsCacheMBean`, exposed to clients as `org.apache. cassandra.auth.PermissionsCache`. We'll discuss this MBean in Chapter 13.

Monitoring with nodetool

We've already explored a few of the commands offered by nodetool in previous chapters, but let's take this opportunity to get properly introduced.

nodetool ships with Cassandra and can be found in *<cassandra-home>/bin*. This is a command-line program that offers a rich array of ways to look at your cluster, understand its activity, and modify it. nodetool lets you get limited statistics about the cluster, see the ranges each node maintains, move data from one node to another, decommission a node, and even repair a node that's having trouble.

Overlap of nodetool and JMX

Many of the tasks in nodetool overlap with functions available in the JMX interface. This is because, behind the scenes, nodetool is invoking JMX using a helper class called org.apache.cassandra .tools.NodeProbe. So JMX is doing the real work, the NodeProbe class is used to connect to the JMX agent and retrieve the data, and the NodeCmd class is used to present it in an interactive command-line interface.

nodetool uses the same environment settings as the Cassandra daemon: *bin/cassandra.in.sh* and *conf/cassandra-env.sh* on Unix (or *bin/cassandra.in.bat* and *conf/cassandra-env.ps1* on Windows). The logging settings are found in the *conf/logback-tools.xml* file; these work the same way as the Cassandra daemon logging settings found in *conf/logback.xml*.

Starting nodetool is a breeze. Just open a terminal, navigate to *<cassandra-home>*, and enter the following command:

```
$ bin/nodetool help
```

This causes the program to print a list of available commands, several of which we will cover momentarily. Running nodetool with no arguments is equivalent to the help command. You can also execute help with the name of a specific command to get additional details.

Connecting to a Specific Node

With the exception of the help command, nodetool must connect to a Cassandra node in order to access information about that node or the cluster as a whole.

You can use the -h option to identify the IP address of the node to connect to with nodetool. If no IP address is specified, the tool attempts to connect to the default port on the local machine, which is the approach we'll take for examples in this chapter.

Getting Cluster Information

There is a variety of information you can get about the cluster and its nodes, which we look at in this section. You can get basic information on an individual node or on all the nodes participating in a ring.

describecluster

The describecluster command prints out basic information about the cluster, including the name, snitch, and partitioner:

```
$ bin/nodetool describecluster
Cluster Information:
    Name: Test Cluster
    Snitch: org.apache.cassandra.locator.DynamicEndpointSnitch
    Partitioner: org.apache.cassandra.dht.Murmur3Partitioner
    Schema versions:
        2d4043cb-2124-3589-b2d0-375759b9dd0a: [127.0.0.1, 127.0.0.2, 127.0.0.3]]
```

The last part of the output is especially important for identifying any disagreements in table definitions, or "schema," between nodes. As Cassandra propagates schema changes through a cluster, any differences are typically resolved quickly, so any lingering schema differences usually indicate a node that is down or unreachable that needs to be restarted.

status

A more direct way to identify the nodes in your cluster and what state they're in, is to use the status command:

```
$ bin/nodetool status
Datacenter: datacenter1
========================
Status=Up/Down
|/ State=Normal/Leaving/Joining/Moving
--  Address    Load      Tokens  Owns  Host ID
UN  127.0.0.1  103.82 KB  256     ?     31d9042b-6603-4040-8aac-fef0a235570b
UN  127.0.0.2  110.9 KB   256     ?     caad1573-4157-43d2-a9fa-88f79344683d
UN  127.0.0.3  109.6 KB   256     ?     e78529c8-ee9f-46a4-8bc1-3479f99a1860
```

The status is organized by data center and rack. Each node's status is identified by a two-character code, in which the first character indicates whether the node is up (currently available and ready for queries) or down, and the second character indicates the state or operational mode of the node. The load column represents the byte count of the data each node is holding.

The owns column indidates the effective percentage of the token range owned by the node, taking replication into account. Because we did not specify a keyspace and the various keyspaces in this cluster have differing replication strategies, nodetool is not able to calculate a meaningful ownership percentage.

info

The info command tells nodetool to connect with a single node and get basic data about its current state. Just pass it the address of the node you want info for:

```
$ bin/nodetool -h 192.168.2.7 info
ID                     : 197efa22-ecaa-40dc-a010-6c105819bf5e
Gossip active          : true
Thrift active          : false
Native Transport active: true
Load                   : 301.17 MB
Generation No          : 1447444152
Uptime (seconds)       : 1901668
Heap Memory (MB)       : 395.03 / 989.88
Off Heap Memory (MB)   : 2.94
Data Center            : datacenter1
Rack                   : rack1
Exceptions             : 0
Key Cache              : entries 85, size 8.38 KB, capacity 49 MB,
   47958 hits, 48038 requests, 0.998 recent hit rate, 14400 save
   period in seconds
Row Cache              : entries 0, size 0 bytes, capacity 0 bytes,
   0 hits, 0 requests, NaN recent hit rate, 0 save period in seconds
Counter Cache          : entries 0, size 0 bytes, capacity 24 MB,
   0 hits, 0 requests, NaN recent hit rate, 7200 save period in seconds
Token                  : (invoke with -T/--tokens to see all 256 tokens)
```

The information reported includes the memory and disk usage ("Load") of the node and the status of various services offered by Cassandra. You can also check the status of individual services by the nodetool commands statusgossip, statusthrift, statusbinary, and statushandoff (note that handoff status is not part of info).

ring

To determine what nodes are in your ring and what state they're in, use the ring command on nodetool, like this:

```
$ bin/nodetool ring
Datacenter: datacenter1
```

```
==========
Address       Rack   Status State   Load      Owns   Token
                                                      9208237582789476801
192.168.2.5   rack1  Up     Normal  243.6 KB  ?      -9203905334627395805
192.168.2.6   rack1  Up     Normal  243.6 KB  ?      -9145503818225306830
192.168.2.7   rack1  Up     Normal  243.6 KB  ?      -9091015424710319286
...
```

This output is organized in terms of vnodes. Here we see the IP addresses of all the nodes in the ring. In this case, we have three nodes, all of which are up (currently available and ready for queries). The load column represents the byte count of the data each node is holding. The output of the describering command is similar but is organized around token ranges.

Other useful status commands provided by nodetool include:

- The getLoggingLevels and setLoggingLevels commands allow dynamic configuration of logging levels, using the Logback JMXConfiguratorMBean we discussed previously.
- The gossipinfo command prints the parameters this node communicates about itself to other nodes via gossip.
- The version command prints the version of Cassandra this node is running.

Getting Statistics

nodetool also lets you gather statistics about the state of your server in the aggregate level as well as down to the level of specific keyspaces and tables. Two of the most frequently used commands are tpstats and tablestats, both of which we examine now.

Using tpstats

The tpstats tool gives us information on the thread pools that Cassandra maintains. Cassandra is highly concurrent, and optimized for multiprocessor/multicore machines. Moreover, Cassandra employs a Staged Event-Driven Architecture (SEDA) internally, so understanding the behavior and health of the thread pools is important to good Cassandra maintenance.

To find statistics on the thread pools, execute nodetool with the tpstats command:

```
$ bin/nodetool tpstats
Pool Name             Active  Pending  Completed  Blocked  All time
                                                           blocked
ReadStage             0       0        216        0        0
MutationStage         1       0        3637       0        0
CounterMutationStage  0       0        0          0        0
ViewMutationStage     0       0        0          0        0
GossipStage           0       0        0          0        0
```

```
RequestResponseStage      0      0      0      0      0
AntiEntropyStage          0      0      0      0      0
MigrationStage            0      0      2      0      0
MiscStage                 0      0      0      0      0
InternalResponseStage     0      0      2      0      0
ReadRepairStage           0      0      0      0      0

Message type          Dropped
READ                        0
RANGE_SLICE                 0
_TRACE                      0
HINT                        0
MUTATION                    0
COUNTER_MUTATION            0
BATCH_STORE                 0
BATCH_REMOVE                0
REQUEST_RESPONSE            0
PAGED_RANGE                 0
READ_REPAIR                 0
```

The top portion of the output presents data on tasks in each of Cassandra's thread pools. You can see directly how many operations are in what stage, and whether they are active, pending, or completed. This output was captured during a write operation, and therefore shows that there is an active task in the MutationStage.

The bottom portion of the output indicates the number of dropped messages for the node. Dropped messages are an indicator of Cassandra's load shedding implementation, which each node uses to defend itself when it receives more requests than it can handle. For example, internode messages that are received by a node but not processed within the `rpc_timeout` are dropped, rather than processed, as the coordinator node will no longer be waiting for a response.

Seeing lots of zeros in the output for blocked tasks and dropped messages means that you either have very little activity on the server or that Cassandra is doing an exceptional job of keeping up with the load. Lots of non-zero values is indicative of situations where Cassandra is having a hard time keeping up, and may indicate a need for some of the techniques described in Chapter 12.

Using tablestats

To see overview statistics for keyspaces and tables, you can use the `tablestats` command. You may also recognize this command from its previous name `cfstats`. Here is sample output on the `hotel` keyspace:

```
$ bin/nodetool tablestats hotel
Keyspace: hotel
    Read Count: 8
    Read Latency: 0.617 ms.
    Write Count: 13
    Write Latency: 0.13330769230769232 ms.
```

```
Pending Flushes: 0
    Table: hotels
    SSTable count: 3
    Space used (live): 16601
    Space used (total): 16601
    Space used by snapshots (total): 0
    Off heap memory used (total): 140
    SSTable Compression Ratio: 0.6277372262773723
    Number of keys (estimate): 19
    Memtable cell count: 8
    Memtable data size: 792
    Memtable off heap memory used: 0
    Memtable switch count: 1
    Local read count: 8
    Local read latency: 0.680 ms
    Local write count: 13
    Local write latency: 0.148 ms
    Pending flushes: 0
    Bloom filter false positives: 0
    Bloom filter false ratio: 0.00000
    Bloom filter space used: 56
    Bloom filter off heap memory used: 32
    Index summary off heap memory used: 84
    Compression metadata off heap memory used: 24
    Compacted partition minimum bytes: 30
    Compacted partition maximum bytes: 149
    Compacted partition mean bytes: 87
    Average live cells per slice (last five minutes): 1.0
    Maximum live cells per slice (last five minutes): 1
    Average tombstones per slice (last five minutes): 1.0
    Maximum tombstones per slice (last five minutes): 1
```

Here we have omitted output for other tables in the keyspace so we can focus on the hotels table; the same statistics are generated for each table. We can see the read and write latency and total number of reads and writes at the keyspace and table level. We can also see detailed information about Cassandra's internal structures for each table, including memtables, Bloom filters and SSTables.

Summary

In this chapter, we looked at ways you can monitor and manage your Cassandra cluster. In particular, we went into some detail on JMX and learned the rich variety of operations Cassandra makes available to the MBean server. We saw how to use JConsole and nodetool to view what's happening in your Cassandra cluster. You are now ready to learn how to perform routine maintenance tasks to help keep your Cassandra cluster healthy.

Maintenance

In this chapter, we look at some things you can do to keep your Cassandra cluster healthy. Our goal here is to provide an overview of the various maintenance tasks available. Because the specific procedures for these tasks tend to change slightly from release to release, you'll want to make sure to consult the DataStax documentation (*http://docs.datastax.com*) for the release you're using to make sure you're not missing any new steps.

Let's put our operations hats on and get started!

Health Check

There are some basic things that you'll want to look for to ensure that nodes in your cluster are healthy:

- Use nodetool status to make sure all of the nodes are up and reporting normal status. Check the load on each node to make sure the cluster is well balanced. An uneven number of nodes per rack can lead to an imbalanced cluster.

- Check nodetool tpstats on your nodes for dropped messages, especially mutations, as this indicates that data writes may be lost. A growing number of blocked flush writers indicates the node is ingesting data into memory faster than it can be flushed to disk. Both of these conditions can indicate that Cassandra is having trouble keeping up with the load. As is usual with databases, once these problems begin, they tend to continue in a downward spiral. Three things that can improve the situation are a decreased load, scaling up (adding more hardware), or scaling out (adding another node and rebalancing).

If these checks indicate issues, you may need to dig deeper to get more information about what is going on:

- Check the logs to see that nothing is reporting at ERROR or WARN level (e.g., an OutOfMemoryError). Cassandra generates warning logs when it detects bad or obsolete configuration settings, operations that did not complete successfully, and memory or data storage issues.

- Review the configuration of the *cassandra.yaml* and *cassandra-env.sh* files for your Cassandra nodes to make sure that they match your intended settings. For example, the heap should be set to its recommended size of 8 GB.

- Verify keyspace and table configuration settings. For example, a frequent configuration error is to forget to update keyspace replication strategies when adding a new data center.

- Beyond the health of your Cassandra nodes, it is always helpful to have a sense of the overall health and configuration of your system, including ensuring network connectivity and that Network Time Protocol (NTP) servers are functioning correctly.

These are a few of the most important things that experienced Cassandra operators have learned to look for. As you gain experience with your own deployments, you can augment this list with additional health checks that are appropriate for your own environment.

Basic Maintenance

There are a few tasks that you'll need to perform before or after more impactful tasks. For example, it makes sense to take a snapshot only after you've performed a flush. So in this section we look at some of these basic maintenance tasks.

Many of the tasks we look at in this chapter work somewhat differently depending on whether you're using virtual nodes or single token nodes. Because vnodes are the default, we'll focus primarily on maintenance of those nodes, but provide pointers if you're using single token nodes.

Flush

To force Cassandra to write data from its memtables to SSTables on the filesystem, you use the flush command on nodetool, like this:

```
$ nodetool flush
```

If you check the server logs, you'll see a series of output statements similar to this, one per table stored on the node:

```
DEBUG [RMI TCP Connection(297)-127.0.0.1] 2015-12-21 19:20:50,794
    StorageService.java:2847 - Forcing flush on keyspace hotel,
    CF reservations_by_hotel_date
```

You can selectively flush specific keyspaces or even specific tables within a keyspace by naming them on the command line:

```
$ nodetool flush hotel
$ nodetool flush hotel reservations_by_hotel_date hotels_by_poi
```

Running flush also allows Cassandra to clear commitlog segments, as the data has been written to SSTables.

The nodetool drain command is similar to flush. This command actually performs a flush and then directs Cassandra to stop listening to commands from the client and other nodes. The drain command is typically used as part of an orderly shutdown of a Cassandra node and helps the node startup to run more quickly, as there is no commitlog to replay.

Cleanup

The cleanup command scans all of the data on a node and discards any data that is no longer owned by the node. You might ask why a node would have any data that it doesn't own.

Say that you've had a cluster running for some time, and you want to change the replication factor or the replication strategy. If you decrease the number of replicas for any data center, then there will be nodes in that data center that no longer serve as replicas for secondary ranges.

Or perhaps you've added a node to a cluster and reduced the size of the token range(s) owned by each node. Then each node may contain data from portions of token ranges it no longer owns.

In both of these cases, Cassandra does not immediately delete the excess data, in case a node goes down while you're in the middle of your maintenance. Instead, the normal compaction processes will eventually discard this data.

However, you may wish to reclaim the disk space used by this excess data more quickly to reduce the strain on your cluster. To do this, you can the nodetool cleanup command.

As with the flush command, you can select to cleanup specific keyspaces and tables. You don't need to automate running cleanup, as you will only need to run it if you have performed one of the actions described earlier.

Repair

As we discussed in Chapter 6, Cassandra's tuneable consistency means that it is possible for nodes in a cluster to get out of sync over time. For example, writes at consistency levels less than ALL may succeed even if some of the nodes don't respond, especially when a cluster is under heavy load. It's also possible for a node to miss mutations if it is down or unreachable for longer than the time window for which hints are stored. The result is that different replicas for a different partition may have different versions of our data.

This is especially challenging when the missed mutations are deletions. A node that is down when the deletion occurs and remains offline for longer than the gc_grace_seconds defined for the table in question can "resurrect" the data when it is brought back online.

Fortunately, Cassandra provides multiple anti-entropy mechanisms to help mitigate against inconsistency. We've already discussed how read repair and higher consistency levels on reads can be used to increase consistency. The final key element of Cassandra's arsenal is the anti-entropy repair or manual repair, which we perform using the nodetool repair command.

We can execute a basic repair as follows:

```
$ nodetool repair
[2016-01-01 14:47:59,010] Nothing to repair for keyspace 'hotel'
[2016-01-01 14:47:59,018] Nothing to repair for keyspace 'system_auth'
[2016-01-01 14:47:59,129] Starting repair command #1, repairing
  keyspace system_traces with repair options (parallelism: parallel,
  primary range: false, incremental: true, job threads: 1,
  ColumnFamilies: [], dataCenters: [], hosts: [], # of ranges: 510)
...
```

The output of this will vary, of course, based on the current state of your cluster. This particular command iterates over all of the keyspaces and tables in our cluster, repairing each one. We can also specify specific keyspaces and even one or more specific tables to repair via the syntax: nodetool repair <keyspace> {<table(s)>}. For example: nodetool repair hotel hotels_by_poi.

Limiting Repair Scope

The repair command can be restricted to run in the local data center via the -local option (which you may also specify via the longer form --in-local-dc), or in a named data center via the -dc <name> option (or --in-dc <name>).

Let's look at what is happening behind the scenes when you run nodetool repair on a node. The node on which the command is run serves as the coordinator node for the request. The `org.apache.cassandra.service.ActiveRepairService` class is responsible for managing repairs on the coordinator node and processes the incoming request. The `ActiveRepairService` first executes a read-only version of a major compaction, also known as *validation compaction*. During a validation compaction, the node examines its local data store and creates Merkle trees containing hash values representing the data in one of the tables under repair. This part of the process is generally expensive in terms of disk I/O and memory usage.

Next, the node initiates a TreeRequest/TreeResponse conversation to exchange Merkle trees with neighboring nodes. If the trees from the different nodes don't match, they have to be reconciled in order to determine the latest data values they should all be set to. If any differences are found, the nodes stream data to each other for the ranges that don't agree. When a node receives data for repair, it stores it in SSTables.

Note that if you have a lot of data in a table, the resolution of Merkle trees will not go down to the individual partition. For example, in a node with a million partitions, each leaf node of the Merkle tree will represent about 30 partitions. Each of these partitions will have to be streamed even if only a single partition requires repair. This behavior is known as *overstreaming*. For this reason, the streaming part of the process is generally expensive in terms of network I/O, and can result in duplicate storage of data that did not actually need repair.

This process is repeated on each node, for each included keyspace and table, until all of the token ranges in the cluster have been repaired.

Although repair can be an expensive operation, Cassandra provides several options to give you flexibility in how the work is spread out.

Full repair, incremental repair, and anti-compaction

In Cassandra releases prior to 2.1, performing a repair meant that all SSTables in a node were examined in a repair, which is now referred to as a *full repair*. The 2.1 release introduced *incremental repair*. With incremental repairs, data that has been repaired is separated from data that has not been repaired, a process known as *anti-compaction*.

This incremental approach improves the performance of the repair process, as there are fewer SSTables to search on each repair. Also the reduced search means that fewer partitions are in scope, leading to smaller Merkle trees and less overstreaming.

Cassandra adds a bit of metadata to each SSTable file in order to keep track of its repair status. You can view the repair time by using the `sstablemetadata` tool. For example, examining an SSTable for our hotel data indicates the data it contains has not been repaired:

```
$ tools/bin/sstablemetadata data/data/hotel/
  hotels-d089fec0677411e59f0ba9fac1d00bce/ma-5-big-Data.db
```

```
SSTable: data/data/hotel/hotels-d089fec0677411e59f0ba9fac1d00bce/ma-5-big
Partitioner: org.apache.cassandra.dht.Murmur3Partitioner
Bloom Filter FP chance: 0.010000
Minimum timestamp: 1443619302081305
Maximum timestamp: 1448201891587000
SSTable max local deletion time: 2147483647
Compression ratio: -1.0
Estimated droppable tombstones: 0.0
SSTable Level: 0
Repaired at: 0
ReplayPosition(segmentId=1449353006197, position=326)
Estimated tombstone drop times:
2147483647:         37
...
```

Transitioning to Incremental Repair

Incremental repair became the default in the 2.2 release, and you must use the -full option to request a full repair. If you are using a version of Cassandra prior to 2.2, make sure to consult the release documentation for any additional steps to prepare your cluster for incremental repair.

Sequential and parallel repair

A sequential repair works on repairing one node at a time, while parallel repair works on repairing multiple nodes with the same data simultaneously. Sequential repair was the default for releases through 2.1, and parallel repair became the default in the 2.2 release.

When a sequential repair is initiated using the -seq option, a snapshot of data is taken on the coordinator node and each replica node, and the snapshots are used to construct Merkle trees. The repairs are performed between the coordinator node and each replica in sequence. During sequential repairs, Cassandra's dynamic snitch helps maintain performance. Because replicas that aren't actively involved in the current repair are able to respond more quickly to requests, the dynamic snitch will tend to route requests to these nodes.

A parallel repair is initiated using the -par option. In a parallel repair, all replicas are involved in repair simultaneously, and no snapshots are needed. Parallel repair places a more intensive load on the cluster than sequential repair, but also allows the repair to complete more quickly.

Partitioner range repair

When you run repair on a node, by default Cassandra repairs all of the token ranges for which the node is a replica. This is appropriate for the situation where you have a single node that is in need of repair—for example, a node that has been down and is being prepared to bring back online.

However, if you are doing regular repairs for preventative maintenance, as recommended, repairing all of the token ranges for each node means that you will be doing multiple repairs over each range. For this reason, the `nodetool repair` command provides the `-pr` option, which allows you to repair only the primary token range or *partitioner range*. If you repair each node's primary range, the whole ring will be repaired.

Subrange repair

Even with the `-pr` option, a repair can still be an expensive operation, as the primary range of a node can represent a large amount of data. For this reason, Cassandra supports the ability to repair by breaking the token range of a node into smaller chunks, a process known as *subrange repair*.

Subrange repair also addresses the issue of overstreaming. Because the full resolution of a Merkle tree is applied to a smaller range, Cassandra can precisely identify individual rows that need repair.

To initiate a subrange repair operation, you will need the start token (`-st`) and end token (`-et`) of the range to be repaired.

```
$ nodetool repair -st <start token> -et <end token>
```

You can obtain tokens for a range programmatically via the DataStax Cassandra drivers. For example, the Java driver provides operations to get the token ranges for a given host and keyspace, and to split a token range into subranges. You could use these operations to automate a repair request for each subrange, or just print out the ranges, as we do in this example:

```
for (Host host : cluster.getMetadata().getAllHosts())
{
  for (TokenRange tokenRange :
      cluster.getMetadata().getTokenRanges("hotel", host))
  {
    for (TokenRange splitRange : tokenRange.splitEvenly(SPLIT_SIZE))
    {
      System.out.println("Start: " + splitRange.getStart().getValue() +
                      ", End: " + splitRange.getEnd().getValue());
    }
  }
}
```

A similar algorithm using subrange repair is implemented by the OpsCenter Repair Service, which we'll examine momentarily.

Best Practices for Repair

In practice, selecting and executing the proper repair strategy is one of the more difficult tasks in maintaining a Cassandra cluster. Here's a checklist to help guide your decision making:

Repair frequency
> Remember that the data consistency your applications will observe depends on the read and write consistency levels you use, but also on the repair strategy you put in place. If you're willing to use read/write consistency levels that don't guarantee immediate consistency, you'll want to do more frequent repairs.

Repair scheduling
> Minimize the impact of repairs on your application by scheduling them at off-peak times for your application. Alternatively, spread the process out by using subrange repairs or stagger repairs for various keyspaces and tables at different start times.

Operations requiring repair
> Don't forget that some operations—such as changing the snitch on a cluster or changing the replication factor on a keyspace—will require a full repair.

Avoiding conflicting repairs
> Cassandra does not allow multiple simultaneous repairs over a given token range, as repair by definition involves interactions between nodes. For this reason, it's best to manage repairs from a single location external to the cluster, rather than trying to implement automated processes on each node to repair their locally owned ranges.
>
> Until a more robust repair status mechanism is put in place (for example, see the JIRA issue CASSANDRA-10302 (*https://issues.apache.org/jira/browse/CASSANDRA-10302*)), you can monitor repairs in progress using `nodetool net stats`.

Rebuilding Indexes

If you're using secondary indexes, they can get out of sync just like any other data. While it is true that Cassandra stores secondary indexes as tables behind the scenes, the index tables only reference values stored on the local node. For this reason, Cassandra's repair mechanisms aren't helpful for keeping indexes up to date.

Because secondary indexes can't be repaired and there is no simple way to check their validity, Cassandra provides the ability to rebuild them from scratch using nodetool's `rebuild_index` command. It is a good idea to rebuild an index after repairing the table on which it is based, as the columns on which the index is based could have been represented among the values repaired. As with repair, remember that rebuilding indexes is a CPU- and I/O-intensive procedure.

Moving Tokens

If you have configured your cluster to use vnodes (which has been the default configuration since the 2.0. release), Cassandra handles the assignment of token ranges to each of the nodes in your cluster. This includes changing these assignments when nodes are added or removed from the cluster. However, if you're using single token nodes, you'll need to reconfigure the tokens manually.

To do this, you first need to recalculate the token ranges for each node using the technique described in Chapter 7. Then we use the `nodetool move` command to assign the ranges. The `move` command takes a single argument, which is the new start token for the node:

```
$ nodetool move 3074457345618258600
```

After adjusting the token of each node, complete the process by running `nodetool cleanup` on each node.

Adding Nodes

We learned briefly in Chapter 7 how to add a node using the Cassandra Cluster Manager (`ccm`), which was a great way for us to get started quickly. Now let's dig a little deeper to discuss some of the motivations and procedures for adding new nodes and data centers.

Adding Nodes to an Existing Data Center

If your application is successful, sooner or later you'll arrive at the point where you need to add nodes to your cluster. This might be as part of a planned increase in capacity, or it might be in reaction to something you've observed in a health check such as running low on storage space, or nodes that are experiencing high memory and CPU utilization, or increasing read and write latencies.

Whatever the motivation for your expansion, you'll start by installing and configuring Cassandra on the machines that will host the new nodes. The process is similar to what we outlined in Chapter 7, but keep the following in mind:

- The Cassandra version must be the same as the existing nodes in the cluster. If you want to do a version upgrade, upgrade the existing nodes to the new version first and then add new nodes.

- You'll want to use the same configuration values as you did for other nodes in files such as *cassandra.yaml* and *cassandra-env.sh*, including the `cluster_name`, `dynamic_snitch`, `partitioner`, and `listen_address`.
- Use the same seed nodes as in the other nodes. Typically, the new nodes you add won't be seed nodes, so there is no need to add the new nodes to the seeds list in your previously existing nodes.
- If you have multiple racks in your configuration, it's a good idea to add nodes to each rack at the same time to keep the number of nodes in each rack balanced. For some reason, this always reminds me of the rule in the classic board game *Monopoly* that requires houses to be spread evenly across properties.
- If you're using single token nodes, you'll have to manually calculate the token range that will be assigned to each node as we discussed in "Moving Tokens" on page 243. A simple and effective way to keep the cluster balanced is to divide each token range in half, doubling the number of nodes in the cluster.
- In most cases, you'll want to configure your new nodes to begin bootstrapping immediately—that is, claiming token ranges and streaming the data for those ranges from other nodes. This is controlled by the `autobootstrap` property, which defaults to `true`. You can add this to your *cassandra.yaml* file to explicitly enable or disable auto bootstrapping.

Once the nodes are configured, you can start them, and use `nodetool status` to determine when they are fully initialized.

You can also watch the progress of a bootstrap operation on a node by running the `nodetool bootstrap` command. If you've started a node with auto bootstrapping disabled, you can also kick off bootstrapping remotely at the time of your choosing with the command `nodetool bootstrap resume`.

After all new nodes are running, make sure to run a `nodetool cleanup` on each of the previously existing nodes to clear out data that is no longer managed by those nodes.

Adding a Data Center to a Cluster

There are several reasons you might want to add an entirely new data center to your cluster. For example, let's say that you are deploying your application to a new data center in order to reduce network latency for clients in a new market. Or perhaps you need an active-active configuration in order to support disaster recovery requirements for your application. A third popular use case is to create a separate data center that can be used for analytics without impacting online customer transactions.

We'll explore some of these deployments further in Chapter 14, but for now let's focus on how we can extend our cluster to a new data center.

The same basic steps we followed for adding a node in an existing data center apply to adding nodes in a new data center. Here are a few additional things you'll want to consider as you configure the *cassandra.yaml* file for each node:

- Make sure to configure an appropriate snitch for your deployment environment using the endpoint_snitch property and any configuration files associated with the snitch. Hopefully you planned for this when first setting up your cluster, but if not, you will need to change the snitch in the initial data center. If you do need to change the snitch, you'll first want to change it on nodes in the existing data center and perform a repair before adding the new data center.
- Select a couple of the nodes in the new data center to be seeds, and configure the seeds property in the other nodes accordingly. Each data center should have its own seeds independent of the other data centers.
- The new data center is not required to have the same token range configuration as any existing data centers within the cluster. You can select a different number of vnodes or use single-token nodes if so desired.
- Disable auto bootstrapping by finding (or adding) the autobootstrap option and setting it to false. This will prevent our new nodes from attempting to stream data before we're ready.

After all of the nodes in the new data center have been brought online, you then configure replication options for the NetworkTopologyStrategy for all keyspaces that you wish to replicate to the new data center.

For example, to extend our hotel keyspace into an additional data center, we might execute the command:

```
cqlsh> ALTER KEYSPACE hotel WITH REPLICATION =
  {'class' : 'NetworkTopologyStrategy', 'dc1' : 3, 'dc2' : 2};
```

Note that the NetworkTopologyStrategy allows us to specify a different number of replicas for each data center.

Next, run the nodetool rebuild command on each node in the new data center. For example, the following command causes a node to rebuild its data by streaming from data center dc1:

```
$ nodetool rebuild -- dc1
```

You can rebuild multiple nodes in parallel if desired; just remember to consider the impact on your cluster before doing this.

Once the rebuilding is complete, your new data center is ready to use. Don't forget to reconfigure the *cassandra.yaml* file for each node in the new data center to remove the autobootstrap: false option, so that the nodes will recover successfully if restarted.

Don't Forget Your Clients

You'll also want to consider how adding another data center affects your existing clients and their usage of LOCAL_* and EACH_* consistency levels. For example, if you have clients using the QUORUM consistency level for reads or writes, queries that used to be confined to a single data center will now involve multiple data centers. You may wish to switch to LOCAL_QUORUM to limit latency, or to EACH_QUORUM to ensure strong consistency in each data center.

Handling Node Failure

From time to time, a Cassandra node may fail. Failure can occur for a variety of reasons, including: hardware failure, a crashed Cassandra process, or a virtual machine that has been stopped or destroyed. A node that is experiencing network connectivity issues may be marked as failed in gossip and reported as down in nodetool status, although it may come back online if connectivity improves.

In this section, we'll examine how to repair or replace failed nodes, as well as how to gracefully remove nodes from a cluster.

Repairing Nodes

The first thing to do when you observe there is a failed node is to try to determine how long the node has been down. Here is a quick rule of thumb to know if repair or replacement may be required:

- If the node has been down for less than the hints delivery window specified by the max_hint_window_in_ms property, the hinted handoff mechanism should be able to recover the node. Restart the node and see whether it is able to recover. You can watch the node's logs or track its progress using nodetool status.
- If the node has been down for less than the repair window defined lowest value of gc_grace_seconds for any of its contained tables, then restart the node. If it comes up successfully, run a nodetool repair.
- If the node has been down for longer than the repair window, it should be replaced, in order to avoid tombstone resurrection.

Recovering from disk failure

A disk failure is one form of hardware failure from which a node may be able to recover. If your node is configured to use Cassandra with multiple disks (JBOD), the disk_failure_policy setting determines what action is taken when a disk failure occurs, and how you may be able to detect the failure:

- If the policy is set to the default (`stop`), the node will stop gossiping, which will cause it to appear as a downed node in `nodetool status`. You can still connect to the node via JMX.
- If the policy is set to `die`, the JVM exits and the node will appear as a downed node in `nodetool status`.
- If the policy is set to `ignore`, there's no immediate way to detect the failure.
- If the policy is set to `best_effort`, Cassandra continues to operate using the other disks, but a WARN log entry is written, which can be detected if you are using a log aggregation tool. Alternatively, you can use a JMX monitoring tool to monitor the state of the `org.apache.cassandra.db.BlacklistedDirectories` `MBean`, which lists the directories for which the node has recorded failures.
- If a disk failure is detected on node startup and the policy is anything besides `best_effort`, the node writes an ERROR log entry and exits.

Once you've detected a disk failure, you may want to try restarting the Cassandra process or rebooting the server. But if the failure persists, you'll have to replace the disk and delete the contents of the *data/system* directory in the remaining disks so that when you restart the node, it comes up in a consistent state. When the node is up, run a repair.

Replacing Nodes

If you've determined that a node can't be repaired, you will most likely want to replace it in order to keep your cluster balanced and maintain the same capacity.

While we could replace a node by removing the old node (as in the next section) and adding a new node, this is not a very efficient approach. Removing and then adding nodes results in excess streaming of data, first to move data away from the old node and then to move it back to the new node.

The more efficient approach is to add a node that takes over the token ranges of an existing node. To do this, we follow the previously outlined procedure for adding a node, with one addition. Edit the *cassandra-env.sh* file for the new node to add the following JVM option (where <address> is the IP address or hostname of the node that is being replaced):

```
JVM_OPTS="$JVM_OPTS -Dcassandra.replace_address=<address>"
```

After the replacement node finishes bootstrapping, you can remove this option, as it is not required for any subsequent restarts of the node.

If you're using a snitch that uses a properties file to record the cluster topology, such as the `GossipingPropertyFileSnitch` or the `PropertyFileSnitch`, you'll need to add the address of your new node to the properties file on each node and do a rolling restart of the nodes in your cluster. It is recommended that you wait 72 hours before removing the address of the old node to avoid confusing the gossiper.

Replacing a Seed Node

If the node you're replacing is a seed node, select an existing non-seed node to promote to a seed node. You'll need to add the promoted seed node to the seeds property in the *cassandra.yaml* file of existing nodes.

Typically, these will be nodes in the same data center, assuming you follow the recommendation of using a different seed list per data center. In this way, the new node we create will be a non-seed node and can bootstrap normally.

There are some additional details if you are using a package installation of Cassandra; consult the documentation for your specific release for additional details.

Removing Nodes

If you decide not to replace a downed node right away, or just want to shrink the size of your cluster, you'll need to remove or decommission the node. The proper technique for removal depends on whether the node being removed is online or able to be brought online. We'll look at three techniques, in order of preference: decommission, remove, and assassinate.

Decommissioning a node

If the node is reporting as up, we *decommission* the node. Decommissioning a node means pulling it out of service. When you execute the `nodetool decommission` command, you're calling the decommission operation on Cassandra's `StorageService` class. The decommission operation assigns the token ranges that the node was responsible for to other nodes and then streams the data to those nodes. This is effectively the opposite of the bootstrapping operation.

While the decommission is running, the node will report that it is in a leaving state in `nodetool status` via the code UL (up, leaving):

```
$ nodetool status

Datacenter: datacenter1
=======================
Status=Up/Down
|/ State=Normal/Leaving/Joining/Moving
--  Address    Load       Tokens  Owns  Host ID                               Rack
UN  127.0.0.1  340.25 KB  256     ?     31d9042b-6603-4040-8aac-...           rack1
UN  127.0.0.2  254.31 KB  256     ?     caad1573-4157-43d2-a9fa-...           rack1
```

```
UN  127.0.0.3  259.45 KB  256     ?     e78529c8-ee9f-46a4-8bc1-...       rack1
UL  127.0.0.4  116.33 KB  256     ?     706a2d42-32b8-4a3a-85b7-...       rack1
```

You can examine the server log of the decommissioned node to see the progress. For example, you'll see a series of statements like this indicating the new home for each token range:

```
DEBUG [RMI TCP Connection(4)-127.0.0.1] 2016-01-07 06:00:20,923
    StorageService.java:2369 - Range (-1517961367820069851,-1490120499577273657]
    will be responsibility of /127.0.0.3
```

After this, you'll see another log statement indicating the beginning of streaming data to other nodes:

```
INFO  [RMI TCP Connection(4)-127.0.0.1] 2016-01-07 06:00:21,274
    StorageService.java:1191 - LEAVING: replaying batch log and
    streaming data to other nodes
```

You can also use `nodetool netstats` to monitor the progress of data streaming to the new replicas.

When the streaming is complete, the node announces its departure to the rest of the cluster for a period of 30 seconds, and then stops:

```
INFO  [RMI TCP Connection(4)-127.0.0.1] 2016-01-07 06:00:22,526
    StorageService.java:3425 - Announcing that I have left the ring for 30000ms
...
WARN  [RMI TCP Connection(4)-127.0.0.1] 2016-01-07 06:00:52,529
    Gossiper.java:1461 - No local state or state is in silent shutdown, not
    announcing shutdown
```

Finally, the decommission is complete:

```
INFO  [RMI TCP Connection(4)-127.0.0.1] 2016-01-07 06:00:52,662
    StorageService.java:1191 - DECOMMISSIONED
```

If you call `decommission` on a node that can't be decommissioned (i.e., one that isn't part of the ring yet, or on the only node available), you'll see an error message to that effect.

Decommissioning Does Not Remove Data Files

Be warned that data is not automatically removed from a decommissioned node. If you decide that you want to reintroduce a previously decommissioned node into the ring with a different range, you'll need to manually delete its data first.

Removing a node

If the node is down, you'll have to use the `nodetool removenode` command instead of `decommission`. If your cluster uses vnodes, the `removenode` command causes Cassandra to recalculate new token ranges for the remaining nodes and stream data from current replicas to the new owner of each token range.

If your cluster does not use vnodes, you'll need to manually adjust the token ranges assigned to each remaining node (as discussed in "Moving Tokens" on page 243) prior to running `removenode` to perform the streaming. The `removenode` command also provides a `-- status` option to allow you to monitor the progress of streaming.

Most `nodetool` commands operate directly on the node identified via the `-h` flag. The syntax of the `removenode` command is a bit different, because it has to run on a node which is not the one being removed. Rather than the IP address, the target node is identified via its host ID, which you can obtain via the `nodetool status` command:

```
$ nodetool status
Datacenter: datacenter1
=======================
Status=Up/Down
|/ State=Normal/Leaving/Joining/Moving
--  Address    Load       Tokens  Owns  Host ID
UN  127.0.0.1  244.71 KB  256     ?     31d9042b-6603-4040-8aac-fef0a235570b
UN  127.0.0.2  224.96 KB  256     ?     caad1573-4157-43d2-a9fa-88f79344683d
DN  127.0.0.3  230.37 KB  256     ?     e78529c8-ee9f-46a4-8bc1-3479f99a1860

$ nodetool removenode  e78529c8-ee9f-46a4-8bc1-3479f99a1860
```

Assassinating a node

If the `nodetool removenode` operation fails, you can also run `nodetool assassinate` as a last resort. The `assassinate` command is similar to `removenode`, except that it does not re-replicate the removed node's data. This leaves your cluster in a state where repair is needed.

Another key difference from `removenode` is that the **assassinate** command takes the IP address of the node to assassinate, rather than the host ID:

```
$ nodetool assassinate 127.0.0.3
```

Don't Forget to Clean Up Seed Node Configuration

Whenever you remove a seed node, make sure you update the *cassandra.yaml* files on remaining nodes to remove the IP address of the node that was removed. You'll also want to make sure you still have an adequate number of seed nodes (at least two per data center).

Upgrading Cassandra

Because Cassandra is a technology that continues to thrive and grow, new releases are made available on a regular basis, offering new features, improved performance, and bug fixes. Just as the Apache community has established a rhythm for its regular releases, you'll also want to plan your adoption of these releases.

Finding a Cassandra Version That Is "Just Right"

You'll want to avoid the extremes of being "too hot" and "too cold" in selecting your Cassandra version.

For example, it's best to avoid deploying major version number releases when they are first available. Historically, major new features tend to be unstable when first released, and you may not want to volunteer your production systems to help shake out the issues.

On the other hand, you don't want to get too far behind either, as the upgrade path becomes more and more complex the longer you wait. The Cassandra email list archives are awash in issues and questions raised against older versions, when fixes are frequently available in newer releases.

When you determine it is time for an upgrade, be careful to consult the *NEWS.txt* file found in the base directory of the new release and follow the upgrade instructions for releases between your current and new releases. An upgrade can be a complex process and it's easy to cause a lot of damage to your cluster if the instructions aren't followed carefully.

You should also consult the overall upgrade guide published by DataStax (*http://docs.datastax.com/en/latest-upgrade/upgrade/cassandra/upgradeCassandra_g.html*). This guide provides an excellent overview of the upgrade process and a summary of any intermediate upgrades that may be required in order to update to and from various versions.

A Cassandra cluster is upgraded via a process known as a *rolling upgrade*, as each node is upgraded one at a time. To perform a rolling upgrade, use the following steps:

1. First, run a `nodetool drain` on the node to clear out any writes that still need to be flushed to disk and stop receiving new writes.
2. Stop the node.
3. Make a backup copy of configuration files such as *cassandra.yaml* and *cassandra-env.sh* so they don't get overwritten.
4. Install the new version.
5. Update the configuration files to match your specific deployment.

Upgrading a major version number (and some minor version upgrades) requires you to run the `nodetool upgradesstables` command to convert your stored data files to the latest format. As with other `nodetool` commands we've examined, you can specify a keyspace or even tables within a keyspace to be upgraded, but in general you'll need to upgrade all of the node's tables. You can also update a node's tables when it is offline via the *bin/sstableupgrade* script.

These steps are repeated for each node in the cluster. Although the cluster remains operational while the rolling upgrade is in process, you should carefully plan your upgrade schedule, taking into account the size of the cluster. While the cluster is still being upgraded, you should avoid making schema changes or run any repairs.

Backup and Recovery

Cassandra is built to be highly resilient to failure, with its support for configurable replication and multiple data centers. However, there are still a number of good reasons for backing up data:

- Defects in application logic could cause good data to be overwritten and replicated to all nodes before the situation becomes known.
- SSTables can become corrupted.

- A multi–data center failure could wipe out your disaster recovery plan.

Cassandra provides two mechanisms for backing up data: *snapshots* and *incremental backups*. Snapshots provide a full backup, while incremental backups provide a way to back up changes a little at a time.

Full, Incremental, and Differential Backups

Database backup approaches typically take one of three forms:

- A *full backup* includes the entire state of a database (or specific tables within a database) and are the most expensive to create.
- An *incremental backup* includes the changes made over a period of time, typically the period of time since the last incremental backup. Taken together, a series of incremental backups provides a differential backup.
- A *differential backup* includes all of the changes made since the previous full backup.

Note that Cassandra does not provide a built-in differential backup mechanism, focusing instead on full and incremental backups.

Cassandra's snapshots and backups are complementary techniques that are used together to support a robust backup and recovery approach.

Both the snapshot and backup mechanisms create hard links to SSTable files, which avoids creating extra files in the short term. However, these files can accumulate over time as compaction occurs and files that are deleted from the data directory are still preserved via the hard links.

The tasks of copying these files to another location and deleting them so they do not fill up disk space are left to the user. However, these tasks are easy to automate and there are various tools that support this such as DataStax OpsCenter, which we'll introduce momentarily. An open source example is Jeremy Grosser's Tablesnap (*https://github.com/JeremyGrosser/tablesnap*).

Taking a Snapshot

The purpose of a snapshot is to make a copy of some or all of the keyspaces and tables in a node and save it to what is essentially a separate database file. This means that you can back up the keyspaces elsewhere or leave them where they are in case you need to restore them later. When you take a snapshot, Cassandra first performs a flush, and then makes a hard link for each SSTable file.

Taking a snapshot is straightforward:

```
$ nodetool snapshot
Requested creating snapshot(s) for [all keyspaces] with snapshot name
   [1452265846037]
Snapshot directory: 1452265846037
```

Here, a snapshot has been taken for all of the keyspaces on the server, including Cassandra's internal `system` keyspace. If you want to specify only a single keyspace to take a snapshot of, you can pass it as an additional argument: `nodetool snapshot hotel`. Alternatively, you can use the `-cf` option to list the name of a specific table.

We can list the snapshots that have been taken with the `nodetool listsnapshots` command:

```
$ nodetool listsnapshots
Snapshot name    Keyspace name   Column family name   True size   Size on disk
1452265846037    hotel           pois_by_hotel        0 bytes     13 bytes
1452265846037    hotel           hotels               0 bytes     13 bytes
...


Total TrueDiskSpaceUsed: 0 bytes
```

To find these snapshots on the filesystem, remember that the contents of the data directory are organized in subdirectories for keyspaces and tables. There is a snapshots directory under each table's directory, and each snapshot is stored in a directory named for the timestamp at which it was taken. For example, we can find the hotels table snapshot at:

$CASSANDRA_HOME/data/data/hotel/hotels-b9282710a78a11e5a0a5fb1a2fbefd47/ snapshots/1452265846037/

Each snapshot also contains a *manifest.json* file, that lists the SSTable files which are included in the snapshot. This is used to make sure that the entire contents of a snapshot are present.

Point-in-Time Snapshots Across Multiple Nodes

The `nodetool snapshot` command only operates on a single server. You will need to run this command at the same time on multiple servers if you want a point-in-time snapshot, using a parallel *ssh* tool such as *pssh*.

Cassandra also provides an *auto snapshot* capability that takes a snapshot on every `DROP KEYSPACE`, `DROP TABLE`, or `TRUNCATE` operation. This capability is enabled by default via the `auto_snapshot` property in the *cassandra.yaml* file to prevent against accidental data loss. There is an additional property, `snapshot_before_compaction`, which defaults to false.

Clearing a Snapshot

You can also delete any snapshots you've made, say, after you've backed them up to permanent storage elsewhere. It is a good idea to delete old snapshots before creating a new one.

To clear your snapshots, you can manually delete the files, or use the `nodetool clear snapshot` command, which takes an optional keyspace option.

Enabling Incremental Backup

After you perform a snapshot, you can enable Cassandra's incremental backup using the `nodetool enablebackup` command. This command applies to all keyspaces and tables in the node.

You can also check whether incremental backups are enabled with `nodetool status backup` and disable incremental backups with `nodetool disablebackup`.

When incremental backups are enabled, Cassandra creates backups as part of the process of flushing SSTables to disk. The backup consists of a hard link to each data file Cassandra writes under a *backups* directory—for example:

$CASSANDRA_HOME/data/data/hotel/hotels-b9282710a78a11e5a0a5fb1a2fbefd47/
backups/

To enable backups across a restart of the node, set the `incremental_backups` property to `true` in the *cassandra.yaml* file.

You can safely clear incremental backups after you perform a snapshot and save the snapshot to permanent storage.

Restoring from Snapshot

The process of restoring a node from backups begins with collecting the most recent snapshot plus any incremental backups since the snapshot. There is no difference in how data files from snapshots and backups are treated.

Before starting a restore operation on a node, you will most likely want to truncate the tables to clear any data changes made since the snapshot.

Don't Forget to Restore the Schema!

Be aware that Cassandra does not include the database schema as part of snapshots and backups. You will need to make sure that the schema is in place before doing any restore operations. Fortunately, this is easy to do using the `cqlsh`'s `DESCRIBE TABLES` operation, which can easily be scripted.

If your cluster topology is the same as when the snapshots were taken, there have been no changes to the token ranges for each node, and there are no changes to the replication factor for the tables in question, you can copy the SSTable data files into the data directory for each node. If the nodes are already running, running the `node tool refresh` command will cause Cassandra to load the data.

If there has been a change to the topology, token ranges, or replication, you'll need to use a tool called `sstableloader` to load the data. In some ways, the `sstableloader` behaves like a Cassandra node: it uses the gossip protocol to learn about the nodes in a cluster, but it does not register itself as a node. It uses Cassandra's streaming libraries to push SSTables to nodes. The `sstableloader` does not copy SSTable files directly to every node, but inserts the data in each SSTable into the cluster, allowing the partitioner and replication strategy of the cluster to do their work.

The `sstableloader` is also useful for moving data between clusters.

SSTable Utilities

There are several utilities found in the *bin* and *tools/bin* directories that operate directly on SSTable data files on the filesystem of a Cassandra node. These files have a *.db* extension. For example:

$CASSANDRA_HOME/data/hotels-b9282710a78a11e5a0a5fb1a2fbefd47/
ma-1-big-Data.db

In addition to the `sstablemetadata`, `sstableloader`, and `sstableupgrade` tools we've seen already, here are a few other SSTable utilities:

- The `sstableutil` utility will list the SSTable files for a provided table name.
- The `sstablekeys` utility lists the partition keys that are stored in a given SSTable.
- The `sstableverify` utility will verify the SSTable files for a provided keyspace and table name, identifying any files that exhibit errors or data corruption. This is an offline version of the `nodetool verify` command.
- The `sstablescrub` utility is an offline version of the `nodetool scrub` command. Because it runs offline, it can be more effective at removing corrupted data from SSTable files. If the tool removes any corrupt rows, you will need to run a repair.
- The `sstablerepairedset` is used to mark specific SSTables as repaired or unrepaired to enable transitioning a node to incremental repair. Because incremental repair is the default as of the 2.2 release, clusters that have been created on 2.2 or later will have no need to use this tool.

Several of the utilities help assist in managing compaction, which we'll examine further in Chapter 12:

- The `sstableexpiredblockers` utility will reveal blocking SSTables that prevent an SSTable from being deleted. This class outputs all SSTables that are blocking other SSTables from getting dropped so you can determine why a given SSTable is still on disk.
- The `sstablelevelreset` utility will reset the level to 0 on a given set of SSTables, which will force the SSTable to be compacted as part of the next compaction operation.
- The `sstableofflinerelevel` utility will reassign SSTable levels for tables using the `LeveledCompactionStrategy`. This is useful when a large amount of data is ingested quickly, such as with a bulk import.
- The `sstablesplit` utility is used to split SSTables files into multiple SSTables of a maximum designated size. This is useful if a major compaction has generated large tables that otherwise would not be compacted for a long time.

Under normal circumstances, you probably won't need to use these tools very often, but they can be quite useful in debugging and gaining a greater understanding of how Cassandra's data storage works. Utilities that modify SSTables such as `sstablelevelreset`, `sstablerepairedset`, `sstablesplit`, `sstableofflinerelevel` must be run when Cassandra is not running on the local host.

Maintenance Tools

While it is certainly possible to maintain a Cassandra cluster entirely via `nodetool`, many organizations, especially those with larger installations, have found it helpful to make use of advanced tools that provide automated maintenance features and improved visualizations.

Let's take a quick look at the capabilities provided by two of these tools: DataStax OpsCenter and Netflix Priam.

DataStax OpsCenter

DataStax OpsCenter is a web-based management and monitoring solution for Cassandra that automates maintenance tasks including those we discussed in this chapter. OpsCenter comes in two editions: the free Community Edition, which manages clusters built on the Apache Cassandra distribution, and the Enterprise version, which manages DataStax Enterprise clusters.

The core of OpsCenter is the dashboard, which provides an immediate visual summary of the health of your cluster, as shown in Figure 11-1.

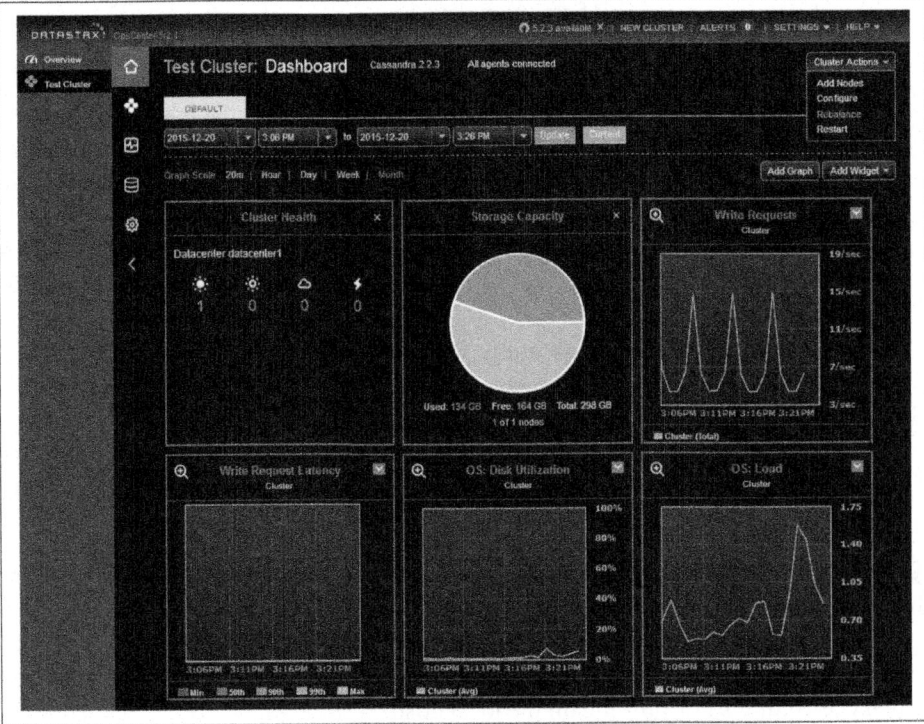

Figure 11-1. DataStax OpsCenter Dashboard for the Test Cluster

In addition to cluster health, the dashboard includes metrics to track capacity and write latency. You can customize the dashboard to add graphs to monitor many other metrics reported by Cassandra via JMX. The Enterprise Edition also allows you to configure thresholds on these metrics for generation of alerts and email notifications.

Operations that can be performed on a cluster are shown at the upper right of the figure and include adding nodes, configuring *cassandra.yaml* settings for all nodes, and restarting the cluster. There is also a "Rebalance" command that can be used to automatically reallocate token ranges in clusters not using vnodes.

DataStax Enterprise Edition also provides a Repair Service which automates repairs across the cluster. The Repair Service runs continuously, using incremental repairs to repair subranges of the cluster. The Repair Service monitors the progress of these subrange repairs and throttles its repairs to minimize impact to the cluster. Once all subranges have been repaired, a new repair cycle is started.

The OpsCenter Nodes view provides a helpful graphical representation of the nodes in the cluster in a ring configuration, as shown in Figure 11-2.

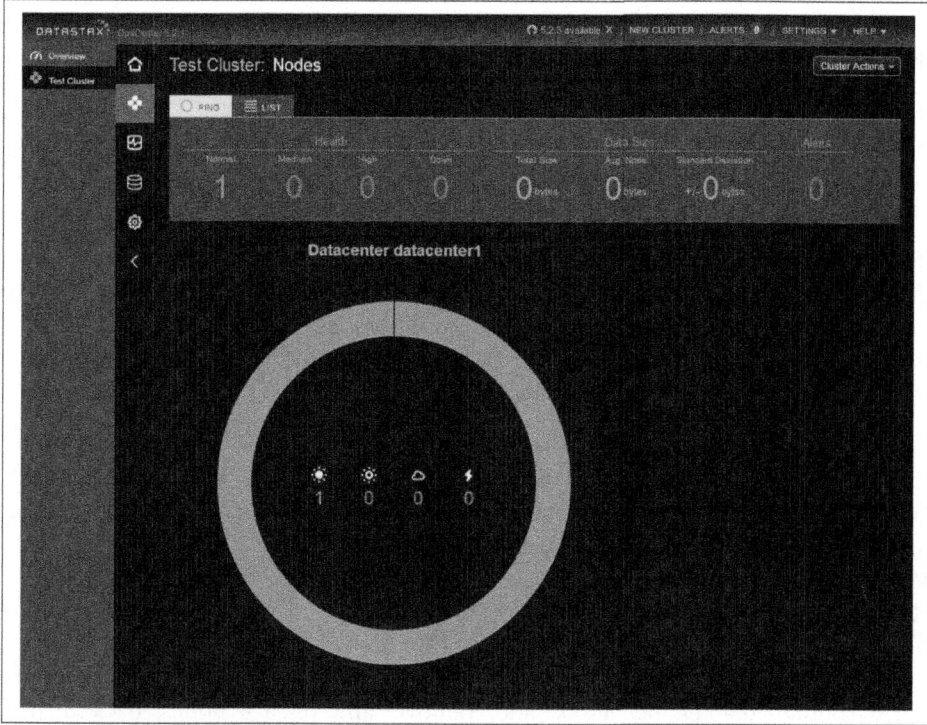

Figure 11-2. DataStax OpsCenter Nodes View

From the Nodes view, we can select an individual node by its position on the ring and view statistics on the node's memory, storage capacity, load, `tpstats` info, and other metrics. We can also start and stop nodes and perform maintenance actions such as cleanup, compaction, flush, repair, decommission, and drain.

Use a Separate Cluster for OpsCenter Data

Behind the scenes, OpsCenter uses Cassandra to store metadata and metrics for the clusters it is managing. While it is possible to configure OpsCenter to put its tables in an existing cluster, the recommended configuration is to create a separate cluster for OpsCenter to store its data. By following this guideline, you will avoid impacting your production clusters.

Netflix Priam

Priam (*https://github.com/Netflix/Priam*) is a tool built by Netflix to help manage its Cassandra clusters. Priam was the King of Troy in Greek mythology, and the father of Cassandra. Priam automates the deployment, starting, and stopping of nodes, as well as backup and restore operations.

Priam is also well integrated with the Amazon Web Services (AWS) cloud environment, although AWS deployment is not required. For example, Priam supports deployment of Cassandra in auto-scaling groups (ASGs), automated backup of snapshots to the Simple Storage Service (S3), and configuration of networking and security groups for Cassandra clusters that span multiple regions.

While Priam does not include a user interface, it does provide a RESTful API that you can use to build your own frontend or access directly via `curl`. The API provides the ability to start and stop nodes, access `nodetool` commands (with JSON-formatted output), and perform backup and restore operations.

Summary

In this chapter, we looked at some of the ways you can interact with Cassandra to perform routine maintenance tasks; add, remove, and replace nodes; back up and recover data with snapshots, and more. We also looked at some tools that help automate these tasks to speed up maintenance and reduce errors.

Performance Tuning

In this chapter, we look at how to tune Cassandra to improve performance. There are a variety of settings in the configuration file and on individual tables. Although the default settings are appropriate for many use cases, there might be circumstances in which you need to change them. In this chapter, we look at how and why to make these changes.

We also see how to use the `cassandra-stress` test tool that ships with Cassandra to generate load against Cassandra and quickly see how it behaves under stress test circumstances. We can then tune Cassandra appropriately and feel confident that we're ready to deploy to a production environment.

Managing Performance

To be effective at achieving and maintaining a high level of performance in your cluster, it's helpful to think of managing performance as a process that begins with the architecture of your application and continues through development and operations.

Setting Performance Goals

Before beginning any performance tuning effort, it is important to have clear goals in mind, whether you are just getting started on deploying an application on Cassandra, or maintaining an existing application.

When planning a cluster, it's important to understand how the cluster will be used: the number of clients, intended usage patterns, expected peak hours, and so on. This will be useful in planning the initial cluster capacity and for planning cluster growth, as we'll discuss further in Chapter 14.

An important part of this planning effort is to identify clear performance goals in terms of both throughput (the number of queries serviced per unit time) and latency (the time to complete a given query).

For example, let's say that we're building an ecommerce website that uses the hotel data model we designed in Chapter 5. We might set a performance goal such as the following for shopping operations on our cluster:

> The cluster must support 30,000 read operations per second from the `available_rooms_by_hotel_date` table with a 95th percentile read latency of 3 ms.

This is a statement that includes both throughput and latency goals. We'll learn how to measure this using `nodetool tablestats`.

Regardless of your specific performance goals, it's important to remember that performance tuning is all about trade-offs. Having well-defined performance goals will help you articulate what trade-offs are acceptable for your application. For example:

- Enabling SSTable compression in order to conserve disk space, at the cost of additional CPU processing.
- Throttling network usage and threads, which can be used to keep network and CPU utilization under control, at the cost of reduced throughput and increased latency.
- Increasing or decreasing number of threads allocated to specific tasks such as reads, writes, or compaction in order to affect the priority relative to other tasks or to support additional clients.
- Increasing heap size in order to decrease query times.

These are just a few of the trade-offs that you will find yourself considering in performance tuning. We'll highlight others throughout the rest of this chapter.

Monitoring Performance

As the size of your cluster grows, the number of clients increases, and more keyspaces and tables are added, the demands on your cluster will begin to pull in different directions. Taking frequent baselines to measure the performance of your cluster against its goals will become increasingly important.

We learned in Chapter 10 about the various metrics that are exposed via JMX, including performance-related metrics for Cassandra's `StorageProxy` and individual tables. In that chapter, we also examined `nodetool` commands that publish performance-related statistics such as `nodetool tpstats` and `nodetool tablestats` and discussed how these can help identify loading and latency issues.

Now we'll look at two additional nodetool commands that present performance statistics formatted as histograms: proxyhistograms and tablehistograms. First, let's examine the output of the nodetool proxyhistograms command:

```
$ nodetool proxyhistograms

proxy histograms
Percentile      Read Latency    Write Latency    Range Latency
                (micros)        (micros)         (micros)
50%                   654.95            0.00            1629.72
75%                   943.13            0.00            5839.59
95%                  4055.27            0.00           62479.63
98%                 62479.63            0.00          107964.79
99%                107964.79            0.00          129557.75
Min                   263.21            0.00             545.79
Max                107964.79            0.00          155469.30
```

The output shows the latency of reads, writes, and range requests for which the requested node has served as the coordinator. The output is expressed in terms of percentile rank as well as minimum and maximum values in microseconds. Running this command on multiple nodes can help identify the presence of slow nodes in the cluster. A large range latency (in the hundreds of milliseconds or more) can be an indicator of clients using inefficient range queries, such as those requiring the ALLOW FILTERING clause or index lookups.

While the view provided by proxyhistograms is useful for identifying general performance issues, we'll frequently need to focus on performance of specific tables. This is what nodetool tablehistograms allows us to do. Let's look at the output of this command against the available_rooms_by_hotel_date table:

```
nodetool tablehistograms hotel available_rooms_by_hotel_date

hotel/available_rooms_by_hotel_date histograms
Percentile  SSTables  Write Latency  Read Latency  Partition Size  Cell Count
                      (micros)       (micros)      (bytes)
50%           0.00      0.00           0.00          2759            179
75%           0.00      0.00           0.00          2759            179
95%           0.00      0.00           0.00          2759            179
98%           0.00      0.00           0.00          2759            179
99%           0.00      0.00           0.00          2759            179
Min           0.00      0.00           0.00          2300            150
Max           0.00      0.00           0.00          2759            179
```

The output of this command is similar. It omits the range latency statistics and instead provides counts of SSTables read per query. The partition size and cell count are provided, and this provides another way of identifying large partitions.

Resetting Metrics

Note that in Cassandra releases through the 3.X series, the metrics reported are lifetime metrics since the node was started. To reset the metrics on a node, you have to restart it. The JIRA issue CASSANDRA-8433 (*https://issues.apache.org/jira/browse/ CASSANDRA-8433*) requests the ability to reset the metrics via JMX and `nodetool`.

Once you've gained familiarity with these metrics and what they tell you about your cluster, you should identify key metrics to monitor and even implement automated alerts that indicate your performance goals are not being met. You can accomplish this via DataStax OpsCenter or any JMX-based metrics framework.

Analyzing Performance Issues

It's not unusual for the performance of a cluster that has been working well to begin to degrade over time. When you've detected a performance issue, you'll want to begin analyzing it quickly to ensure the performance doesn't continue to deteriorate. Your goal in these circumstances should be to determine the root cause and address it.

In this chapter, we'll be looking at many configuration settings that can be used to tune the performance of each node in a cluster as a whole, across all keyspaces and tables. It's also important to try to narrow performance issues down to specific tables and even queries.

In fact, the quality of the data model is usually the most influential factor in the performance of a Cassandra cluster. For example, a table design that results in partitions with a growing number of rows can begin to degrade the performance of the cluster and manifest in failed repairs, or streaming failures on addition of new nodes. Conversely, partitions with partition keys that are too restrictive can result in rows that are too narrow, requiring many partitions to be read to satisfy a simple query.

Beware the Large Partition

In addition to the `nodetool tablehistograms` discussed earlier, you can detect large partitions by searching logs for WARN messages that reference "Writing large partition" or "Compacting large partition". The threshold for warning on compaction of large partitions is set by the `compaction_large_partition_warning_thresh old_mb` property in the *cassandra.yaml* file.

You'll also want to learn to recognize instances of the anti-patterns discussed in Chapter 5 such as queues, or other design approaches that generate a large amount of tombstones.

Tracing

If you can narrow your search down to a specific table and query of concern, you can use tracing to gain detailed insight. Tracing is an invaluable tool for understanding the communications between clients and nodes involved in each query and the time spent in each step. This helps us see the performance implications of design decisions we make in our data models and choice of replication factors and consistency levels.

There are several ways to access trace data. We'll start by looking at how tracing works in cqlsh. First we'll enable tracing, and then execute a simple command:

```
cqlsh:hotel> TRACING ON
Now Tracing is enabled
cqlsh:hotel> SELECT * from hotels where id='AZ123';

 id    | address | name                          | phone          | pois
-------+---------+-------------------------------+----------------+------
 AZ123 |    null | Super Hotel Suites at WestWorld | 1-888-999-9999 | null

(1 rows)

Tracing session: 6669f210-de99-11e5-bdb9-59bbf54c4f73

 activity            | timestamp                  | source    | source_elapsed
---------------------+----------------------------+-----------+----------------
 Execute CQL3 query  | 2016-02-28 21:03:33.503000 | 127.0.0.1 |              0
 Parsing SELECT *... | 2016-02-28 21:03:33.505000 | 127.0.0.1 |          41491
 ...
```

We've truncated the output quite a bit for brevity, but if you run a command like this, you'll see activities such as preparing statements, read repair, key cache searches, data lookups in memtables and SSTables, interactions between nodes, and the time associated with each step in microseconds.

You'll want to be on the lookout for queries that require a lot of inter-node interaction, as these may indicate a problem with your schema design. For example, a query based on a secondary index will likely involve interactions with most or all of the nodes in the cluster.

Once you are done using tracing in cqlsh, you can turn it off using the TRACING OFF command.

Tracing information is also available to clients using the DataStax drivers. Let's modify one of our examples from Chapter 8 to see how to interact with traces via the DataStax Java Driver. The highlighted code enables tracing on a query and prints out the trace results:

```
SimpleStatement hotelSelect = session.newSimpleStatement(
            "SELECT * FROM hotels WHERE id='AZ123'");
hotelSelect.enableTracing();
```

```
ResultSet hotelSelectResult = session.execute(hotelSelect);

QueryTrace queryTrace = hotelSelectResult.getExecutionInfo().getQueryTrace();

System.out.printf("Trace id: %s\n\n", queryTrace.getTraceId());
System.out.printf("%-42s | %-12s | %-10s \n", "activity",
                  "timestamp", "source");

System.out.println("-------------------------------------------"
 + "-------------+-----------");

SimpleDateFormat dateFormat = new SimpleDateFormat("HH:mm:ss.SSS");

for (QueryTrace.Event event : queryTrace.getEvents()) {
  System.out.printf("%42s | %12s | %10s\n",
    event.getDescription(),
    dateFormat.format((event.getTimestamp())),
    event.getSource());
}
```

Tracing is individually enabled on each `Statement` or `PreparedStatement` using the `enableTracing()` operation. To obtain the trace of a query, we look at the query results. You may have noticed in our previous examples that the `Session.execute()` operation always returns a `ResultSet` object, even for queries other than SELECT queries. This enables us to obtain metadata about the request via an `ExecutionInfo` object, even when there are no results to be returned. This metadata includes the consistency level that was achieved, the coordinator node and other nodes involved in the query, and information about tracing and paging.

Executing this code produces output that is quite similar to what we saw in `cqlsh`:

```
Trace id: 58b22960-90cb-11e5-897a-a9fac1d00bce

activity                                      |  timestamp   |  source
----------------------------------------------+--------------+-----------
         Parsing SELECT * FROM hotels WHERE id=? |  20:44:34.550 |  127.0.0.1
                            Preparing statement |  20:44:34.550 |  127.0.0.1
                            Read-repair DC_LOCAL |  20:44:34.551 |  127.0.0.1
     Executing single-partition query on hotels |  20:44:34.551 |  127.0.0.1
                     Acquiring sstable references |  20:44:34.551 |  127.0.0.1
                       Merging memtable contents |  20:44:34.551 |  127.0.0.1
                    Merging data from sstable 3 |  20:44:34.552 |  127.0.0.1
        Bloom filter allows skipping sstable 3 |  20:44:34.552 |  127.0.0.1
                    Merging data from sstable 2 |  20:44:34.552 |  127.0.0.1
        Bloom filter allows skipping sstable 2 |  20:44:34.552 |  127.0.0.1
                    Read 1 live and 0 tombstone cells |  20:44:34.552 |  127.0.0.1
```

Tracing is also supported in DataStax DevCenter, where it is enabled by default. You can immediately view the trace of any request you make in DevCenter by selecting the "Query Trace" tab in the lower middle of the screen, as shown in Figure 12-1.

(The "Connection", "CQL Scripts", "Schema", and "Outline" panels have been minimized to enable readability.)

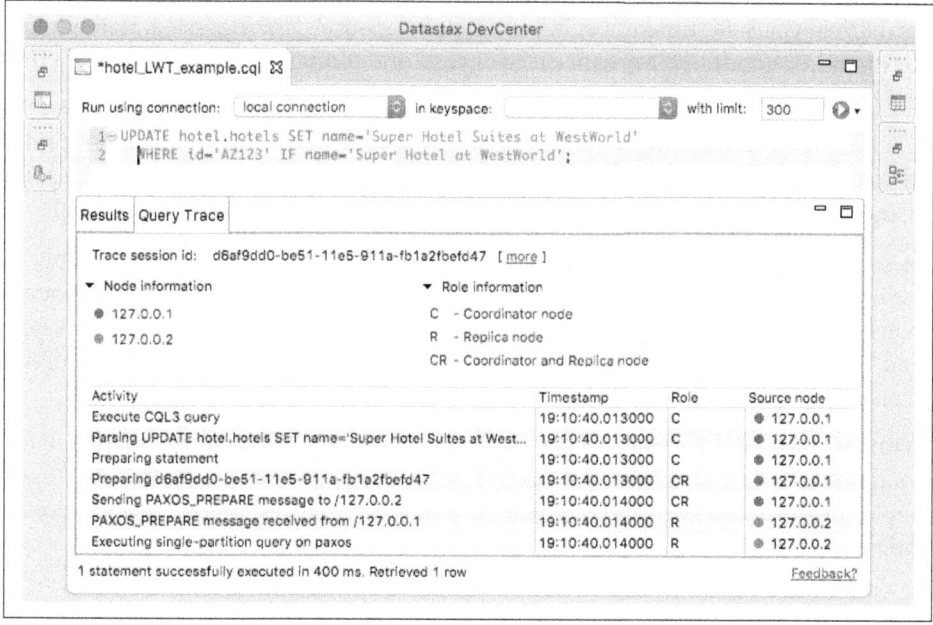

Figure 12-1. Viewing query traces in DataStax DevCenter

You can configure individual nodes to trace some or all of their queries via the node tool settraceprobability command. This command takes a number between 0.0 (the default) and 1.0, where 0.0 disables tracing and 1.0 traces every query. This does not affect tracing of individual queries as requested by clients. Exercise care in changing the trace probability, as a typical trace session involves 10 or more writes. Setting a trace level of 1.0 could easily overload a busy cluster, so a value such as 0.01 or 0.001 is typically appropriate.

Traces Aren't Forever

Cassandra stores query trace results in the system_traces keyspace. Since the 2.2 release, Cassandra also uses tracing to store the results of repair operations. Cassandra limits the TTL on these tables to prevent them from filling up your disk over time. You can configure these TTL values by editing the tracetype_query_ttl and tracetype_repair_ttl properties in the *cassandra.yaml* file.

Tuning Methodology

Once you've identified the root cause of performance issues related to one of your established goals, it's time to begin tuning performance. The suggested methodology for tuning Cassandra performance is to change one configuration parameter at a time and test the results.

It is important to limit the amount of configuration changes you make when tuning so that you can clearly identify the impact of each change. You may need to repeat the change process multiple times until you've reached the desired performance goal.

In some cases, it may be that you can get the performance back in line simply by adding more resources such as memory or extra nodes, but make sure that you aren't simply masking underlying design or configuration issues. In other cases, you may find that you can't reach your desired goals through tuning alone, and that design changes are needed.

With this methodology in mind, let's look at some of the various options that you can configure to tune your Cassandra clusters. We'll highlight node configuration properties in the *cassandra.yaml* and *cassandra-env.sh* files as well as options that are configured on individual tables using CQL.

Caching

Caches are used to improve responsiveness to read operations. Additional memory is used to hold data, to minimize the number of disk reads that must be performed. As the cache size increases, so does the number of "hits" that can be served from memory.

There are three caches built into Cassandra: the key cache, row cache, and counter cache. The row cache caches a configurable number of rows per partition. If you are using a row cache for a given table, you will not need to use a key cache on it as well.

Your caching strategy should therefore be tuned in accordance with a few factors:

- Consider your queries, and use the cache type that best fits your queries.
- Consider the ratio of your heap size to your cache size, and do not allow the cache to overwhelm your heap.
- Consider the size of your rows against the size of your keys. Typically keys will be much smaller than entire rows.

Let's consider some specific tuning and configuration options for each cache.

Key Cache

Cassandra's key cache stores a map of partition keys to row index entries, facilitating faster read access into SSTables stored on disk. We can configure usage of the key cache on a per-table basis. For example, let's use `cqlsh` to examine the caching settings on our hotels table:

```
cqlsh:hotel> DESCRIBE TABLE hotels;

CREATE TABLE hotel.hotels (
    id text PRIMARY KEY,
    address frozen<address>,
    name text,
    phone text,
    pois set<text>
) WITH bloom_filter_fp_chance = 0.01
    AND caching = {'keys': 'ALL', 'rows_per_partition': 'NONE'}
    ...
```

Because the key cache greatly increases reads without consuming a lot of additional memory, it is enabled by default; that is, key caching is enabled if you don't specify a value when creating the table. We can disable key caching for this table with the `ALTER TABLE` command:

```
cqlsh:hotel> ALTER TABLE hotels
    WITH caching = { 'keys' : 'NONE', 'rows_per_partition' : 'NONE' };
```

The legal options for the `keys` attribute are `ALL` or `NONE`.

The `key_cache_size_in_mb` setting indicates the maximum amount of memory that will be devoted to the key cache, which is shared across all tables. The default value is either 5% of the total JVM heap, or 100 MB, whichever is less.

Row Cache

The row cache caches entire rows and can speed up read access for frequently accessed rows, at the cost of more memory usage.

You'll want to use the row cache size setting carefully, as this can easily lead to more performance issues than it solves. In many cases, a row cache can yield impressive performance results for small data sets when all the rows are in memory, only to degrade on larger data sets when the data must be read from disk.

If your table gets far more reads than writes, then configuring an overly large row cache will needlessly consume considerable server resources. If your table has a lower ratio of reads to writes, but has rows with lots of data in them (hundreds of columns), then you'll need to do some math before setting the row cache size. And unless you have certain rows that get hit a lot and others that get hit very little, you're not going to see much of a boost here.

For these reasons, row caching tends to yield fewer benefits than key caching. You may want to explore file caching features supported by your operating system as an alternative to row caching.

As with key caching, we can configure usage of the row cache on a per-table basis. The rows_per_partition setting specifies the number of rows that will be cached per partition. By default, this value is set to NONE, meaning that no rows will be cached. Other available options are positive integers or ALL. The following CQL statement sets the row cache to 200 rows:

```
cqlsh:hotel> ALTER TABLE hotels
    WITH caching = { 'keys' : 'NONE', 'rows_per_partition' : '200' };
```

The implementation of the row cache is pluggable via the row_cache_class_name property. This defaults to the off-heap cache provider implemented by the org.apache.cassandra.OHCProvider class. The previous implementation was the SerializingCacheProvider.

Counter Cache

The counter cache improves counter performance by reducing lock contention for the most frequently accessed counters. There is no per-table option for configuration of the counter cache.

The counter_cache_size_in_mb setting determines the maximum amount of memory that will be devoted to the counter cache, which is shared across all tables. The default value is either 2.5% of the total JVM heap, or 50 MB, whichever is less.

Saved Cache Settings

Cassandra provides the ability to periodically save caches to disk, so that they can be read on startup as a way to quickly warm the cache. The saved cache settings are similar across all three cache types:

- Cache files are saved under the directory specified by the saved_caches property. The files are written at the interval in seconds specified by the key_ cache_ save_period, row_cache_save_period, and counter_cache_ save_period, which default to 14000 (4 hours), 0 (disabled), and 7200 (2 hours), respectively.
- Caches are indexed by key values. The number of keys to save in the file are indicated by the key_cache_keys_to_save, row_cache_keys_to_save, and counter_ cache_keys_to_save properties.

Cassandra also provides capabilities for managing caching via node
tool:

- You can clear caches using the invalidatekeycache, invalid
  aterowcache, and invalidatecountercache commands.
- Use the setcachecapacity command to override the configured settings for key and row cache capacity.
- Use the setcachekeystosave command to override the configured settings for how many key and row cache elements to
  save to a file.

Remember that these settings will revert to the values set in the *cas-
sandra.yaml* file on a node restart.

Memtables

Cassandra uses memtables to speed up writes, holding a memtable corresponding to
each table it stores. Cassandra flushes memtables to disk as SSTables when either the
commit log threshold or memtable threshold has been reached.

Cassandra stores memtables either on the Java heap, off-heap (native) memory, or
both. The limits on heap and off-heap memory can be set via the properties
memtable_heap_space_in_mb and memtable_offheap_space_in_mb, respectively.
By default, Cassandra sets each of these values to 1/4 of the total heap size set in the
cassandra-env.sh file. Allocating memory for memtables reduces the memory available for caching and other internal Cassandra structures, so tune carefully and in
small increments.

You can influence how Cassandra allocates and manages memory via the
memtable_allocation_type property. This property configures another of Cassandra's pluggable interfaces, selecting which implementation of the abstract class
org.apache.cassandra.utils.memory.MemtablePool is used to control the memory
used by each memtable. The default value heap_buffers causes Cassandra to allocate
memtables on the heap using the Java New I/O (NIO) API, while offheap_buffers
uses Java NIO to allocate a portion of each memtable both on and off the heap. The
offheap_objects uses native memory directly, making Cassandra entirely responsible for memory management and garbage collection of memtable memory. This is a
less-well documented feature, so it's best to stick with the default here until you can
gain more experience.

Another element related to tuning the memtables is memtable_flush_writers. This
setting, which is 2 by default, indicates the number of threads used to write out the
memtables when it becomes necessary. If your data directories are backed by SSD,

you should increase this to the number of cores, without exceeding the maximum value of 8. If you have a very large heap, it can improve performance to set this count higher, as these threads are blocked during disk I/O.

You can also enable metered flushing on each table via the CQL `CREATE TABLE` or `ALTER TABLE` command. The `memtable_flush_period_in_ms` option sets the interval at which the memtable will be flushed to disk.

Setting this property results in more predictable write I/O, but will also result in more SSTables and more frequent compactions, possibly impacting read performance. The default value of 0 means that periodic flushing is disabled, and flushes will only occur based on the commit log threshold or memtable threshold being reached.

Commit Logs

There are two sets of files that Cassandra writes to as part of handling update operations: the commit log and the SSTable files. Their different purposes need to be considered in order to understand how to treat them during configuration.

Remember that the *commit log* can be thought of as short-term storage that helps ensure that data is not lost if a node crashes or is shut down before memtables can be flushed to disk. That's because when a node is restarted, the commit log gets replayed. In fact, that's the only time the commit log is read; clients never read from it. But the normal write operation to the commit log blocks, so it would damage performance to require clients to wait for the write to finish.

You can set the value for how large the commit log is allowed to grow before it stops appending new writes to a file and creates a new one. This value is set with the `commitlog_segment_size_in_mb` property. By default, the value is 32 MB. This is similar to setting log rotation on a logging engine such as Log4J or Logback.

The total space allocated to the commit log is specified by the `commitlog_total_space_in_mb` property. Setting this to a larger value means that Cassandra will need to flush tables to disk less frequently.

The commit logs are periodically removed, following a successful flush of all their appended data to the dedicated SSTable files. For this reason, the commit logs will not grow to anywhere near the size of the SSTable files, so the disks don't need to be as large; this is something to consider during hardware selection.

To increase the amount of writes that the commit log can hold, you'll want to enable log compression via the `commitlog_compression` property. The supported compression algorithms are LZ4, Snappy, and Deflate. Using compression comes at the cost of additional CPU time to perform the compression.

Additional settings relate to the commit log sync operation, represented by the `commitlog_sync` element. There are two possible settings for this: `periodic` and `batch`. The default is `periodic`, meaning that the server will make writes durable only at specified intervals. The interval is specified by the `commitlog_sync_period_in_ms` property, which defaults to 10000 (10 seconds).

In order to guarantee durability for your Cassandra cluster, you may want to examine this setting. When the server is set to make writes durable periodically, you can potentially lose the data that has not yet been synced to disk from the write-behind cache.

If your commit log is set to `batch`, it will block until the write is synced to disk (Cassandra will not acknowledge write operations until the commit log has been completely synced to disk). Changing this value will require taking some performance metrics, as there is a necessary trade-off here: forcing Cassandra to write more immediately constrains its freedom to manage its own resources. If you do set `commitlog_sync` to `batch`, you need to provide a suitable value for `commit_log_sync_batch_window_in_ms`, where `ms` is the number of milliseconds between each sync effort.

SSTables

Unlike the commit log, Cassandra writes SSTable files to disk asynchronously. If you're using hard disk drives, it's recommended that you store the datafiles and the commit logs on separate disks for maximum performance. If you're deploying on solid state drives (SSDs), it is fine to use the same disk.

Cassandra, like many databases, is particularly dependent on the speed of the hard disk and the speed of the CPUs. It's more important to have several processing cores than one or two very fast ones, to take advantage of Cassandra's highly concurrent construction. So make sure for QA and production environments to get the fastest disks you can—SSDs if you can afford them. If you're using hard disks, make sure there are at least two so that you can store commit log files and the datafiles on separate disks and avoid competition for I/O time.

When reading SSTable files from disk, Cassandra uses a *buffer cache* (also known as a *buffer pool*), to help reduce database file I/O. This cache uses off-heap memory, but its size defaults to either 512 MB, or 1/4 of the Java heap, whichever is smaller. You can set the cache size using the `file_cache_size_in_mb` property in *cassandra.yaml*. You can also allow Cassandra to use the Java heap for buffers once the off-heap cache is full by setting `buffer_pool_use_heap_if_exhausted` to `true`.

As we discussed in Chapter 9, Cassandra maintains SSTable index summaries in memory in order to speed access into SSTable files. By default, Cassandra allocates

5% of the Java heap to these indexes, but you can override this via the `index_summary_capacity_in_mb` property in *cassandra.yaml*. In order to stay within the allocated limit, Cassandra will shrink indexes associated with tables that are read less frequently. Because read rates may change over time, Cassandra also resamples indexes from files stored on disk at the frequency specified by the `index_summary_resize_interval_in_minutes` property, which defaults to 60.

Cassandra also provides a mechanism to influence the relative amount of space allocated to indexes for different tables. This is accomplished via the `min_index_interval` and `max_index_interval` properties, which can be set per via the CQL `CREATE TABLE` or `ALTER TABLE` commands. These values specify the minimum and maximum number of index entries to store per SSTable.

Hinted Handoff

Hinted handoff is one of several mechanisms that Cassandra provides to keep data in sync across the cluster. As we've learned previously, a coordinator node can keep a copy of data on behalf of a node that is down for some amount of time. We can tune hinted handoff in terms of the amount of disk space we're willing to use to store hints, and how quickly hints will be delivered when a node comes back online.

We can control the bandwidth utilization of hint delivery using the property `hinted_handoff_throttle_in_kb`, or at runtime via `nodetool sethintedhandoff throttlekb`.

This throttling limit has a default value of 1024, or 1 MB/second, and is used to set an upper threshold on the bandwidth that would be required of a node receiving hints. For example, in a cluster of three nodes, each of the two nodes delivering hints to a third node would throttle its hint delivery to half of this value, or 512KB/second.

Note that configuring this throttle is a bit different than configuring other Cassandra features, as the behavior that will be observed by a node receiving hints is entirely based on property settings on other nodes. You'll definitely want to use the same values for these settings in sync across the cluster to avoid confusion.

In releases prior to 3.0, Cassandra stores hints in a table which is not replicated to other nodes, but starting with the 3.0 release, Cassandra stores hints in a directory specified by the `hints_directory` property, which defaults to the *data/hints* directory under the Cassandra installation. You can set a cap on the amount of disk space devoted to hints via the `max_hints_file_size_in_mb` property.

You can clear out any hints awaiting delivery to one or more nodes using the `nodetool truncatehints` command with a list of IP addresses or hostnames. Hints eventually expire after the value expressed by the `max_hint_window_in_ms` property.

It's also possible to enable or disable hinted handoff entirely, as we learned in Chapter 10. While some would use this as a way to conserve disk and bandwidth, in general the hinted handoff mechanism does not consume a lot of resources in comparison to the extra layer of consistency it helps to provide, especially compared to the cost of repairing a node.

Compaction

Cassandra provides configuration options for compaction including the resources used by compaction on a node, and the compaction strategy to be used for each table.

Choosing the right compaction strategy for a table can certainly be a factor in improving performance. Let's review the available strategies and discuss when they should be used.

SizeTieredCompactionStrategy

> The SizeTieredCompactionStrategy (STCS) is the default compaction strategy, and it should be used in most cases. This strategy groups SSTables into tiers organized by size. When there are a sufficient number of SSTables in a tier (4 or more by default), a compaction is run to combine them into a larger SSTable. As the amount of data grows, more and more tiers are created. STCS performs especially well for write-intensive tables, but less so for read-intensive tables, as the data for a particular row may be spread across an average of 10 or so SSTables.

LeveledCompactionStrategy

> The LeveledCompactionStrategy (LCS) creates SSTables of a fixed size (5 MB by default) and groups them into levels, with each level holding 10 times as many SSTables as the previous level. LCS guarantees that a given row appears in at most one SSTable per level. LCS spends additional effort on I/O to minimize the number of SSTables a row appears in; the average number of SSTables for a given row is 1.11. This strategy should be used if there is a high ratio of reads to writes or predictable latency is required. LCS will tend to not perform as well if a cluster is already I/O bound. If writes dominate reads, Cassandra may struggle to keep up.

DateTieredCompactionStrategy

> The DateTieredCompactionStrategy (DTCS) was introduced in the 2.0.11 and 2.1.1 releases. It is intended to improve read performance for time series data, specifically for access patterns that involve accessing the most recently written data. It works by grouping SSTables in windows organized by the write time of the data. Compaction is only performed within these windows. Because DTCS is relatively new and targeted at a very specific use case, make sure you research carefully before making use of it.

Each strategy has its own specific parameters that can be tuned. Check the documentation for your release for further details.

Testing Compaction Strategies with Write Survey Mode

If you'd like to test out using a different compaction strategy for a table, you don't have to change it on the whole cluster in order to see how it works. Instead, you can create a test node running in *write survey mode* to see how the new compaction strategy will work.

To do this, add the following options to the *cassandra-env.sh* file for the test node:

```
JVM_OPTS="$JVM_OPTS -Dcassandra.write_survey=true"
JVM_OPTS="$JVM_OPTS -Djoin_ring=false"
```

Once the node is up, you can then access the `org.apache.cassandra.db.Col umnFamilyStoreMBean` for the table under `org.apache.cassandra.db > Tables` in order to configure the compaction strategy. Set the `CompactionStrategyClass` attribute to the fully qualified compaction strategy class name.

After this configuration change, add the node to the ring via `nodetool join` so that it can start receiving writes. Writes to the test node place a minimal additional load on the cluster and do not count toward consistency levels. You can now monitor the performance of writes to the node using `nodetool tablestats` and `tablehistograms`.

You can test the impact of new compaction strategy on reads by stopping the node, bringing it up as a standalone machine, and then testing read performance on the node.

Write survey mode is also useful for testing out other configuration changes or even a new version of Cassandra.

Another per-table setting is the *compaction threshold*. The compaction threshold refers to the number of SSTables that are in the queue to be compacted before a minor compaction is actually kicked off. By default, the minimum number is 4 and the maximum is 32. You don't want this number to be too small, or Cassandra will spend time fighting with clients for resources to perform many frequent, unnecessary compactions. You also don't want this number to be too large, or Cassandra could spend a lot of resources performing many compactions at once, and therefore will have fewer resources available for clients.

The compaction threshold is set per table using the CQL CREATE TABLE or ALTER TABLE commands. However, you can inspect or override this setting for a particular node using the `nodetool getcompactionthreshold` or `setcompactionthreshold` commands:

```
$ nodetool getcompactionthreshold hotel hotels
Current compaction thresholds for hotel/hotels:
 min = 4,  max = 32
$ nodetool setcompactionthreshold hotel hotels 8 32
```

Compaction can be intensive in terms of I/O and CPU, so Cassandra provides the ability to monitor the compaction process and influence when compaction occurs.

You can monitor the status of compaction on a node using the `nodetool compaction stats` command, which lists the completed and total bytes for each active compaction (we've omitted the ID column for brevity):

```
$ nodetool compactionstats

pending tasks: 1
   id  compaction type  keyspace  table   completed  total      unit   progress
   ... Compaction           hotel     hotels  57957241   127536780  bytes  45.44%
Active compaction remaining time :   0h00m12s
```

If you see that the pending compactions are starting to stack up, you can use the node tool commands `getcompactionthroughput` and `setcompactionthroughput` to check and set the throttle that Cassandra applies to compactions across the cluster. This corresponds to the property `compaction_throughput_mb_per_sec` in the *cassandra.yaml* file. Setting this value to 0 disables throttling entirely, but the default value of 16 MB/s is sufficient for most non-write-intensive cases.

If this does not fix the issue, you can increase the number of threads dedicated to compaction by setting the `concurrent_compactors` property in *cassandra.yaml* file, or at runtime via the `CompactionManagerMBean`. This property defaults to the minimum of the number of disks and number of cores, with a minimum of 2 and a maximum of 8.

Although it is not very common, a large compaction could negatively impact the performance of the cluster. You can use the `nodetool stop` command to stop all active compactions on a node. You can also identify a specific compaction to stop by ID, where the ID is obtained from the `compactionstats` output. Cassandra will reschedule any stopped compactions to run later.

You can force a major compaction via the `nodetool compact` command. Before kicking off a major compaction manually, remember that this is an expensive operation. The behavior of `nodetool compact` during compaction varies depending on the compaction strategy in use. We'll discuss the implications of each compaction strategy on disk usage in Chapter 14.

The `nodetool compactionhistory` command prints statistics about completed compactions, including the size of data before and after compaction and the number of rows merged. The output is pretty verbose, so we've omitted it here.

Concurrency and Threading

Cassandra differs from many data stores in that it offers much faster write performance than read performance. There are two settings related to how many threads can perform read and write operations: `concurrent_reads` and `concurrent_writes`. In general, the defaults provided by Cassandra out of the box are very good.

The `concurrent_reads` setting determines how many simultaneous read requests the node can service. This defaults to 32, but should be set to the number of drives used for data storage × 16. This is because when your data sets are larger than available memory, the read operation is I/O bound.

The `concurrent_writes` setting behaves somewhat differently. This should correlate to the number of clients that will write concurrently to the server. If Cassandra is backing a web application server, you can tune this setting from its default of 32 to match the number of threads the application server has available to connect to Cassandra. It is common in Java application servers to prefer database connection pools no larger than 20 or 30, but if you're using several application servers in a cluster, you'll need to factor that in as well.

Two additional settings—`concurrent_counter_writes` and `concurrent_material ized_view_writes`—are available for tuning special forms of writes. Because counter and materialized view writes both involve a read before write, it is best to set this to the lower of `concurrent_reads` and `concurrent_writes`.

There are several other properties in the *cassandra.yaml* file which control the number of threads allocated to the thread pools which implement various stages in Cassandra's SEDA approach. We've looked at some of these already, but here is a summary:

`max_hints_delivery_threads`
: Maximum number of threads devoted to hint delivery

`memtable_flush_writers`
: Number of threads devoted to flushing memtables to disk

`concurrent_compactors`
: Number of threads devoted to running compaction

`native_transport_max_threads`
: Maximum number of threads devoted to processing incoming CQL requests (you may also notice the similar properties `rpc_min_threads` and `rpc_ max_ threads`, which are for the deprecated Thrift interface)

Note that some of these properties allow Cassandra to dynamically allocate and deallocate threads up to a maximum value, while others specify a static number of threads. Tuning these properties up or down affects how Cassandra uses its CPU time and how much I/O capacity it can devote to various activities.

Networking and Timeouts

As Cassandra is a distributed system, it provides mechanisms for dealing with network and node issues including retries, timeouts, and throttling. We've already discussed a couple of the ways Cassandra implements retry logic, such as the RetryPolicy in the DataStax client drivers, and speculative read execution in drivers and nodes.

Now let's take a look at the timeout mechanisms that Cassandra provides to help it avoid hanging indefinitely waiting for other nodes to respond. The timeout properties listed in Table 12-1 are set in the *cassandra.yaml* file.

Table 12-1. Cassandra node timeouts

Property Name	Default Value	Description
read_request_timeout_in_ms	5000 (5 seconds)	How long the coordinator waits for read operations to complete
range_request_timeout_in_ms	10000 (10 seconds)	How long the coordinator should wait for range reads to complete
write_request_timeout_in_ms	2000 (2 seconds)	How long the coordinator should wait for writes to complete
counter_write_request_timeout_in_ms	5000 (5 seconds)	How long the coordinator should wait for counter writes to complete
cas_contention_timeout_in_ms	1000 (1 second)	How long a coordinator should continue to retry a lightweight transaction
truncate_request_timeout_in_ms	60000 (1 minute)	How long the coordinator should wait for truncates to complete (including snapshot)
streaming_socket_timeout_in_ms	3600000 (1 hour)	How long a node waits for streaming to complete
request_timeout_in_ms	10000 (10 seconds)	The default timeout for other, miscellaneous operations

The values for these timeouts are generally acceptable, but you may need to adjust them for your network environment.

Another property related to timeouts is cross_node_timeout, which defaults to false. If you have NTP configured in your environment, consider enabling this so that nodes can more accurately estimate when the coordinator has timed out on long-running requests and release resources more quickly.

Cassandra also provides several properties that allow you to throttle the amount of network bandwidth it will use for various operations. Tuning these allows you to prevent Cassandra from swamping your network, at the cost of longer time to complete these tasks. For example, the `stream_throughput_outbound_megabits_per_sec` and `inter_dc_stream_throughput_outbound_megabits_per_sec` properties specify a per-thread throttle on streaming file transfers to other nodes in the local and remote data centers, respectively.

The throttles for hinted handoff and batchlog replay work slightly differently. The values specified by `hinted_handoff_throttle_in_kb` and `batchlog_replay_throt tle_in_kb` are considered maximum throughput values for the cluster and are therefore spread proportionally across nodes according to the formula:

$$T_x = \frac{T_t}{N_n - 1}$$

That is, the throughput of a node x (T_x) is equal to the total throughput (T_t) divided by one less than the number of nodes in the cluster (N_n).

Finally, there are several properties that you can use to limit traffic to the native CQL port on each node. These may be useful in situations where you don't have direct control over the client applications of your cluster. The default maximum frame size specified by the `native_transport_max_frame_size_in_mb` property is 256. Frame requests larger than this will be rejected by the node.

The node can also limit the maximum number of simultaneous client connections, via the `native_transport_max_concurrent_connections` property, but the default is -1 (unlimited). If you configure this value, you'll want to make sure it makes sense in light of the `concurrent_readers` and `concurrent_writers` properties.

To limit the number of simultaneous connections from a single source IP address, configure the `native_transport_max_concurrent_connections_per_ip` property, which defaults to -1 (unlimited).

JVM Settings

Cassandra allows you to configure a variety of options for how the server JVM should start up, how much Java memory should be allocated, and so forth. In this section, we look at how to tune the startup.

If you're using Windows, the startup script is called *cassandra.bat*, and on Linux it's *cassandra.sh*. You can start the server by simply executing this file, which sets several defaults. But there's another file in the *conf* directory that allows you to configure a variety of settings related to how Cassandra starts. This file is called *cassandra-env.sh* (*cassandra-env.ps1* on Windows) and it separates certain options, such as the JVM settings, into a different file to make it easier to update.

Try tuning the options passed to the JVM at startup for better performance. The key JVM options included in *cassandra-env.sh* and guidelines for how you might tweak them are discussed momentarily. If you want to change any of these values, simply open the *cassandra-env.sh* file in a text editor, change the values, and restart.

The jvm.options File

The Cassandra 3.0 release introduced another settings file in the *conf* directory called *jvm.options*. The purpose of this file is to move JVM settings related to heap size and garbage collection out of *cassandra.in.sh* file to a separate file, as these are the attributes that are tuned most frequently. The *jvm.options* and *cassandra.in.sh* are included (sourced) by the *cassandra-env.sh* file.

Memory

By default, Cassandra uses the following algorithm to set the JVM heap size: if the machine has less than 1 GB of RAM, the heap is set to 50% of RAM. If the machine has more than 4 GB of RAM, the heap is set to 25% of RAM, with a cap of 8 GB. To tune the minimum and maximum heap size, use the -Xms and -Xmx flags. These should be set to the same value to allow the entire heap to be locked in memory and not swapped out by the OS. It is not recommended to set the heap larger than 8GB if you are using the Concurrent Mark Sweep (CMS) garbage collector, as heap sizes larger than this value tend to lead to longer GC pauses.

When performance tuning, it's a good idea to set only the heap min and max options, and nothing else at first. Only after real-world usage in your environment and some performance benchmarking with the aid of heap analysis tools and observation of your specific application's behavior should you dive into tuning the more advanced JVM settings. If you tune your JVM options and see some success, don't get too excited. You need to test under real-world conditions.

In general, you'll probably want to make sure that you've instructed the heap to dump its state if it hits an out-of-memory error, which is the default in *cassandra-env.sh*, set by the -XX:+HeapDumpOnOutOfMemory option. This is just good practice if you start experiencing out-of-memory errors.

Garbage Collection

The Java heap is broadly divided into two object spaces: young and old. The young space is subdivided into one for new object allocation (called "eden space") and another for new objects that are still in use (the "survivor space").

Cassandra uses the parallel copying collector in the young generation; this is set via the `-XX:+UseParNewGC` option. Older objects still have some reference, and have therefore survived a few garbage collections, so the Survivor Ratio is the ratio of eden space to survivor space in the young object part of the heap. Increasing the ratio makes sense for applications with lots of new object creation and low object preservation; decreasing it makes sense for applications with longer-living objects. Cassandra sets this value to 8 via the `-XX:SurvivorRatio` option, meaning that the ratio of eden to survivor space is 1:8 (each survivor space will be 1/8 the size of eden). This is fairly low, because the objects are living longer in the memtables.

Every Java object has an age field in its header, indicating how many times it has been copied within the young generation space. Objects are copied into a new space when they survive a young generation garbage collection, and this copying has a cost. Because long-living objects may be copied many times, tuning this value can improve performance. By default, Cassandra has this value set at 1 via the `-XX:MaxTenuringThreshold` option. Set it to 0 to immediately move an object that survives a young generation collection to the old generation. Tune the survivor ratio together along with the tenuring threshold.

By default, modern Cassandra releases use the Concurrent Mark Sweep (CMS) garbage collector for the old generation; this is set via the `-XX:+UseConcMarkSweepGC` option. This setting uses more RAM and CPU power to do frequent garbage collections while the application is running, in order to keep the GC pause time to a minimum. When using this strategy, it's important to set the heap min and max values to the same value, in order to prevent the JVM from having to spend a lot of time growing the heap initially.

Moving to the Garbage First Garbage Collector

The Garbage First garbage collector (also known as G1GC) was introduced in Java 7 as an improvement and eventual replacement for CMS GC, especially on multiprocessor machines with more memory.

G1GC divides the heap into multiple equal size regions and allocates these to eden, survivor, and old generations dynamically, so that each generation is a logical collection of regions that need not be consecutive regions in memory. This approach enables garbage collection to run continually and require fewer of the "stop the world" pauses that characterize traditional garbage collectors.

G1GC generally requires fewer tuning decisions; the intended usage is that you need only define the min and max heap size and a pause time goal. A lower pause time will cause GC to occur more frequently.

G1GC was on course to become the default for the Cassandra 3.0 release, but was backed out as part of the JIRA issue CASSANDRA-10403 (*https://issues.apache.org/*

---

jira/browse/CASSANDRA-10403), due to the fact that it did not perform as well as the CMS for heap sizes smaller than 8 GB.

If you'd like to experiment with using G1GC and a larger heap size on a Cassandra 2.2 or later release, the settings are readily available in the *cassandra-env.sh* file (or *jvm.options*) file.

Look for G1GC to become the default in a future Cassandra release, most likely in conjunction with support for Java 9, in which G1GC will become the Java default.

To get more insight on garbage collection activity in your Cassandra nodes, there are a couple of options. The gc_warn_threshold_in_ms setting in the *cassandra.yaml* file determines the pause length that will cause Cassandra to generate log messages at the WARN logging level. This value defaults to 1000 ms (1 second). You can also instruct the JVM to print garbage-collection details by setting options in the *cassandra-env.sh* or *jvm.options* file.

Using cassandra-stress

Cassandra ships with a utility called cassandra-stress that you can use to run a stress test on your Cassandra cluster. To run cassandra-stress, navigate to the *<cassandra-home>/tools/bin* directory and run the command:

```
$ cassandra-stress write n=1000000
Connected to cluster: test-cluster
Datatacenter: datacenter1; Host: localhost/127.0.0.1; Rack: rack1
Datatacenter: datacenter1; Host: /127.0.0.2; Rack: rack1
Datatacenter: datacenter1; Host: /127.0.0.3; Rack: rack1
Created keyspaces. Sleeping 1s for propagation.
Sleeping 2s...
Warming up WRITE with 50000 iterations...
Running WRITE with 200 threads for 1000000 iteration
...
```

The output lists the nodes to which the tool is connected (in this case, a cluster created using *ccm*) and creates a sample keyspace and table to which it can write data. The test is warmed up by doing 50,000 writes, and then the tool begins to output metrics as it continues to write, which we've omitted for brevity. The tool creates a pool of threads (defaulting on my system to 200) that perform one write after another, until it inserts one million rows. Finally, it prints a summary of results:

```
Results:
op rate                  : 7620 [WRITE:7620]
partition rate           : 7620 [WRITE:7620]
row rate                 : 7620 [WRITE:7620]
latency mean             : 26.2 [WRITE:26.2]
latency median           : 2.6 [WRITE:2.6]
latency 95th percentile  : 138.4 [WRITE:138.4]
```

```
latency 99th percentile  : 278.8 [WRITE:278.8]
latency 99.9th percentile : 393.3 [WRITE:393.3]
latency max              : 820.9 [WRITE:820.9]
Total partitions         : 1000000 [WRITE:1000000]
Total errors             : 0 [WRITE:0]
total gc count           : 0
total gc mb              : 0
total gc time (s)        : 0
avg gc time(ms)          : NaN
stdev gc time(ms)        : 0
Total operation time     : 00:02:11
```

Let's unpack this a bit. What we've done is generated and inserted one million values into a completely untuned three-node cluster in a little over two minutes, which represents a rate of 7,620 writes per second. The median latency per operation is 2.6 milliseconds, although a small number of writes took longer.

Now that we have all of this data in the database, let's use the test to read some values too:

```
$ cassandra-stress read n=200000
...
Running with 4 threadCount
Running READ with 4 threads for 200000 iteration
```

If you examine the output, you will see that it starts out with a small number of threads and ramps up. On one test run, it peaked at over 600 threads, as shown here:

```
Results:
op rate                  : 13828 [READ:13828]
partition rate           : 13828 [READ:13828]
row rate                 : 13828 [READ:13828]
latency mean             : 67.1 [READ:67.1]
latency median           : 9.9 [READ:9.9]
latency 95th percentile  : 333.2 [READ:333.2]
latency 99th percentile  : 471.1 [READ:471.1]
latency 99.9th percentile : 627.9 [READ:627.9]
latency max              : 1060.5 [READ:1060.5]
Total partitions         : 200000 [READ:200000]
Total errors             : 0 [READ:0]
total gc count           : 0
total gc mb              : 0
total gc time (s)        : 0
avg gc time(ms)          : NaN
stdev gc time(ms)        : 0
Total operation time     : 00:00:14
Improvement over 609 threadCount: 7%
```

The tool periodically prints out statistics about the last several writes. The preceding output came from the last block of statistics. As you can see, Cassandra doesn't read nearly as fast as it writes; the mean read latency was around 10 ms. Remember, though, that this is out of the box, untuned, single-threaded, on a regular workstation running other programs, and the database is approximately 2 GB in size. Regardless, this is a great tool to help you do performance tuning for your environment and to get a set of numbers that indicates what to expect in your cluster.

We can also run `cassandra-stress` on our own tables by creating a specification in a *yaml* file. For example, we could create a *cqlstress-hotel.yaml* file to describe queries that read from tables in our hotel keyspace. This file defines queries that we would use to stress the `available_rooms_by_hotel_date` table:

```
keyspace: hotel
table: available_rooms_by_hotel_date

columnspec:
  - name: date
    cluster: uniform(20..40)

insert:
  partitions: uniform(1..50)
  batchtype: LOGGED
  select: uniform(1..10)/10

queries:
  simple1:
    cql: select * from available_rooms_by_hotel_date
      where hotel_id = ? and date = ?
    fields: samerow
  range1:
    cql: select * from available_rooms_by_hotel_date
      where hotel_id = ? and date >= ? and date <= ?
    fields: multirow
```

We can then execute these queries in a run of `cassandra-stress`. For example, we might run a mixed load of writes, single item queries, and range queries, as follows:

```
$ cassandra-stress user profile=~/cqlstress-hotel.yaml
  ops\(simple1=2,range1=1,insert=1\) no-warmup
```

The numbers associated with each query indicate the desired ratio of usage. This command performs three reads for every write.

Additional Help on cassandra-stress

There are a number of options. You can execute `cassandra-stress help` to get the list of supported commands and options, and `cassandra-stress help <command>` to get more information on a specific command.

You may also want to investigate `cstar_perf`, an open source performance testing platform for Cassandra provided by DataStax. This tool supports automation of stress testing, including the ability to spin up clusters and run performance tests across multiple Cassandra versions, or separate clusters with different configuration settings for the purpose of comparison. It provides a web-based user interface for creating and running test scripts and viewing test results. You can download `cstar_perf` and read the documentation at *http://datastax.github.io/cstar_perf/setup_cstar_perf_tool.html*.

Summary

In this chapter, we looked at managing Cassandra performance and the settings available in Cassandra to aid in performance tuning, including caching settings, memory settings, and hardware concerns. We also set up and used the `cassandra-stress` test tool to write and then read one million rows of data.

If you're somewhat new to Linux systems and you want to run Cassandra on Linux (which is recommended), you may want to check out Al Tobey's blog post on tuning Cassandra (*https://tobert.github.io/pages/als-cassandra-21-tuning-guide.html*). This walks through several Linux performance monitoring tools to help you understand the performance of your underlying platform so that you can troubleshoot in the right place. Although the post references Cassandra 2.1, the advice it contains is broadly applicable.

Security

Making data accessible has been one of the key tenets of the Big Data movement, enabling huge strides in data analytics and bringing tangible benefits to business, academia, and the general public. At the same time, this data accessibility is held in tension with growing security and privacy demands. Internet scale systems are exposed to an ever-changing collection of attacks, with the data held by these systems being the most common target. We're all aware of multiple high-profile breaches resulting in significant losses of data, including personal data, payment information, military intelligence, and corporate trade secrets. And these are just the breaches that have made the news.

One result of this heightened threat environment has been increased regulatory and compliance regimens in many industries:

- The U.S. Health Insurance Portability and Accountability Act (HIPAA) of 1996 prescribes controls for the protection and handling of individual health information.
- Germany's Federal Data Protection Act (known as Bundesdatenschutzgesetz or BDSG) was revised in 2009 to regulate the collection and transfer of personally identifiable information (PII), including restrictions on movement of such data outside of Germany and the European Union.
- The Payment Card Industry Data Security Standard (PCI DSS), first released in 2006, is an industry-defined set of standards for the secure handling of payment card data.
- The U.S. Sarbanes-Oxley Act of 2002 regulates corporate auditing and reporting, including data retention, protection, and auditing.

These are just a few examples of regulatory and compliance standards. Even if none of these examples apply directly to your application, chances are there are regulatory guidelines of some kind that impact your system.

All of this publicity and regulatory rigor has resulted in a much increased level of visibility on enterprise application security in general, and more pertinently for our discussions, on NoSQL database security. Although a database is by definition only a part of an application, it certainly forms a vital part of the attack surface of the application, because it serves as the repository of the application's data.

Is Security a Weakness of NoSQL?

A 2012 Information Week report (*http://reports.information week.com/abstract/2/8758/Business-Continuity/strategy-why-nosql-equals-nosecurity.html*) took the NoSQL community to task for a perceived complacency and lack of prioritization of security features in NoSQL databases. While the security of many NoSQL technologies, including Cassandra, has improved significantly since then, the paper serves as a healthy reminder of our responsibilities and the need for continued vigilance.

Fortunately, the Cassandra community has demonstrated a commitment to continuous improvement in security over its relatively short lifespan, as we've seen already in the release history in Chapter 2.

Cassandra's security features include authentication, role-based authorization, and encryption, as shown in Figure 13-1.

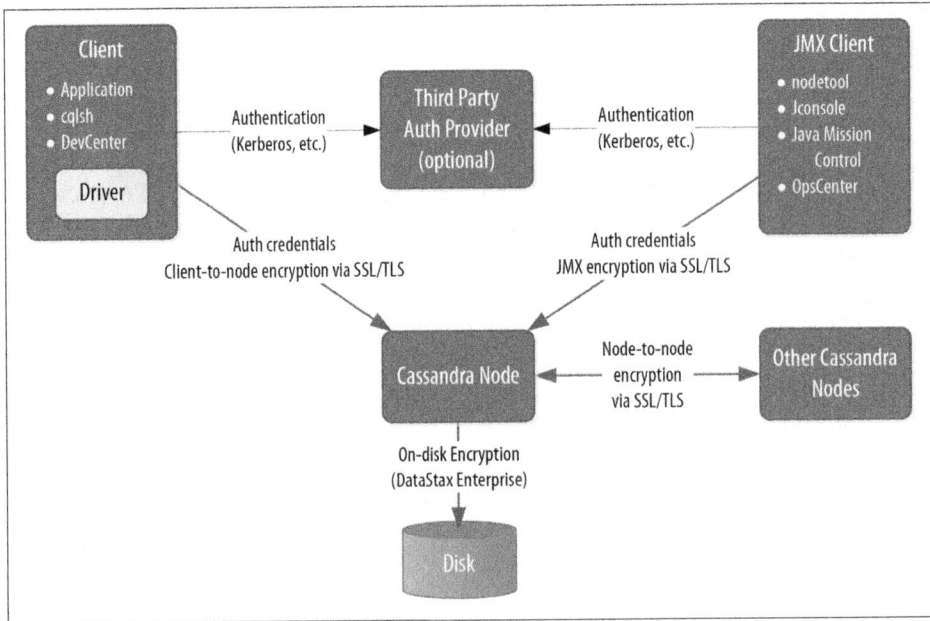

Figure 13-1. Cassandra's security features

In this chapter, we'll explore these security features and how to access them via `cqlsh` and other clients, with some thoughts along the way for how Cassandra fits into a broader application security strategy.

Authentication and Authorization

Let's take a look at Cassandra's authentication and authorization features.

Password Authenticator

By default, Cassandra allows any client on your network to connect to your cluster. This does not mean that no security is set up out of the box, but rather that Cassandra is configured to use an authentication mechanism that allows all clients, without requiring that they provide credentials. The security mechanism is pluggable, which means that you can easily swap out one authentication method for another, or write your own.

The authenticator that's plugged in by default is the `org.apache.cassandra.auth.AllowAllAuthenticator`. If you want to force clients to provide credentials, another alternative ships with Cassandra, the `org.apache.cassandra.auth.PasswordAuthenticator`. In this section, we see how to use this second authenticator.

Configuring the authenticator

First, let's shut down our cluster so that we can change the security configuration. We'll open the *cassandra.yaml* file and search for "authenticator". You'll find the following line:

```
authenticator: AllowAllAuthenticator
```

Let's change this line to use the `PasswordAuthenticator`:

```
authenticator: PasswordAuthenticator
```

If you're using Cassandra 2.2 or later, you'll see a note in the *cassandra.yaml* file indicating that the `CassandraRoleManager` must be used if the `PasswordAuthenticator` is used. The `CassandraRoleManager` is part of Cassandra's authorization capability and we'll discuss it in more depth momentarily.

Additional authentication providers

You can provide your own method of authenticating to Cassandra, such as a Kerberos ticket, or if you want to store passwords in a different location, such as an LDAP directory. In order to create your own authentication scheme, simply implement the `IAuthenticator` interface. DataStax Enterprise Edition provides additional authentication integrations.

Cassandra also supports pluggable authentication between nodes via the IInternode Authenticator interface. The default implementation AllowAllInternodeAuthenticator performs no authentication, but you are free to implement your own authenticator as a way to protect a node from making connections to untrusted nodes.

Adding users

Now we'll save the *cassandra.yaml* file and restart our node or cluster, and try logging in with cqlsh. Immediately we run into a problem:

```
$ bin/cqlsh
Connection error: ('Unable to connect to any servers',
    {'127.0.0.1': AuthenticationFailed('Remote end requires
    authentication.',)})
```

Prior versions of Cassandra might allow login, but would not allow any access. Versions of Cassandra 2.2 and later require a password even to log in. Cassandra comes with a default user known as *cassandra*, with "cassandra" as the password. Let's try logging in again with these credentials:

```
$ bin/cqlsh -u cassandra -p cassandra
Connected to Test Cluster at 127.0.0.1:9042.
[cqlsh 5.0.1 | Cassandra 3.0.0-rc1 | CQL spec 3.3.1 |
    Native protocol v4]
Use HELP for help.
cassandra@cqlsh>
```

Once we've logged in successfully, we see that the prompt indicates that we are logged in as the user *cassandra*. One of the first things we'll want to do to begin securing our installation is to change the password for this very important user. We've used a random password generator here as an example:

```
cassandra@cqlsh> ALTER USER cassandra WITH PASSWORD 'Kxl0*nGpB6'
```

Make sure to store the *cassandra* user's password in a secure location.

Now, let's create a new user account. We'll specify a username and password. The password is optional, but of course recommended.

```
cassandra@cqlsh> CREATE USER jeff WITH PASSWORD 'i6XJsj!k#9';
```

The CREATE USER command also supports the IF NOT EXISTS syntax to avoid errors on multiple attempts to create a user. Now, we'll check to see that we've created the user successfully by using the LIST USERS command:

```
cassandra@cqlsh> LIST USERS;

 name      | super
-----------+-------
 cassandra |  True
      jeff | False
```

```
(2 rows)
```

You'll note that the user *cassandra* is listed as being a superuser. The superuser designates the ability to perform all supported actions. Only a superuser can create other users. We've already changed the password for the built-in user *cassandra*. You may also want to create another superuser and remove the *cassandra* account's superuser status for additional security.

Configuring Automatic Login

To avoid having to enter a username and password on every login to `cqlsh`, create a file in your home directory called *.cqlshrc*. You can enter login credentials through lines like this:

```
; Sample ~/.cqlshrc file.
[authentication]
username = jeff
password = i6XJsj!k#9
```

Obviously, you'll want to make sure this file is secure so that only authorized users (such as your account) have access to the password.

Other operations on users include the `ALTER USER` command, which allows us to change a user's password or superuser status, as well as the `DROP USER` command, which we use to delete a user. A non-superuser can alter their own password using the `ALTER USER` command, but all other operations require superuser status.

We can use the `LOGIN` command to switch users within `cqlsh` without restart:

```
cassandra@cqlsh> login jeff 'i6XJsj!k#9'
jeff@cqlsh>
```

You may choose to omit the password from the command, in which case `cqlsh` will prompt you to enter the password. It's preferable to enter passwords at the shell prompt, rather than the command line, as `cqlsh` saves all of your commands to a file called *.cassandra/cqlsh_history* under your home directory, including any passwords you include on the command line when using the `LOGIN` command.

Authenticating via the DataStax Java driver

Of course, your applications don't use `cqlsh` to access Cassandra, so it will be helpful for us to learn how to authenticate to the client using the DataStax client drivers. Building on the simple Java driver example from Chapter 8, let's use the `Cluster.Builder.withCredentials()` operation to provide the user name and password when we construct our `Cluster` instance:

```
Cluster cluster = Cluster.builder().addContactPoint("127.0.0.1").
    withCredentials("jeff", "i6XJsj!k#9").
    build();
```

This is a simple example that hardcodes the login credentials, but you could just as easily use values stored in a secure configuration file or provided by an application user. The login syntax is quite similar for the other DataStax drivers.

If you've configured an authenticator on your nodes other than the default, you'll also need to configure a compatible authenticator in your clients as well. Client authentication providers implement the `com.datastax.driver.core.AuthProvider` interface. The default implementation is the `PlainTextAuthProvider` class, an instance of which is registered when we call the `Cluster.Builder.withCredentials()` operation.

Other implementations provided with the driver are found in the `com.datastax.driver.auth` package. These include the `DseAuthProvider` for connecting to DataStax Enterprise clusters, and the `KerberosAuthenticator`.

You select these providers when constructing your `Cluster` object by calling the `Cluster.Builder.withAuthProvider()` operation.

Using CassandraAuthorizer

It is certainly possible to only use authentication, although in most cases you'll want to make use of Cassandra's authorization capabilities as well. Cassandra's out-of-the-box configuration authorizes all clients to access all keyspaces and tables in your cluster. As with authentication, the authentication mechanism is pluggable.

The authorizer that's plugged in by default is the `org.apache.cassandra.auth.AllowAllAuthorizer`. To enable Cassandra's role-based access control, we'll need to configure the `org.apache.cassandra.auth.CassandraAuthorizer`.

Again, we'll shut down the cluster to enable us to change the authorizer. In the *cassandra.yaml* file, we'll search for "authorizer". We'll find the line:

```
authorizer: AllowAllAuthorizer
```

and change it to:

```
authorizer: CassandraAuthorizer
```

Once we restart our cluster, we can log into `cqlsh` again as our regular user to see what we can access, making use of the hotel data we've stored in our cluster in previous chapters:

```
$ cqlsh -u jeff -p 'i6XJsj!k#9'
...
jeff@cqlsh> DESCRIBE KEYSPACES;
```

```
hotel  system_schema  system_auth  system  system_distributed
   system_traces

jeff@cqlsh> USE hotel;
jeff@cqlsh:hotel> DESCRIBE TABLES;

hotels

jeff@cqlsh:hotel> select * from hotels;
Unauthorized: code=2100 [Unauthorized] message="User jeff has no
   SELECT permission on <table hotel.hotels> or any of its parents"
```

As you can see, we are able to navigate through cqlsh to view the names of the various keyspaces and tables, but once we attempt to access data, we are denied access.

To fix this, we'll need to switch back into a superuser role and grant our user some permissions. For example, let's allow our user to access the hotels table:

```
cassandra@cqlsh> GRANT SELECT ON hotel.hotels TO jeff;
```

Now, if we log back in as our regular user and run our SELECT command again, we'll see the data we've stored in our hotel table previously.

Getting Help with Permissions

Use the cqlsh commands HELP GRANT and HELP PERMISSIONS to get additional information on configuring permissions.

Role-Based Access Control

In a large Cassandra cluster, there might be a lot of different keyspaces and tables, with many different potential users. It would be difficult to keep track of the permissions assigned to many different users. While it's tempting to share login information with multiple support staff, there is a better way.

Starting with the 2.2 release, Cassandra provides a role-based access control (RBAC) capability. This allows us to create roles and assign permissions to these roles. Roles can be granted to individual users in any combination. Roles can themselves contain other roles.

To see how this works, let's create a hotel management role and grant it all permissions to all of the tables in the hotel keyspace:

```
cassandra@cqlsh> CREATE ROLE hotel_management;
cassandra@cqlsh> GRANT ALL ON KEYSPACE hotel TO hotel_management;
```

We've created a simple role here to which you can't log in to directly. You can also create roles that have superuser privileges, and roles that support login and take a password.

Now we'll apply this role to our regular user:

```
cassandra@cqlsh> GRANT hotel_management TO jeff;
```

Roles are additive in Cassandra, meaning that if any of the roles granted to a user have a specific permission granted, then that permission is granted to the user.

Behind the scenes, Cassandra stores users and roles in the system_auth keyspace. If we've configured authorization for our cluster, only administrative users can access this keyspace, so let's examine its contents in cqlsh using our administrator login:

```
cassandra@cqlsh> DESCRIBE KEYSPACE system_auth

CREATE KEYSPACE system_auth WITH replication = {'class': 'SimpleStrategy',
    'replication_factor': '1'}  AND durable_writes = true;

...
```

We've truncated the output, but if you run this command, you'll see the tables that store the roles, their permissions, and role assignments. There is actually no separate concept of a user at the database level—Cassandra uses the role concept to track both users and roles.

Changing the system_auth replication Factor

It's important to note that the system_auth keyspace is configured out of the box to use the SimpleStrategy with a replication factor of one.

This means that by default, any users, roles, and permissions we configure will not be distributed across the cluster until we reconfigure the replication strategy of the system_auth keyspace to match our cluster topology.

Encryption

Protecting user privacy is an important aspect of many systems, especially with respect to health, financial, and other personal data. Typically we protect privacy by encrypting data, so that if the data is intercepted, it is unusable to an attacker who does not have the encryption key. Data can be encrypted as it moves around the public Internet and within our internal systems, also known as *data in motion*, or it can be encrypted on systems where it is persisted. This is known as *data at rest*.

As of the 3.0 release, Cassandra secures data in motion via encryption between clients and servers (nodes) and encryption between nodes. As of Cassandra 3.0, encryption of data files (data at rest) is only supported in DataStax Enterprise releases of Cassandra.

Data File Encryption Roadmap

There are several Cassandra JIRA requests targeted for the 3.X release series that provide encryption features. For example, the following were added in the 3.4 release:

- CASSANDRA-11040 - encryption of hints (*https:// issues.apache.org/jira/browse/CASSANDRA-11040*)
- CASSANDRA-6018 - encryption of commit logs (*https:// issues.apache.org/jira/browse/CASSANDRA-6018*)

See also CASSANDRA-9633 on encryption of SSTables (*https:// issues.apache.org/jira/browse/CASSANDRA-9633*), and CASSANDRA-7922, which serves as an umbrella ticket for file-level encryption requests (*https://issues.apache.org/jira/browse/ CASSANDRA-7922*).

Before we start configuring nodes to enable encryption, we have some preparation work to do to create security certificates that are a key part of the machinery.

SSL, TLS, and Certificates

Cassandra uses Transport Layer Security (TLS) for encrypting data in motion. TLS is often referenced by the name of its predecessor, Secure Sockets Layer (SSL). TLS is a cryptographic protocol for securing communications between computers to prevent eavesdropping and tampering. More specifically, TLS makes use of public key cryptography (also known as asymmetric cryptography), in which a pair of keys is used to encrypt and decrypt messages between two endpoints: a client and a server.

Prior to establishing a connection, each endpoint must possess a certificate containing a public and private key pair. Public keys are exchanged with communication partners, while private keys are not shared with anyone.

To establish a connection, the client sends a request to the server indicating the cipher suites it supports. The server selects a cipher suite from the list that it also supports and replies with a certificate that contains its public key. The client optionally validates the server's public key. The server may also require that the client provide its public key in order to perform two-way validation. The client uses the server's public key to encrypt a message to the server in order to negotiate a session key. The session key is a symmetric key generated by the selected cipher suite which is used for subsequent communications.

For many applications of public key cryptography, the certificates are obtained from a certificate authority, but because we typically control both the clients and our Cassandra nodes, we don't need quite that level of validation. For our purposes, we can generate our certificates with a simple tool that is provided with Java, the keytool.

The following command gives an example of how we can use the -genkey switch on keytool to generate a public/private key pair:

```
$ keytool -genkey -keyalg RSA -alias node1 -keystore node1.keystore
    -storepass cassandra -keypass cassandra
    -dname "CN=Jeff Carpenter, OU=None, O=None, L=Scottsdale, C=USA"
```

This command generates the keypair for one of our Cassandra nodes, which we'll call "node1", and places the keypair in a file called a *keystore*. We call our keystore *node1.keystore*. We provide passwords for the keystore and for the keypair, and a distinguished name specified according to the Lightweight Directory Access Prototol (LDAP) format.

The example command we've shown here provides the bare minimum set of attributes for generating a key. We could also provide fewer attributes on the command line and allow keytool to prompt us for the remaining ones, which is more secure for entering passwords.

Then we export the public key of each certificate to a separate file that we can share with others:

```
$ keytool -export -alias node1 -file node0.cer -keystore node1.keystore
Enter keystore password:
Certificate stored in file <node0.cer>
```

We identify the key we want to export from the keystore via the same alias as before, and provide the name of the output file. keytool prompts us for the keystore password and generates the certificate file.

We repeat this procedure to generate keys for each node and client.

Node-to-Node Encryption

Now that we have keys for each of our Cassandra nodes, we are ready to enable node-to-node configuration by setting the server_encryption_options in the *cassandra.yaml* file:

```
server_encryption_options:
    internode_encryption: none
    keystore: conf/.keystore
    keystore_password: cassandra
    truststore: conf/.truststore
    truststore_password: cassandra
    # More advanced defaults below:
    # protocol: TLS
    # algorithm: SunX509
    # store_type: JKS
    # cipher_suites: [TLS_RSA_WITH_AES_128_CBC_SHA,...]
    # require_client_auth: false
```

First, we set the `internode_encryption` option. We can select `all` to encrypt all inter-node communications, `dc` to encrypt between data centers, and `rack` to encrypt between racks. We provide the password for the keystore and set its path, or we can place the keystore file we created earlier at the default locations in the *conf* directory.

Next, we configure options for a file similar to the keystore called the *truststore*. We generate a truststore for each node containing the public keys of all the other nodes in our cluster. Each command looks something like the following:

```
$ keytool -import -v -trustcacerts -alias node1 -file node1.cer
  -keystore node1.truststore
Enter keystore password:
Re-enter new password:
Owner: CN=Jeff Carpenter, OU=None, O=None, L=Scottsdale, C=USA
Issuer: CN=Jeff Carpenter, OU=None, O=None, L=Scottsdale, C=USA
Serial number: 52cf9209
Valid from: Thu Dec 17 17:01:03 MST 2015 until: Wed Mar 16 17:01:03 MST 2016
Certificate fingerprints:
        MD5:   E2:B6:07:C0:AA:BB:71:E8:47:8A:2A:81:FE:48:2F:AB
        SHA1: 42:3E:9F:85:0D:87:02:50:A7:CD:C5:EF:DD:D1:6B:C2:78:2F:B0:E7
        SHA256: C1:F0:51:5B:B6:C7:B5:8A:57:7F:D0:F2:F7:89:C7:34:30:79:30:
          98:0B:65:75:CE:03:AB:AA:A6:E5:F5:6E:C0
        Signature algorithm name: SHA256withRSA
        Version: 3

Extensions:

#1: ObjectId: 2.5.29.14 Criticality=false
SubjectKeyIdentifier [
KeyIdentifier [
0000: C2 32 58 D0 55 27 5C D2   FB 1E 50 C9 76 21 30 5C   .2X.U'\...P.v!0\
0010: E6 1A 7D CF                                         ....
]
]

Trust this certificate? [no]:  y
Certificate was added to keystore
[Storing truststore.node1]
```

`keytool` prompts us to enter a password for the new truststore and then prints out summary information about the key we're importing.

The *cassandra.yaml* file also presents us with a series of "advanced" options to config-ure the cryptography. These options provide you the ability to select from Java's menu of supported cryptographic algorithms and libraries. For example, for Java 8, you can find the descriptions of these items at *http://docs.oracle.com/javase/8/docs/technotes/guides/security/StandardNames.html*.

The defaults will be sufficient in most cases, but it's helpful to understand what options are available. We can see how these options are used in Cassandra by examining the class `org.apache.cassandra.security.SSLFactory`, which Cassandra uses to generate secure sockets.

The `protocol` option specifies the protocol suite that will be used to instantiate a `javax.net.ssl.SSLContext`. As of Java 8, the supported values include `SSLv2`, `SSLv3`, `TLSv1`, `TLSv1.1`, or `TLSv1.2`. You can also use the shortcuts `SSL` or `TLS` to get the latest supported version of either suite.

The `algorithm` option specifies the setting provided to obtain an instance of `javax.net.ssl.TrustManagerFactory`. This defaults to the X.509 certificate.

The `store_type` option specifies the setting provided to obtain an instance of `java.security.KeyStore`. The default value `jks` indicates a keystore built by `keytool`, which is exactly what we have.

The `cipher_suites` option is a list of encryption algorithms in order of preference. The cipher suite to use is determined by the client and server in negotiating their connection, based on the priority specified in this list. The same technique is used by your browser in negotiating with web servers when you visit websites using *https:* URLs. As demonstrated by the defaults, you'll typically want to prefer stronger cipher suites by placing them at the front of the list. If you don't have total control over your clients, you may even wish to remove weaker suites entirely to eliminate the threat of a downgrade attack.

Finally, we can also enable two-way certificate authentication in which the client authenticates the server as well by setting `require_client_auth` to `true`.

Client-to-Node Encryption

Client-to-node encryption protects data as it moves from client machines to nodes in the cluster. The `client_encryption_options` in the *cassandra.yaml* file are quite similar to the node-to-node options:

```
# enable or disable client/server encryption.
client_encryption_options:
    enabled: false
    optional: false
    keystore: conf/.keystore
    keystore_password: cassandra
    # require_client_auth: false
    # Set truststore and truststore_password if require_client_auth is true
    # truststore: conf/.truststore
    # truststore_password: cassandra
    # More advanced defaults below:
    # protocol: TLS
    # algorithm: SunX509
    # store_type: JKS
    # cipher_suites: [TLS_RSA_WITH_AES_128_CBC_SHA,...]
```

The primary differences from the `server_encryption_options` are the `enabled` option, which serves as the on/off switch for client-to-node encryption, and the `optional` option, which indicates whether clients may choose either encrypted or unencrypted connections.

The *keystore* and *truststore* settings will typically be the same as those in the `server_encryption_options`, although it is possible to have separate files for the client options.

Note that setting `require_client_auth` for clients means that the *truststore* for each node will need to have a public key for each client that will be using a encrypted connection.

Simplified Certificate Management

Configuring *truststores* for Cassandra nodes can become something of a logistical problem if you're adding nodes to your cluster or additional clients on a regular basis. A common practice is to reuse the same certificate for all of the nodes in a cluster, and a second certificate for all of the clients.

This approach simplifies the process of managing your cluster greatly as you won't have to reconfigure *truststores* and restart nodes in order to add nodes and clients. This comes at the cost of fine-grained control over the trust you assign to individual nodes and clients.

Whatever scheme you choose to manage your certificates, the overall security of your Cassandra cluster depends on limiting access to the computers on which your nodes are running so that the configuration can't be tampered with.

JMX Security

We learned how Cassandra exposes a monitoring and management capability via JMX in Chapter 10. In this section, we'll learn how to make that management interface secure, and what security-related options we can configure using JMX.

Securing JMX Access

By default, Cassandra only makes JMX accessible from localhost. This is fine for situations where you have direct machine access, but if you're running a large cluster, it may not be practical to log in to the machine hosting each node in order to access with tools such as `nodetool` or OpsCenter.

For this reason, Cassandra provides the ability to expose its JMX interface for remote access. Of course, it would be a waste to invest our efforts in securing access to Cassandra via the native transport, and leave a major attack surface like JMX vulnerable. So let's see how to enable remote JMX access in a way that is secure.

First, we'll stop our node or cluster and edit the *conf/cassandra-env.sh* file (or *cassandra-env.ps1* on Windows). Look for the setting LOCAL_JMX, and change it as follows:

```
LOCAL_JMX=no
```

Setting this value to anything other than "yes" causes several additional properties to be set, including properties that enable the JMX port to be accessed remotely:

```
JVM_OPTS="$JVM_OPTS -Dcom.sun.management.jmxremote.port=$JMX_PORT"
JVM_OPTS="$JVM_OPTS -Dcom.sun.management.jmxremote.rmi.port=$JMX_PORT"
```

Next, there is a property that configures whether SSL is used to encrypt JMX connections (we'll discuss it in more depth momentarily):

```
JVM_OPTS="$JVM_OPTS -Dcom.sun.management.jmxremote.ssl=false"
```

Finally, there are properties that configure remote authentication for JMX:

```
JVM_OPTS="$JVM_OPTS -Dcom.sun.management.jmxremote.authenticate=true"
JVM_OPTS="$JVM_OPTS -Dcom.sun.management.jmxremote.password.file=
    /etc/cassandra/jmxremote.password"
```

The location of the *jmxremote.password* file is entirely up to you. Keep in mind that you'll want to specify a location for the file that is accessible only to users that you intend to have access. We'll configure the *jmxremote.password* file in just a minute, but first let's finish up our configuration edits by saving the *cassandra-env.sh* file.

Your JRE installation comes with a template *jmxremote.password* file under the *jre/lib/ management* directory. Typically you will find installed JREs under *C:\Program Files \Java* on Windows, */Library/Java/JavaVirtualMachines* on Mac OS, and */usr/lib/java* on Linux. Copy the *jmxremote.password* file to the location you set previously in *cassandra-env.sh* and edit the file, adding a line with our administrator username and password, as shown in bold here:

```
...
# monitorRole   QED
# controlRole   R&D
cassandra cassandra
```

We'll also edit the *jmxremote.access* file under the *jre/lib/management* directory to add read and write MBean access for our administrative user:

```
monitorRole readonly
controlRole readwrite \
        create javax.management.monitor.*,javax.management.timer.* \
        unregister
cassandra readwrite
```

Configure the permissions on the *jmxremote.password* and *jmxremote.access*. Ideally, the account under which you run Cassandra should have read-only access to this file, and other non-administrative users should have no access.

Finally, we restart Cassandra and test that we've configured secure access correctly by calling nodetool:

```
$ nodetool status -u cassandra -pw cassandra
```

We can also configure SSL for our JMX connection. To do this, we need to add a few more JVM options in the *cassandra-env* file:

```
JVM_OPTS="${JVM_OPTS} -Dcom.sun.management.jmxremote.ssl=true"
JVM_OPTS="${JVM_OPTS} -Djavax.net.ssl.keyStore=conf/node1.keystore"
JVM_OPTS="${JVM_OPTS} -Djavax.net.ssl.keyStorePassword=cassandra"
JVM_OPTS="${JVM_OPTS} -Djavax.net.ssl.trustStore=conf/node1.truststore"
JVM_OPTS="${JVM_OPTS} -Djavax.net.ssl.trustStorePassword=cassandra"
JVM_OPTS="${JVM_OPTS} -Dcom.sun.management.jmxremote.ssl.need.client.auth=true"
```

Security MBeans

We learned about the various MBeans exposed by Cassandra in Chapter 10. For understandable reasons, there are not many security-related configuration parameters that are accessible remotely via JMX, but there are some capabilities exposed via the org.apache.cassandra.auth domain.

PermissionsCacheMBean

By default, Cassandra caches information about roles and permissions as a performance optimization. The amount of time permissions are cached is set in the *cassandra.yaml* file by the permissions_validity_in_ms property, defaulting to 2 seconds. The PermissionsCacheMBean allows you to override this value to extend or shorten the cache time, and also provides a command to invalidate all of the permissions in cache. This could be a useful operation if you need to change permissions in your cluster and need them to take effect immediately.

Summary

Cassandra is just one part of an enterprise application, but performs an important part nonetheless. In this chapter, we learned how to configure Cassandra's pluggable authentication and authorization capabilities, and how to manage and grant permissions to users and roles. We enabled encryption between clients and nodes and learned how to secure the JMX interface for remote access.

Deploying and Integrating

In this, our final chapter, it's time to share a few last pieces of advice as you work toward deploying Cassandra in production. We'll discuss options to consider in planning deployments and explore options for deploying Cassandra in various cloud environments. We'll close with a few thoughts on some technologies that complement Cassandra well.

Planning a Cluster Deployment

A successful deployment of Cassandra starts with good planning. You'll want to consider the amount of data that the cluster will hold, the network environment in which the cluster will be deployed, and the computing resources (whether physical or virtual) on which the instances will run.

Sizing Your Cluster

An important first step in planning your cluster is to consider the amount of data that it will need to store. You will, of course, be able to add and remove nodes from your cluster in order to adjust its capacity over time, but calculating the initial and planned size over time will help you better anticipate costs and make sound decisions as you plan your cluster configuration.

In order to calculate the required size of the cluster, you'll first need to determine the storage size of each of the supported tables using the formulas we introduced in Chapter 5. This calculation is based on the columns within each table as well as the estimated number of rows and results in an estimated size of one copy of your data on disk.

In order to estimate the actual physical amount of disk storage required for a given table across your cluster, you'll also need to consider the replication factor for the table's keyspace and the compaction strategy in use. The resulting formula for the total size T_t is as follows:

$$T_t = S_t * RF_k * CSF_t$$

Where S_t is the size of the table calculated using the formula referenced above, RF_k is the replication factor of the keyspace, and CSF_t is a factor representing the compaction strategy of the table, whose value is as follows:

- 2 for the `SizeTieredCompactionStrategy`. The worst case scenario for this strategy is that there is a second copy of all of the data required for a major compaction.
- 1.25 for other compaction strategies, which have been estimated to require an extra 20% overhead during a major compaction.

Once we know the total physical disk size of the data for all tables, we can sum those values across all keyspaces and tables to arrive at the total for our cluster.

We can then divide this total by the amount of usable storage space per disk to estimate a required number of disks. A reasonable estimate for the usable storage space of a disk is 90% of the disk size.

Note that this calculation is based on the assumption of providing enough overhead on each disk to handle a major compaction of all keyspaces and tables. It's possible to reduce the required overhead if you can ensure such a major compaction will never be executed by an operations team, but this seems like a risky assumption.

Sizing Cassandra's System Keyspaces

Alert readers may wonder about the disk space devoted to Cassandra's internal data storage in the various `system` keyspaces. This is typically insignificant when compared to the size of the disk. We created a three-node cluster and measured the size of each node's data storage at about 18 MB with no additional keyspaces.

Although this could certainly grow considerably if you are making frequent use of tracing, the `system_traces` tables do use TTL to allow trace data to expire, preventing these tables from overwhelming your data storage over time.

Once you've made calculations of the required size and number of nodes, you'll be in a better position to decide on an initial cluster size. The amount of capacity you build into your cluster is dependent on how quickly you anticipate growth, which must be balanced against cost of additional hardware, whether it be physical or virtual.

Selecting Instances

It is important to choose the right computing resources for your Cassandra nodes, whether you are running on physical hardware or in a virtualized cloud environment. The recommended computing resources for modern Cassandra releases (2.0 and later) tend to differ for development versus production environments:

Development environments
> Cassandra nodes in development environments should generally have CPUs with at least two cores and 8 GB of memory. Although Cassandra has been successfully run on smaller processors such as Raspberry Pi with 512 MB of memory, this does require a significant performance-tuning effort.

Production environments
> Cassandra nodes in production environments should have CPUs with at least eight cores (although four cores are acceptable for virtual machines), and anywhere from 16 MB to 64 MB of memory.

Docker and Other Container Deployments

Another deployment option that has been rapidly gaining in popularity, especially in the Linux community, is software containers such as Docker.

The value proposition of containers is often phrased as "build once, deploy anywhere." Container engines support the ability to create lightweight, portable containers for software that can be easily moved and deployed on a wide variety of hardware platforms.

In Docker, each container is a lightweight virtual machine that provides process isolation, and a separate filesystem and network adapter. The Docker engine sits between the application and the OS.

The primary challenges in deploying Cassandra in Docker have to do with networking and data directories. The default deployment in Docker uses software-defined routing. At the time of writing, the performance of this layer currently reduces Cassandra throughput by somewhere around 50%, so the recommended configuration is to use the host network stack directly. This limits the deployment to a single Cassandra node per container.

If you do attempt to run multiple Cassandra instances in a container, this is really only appropriate for a development environment. You'll want to carefully consider the memory settings we discussed in Chapter 12.

From a data management perspective, you will want to configure data directories to be outside of the container itself. This will allow you to preserve your data when you want to upgrade or stop containers.

These same considerations apply in other container technologies, although the details will be slightly different. This is an emerging area that is likely to see continuing change over the coming months and years.

Storage

There are a few factors to consider when selecting and configuring storage, including the type and quantities of drives to use:

HDDs versus SSDs

Cassandra supports both hard disk drives (HDDs, also called "spinning drives") and solid state drives (SSDs) for storage. Although Cassandra's usage of append-based writes is conducive to sequential writes on spinning drives, SSDs provide higher performance overall because of their support for low-latency random reads.

Historically, HDDs have been the more cost-effective storage option, but the cost of using SSDs has continued to come down, especially as more and more cloud platform providers support this as a storage option.

Disk configuration

If you're using spinning disks, it's best to use separate disks for data and commit log files. If you're using SSDs, the data and commit log files can be stored on the same disk.

JBOD versus RAID

Traditionally, the Cassandra community has recommended using multiple disks for data files, with the disks configured as a Redundant Array of Independent Disks (RAID). Because Cassandra uses replication to achieve redundancy across multiple nodes, the RAID 0 (or "striped volume") configuration is considered sufficient.

More recently, Cassandra users have been using a Just a Bunch of Disks (JBOD) deployment style. The JBOD approach provides better performance and is a good choice if you have the ability to replace individual disks.

Avoid shared storage

When selecting storage, avoid using Storage Area Networks (SAN) and Network Attached Storage (NAS). Neither of these storage technologies scale well—they consume additional network bandwidth in order to access the physical storage over the network, and they require additional I/O wait time on both reads and writes.

Network

Because Cassandra relies on a distributed architecture involving multiple networked nodes, here are a few things you'll need to consider:

Throughput

First, make sure your network is sufficiently robust to handle the traffic associated with distributing data across multiple nodes. The recommended network bandwidth is 1 GB or higher.

Network configuration

Make sure that you've correctly configured firewall rules and IP addresses for your nodes and network appliances to allow traffic on the ports used for the CQL native transport, inter-node communication (the listen_address), JMX, and so on. This includes networking between data centers (we'll discuss cluster topology momentarily).

The clocks on all nodes should be synchronized using Network Time Protocol (NTP) or other methods. Remember that Cassandra only overwrites columns if the timestamp for the new value is more recent than the timestamp of the existing value. Without synchronized clocks, writes from nodes that lag behind can be lost.

Avoid load balancers

Load balancers are a feature of many computing environments. While these are frequently useful to spread incoming traffic across multiple service or application instances, it's not recommended to use load balancers with Cassandra. Cassandra already provides its own mechanisms to balance network traffic between nodes, and the DataStax drivers spread client queries across replicas, so strictly speaking a load balancer won't offer any additional help. Besides this, putting a load balancer in front of your Cassandra nodes actually introduces a potential single point of failure, which could reduce the availability of your cluster.

Timeouts

If you're building a cluster that spans multiple data centers, it's a good idea to measure the latency between data centers and tune timeout values in the *cassandra.yaml* file accordingly.

A proper network configuration is key to a successful Cassandra deployment, whether it is in a private data center, a public cloud spanning multiple data centers, or even a hybrid cloud environment.

Cloud Deployment

Now that we've learned the basics of planning a cluster deployment, let's examine our options for deploying Cassandra in three of the most popular public cloud providers.

There are a couple of key advantages that you can realize by using commercial cloud computing providers. First, you can select from multiple data centers in order to maintain high availability. If you extend your cluster to multiple data centers in an active-active configuration and implement a sound backup strategy, you can avoid having to create a separate disaster recovery system.

Second, using commercial cloud providers allows you to situate your data in data centers that are closer to your customer base, thus improving application response time. If your application's usage profile is seasonal, you can expand and shrink your clusters in each data center according to the current demands.

You may want to save time by using a prebuilt image that already contains Cassandra. There are also companies that provide Cassandra as a managed service in a Software-as-a-Service (SaaS) offering.

Don't Forget Cloud Resource Costs

In planning a public cloud deployment, you'll want to make sure to estimate the cost to operate your cluster. Don't forget to account for resources including compute services, node and backup storage, and networking.

Amazon Web Services

Amazon Web Services (AWS) has been a popular deployment option for Cassandra, as evidenced by the presence of AWS-specific extensions in the Cassandra project such as the `Ec2Snitch`, `Ec2MultiRegionSnitch`, and the `EC2MultiRegion Address Translator` in the DataStax Java Driver.

Cluster layout

AWS is organized around the concepts of regions and availability zones, which are typically mapped to the Cassandra constructs of data centers and racks, respectively. A sample AWS cluster topology spanning the us-east-1 (Virginia) and eu-west-1 (Ireland) regions is shown in Figure 14-1. The node names are notional—this naming is not a required convention.

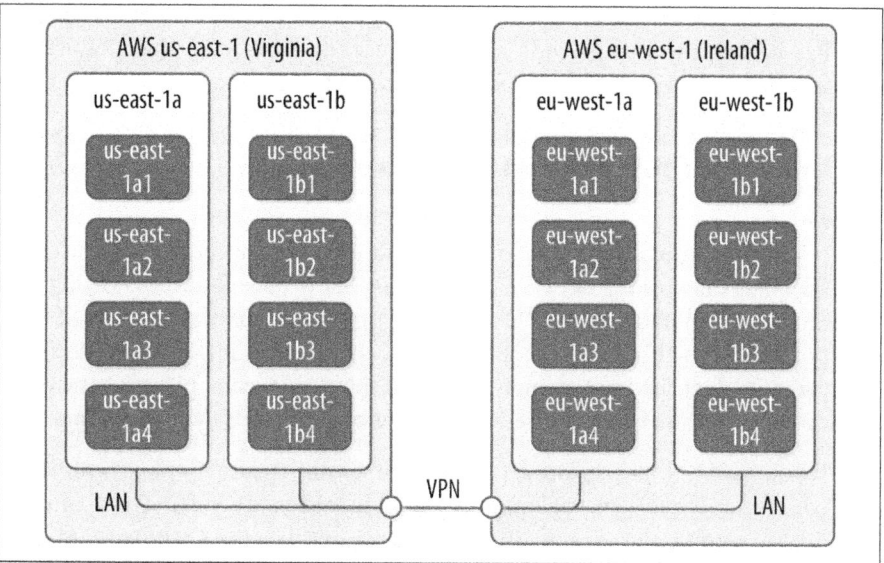

Figure 14-1. Topology of a cluster in two AWS regions

EC2 instances

The Amazon Elastic Compute Cloud (EC2) provides a variety of different virtual hardware instances grouped according to various classes. The two classes most frequently recommended for Cassandra deployments are the M-class and the I-class.

M-class instances are general-purpose instances that balance compute, memory, and network resources and are generally acceptable for development and light production environments. Later M-class instances such as M3 and M4 are SSD-backed.

The I-class instances are all SSD-backed and designed for high I/O. These instances come at a higher cost that generally pays off for heavily loaded production clusters.

You can find more information about the various instance types available at *https://aws.amazon.com/ec2/instance-types*.

DataStax Enterprise provides a prebuilt Amazon Machine Image (AMI) to simplify deployment (an AMI for DataStax Community Edition was discontinued after the Cassandra 2.1 release).

Data storage

Historically, the recommended disk option in AWS was to use ephemeral storage attached to each instance. The drawback of this is that if an instance on which a node is running is terminated (as happens occasionally in AWS), the data is lost.

By late 2015, the network-attached storage known as Elastic Block Store (EBS) has been proven to provide a reliable place to store data that doesn't go away when EC2 instances are dropped, at the cost of additional latency.

AWS Services such as S3 and Glacier are a good option for short- to medium-term and long-term storage of backups, respectively.

Networking
If you're running a multi-region configuration, you'll want to make sure you have adequate networking between the regions. Many have found that using elements of the AWS Virtual Private Cloud (VPC) provides an effective way of achieving reliable, high-throughput connections between regions. AWS Direct Connect provides dedicated private networks, and there are virtual private network (VPN) options available as well. These services of course come at an additional cost.

If you have a single region deployment or a multi-region deployment using VPN connections between regions, use the `Ec2Snitch`. If you have a multi-region deployment that uses public IP between regions, use the `Ec2MultiRegionSnitch`. For either snitch, increasing the `phi_convict_threshold` value in the *cassandra.yaml* file to 12 is generally recommended in the AWS network environment.

Microsoft Azure

DataStax and Microsoft have partnered together to help improve deployment of Cassandra in Microsoft's Azure on both Windows and Ubuntu Linux OSs.

Cluster layout
Azure provides data centers in locations worldwide, using the same term "region" as AWS. The concept of *availability sets* is used to manage collections of VMs. Azure manages the assignment of the VMs in an availability set across *update domains*, which equate to Cassandra's racks.

Virtual machine instances
Similar to AWS, Azure provides several classes of VMs. The D series, D series v2, and G series machines are all SSD-backed instances appropriate for Cassandra deployments. The G series VMs provide additional memory as required for integrations such as those described next. You can find more information about Azure VM types at *https://azure.microsoft.com/en-us/pricing/details/virtual-machines*.

Data storage
Azure provides a standard SSD capability on the previously mentioned instances. In addition, you can upgrade to use Premium Storage, which provides network-attached SSDs in larger sizes up to 1 TB.

Networking

Public IP addresses are recommended for both single-region and multi-region deployments. Use the `GossipingPropertyFileSnitch` to allow your nodes to detect the cluster topology. Networking options between regions include VPN Gateways and the Express Route, which provides up to 2 GB/s throughput.

Google Cloud Platform

Google Cloud Platform provides cloud computing, application hosting, networking, storage, and various Software-as-a-Service (SaaS) offerings such as Google's Translate and Prediction APIs.

Cluster layout

The Google Compute Environment (GCE) provides regions and zones, corresponding to Cassandra's data centers and racks, respectively.

Virtual machine instances

GCE's *n1-standard* and *n1-highmemory* machine types are recommended for Cassandra deployments. You can launch Cassandra quickly on the Google Cloud Platform using the Cloud Launcher. For example if you search the launcher at *https://cloud.google.com/launcher/?q=cassandra*, you'll find options for creating a cluster in just a few button clicks.

Data storage

GCE provides both spinning disk (*pd-hdd)* and solid state disk options for both ephemeral drives (*local-ssd*) and network-attached drives (*pd-ssd*). There are three storage options that can be used to store Cassandra backups, each with different cost and availability profiles: Standard, Durable Reduced Availability (DRA), and Nearline.

Networking

The `GoogleCloudSnitch` is a custom snitch designed just for the GCE. VPN networking is available between regions.

Integrations

As we learned in Chapter 2, Cassandra is a great solution for many applications, but that doesn't guarantee that it provides everything you need for your application or enterprise. In this section, we'll discuss several technologies that can be paired with Cassandra in order to provide more robust solutions for features such as searching and analytics.

Apache Lucene, SOLR, and Elasticsearch

One of the features that is commonly required in applications built on top of Cassandra is full text searching. This capability can be added to Cassandra via Apache Lucene (*http://lucene.apache.org/*), which provides an engine for distributed indexing and searching, and its subproject, Apache Solr (*http://lucene.apache.org/solr*), which adds REST and JSON APIs to the Lucene search engine.

Elasticsearch (*https://github.com/elastic/elasticsearch*) is another popular open source search framework built on top of Apache Lucene. It supports multitenancy and provides Java and JSON over HTTP APIs.

Stratio has provided a plugin (*https://github.com/Stratio/cassandra-lucene-index*) that can be used to replace Cassandra's standard secondary index implementation with a Lucene index. When using this integration, there is a Lucene index available on each Cassandra node that provides high performance search capability.

Apache Hadoop

Apache Hadoop is a framework that provides distributed storage and processing of large data sets on commodity hardware. This work originated at Google in the early 2000s. Google found that several internal groups had been implementing similar functionality for data processing, and that these tools commonly had two phases: a map phase and a reduce phase. A map function operates over raw data and produces intermediate values. A reduce function distills those intermediate values, producing the final output. In 2006, Doug Cutting wrote open source implementations of the Google File System (*http://research.google.com/archive/gfs.html*), and MapReduce (*http://research.google.com/archive/mapreduce.html*), and thus, Hadoop was born.

Similar to Cassandra, Hadoop uses a distributed architecture with nodes organized in clusters. The typical integration is to install Hadoop on each Cassandra node that will be used to provide data. You can use Cassandra as a data source by running a Hadoop Task Tracker and Data Node on each Cassandra node. Then, when a MapReduce job is initiated (typically on a node external to the Cassandra cluster), the Job Tracker can query Cassandra for data as it tracks map and reduce tasks, as shown in Figure 14-2.

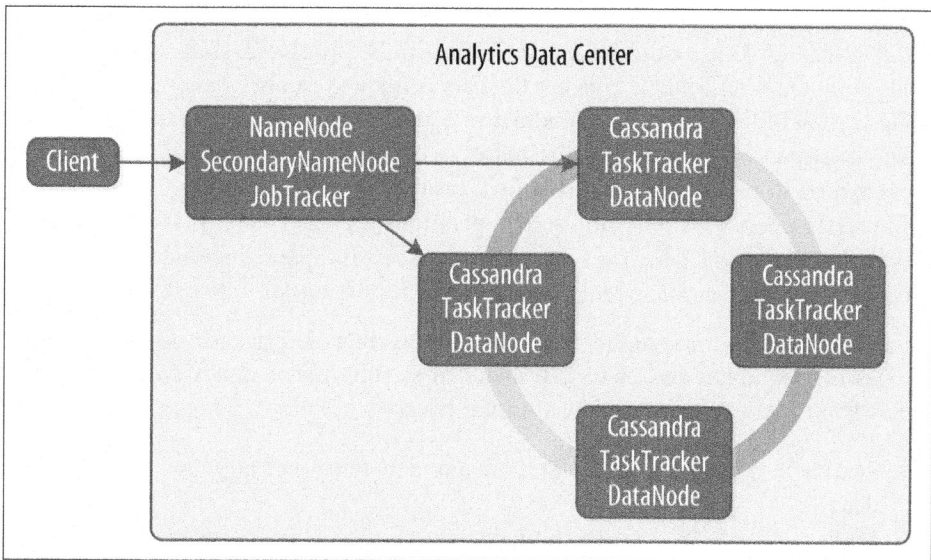

Figure 14-2. Topology of a Hadoop-Cassandra cluster

Starting in the late 2000s, Hadoop has been a huge driver of interest and growth in the Big Data community. Due to its popularity, a large ecosystem of extensions has developed around Hadoop, such as Apache Pig, which provides a framework and language for data analysis, and Apache Hive, a data warehouse tool. The Hadoop community has begun moving away from MapReduce because of its relatively slow performance (all data is written to disk, even for intermediate processing steps), high memory use, non-intuitive API, and batch-only processing mode. For this reason, the emergence of the Apache Spark project has been a significant development.

Apache Spark

with Patrick McFadin

Apache Spark (*http://spark.apache.org*) is an emerging data analytics framework that provides a massively parallel processing framework to enable simple API calls across large volumes of data. Originally developed in 2009 at UC Berkeley as an improvement to MapReduce, Spark was open sourced in 2010, and became an Apache project in 2014.

Unlike Hadoop, which writes intermediate results to disk, the Spark core processing engine is designed to maximize memory usage while minimizing disk and network access. Spark uses streaming instead of batch-oriented processing to achieve processing speeds up to 100 times faster than Hadoop. In addition, Spark's API is much simpler to use than Hadoop.

The basic unit of data representation in Spark is the Resilient Distributed Dataset (RDD). The RDD is a description of the data to be processed, such as a file or data collection. Once an RDD is created, the data contained can be transformed with API calls as if all of the data were contained in a single machine. However, in reality, the RDD can span many nodes in the network by partitioning. Each partition can be operated on in parallel to produce a final result. The RDD supports the familiar `map` and `reduce` operations plus additional operations such as `count`, `filter`, `union`, and `distinct`. For a full list of transformations, see the Spark documentation (*http://spark.apache.org/docs/latest/programming-guide.html#transformations*).

In addition to the core engine, Spark includes further libraries for different types of processing requirements. These are included as subprojects that are managed separately from Spark core, but follow a similar release schedule:

- SparkSQL provides familiar SQL syntax and relational queries over structured data.
- MLlib is Spark's machine learning library.
- SparkR provides support for using the R statistics language in Spark jobs.
- GraphX is Spark's library for graph and collection analytics.
- Spark Streaming provides near real-time processing of live data streams.

Use cases for Spark with Cassandra

As we've discussed in this book, Apache Cassandra is a great choice for transactional workloads that require high scale and maximum availability. Apache Spark is a great choice for analyzing large volumes of data at scale. Combining the two enables many interesting use cases that exploit the power of both technologies.

An example use case is high-volume time-series data. A system for ingesting weather data from thousands of sensors with variable volume is a perfect fit for Cassandra. Once the data is collected, further analysis on data stored in Cassandra may be difficult given that the analytics capabilities available using CQL are limited. At this point, adding Spark to the solution will open many new uses for the collected data. For example, we can pre-build aggregations from the raw sensor data and store those results in Cassandra tables for use in frontend applications. This brings analytics closer to users without the need to run complex data warehouse queries at runtime.

Or consider the hotel application we've been using throughout this book. We could use Spark to implement various analytic tasks on our reservation and guest data, such as generating reports on revenue trends, or demographic analysis of anonymized guest records.

One use case to avoid is using Spark-Cassandra integration as an alternative to a Hadoop workload. Cassandra is suited for transactional workloads at high volume and shouldn't be considered as a data warehouse. When approaching a use case where both technologies might be needed, first apply Cassandra to solving a problem suited for Cassandra, such as those we discuss in Chapter 2. Then consider incorporating Spark as a way to analyze and enrich the data stored in Cassandra without the cost and complexity of extract, transform, and load (ETL) processing.

Deploying Spark with Cassandra

Cassandra places data per node based on token assignment. This existing data distribution can be used as an advantage to parallelize Spark jobs. Because each node contains a subset of the cluster's data, the recommended configuration for Spark-Cassandra integrations is to co-locate a Spark Worker on each Cassandra node in a data center, as shown in Figure 14-3.

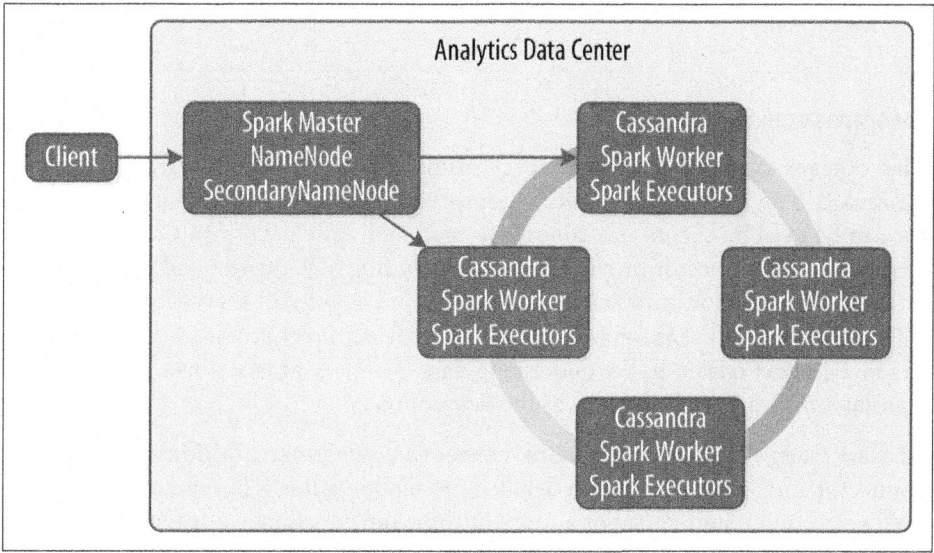

Figure 14-3. Topology of a Spark-Cassandra cluster

When a job is submitted to the Spark Master, the Spark Workers on each node spawn Spark Executors to complete the work. Using the `spark-cassandra-connector` as a conduit, he data required for each job is sourced from the local node as much as possible. We'll learn more about the connector momentarily.

Because each node contains a portion of the entire data in the cluster, each Spark Worker will only need to process that local subset of data. An example is a count action on a table. Each node will have a range of the table's data. The count is calculated locally and then merged from every node to produce the total count.

This design maximizes data locality, resulting in improved throughput and lower resource utilization for analytic jobs. The Spark Executors only communicate over the network when data needs to be merged from other nodes. As cluster sizes get larger, the efficiency gains of this design are much more pronounced.

Using a Separate Data Center for Analytics

A common deployment model for Cassandra and analytics toolsets such as Spark is to create a separate data center for analytic processing. This has the advantage of isolating the performance impact of analytics workloads from the rest of the cluster. The analytics data center can be constructed as a "virtual" data center where the actual hardware exists in the same physical location as another data center within the cluster. Using the NetworkTopologyStrategy, you can specify a lower replication factor for the analytics data center, as your required availability in this data center will typically be lower.

The spark-cassandra-connector

The spark-cassandra-connector (*https://github.com/datastax/spark-cassandra-connector*) is an open source project sponsored by DataStax on GitHub. The connector can be used by clients as a conduit to read and write data from Cassandra tables via Spark. The connector provides features including SQL queries and server-side filtering. The connector is implemented in Scala, but a Java API is available as well. API calls from the spark-cassandra-connector provide direct access to data in Cassandra in a context related to the underlying data. As Spark accesses data, the connector translates to and from Cassandra as the data source.

To start using the spark-cassandra-connector, you'll need to download both the connector and Spark. Although a detailed installation guide is beyond our scope here, we'll give a quick summary. For a more fulsome introduction, we suggest the O'Reilly book *Learning Spark* (*http://shop.oreilly.com/product/0636920028512.do*). You can download either a pre-built version of Spark, or you can build Spark yourself from the source.

If you're building an application in Java or Scala and using Maven, you'll want to add dependencies such as the following to your project's *pom.xml* file to access the Spark core and connector:

```
<dependency>
    <groupId>org.apache.spark</groupId>
    <artifactId>spark-core_2.10</artifactId>
    <version>1.5.2</version>
</dependency>
<dependency>
    <groupId>com.datastax.spark</groupId>
    <artifactId>spark-cassandra-connector_2.10</artifactId>
    <version>1.5.0</version>
</dependency>
```

Spark supports two modes of deployment: *local* and *cluster*. Cluster mode involves a central Spark Master and many compute nodes. Local mode runs entirely on the local host; this mode is best suited for development. For this example, we will run in local mode, but clustering requires only a few more steps.

Let's review the common API elements used for most Spark jobs accessing data in Cassandra. In this section, we've chosen to write our examples in Scala because of its simplicity and readability, as well as the fact that Spark and many Spark applications are written in Scala. The Java API is similar but quite a bit more verbose; we've provided a Java version of this example code in the GitHub repository (*https://github.com/jeffreyscarpenter/cassandra-guide/*) for this book. To connect your Spark application to Cassandra, you will first need to create a `SparkContext` containing connection parameters:

```
val conf = new SparkConf(true)
    .set("spark.cassandra.connection.host", "127.0.0.1")
    .setMaster("local[*]")
    .setAppName(getClass.getName)
    // Optionally
    .set("cassandra.username", "cassandra")
    .set("cassandra.password", "cassandra")

val sc = new SparkContext(conf)
```

Establishing a connection between Cassandra and Spark is simply the process of pointing to the running Cassandra cluster and Spark Master. This example configuration shows how to connect to a local Cassandra node and Spark Master. You can also provide Cassandra login credentials if required.

Once the `SparkContext` is created, you can then operate on Cassandra data by creating an RDD representing a Cassandra table. For example, let's create an RDD representing the `reservations_by_hotel_date` table from the `reservation` keyspace introduced in Chapter 5:

```
val rdd = sc.cassandraTable("reservation",
  "reservations_by_hotel_date")
```

Once you've created an RDD, you can perform transformations and actions on it. For example, to get the total number of reservations, create the following action to count every record in the table:

```
println("Number of reservations: " + rdd.count)
```

Because this is running as an analytics job in parallel with Cassandra, it is much more efficient than running a `SELECT count(*) FROM reservations` from cqlsh.

As the underlying structure of the RDD is a Cassandra table, you can use CQL to filter the data and select rows. In Cassandra, filter queries using native CQL require a partition key to be efficient, but that restriction is removed when running queries as Spark jobs.

For example, you might derive a use case to produce a report listing reservations by end date, so that each hotel can know who is checking out on a given day. In this example, end_date is not a partition key or clustering column, but you can scan the entire cluster's data looking for reservations with a checkout date of September 8, 2016:

```
val rdd = sc.cassandraTable("reservation",
  "reservations_by_hotel_date")
  .select("hotel_id", "confirm_number")
  .where("end_date = ?", "2016-09-08")

// Invoke the action to run the spark job
rdd.toArray.foreach(println)
```

Finding and retrieving data is only half of the functionality available—you can also save data back to Cassandra. Traditionally, data in a transactional database would require extraction to a separate location in order to perform analytics. With the spark-cassandra-connector, you can extract data, transform in place, and save it directly back to a Cassandra table, eliminating the costly and error-prone ETL process. Saving data back to a Cassandra table is amazingly easy:

```
// Create a collection of guests with simple identifiers
val collection = sc.parallelize(Seq(("1", "Delaney", "McFadin"),
  ("2", "Quinn", "McFadin")))

// Save to the guests table
collection.saveToCassandra("reservation", "guests",
  SomeColumns("guest_id", "first_name", "last_name"))
```

This is a simple example, but the basic syntax applies to any data. A more advanced example would be to calculate the average daily revenue for a hotel and write the results to a new Cassandra table. In a sensor application, you might calculate high and low temperatures for a given day and write those results back out to Cassandra.

Querying data is not just limited to Spark APIs. With SparkSQL, you can use familiar SQL syntax to perform complex queries on data in Cassandra, including query options not available in CQL. It's easy to create enhanced queries such as aggregations, ordering, and joins.

To embed SQL queries inside your code, you need to create a CassandraSQLContext:

```
// Use the SparkContext to create a CassandraSQLContext
val cc = new CassandraSQLContext(sc)

// Set the keyspace
cc.setKeyspace("reservation")
val rdd = cc.cassandraSql("
```

```
SELECT hotel_id, confirm_number
FROM reservations_by_hotel_date
WHERE end_date = '2016-09-08'
ORDER BY hotel_id")

// Perform action to run SQL job
rdd.collect().foreach(println)
```

The SQL syntax is similar to the Spark job from before, but is more familiar to users with a traditional database background. To explore data outside of writing Spark jobs, you can also use the spark-sql shell, which is available under the *bin* directory in your Spark installation.

Integrations in DataStax Enterprise

DataStax Enterprise is a productized version of Cassandra that supports many of the integrations described in this chapter. Specifically, DSE Search provides integration with Solr, while DSE Analytics provides integration with Apache Spark and elements of the Hadoop ecosystem such as MapReduce, Hive, and Pig.

Additional DSE features include additional security provider plugins and an in-memory configuration suitable for applications that require extremely fast response times.

Summary

In this chapter, we've just scratched the surface of the many deployment and integration options available for Cassandra. Hopefully we've piqued your interest in the wide range of directions you can take your applications using Cassandra and related technologies.

And now we've come to the end of our journey together. If we've achieved our goal, you now have an in-depth understanding of the right problems to solve using Cassandra, and how to design, implement, deploy, and maintain successful applications.

Index

Symbols

2PC (see two-phase commit)
? command, getting help in cqlsh, 50

A

AbstractCompactionStrategy, 121
AbstractReplicationStrategy, 112
accrual failure detection, 107
ACID (atomic, consistent, isolated, durable), 6
ActiveRepairService, 239
AddressTranslator interface, 167
aggregates, 198, 200-202
    built-in, 202
    defined in Java and JavaScript, native support for, 199
    user-defined, 129, 200
ALL consistency level, 113, 180, 191
    speculative retry and, 205
allocate_tokens_keyspace property, 138
ALLOW FILTERING keyword, 197, 263
AllowAllAuthenticator, 289
AllowAllAuthorizer, 292
AllowAllInternodeAuthenticator, 290
ALTER TABLE command, 62
ALTER USER command, 291
Amazon Dynamo, 17, 22
Amazon EC2, 109, 140
Amazon Web Services (AWS), 5
    Cassandra deployment on, 308
    Priam, integration with, 260
    snitches for, 140
analysis, using Cassandra for, 36
analytics
    Apache Spark, 313

using a separate data center for, 316
Ant
    additional build targets, 43
    downloading, 41
    executing and compiling Cassandra source, 42
    more build output with -v option, 42
anti-compaction, 239
anti-entropy, 122
    meaning in Cassandra, 122
    node repair via, 181
anti-entropy repair, 123
anticompaction, 122
ANY consistency level, 117, 180, 182
AP, primarily supporting availability and partition tolerance, 26
Apache Cassandra (see Cassandra)
Apache Cassandra Wiki, 37
Apache Cloudstack, 109, 140
Apache Hadoop, 30, 312
Apache Lucene, 312
Apache Solr, 312
Apache Spark (see Spark)
append-only writes, 179
APPLY BATCH command, 189
architecture (Cassandra), 105-130
    anti-entropy, repair, and Merkle trees, 122
    Bloom filters, 120
    compaction, 121
    consistency levels, 113
    data centers and racks, 105
    gossip and failure detection, 106-108
    hinted handoff, 117
    managers and services, 125-128

CQL commands operating in terms of, 62
in Cassandra, 58, 61, 61
number in a partition, 97
rows_per_partition, 270
row_cache_class_name property, 270
rpc_address property, 167
rpc_keepalive property, 142
rpc_port property, 142
rpc_timeout_in_ms property, 191
Ruby, DataStax Ruby driver, 174
running Cassandra, 43-48
on Linux, 45
on Windows, 44
required Java version, 43
starting the server, 45

S

SASI indexes, 78
saved_caches property, 270
Scala, 199
scalability, 19
problems with relational databases, 3
scaling
horizontal scalability in NoSQL databases, 14
in relational databases, problems with, 12
Web scale, 13
Web scale data solutions, 12
SchemaBuilder, 171
SchemaChangeListener, 170
schemas
accessing schema in a cluster, 170
avoiding conflics using programmatic definition, 171
defining a database schema, 100-103
identifying conflicts in, 230
in relational databases, 9
restoring, 255
schema-free data model, Cassandra and, 27
using transactions on schema creation, 187
SchemaStatement, 171
secondary indexes, 76-78
materialized views and, 94
rebuilding, 242
security, 287-301
authentication and authorization, 289-294
Cassandra's security features, 288
encryption, 294-299
JMX, 299-301

security MBeans, 301
MBeans, 228
possible weakness of NoSQL, 288
regulatory and compliance concerns, 287
SEDA (staged event-driven architecture), 124-125, 228
"SEDA: An Architecture for Well-Conditioned, Scalable Internet Services", 124
seed nodes, 132, 135, 245
removing, 250
replacing, 248
SeedProvider interface, 136
SELECT command, 55, 62
building with QueryBuilder, 161
range queries, ordering and filtering, 195-198
using TTL() function with, 64
SELECT COUNT command, 55
sequential consistency (see strict consistency)
sequential repair, 240
serial consistency levels, 187
SerializingCacheProvider, 270
server version, determining in cqlsh, 52
servers
setting to be seeds, 136
starting the Cassandra server, 45-47
stopping the Cassandra server, 47
server_encryption_options, 296, 299
services
CassandraDaemon, 125
EmbeddedCassandraService, 126
MessagingService class, 127
service MBeans, 228
StorageProxy class, 126
StorageService class, 126
session key, 295
sessions
creating using DataStax C/C++ driver, 176
creating using DataStax Java driver, 155
creating using DataStax Ruby driver, 174
set type, 71
other set operations, 71
sets, testing if element is a member of, 120
sharding, 10
as shared-nothing architecture, 11
strategies for determining shard structure, 11
shared storage, avoiding, 306
shared-nothing architecture, 11

About the Authors

Eben Hewitt is Chief Technology Officer for Choice Hotels International, one of the largest hotel companies in the world. He is the author of several books on architecture, distributed systems, and programming. He has consulted for venture capital firms, and is a frequently invited speaker on technology and strategy.

Jeff Carpenter is a Systems Architect for Choice Hotels International, with 20 years of experience in the hospitality and defense industries. Jeff's interests include SOA/microservices, architecting large-scale systems, and data architecture. He has worked on projects ranging from complex battle planning systems to a cloud-based hotel reservation system. Jeff is passionate about disruptive projects that change industries, mentoring architects and developers, and the next challenge.

Colophon

The bird on the cover of *Cassandra: The Definitive Guide* is a paradise flycatcher. Part of the family of monarch flycatchers (*Monarchidae*), paradise flycatchers are passerine (perching) insectivores. They're the most widely distributed of the monarch flycatchers and can be found from sub-Saharan Africa to Southeast Asia and on many Pacific islands. While most species are resident, others, including the Japanese paradise flycatcher and the Satin flycatcher, are migratory.

Most species of paradise flycatcher are sexually dimorphic, meaning that males and females look different. Females of most species tend to be less brilliantly colored than their male counterparts, which are also characterized by long tail feathers that vary in length according to species. For example, the male Asian paradise flycatcher's tail streamers can be approximately 15 inches long. Female flycatchers are believed to select their mate based on tail length. Paradise flycatchers are monogamous, which makes their distinctive coloring and plumage unusual, as this form of sexual display is usually reserved for non-monogamous species.

Because they're so widely distributed, paradise flycatchers can be found in a variety of habitats, including savannas, bamboo groves, rain forests, deciduous forests, and even cultivated gardens. Most species catch their food on the wing, thanks in part to their quick reflexes and sharp eyesight.

The cover image is from *Cassell's Natural History, Vol. IV*. The cover fonts are URW Typewriter and Guardian Sans. The text font is Adobe Minion Pro; the heading font is Adobe Myriad Condensed; and the code font is Dalton Maag's Ubuntu Mono.

Get even more for your money.

Join the O'Reilly Community, and register the O'Reilly books you own. It's free, and you'll get:

- $4.99 ebook upgrade offer
- 40% upgrade offer on O'Reilly print books
- Membership discounts on books and events
- Free lifetime updates to ebooks and videos
- Multiple ebook formats, DRM FREE
- Participation in the O'Reilly community
- Newsletters
- Account management
- 100% Satisfaction Guarantee

Signing up is easy:

1. Go to: oreilly.com/go/register
2. Create an O'Reilly login.
3. Provide your address.
4. Register your books.

Note: English-language books only

To order books online:
oreilly.com/store

For questions about products or an order:
orders@oreilly.com

To sign up to get topic-specific email announcements and/or news about upcoming books, conferences, special offers, and new technologies:
elists@oreilly.com

For technical questions about book content:
booktech@oreilly.com

To submit new book proposals to our editors:
proposals@oreilly.com

O'Reilly books are available in multiple DRM-free ebook formats. For more information:
oreilly.com/ebooks

O'REILLY®

Have it your way.

O'Reilly eBooks

- Lifetime access to the book when you buy through oreilly.com
- Provided in up to four, DRM-free file formats, for use on the devices of your choice: PDF, .epub, Kindle-compatible .mobi, and Android .apk
- Fully searchable, with copy-and-paste, and print functionality
- We also alert you when we've updated the files with corrections and additions.

oreilly.com/ebooks/

Safari Books Online

- Access the contents and quickly search over 7000 books on technology, business, and certification guides
- Learn from expert video tutorials, and explore thousands of hours of video on technology and design topics
- Download whole books or chapters in PDF format, at no extra cost, to print or read on the go
- Early access to books as they're being written
- Interact directly with authors of upcoming books
- Save up to 35% on O'Reilly print books

See the complete Safari Library at safaribooksonline.com

CPSIA information can be obt
at www.ICGtesting.com
Printed in the USA
BVOW11s0239010716
454166BV00005I